WILFRED OWEN

WILFRED OWEN

GUY CUTHBERTSON

YALE UNIVERSITY PRESS
NEW HAVEN AND LONDON

For information about this and other Yale University Press publications, please contact:

U.S. Office: sales.press@yale.edu   www.yalebooks.com
Europe Office: sales@yaleup.co.uk   www.yalebooks.co.uk

Set in Adobe Caslon Pro by IDSUK (DataConnection) Ltd
Printed in Great Britain by TJ International Ltd, Padstow, Cornwall

Library of Congress Cataloging-in-Publication Data

Cuthbertson, Guy, 1975–
   Wilfred Owen / Guy Cuthbertson.
     pages cm
     ISBN 978-0-300-15300-2 (hardback)
1. Owen, Wilfred, 1893–1918. 2. Poets, English—20th century—Biography.
3. World War, 1914–1918—Great Britain—Literature and the war. I. Title.
   PR6029.W4Z626 2014
   821'.912—dc23
   [B]
                                                                    2013037642

A catalogue record for this book is available from the British Library.

10 9 8 7 6 5 4 3 2 1

Contents

A Note of Introduction

THE Caledonian Hotel, a rosy-coloured Victorian building, stands regally at the western end of Princes Street in Edinburgh, and its opulent interior has long been a place for special dinners and romantic assignations. There, one evening in September 1917, the artist Cecile Walton was at a glamorous dinner when 'with a certain amount of fuss' she was handed a note.[1] The piece of paper told her to be nice to the man sitting on her left, who was 'a <u>dear</u> a real <u>dear</u>', an officer called Owen. The beautiful twenty-six-year-old woman, a lady seen in many paintings, turned to Lieutenant Owen and was pleased to discover that the young man was charming. The dinner went very well, she enjoyed herself and the young man found it 'jolly'.[2] Later, the lady who had handed her the note, Maidie Gray, who was by now in tears, confessed to being in love with this Wilfred Owen and asked whether Cecile loved dear Owen too. Maidie said that it was 'all quite spiritual' and 'there's no sex about it', but 'Owen is so charming you can't help loving him'. Cecile, for her part, had enjoyed his company but found him a young man with a restricted range of conversation based upon 'Oh rather' and 'I should just think so'.[3] A married woman, she told her husband that Owen was a 'very young boy'.[4] Even married Maidie saw 'her precious Owen'[5] as essentially sexless, like a child, observing that 'individual development can hardly be said to have existed for him', and when he was with her baby 'the tacit understanding between him and the child was almost uncanny'.[6]

Maybe Cecile Walton was keen to portray Owen as a very young boy so that her husband, who was away, would not be worried, and perhaps Maidie Gray was trying to explain why her advances had been spurned, but their remarks are corroborated by many other people who knew Owen. Owen was childlike to the end. At times Owen suggested, somewhat regretfully, that he believed he had grown up, but even the war had not changed him by the time he met Cecile Walton.[7] The following year, he met Conal O'Riordan, who later recalled the twenty-five-year-old's schoolboy chuckle and boyish sense of humour, 'a smiling schoolboy face [. . .] his charming face; a child's [. . .] he seemed quite the youngest officer who came my way'.[8] Owen's brother Harold remembered his innocence and boyishness, which were especially noticeable in Owen's relationship with their parents – Harold recalled Owen once saying angrily, 'I don't want to be a man' (sounding like Peter Pan), in response to his father's desire for him to be 'manly'.[9]

Wilfred Owen was always close to his mother. The apron strings were never cut – not even by the bullets of the Western Front. As Owen wrote to her late one night in July 1917, it was at the Caledonian Hotel that 'I saw you gliding up to me, veiled in azure [. . .] I thought you looked very very beautiful and well, through the veil'.[10] He had been exulted, and made it sound as if she was his young bride; yet 'without the veil I saw better the supremer beauty of the ashes of all your Sacrifices: for Father, for me, and for all of us'.[11] In late January 1917, Wilfred Owen and his platoon spent days in the advanced front line, lying in the snow with no dug-out, exposed to the fierce winter wind and whizz-bangs, and hidden from the Germans' periscope only by a little ridge. They needed food, and could not melt the ice in the water-cans. One of the men froze to death, and they were all on the verge of dying. A bird of prey circled above them ominously. Yet Owen was kept from death by thoughts of home, and of his mother especially. Describing the horrific experience in a letter to 'My own dear Mother' on 4 February 1917, he said that 'The intensity of your Love reached me and kept me living'.[12] Owen's letters, which are mostly to his mother, are testimony to the strength of the bond. He was 'Your lovingest of Boys', 'your adoring Wilfred', 'Your devoted son', 'Mother's Son'. His first letter to her, at the age of five, ended 'With love from Wilfred I remain your loving son Wilfred'; a few days before his death he ended with 'All my dearest love, my darling Mother'. He wrote, in the last summer of the war, that:

> Taking the world as it really is, not everybody of my years can boast, (or as many would say, confess) that their Mother is absolute in their affections.
> But I believe it will always be so with me, always.
> There is nothing in heaven or earth like you, and that is why I can't write a poem for you.[13]

His letters also show that he delighted in the company of children – as their teacher, tutor and friend, and as an equal who saw himself in them. As an adult, he played happily 'in the garden of boyhood'.[14] Years after leaving school, when he was a veteran of the Front, he was excitedly reading the boarding-school stories *The Hill* and *The Loom of Youth*. There is a photograph of Wilfred Owen as a child posing as a proud soldier with a gun in one hand, a sword at his belt and a small military tent nearby, and in another photograph the little boy is a soldier again, carrying a sword and a determined and heroic look – as an army officer aged twenty-five, had he changed so very much? Owen was still a boy when he wrote as a twenty-one-year-old that 'After all my years of playing soldiers, and then of reading History, I have almost a mania to be in the East, to see fighting, and to serve'.[15]

But then there is the poetry. Cecile Walton's encounter with Wilfred Owen under the electric chandeliers of the Caledonian's dining room was superficial but revealing: her letters to her husband do not mention that Owen writes poetry – she offers us not the poet but a shy, straightforward young officer who, she feared, was getting rather too close to her friend Maidie. It is as if there were two Wilfred Owens. During the war he produced sophisticated, inventive, courageous, original work: Owen was mature beyond his years. And alongside the impression of arrested development, there was a determination to improve himself, to educate himself, to achieve 'progress'. His reading was eclectic and not driven by any canon, but it was wide and not always adolescent.

It does seem to be a recurring characteristic of the English poet that he can be both childlike and sophisticated: a John Betjeman travelling with his teddy bear in his briefcase on top of volumes of Victorian poetry, or an Alfred Tennyson who was both the grand man of letters and the boy who needed to be mothered. Owen was an eager reader of biographies of the poets, and knew about Tennyson: 'Tennyson, it seems, was always a great child'.[16] Philip Larkin was an enthusiastic fan of Beatrix Potter's tales – he was also, indeed, a big fan of school-themed pornography. Edward Thomas felt that poets must play with words in the way a child does. W. H. Auden was obsessed with schools and boyish game-playing. Ernest Dowson described himself as always remaining four years old, never growing old; Arthur Symons observed that Dowson 'was a child, clamouring for so many things, all impossible'.[17] The Romantics' obsession with childhood seems to have created a literary tradition in which the poet must retain the child within himself. Owen claimed that a poet, any true poet, is 'childish':[18] he asked, 'Now, what's your Poet, but a Child of Nine?'[19]

In Owen's case, the child and childhood feature in his poetry again and again. In *The Poems of Wilfred Owen*, of the 87 poems written after Owen's twenty-first birthday, 36 involve the child and others refer to lads or youths. The child remained a characteristic of his poetry and his life, and the poetry grew out of the boyishness, and out of his sense of affinity with children, even though Owen's own childhood does not feature prominently in his poetry. In many ways, he was trying to escape his childhood while retaining a longing to be a child. And the child is a focus for his portrayal of the war. His penultimate letter talks of British shells 'burying little children alive'.[20] Children ardent for some desperate glory were told with such high zest 'The old Lie: Dulce et decorum est / Pro patria mori'. And many of the soldiers were just lads, barely more than children in uniform. W. B. Yeats, who disliked Owen's poetry, famously complained that Owen 'is all blood, dirt and sucked sugar-stick'[21] – but that is in fact part of Owen's brilliance: he sees the child's sucked sugar stick among the blood and dirt of war. We must look at the relationship between the child and the man, the relationship between the man and the poetry, and the relationship between the child and the Western Front.

> Let the boy try along this bayonet-blade
> How cold steel is, and keen with hunger of blood[22]

CHAPTER I

Lands of Our Fathers

Here I turned and looked at the hills I had come across. There they
stood, darkly blue, a rain cloud, like ink, hanging over their summits.
Oh, the wild hills of Wales, the land of old renown and of wonder, the
land of Arthur and Merlin!
GEORGE BORROW, *Wild Wales*, 1862[1]

His beauty, dress, and manner struck me as so out of place in such a
street, that I could not possibly divine what had transplanted this delicate
exotic from the conservatories of some Regent-street to the untidy
potato-patches of Liverpool.
HERMAN MELVILLE, *Redburn*, 1849[2]

FIGHTING in 1918, Wilfred Owen scrambled out of a trench and
confronted the machine guns with 'quick bounds from cover to
cover', 'remembering my own duty, and remembering also my forefa-
thers the agile Welshmen of the Mountains'.[3] The Owens seem to have
come, some way back, from the north-west of Wales, wild Wales, and
Wilfred Owen's father Tom certainly liked to believe that he was
descended from a certain Baron Lewis Owen, knight of the shire and
baron of the exchequer under the Tudors, a member of parliament, an
usher of the chamber and sheriff of mountainous Merionethshire: 'it
was a family belief and the legend, it is known, has been passed down
orally from father to eldest son for many generations'.[4] Descended from

Gwrgan ab Ithel, a prince of Powys, with a wife said to be descended from the mother of Richard II,[5] this Welsh magnate lived in a substantial house ('the great barn of the Baron') at Dolgelly that was reputed to have once been a meeting house for Owen Glendower's parliament, and the Baron was something of a principled Welsh leader in the tradition of Glendower. Owen is a common name, especially in that corner of Wales,[6] where, north of Dolgelly, the mountains include Moel Hafod-Owen, standing above the River Wen, and plenty of the mountains' grubby slate-quarrymen and illiterate sheep-farmers have possessed the name – which might mean 'well born' or 'noble' but could also derive from the Welsh for lamb, *oen*. There is still no real evidence for the connection between Wilfred and Lewis Owen, but Lewis Owen probably had seven sons and four daughters, and those children had many children too (his eldest son, for instance, had ten), and this continued down the generations, so if one throws in illegitimate children along the way then the Lewis Owen clan is large and genealogists have their work cut out. Such was the fertility of the Owen clan, and the fame of the Baron, that in 1886 the National Eisteddfod offered a prize of £20 for an essay on the descendants of Baron Owen.[7]

If the Baron was famous in Wales, it was really his death that he was famous for. In October 1555, Lewis Owen was near Dinas Mawddwy, to the east of Dolgelly, when he was ambushed and murdered. It has always been said that his death was at the hands of the Red Bandits,[8] a gang of red-haired rogues and profligates so feared in those parts that the locals put scythes in their chimneys to protect against the intruding ginger killers. Legend has it that, at the spot now known as Baron's Gate,[9] these *banditti* lay in wait in an upland wood, where, although it was autumn, the trees still allowed a man to hide, and their red hair would have been camouflage among the scarlet and copper leaves. Knowing that the Baron would be travelling that way with his retinue, they put trees in the road in order to halt the travellers (a tactic later used by German troops in the First World War), and as the Baron's attendants tried to move the trees they received a shower of arrows from the hidden gang and fled, leaving the Baron with only his kinsman,

John Lloyd, for company. When the bandits came out of hiding and took to their victims with swords and daggers, these two men put up a brave fight, but Lloyd and Owen were outnumbered and their butchered bodies were unceremoniously left in the road without palls, orisons, candles or passing-bells. But five poets wrote elegies when the Baron died, and a cross was erected at the spot where he fell; the woods became known as Ffridd-y-Groes, the enclosure of the cross. The law's response to the Baron's murder was so brutal and unstinting that 'the horde of desperadoes'[10] were quickly executed or driven out of Wales, hence the comment by one seventeenth-century descendant, Robert Vaughan, that 'with the loss of his life he purchased peace and quietness to his country, the which God be praised we enjoy even to our days'.[11]

In the summer of 1917, Wilfred Owen wrote a faux-medieval poem called the 'Ballad of Lady Yolande', and when writing it he might have had Baron Owen in mind: it is about Baron Oberon or Oberond and his rival for the heart of Lady Yolande is a red lad – not a red-haired bandit, but he is dressed in scarlet silk and 'His cheek was red as bin her owne / And full as red his lips'.[12] The Baron journeys westward, deep into Wales: Owen mentions 'the western shore', 'the western march' and 'the wild welsh march' and another character has the Welsh name Sir Price and lives in a Welsh *plas* ('plas' is Welsh for hall or mansion, hence the Baron's house called Cwrt Plas yn Dre).[13] The Baron defeats Sir Price in this Welsh landscape, but there the poem ends, unfinished, and one is left to wonder whether he would eventually have been defeated by the red youth – as, in a sense, he already has been, because it was this lad and not the Baron who had won Lady Yolande's heart.

Wilfred Owen looked Welsh – one person who knew him before the war stressed that Owen 'could only have come from the "Celtic fringes" in these islands', recalling him as 'a rather small, good-looking, young Welshman'[14] (dark and little-legged like the classic Welshman, Owen would grow up to be just 5 feet 5 ½ inches).[15] There have been unconvincing attempts to suggest that Owen had a Celtic temperament – emotional, wistful, sentimental, passionate. Later in his life, he would make a number of admiring references to the Welsh, and would refer to his Welsh ancestry. 'It is pleasant to be among the Welsh,' he wrote in June 1917.[16] Then in May 1918, Owen looked forward to writing blank-verse plays on old Welsh themes, turning to stories that his Welsh ancestors would have known – possibly tales of famous Owens like Owen Laurgoch, 'Owen of the Red Hand', seven feet tall and a popular hero in Welsh ballads, who is sometimes given legends that are elsewhere linked with King Arthur; or Owain, the son of Arthur's sister Modron or of Morgan le Fay; or perhaps even Baron Lewis Owen. But Wilfred Owen was not quite a Welshman. As Dylan Thomas discovered, 'any claim we may make to Wilfred Owen as a Welshman has been repudiated, Anglo-Saxonly and indignantly, by his brother and, I think, his mother'.[17] One of his forefathers left the mountains, and the Owens became English. Tom Owen was a Cheshire lad from Nantwich. Any longing for the west was a residual instinct seen in Tom Owen's love for 'Men of Harlech' (Harlech being in their ancestral corner of Wales), his favourite gramophone record, which Wilfred thought 'beastly',[18] and in the Owens' occasional holidays in towns like Aberystwyth. It also seems that Tom Owen's voice could throw itself back to Wales on occasions – his son Harold remembered a startling reversion:

My father in his unbelievably rare and so quickly suppressed flashes of emotional tenderness always lapsed into a sort of hybrid Welsh in the choice of his words. His voice and inflections at these times were purely Welsh and very beautiful indeed.[19]

Wilfred Edward Salter Owen was born at Oswestry, a rather Welsh town in Shropshire, early in the morning of Saturday 18 March 1893. Only five miles from the Welsh–English border, Oswestry combined the two cultures, the two languages. Welsh was still spoken by some of the residents, and the literary associations of Oswestry are mostly Welsh, for example with the scholar Edward Lloyd (or Lhuyd) and the poets Goronwy Owen, Wiliam Llŷn and Guto'r Glyn. Many people would say that Oswestry is really a bit of Wales that just happens to be in England. Wilfred Owen was almost a Welsh writer by birth. Many of the inhabitants had, and have, Welsh names – one of them was Edward Thomas, the Oswestry ironmonger whose granddaughter Barbara Pym, the quintessentially English novelist, was born in the town in 1913.[20] Owen's birthplace had a Welsh *plas* as its name: Plas Wilmot. And given that it was March when Owen was born, there might even have been a few Welsh daffodils in the south-facing garden. Oswestry was the hometown of Owen's mother, Susan; and his mother's family was English, carrying the un-Welsh surname Shaw, although like the Owens they might have had some Welsh blood from some way back.

The name Wilfred was not a family name, and is usually associated with the north of England because of the cult of St Wilfrid (or Wilfred), a seventh-century bishop from Northumbria who is associated above all with York, Ripon and Hexham. But St Wilfrid also played an important part in the cult of another seventh-century Northumbrian saint, Oswald, a king and martyr who was buried at Oswestry ('Oswald's Tree'). Susan and Tom Owen had married on 8 December 1891 in St Oswald's Church, where, appropriately, Wilfred Owen was later christened. The Christian name appears to haunt his writing, so, for instance, when in 'Insensibility' he rhymes 'red' and 'rid' he seems to be playing with the fact that 'Wilfred' is pronounced 'Wilfrid', and is there not a hint of his name in 'killed' and 'friend' in the famous line 'I am the enemy you killed, my friend'? In the same way, his mother's maiden name is alluded to elsewhere with 'nuzzling boars ran grunting through the shaw'.[21]

*

Owen's mother, Susan Shaw, was born at Plas Wilmot on 17 March 1867: mother and son were born in the same room of the same house on 17 March and 18 March, respectively.[22] The detached house was pretty, and essentially rural, located at the edge of the market town, and no doubt the births of these two spring babies were attended, at a respectful distance, by chiffchaffs, newly arrived that week, and even a swallow or two. But 16 March would not be a day for celebrations: Owen's grandfather Edward Shaw (born in 1821) lived until 15 January 1897, and then Plas Wilmot was sold that year, its contents being auctioned at the house on 16 March, the day before Susan's thirtieth birthday and two days before Owen's fourth. The loss of his grandfather and the house seems to chime with a feeling, in that year of the Diamond Jubilee, that the Victorian Age, with all its success and confidence, was passing away; a feeling enhanced by the deaths of magisterial Victorians, such as Arnold in 1888, Browning in 1889, Cardinal Newman in 1890, Tennyson and Cardinal Manning in 1892, and Millais and William Morris in 1896. Plas Wilmot was an expense that no one could afford, not even Edward Shaw, who had achieved some affluence as an ironmonger and some status as mayor. The house had been built by Wilfred Owen's maternal grandmother's family, the Salters, and was occupied by the Shaws: Edward Shaw married Mary Salter on 30 April 1857, another spring event, and she was already the owner of Plas Wilmot as the eldest of the children of the couple who built the house, Edward and Mary Salter. Edward and Mary Shaw then had a son called Edward, a daughter called Mary, a daughter called Emma and a daughter called (Harriett) Susan. Wilfred Edward Salter Owen, Susan's first child, had within his name the name of the man who had created Plas Wilmot.

The house still stands, on Weston Lane which, although a little more suburban now, is still a beautiful rural lane and Plas Wilmot is a largish residence peering from behind tall trees, iron gates, garden greenery and an old garden wall, and taking in the view of the unspoilt Shropshire landscape. Susan loved the house. She drew a picture of Plas Wilmot in about 1885, and, looking up to the house from the bottom of the drive, the picture emphasises the grandeur of her home, as if it's a country house accessed down a long driveway through a vast estate. A black-coated, black-hatted figure, presumably her father, strides towards the door, while above, a number of carefree birds wheel elegantly. The drawing speaks of seclusion and security. It is also a remnant of her artistic ambitions. Susan had taken art classes for some time in her youth, her art teacher urging her to further her art education, and Susan believed for the rest of her life that she could have become a proper artist if she hadn't had to stay at home and care for her parents (her mother died in 1891). So that sketch of Plas Wilmot represents the life that she gave up art for, but she wanted her son to inherit both the house and her artistic sensibility. When she preserved a lock of her baby's hair with the words 'The hair of Sir Wilfred Edward Salter-Owen at the age of 11½ months – in the year 1894', the surname gave him the double-barrelled distinctiveness of the upper classes; however, it may also have been a reference to the painter Sir Edward Coley Burne-Jones, whom Owen later referred to as one of 'the mighty ones',[23] who, when Owen was 10½ months old, became a baronet, and his double-barrelled surname was officially adopted, the artist having 'in the natural yearning of mortal man not to be lost in the million of Joneses, put another family name before it, [. . .] but solely from dread of annihilation'.[24] Yet when her father died it became clear that while her son might become an artist and a baronet he would not inherit the home Edward Salter built. Looked at again, the sketch of Plas Wilmot could show a black-clad undertaker, or Death himself, approaching the house while ominous birds of prey circle overhead.

Wilfred Owen only lived in Oswestry for four years, but even so, he had fond memories of Plas Wilmot. Susan recorded that Owen remembered Plas Wilmot garden and his grandad. In September 1911, Owen visited Nellie, once a maid at Plas Wilmot, and 'Spent the time very pleasantly in recalling our reminiscences of the common fountain-head of our existences, known by all as the "old Home"'.[25] She had an album of old photographs of the family. One Plas Wilmot photograph from 1895 depicts Owen with his bow-legged grandfather, the wee boy holding his grandfather's walking stick as if he had inherited a sword. Both figures look wary and ill at ease, and the photograph suggests fragility – the stick props up the boy and the old man bends slightly to hold his grandson's hand. Another photograph from that year is especially powerful, depicting a caged parrot, a faceless doll, Grandfather Shaw in a top hat with a reluctant cat on his knee, Susan's sister Emma Gunston and her three cherubic children, three members of staff, looking wistful, and, centre stage, Susan Owen holding a serious-looking Wilfred. There aren't many smiles but the family looks just a little like a small travelling circus. The ringmaster died two years later, the contents of the house were sold, and presumably the servants had to move elsewhere. What happened to the parrot called Jubilee? Who looked after the cat? Even now, the photograph carries some sadness because we know what happened next – the death of the old man, and then the coming of the Great War. Presumably the young male servant with the wistful look fought in the war, and although the Gunston boy didn't, the Owen boy did. We can see the famous 1916 photograph of Second Lieutenant Owen (uniformed, confident and sensitive) in the baby who doesn't show his full face to the camera, but, exposing his left cheek, meets the camera with his eyes – both photographs were taken, twenty-one years apart, by John Gunston, husband of Emma. Susan's other sister, Mary ('May') had married in 1884 a Dr Richard Loughrey, who worked on the Mile End Road in the East End (they were there in 1888 when the Jack the Ripper murders took place) but she died three years after Owen was born, leaving four children; within a year, Susan had to cope with the death of her oldest sister, the death of her father and the loss of her home.

According to Susan, Owen dearly loved his Grandfather Shaw, and Plas Wilmot must have been a jolly place for a little boy because it had a large garden and various animals. Edward Shaw was an expert bird-keeper, much involved with bird-fanciers' competitions, and he seems to have shared this hobby with his young grandson: at the Oswestry Flower Show in 1894, when this grandson was a year and a half old, a Wilfred Owen won second prize for 'Best pen of fantails' and first prize for 'Best pen of game bantams'. Was this the famous poet's first public success, with some assistance from his beloved grandad?[26] In Susan Owen's recollections we can see that at Plas Wilmot the little boy had looked up to his grandfather above all:

Another winter day when his father fell into our little skating pool 'and crawled out like a horse' as he said he (W) did not seem frightened until he got near the house when he sobbed 'because Grandad would be so cross with my Daddie. I heard him tell Daddie to be careful not to fall in as the ice was thin in places'.

Susan saw this response as evidence of Owen's love for his father – 'little darling he, in those early days looked upon his dear Daddie as a brother – and indeed he was "as a brother" all his life'[27] – but it really shows that the difficulties between Tom and Wilfred Owen went back to Plas Wilmot, and it shows, too, the influence of Edward Shaw, who when he died left a great hole in the family's lives, even that of a three-year-old. Soon after the old man died, Owen hoped that 'God would see that Grandad had his prunes after lunch each day'. Another day the little boy declared, 'I do hope Grandad has the "Echo" every eve[n]ing in Heaven 'cos I know he likes it and we can't send it to him now can we?'[28] For Susan this was evidence of the sweetness and high intelligence of her firstborn. The fascination with heaven and its domestic comforts would continue into his war poetry, such as 'Asleep', where Owen asks:

Whether his deeper sleep lie shaded by the shaking
Of great wings, and the thoughts that hung the stars,
High-pillowed on calm pillows of God's making,
Above these clouds, these rains, these sleets of lead,
And these winds' scimitars

When he was twenty, Owen attempted a poem that looks back to Plas Wilmot and to himself as the young child mesmerised by the fireplace there. Owen wrote about how we have all as children looked 'from between our Mother's knees', with 'fascinated' eyes into the fire – 'the eyes of youth' see 'a rosy, beauteous Hell'.[29] This Hell would become a constant companion in his childhood – Plas Wilmot was an evangelical home and Susan inherited her father's faith even if she couldn't inherit his house – and this fascination with the fire would continue through his life from Plas Wilmot into the war poems 'Miners' and 'Exposure', and into his last letter, where a smoky fire is fed damp wood (appropriately, the letters f, i, r and e are there in the name 'Wilfred'). 'Miners' recreates that early experience of staring into the fireplace – 'There was a whispering in my hearth [. . .] And I saw white bones in the cinder-shard' – and he finds there a hell of underground fire, although rather than Owen it is the coal that recalls its origins. In 'Exposure', home is revisited with a child's eye – the fire has 'dark-red jewels'.

These dark-red jewels were also at the heart of his father's life. Coal fuelled the railways that gave Tom Owen his career and fed his family – not just Susan and Wilfred, but also Wilfred's sister Mary, born in Oswestry in 1895, and his two brothers Harold, born in 1897, and Colin, born in 1900. Tom Owen joined the LNWR and GWR joint railway in December 1884, acquiring a secure career and a powerful employer. In fact, during Tom Owen's career these railways gradually expanded their empires, building new lines and stations and gobbling up smaller railway companies – the LNWR even used the Roman Empire and 'Veni, vidi, vici' on a poster in 1909. In 1910, the GWR ran well over a million passenger trains and by 1913 employed over 73,000 people.[30] In the Golden Age of Steam, a son could be proud of a father who worked with trains, especially a father who became a stationmaster and then, eventually, chief clerk to the superintendent and acting superintendent. The young Wilfred Owen admired his uniformed father and took an interest in trains when he was growing up, as many boys did. In 1906 – the year *The Railway Children* was published – he described a miniature railway in Wales and compared it with one at Eaton Hall, Cheshire, which the family had visited. In 1907 Owen signed a letter with a monogram (of WEO) that was probably based on the monogram of the GWR, and this WEO monogram remains in some of his books. When, later, he wrote about how soldiers 'lined the train with faces grimly gray' and how 'signals nodded, and a lamp / Winked to the guard', that was his father's world.[31]

When Plas Wilmot was sold, Tom's career took him and the family briefly to Shrewsbury, then Birkenhead. At Birkenhead he was stationmaster at Woodside Station, a baronial building with an open timber roof that gave it the feel of a Great Hall in a castle. Owen was a Birkenhead boy until 1907. Birkenhead is on the Wirral, but it was only a penny's short but exciting ferry ride away from Liverpool: indeed, to many people, Birkenhead is part of Liverpool, and from

Woodside's station and ferry stage there was a wonderful view of the great city across the Mersey. In a succession of houses, 7 Elm Grove, 14 Willmer Road and 51 Milton Road, on neighbouring streets, the Owens were not far from the station and the river, but also deep in a territory of humble semis and humbler terraces, all looking on to brick and paving stones, although their Birkenhead homes were not houses to be ashamed of – and much of Birkenhead was middle-class.

In his autobiographical novel *Ultramarine* (1933), Malcolm Lowry – who was born in 1909 at New Brighton, the holiday resort on the northern edge of Birkenhead,[32] where a young Wilfred Owen had enjoyed himself among its horses, donkeys, photographers, and children digging in the sand – describes the Birkenhead that Owen knew: the river is 'a vast camera film, slowly and inexorably winding',[33] and at Birkenhead ships came from 'Rio and the Plata: Cuba and Colon: Pernambuco, Rangoon', with tea, sugar, 'rich and romantic cargoes'.[34] At Liverpool, J. B. Priestley saw 'the gateway to the bronze ramparts of Arabia, to the temples and elephants of Ceylon, to flying fish and humming birds and hibiscus'.[35] Terraced streets, named after Oxbridge colleges, Shakespearean characters, composers, writers, and naval heroes, led down to the magic, colour and excitement of the docks. The River Mersey, running between Birkenhead and Liverpool, was a shifting forest of masts and funnels back then – Henry James described 'the black steamers knocking about in the yellow Mersey, under a sky so low that they seemed to touch it with their funnels, and in the thickest, windiest light'.[36] Ships, like the Wise Men, brought luxurious gifts from the East. Owen would return to boats, docks and water in his poetry, and he would write about mermaids, mariners and drowning, and during the war, he would fondly recall the Pier Head at Liverpool, which is famous today for its three mighty buildings, The Three Graces (although only one, the domed Port of Liverpool Building, could be seen when Owen was a child there). When he heard a Liverpool accent during the war it made him think of the docks: 'a delightful Liverpool brogue (delightful <u>Now</u> and <u>here</u>)'; it reminded him of 'Tranmere, the Pier Head, Sefton Park, and such like'.[37]

Because they were ports, Birkenhead and Liverpool were rather multi-racial, and many nationalities and languages were to be encountered there. Indeed, Birkenhead was a somewhat Welsh town, where the Welsh language could easily be heard, and at 7 Elm Grove the Owens were surrounded by neighbours with Somewhat names – next door on one side they had a Thomas Hughes and on the other a John Evans; at 13 there was a Samuel Jones, and on the other side of the short street there were Thomases, Edwardses, and another Owen. Welsh-language writer and prominent Welsh Nationalist Saunders Lewis was born at Wallasey, next to Birkenhead on the Wirral in 1893: he pointed out that he was not born in 'English England': 'I am fairly certain that there was somewhere in the region of a hundred thousand Welsh-speaking Welshmen in Liverpool throughout my boyhood period. And I should say that at least half of these were monoglot Welsh-speakers who had hardly any English'.[38] Liverpool, with its many Welsh (the *Cymry Lerpwl*) has been described as the capital of Wales. In a letter, Owen alludes to Owen Owen the large Liverpool store established by a Welshman. The National Eisteddfod has been held in both Birkenhead and Liverpool – when it took place in Liverpool in September 1900, the Lord Mayor drew attention to the number of Welsh surnames in the city.

Owen was technically not a Scouser but he was a northerner for some time, although he is rarely seen as such. Perhaps Owen belongs with 'the Liverpool Poets' and the Beatles – Britain's two great anti-war icons of modern times, Wilfred Owen and John Lennon, were lower-middle-class dreamers who longed for a more glamorous elsewhere and began their artistic lives in unremarkable bedrooms in quiet semi-detached Merseyside homes, growing up about six miles and forty years apart.[39] Lennon had his Strawberry Field in Liverpool, and Owen enjoyed the parks of Liverpool and Birkenhead. Birkenhead Park, designed by Joseph Paxton and one of the first and grandest of Victorian parks, was probably the town's chief attraction from the moment of its creation in 1847. Owen mentions 'B'head Park' in an early letter, and Liverpool's parks are mentioned too: in July 1915 he fondly recalled Sefton Park, and 'the Park' in a letter of 1908 was Stanley Park. Parks were places of fantasy and enchantment. Birkenhead's had a princely triumphal entrance and an oriental bridge; Sefton Park had the Grotto, the gnomed Children's Gardens, a very Victorian 'Fairy Glen', an aviary, a Palm House, and statues of explorers, botanists, Highland Mary and 'The Angel's Whisper'; Stanley Park had the Gladstone Conservatory, an aviary, a rustic bridge. It seems appropriate that George Melly, the colourful jazz singer, surrealist and fedora-wearer, was born at the edge of exotic Sefton Park in 1926 (one of Owen's Birkenhead letters mentions a Mr Melly, who would have been a fellow member of this well-known Liverpool family).

The parks also seemed to speak of Progress, that Victorian obsession. Where there had been no flowers apart from weeds, colourful flowerbeds appeared in the nineteenth century, paid for with industry's hard-earned money. Where there were marshes until the Victorian era, beautiful boating lakes appeared. No example of nature was so beautiful that it could not be improved by the addition of an ornamental bridge or a statue of Darwin. Native plants are all very well, but plants from India and the Pacific could make a place magical.

Beyond the parks, Birkenhead and Liverpool were both very modern with only the tiniest architectural evidence of their past lives. To much rejoicing, Edward VII and Queen Alexandra visited Liverpool in 1904 to lay the foundation stone of the Anglican Cathedral and, although the building was to be in the medieval style, it was an expression of the growth, wealth and pride of a city that considered itself the Second City of the Empire and was 'an almost pure product of the nineteenth century, a place empty of memorials'.[40] Birkenhead had ruins of a priory, but otherwise it was a nineteenth-century invention flush with the optimism of the most powerful country in the world. Birkenhead was supposed to show that Britain was ever-improving, and its improvement was the natural consequence of trade and industry:

> Along the coast-way grind the wheels
>   Of endless carts of coal;
> And on the sides of giant keels
>   The shipyard hammers roll.[41]

Tom Owen's railway was the more literal aspect of this progress. In his novel *Tancred* (1847), Benjamin Disraeli was probably being his usual cynical self when he praised Damascus as 'full of life, wealth, and enjoyment' and continued to say that 'the disciples of progress have not been able exactly to match this instance of Damascus, but, it is said that they have great faith in the future of Birkenhead';[42] even so Birkenhead was going places. Growing up in Birkenhead later in the nineteenth century, and attending the highly-regarded Birkenhead School, F. E. Smith imbibed the spirit of progress that made him the 1st Earl of Birkenhead and one of the most successful – and ambitious – men of his age: it was entirely appropriate that the name Birkenhead should have been taken by a politician who famously believed that 'human societies passed through a ceaseless process of evolution' and that 'The world continues to offer glittering prizes to those who have stout hearts and sharp swords'.[43] At the less prestigious Birkenhead Institute between 1900 and 1907, where, at the modern rather unprepossessing premises on Whetstone Lane, Owen received a solid day-school education, he was taught to be proud of his town and the modern age, proud of what the Victorians had achieved, and he would become a fan of brilliant 'F. E.'. Unlike his father, Owen was not interested in team sports, and Birkenhead Institute didn't have playing fields, but at school he could compete for modest academic prizes – he and his friend Alec Paton were picked on for being swots – and began to hope for a successful career. A military career was not on the cards, but he enjoyed playing toy soldiers with Alec.

Yet Owen also associated the Birkenhead years with dirt and misery. They were 'the old dark days'.[44] During the war, when so many men were striving and failing to survive the Somme, it was Birkenhead he was referring to when he said to his mother, 'Can't think how We ever survived the place'.[45] He associated Liverpool with the 'detestably sordid'.[46] Later in life, Owen remembered 'dirty lace curtains in Birkenhead windows'.[47] At Willmer Road, Milton Road and Elm Grove, the Owens were surrounded by roads with sylvan names – Larch, Hazel, Ash, Beech, Laurel, Sycamore, Chestnut, Spruce – but Owen's homes were utterly

towny, and no Eden. The countryside had been left behind. The Mersey
was dirtier then than it is now, and the skies were darkened by many coal
fires and factory chimneys. Birkenhead was a blackened town where
plenty of aching women could be seen cleaning windows and steps.
Malcolm Lowry saw, beyond the exotic docks, lives of heartbreak, dirt
and gloom and the Mersey as 'an enormous open drain'; J. B. Priestley
saw 'gloom and emptiness and decay',[48] 'a heart of darkness'.[49] Certainly,
Harold Owen's memoir becomes a misery memoir when he describes the
Birkenhead years. Susan Owen was still heartbroken about the loss of
Plas Wilmot, and the houses they lived in were shabby in comparison:
brokenhearted by the waters of Birkenhead, Susan sat down and wept
when she remembered Oswestry. Much of Harold's description of
Birkenhead suggests dirt, ill health, degeneracy, pollution, poverty, noise
and ugliness.

When he was fifteen, Wilfred Owen, who was known in his family
as 'Lone Wolf', wrote a story called 'The Autobiography of a Dog', and
it begins by announcing that 'The first place that I can well remember
was a large old country house, where the early part of my life was spent',
but the dog has to leave, encounters unhappiness, and longs for this
paradisal lost home. The dog had moved from the happy countryside
to the rough, violent world of the city: 'I found it a very different life
from the country I had been accustomed to [. . .] I longed to be free
again, to race & swim & hunt rats as in the old life in the country'.[50]
Years later, in 'Exposure', Owen would write about escaping from an
unhappy place into 'grassier ditches [. . .] Littered with blossoms trick-
ling where the blackbird fusses'. No doubt he looked back fondly on
Plas Wilmot, and during the Birkenhead years he seems to have been
happier when visiting the countryside of Wales or Cheshire. The poet
was born in the country, and so too was his poethood: he became a
poet, he said, when he was on holiday with his mother in about 1904:

>   the weeks at Broxton, by the Hill
>   Where first I felt my boyhood fill
>   With uncontainable fancies and strange movements[51]

The beauty of Broxton brought about a change. Broxton was a small village in Cheshire, in the same county as Birkenhead, but somehow in a different world, with its magical hills 'of individual, peculiar and even fantastic forms which rise freakishly from the flat Cheshire plain',[52] and its strong connection to the past through its old timber houses, such as Broxton Hall, its legends and the site of the ancient hill fort called Maiden Castle.

Owen was increasingly drawn to the past: if the present was ugly, then, contrary to 'Progress', he could find happiness in the past. At school he discovered Shakespeare and the medieval worlds of Sir Walter Scott, and was introduced to ancient Rome, and he began to take an interest in the riches of museums and galleries.[53] He would express the museum-goer's sensibility in a poem called 'Perversity', saying:

How singular and sad that I should see
More loveliness in Grecian marbles clear
Than modern flesh

He loved 'Portraits' and 'dark ladies in dark tales antique'. He was unlikely to follow his father into a career with the railways. This backward look was partly a result of his religious upbringing: like many Victorians, he might have been living in the most advanced country in the world, but much of his life was spent among the distant inhabitants of the biblical Middle East. He delighted in the Bible and he also took an interest in the history of the Church. In an early letter, from 1904, he proudly announces that he got ten marks for an essay on St Thomas Becket. For her birthday in 1904, Susan Owen received from her husband *The Pilgrim's Progress from This World to That Which Is to Come* by John Bunyan. This was in fact a gift to the whole family since Tom would read it out to them all, and the book offered an alternative 'Progress', an alternative religion, a Christian's Progress rather than the capitalist's belief in industry and trade.

CHAPTER 2

The Struggle for Existence

I ask not for a Defence from Life-Troubles or an Excuse for not
labouring, but I ask for a Weapon. I <u>will</u> fight through Life;
(have I not fought?)
WILFRED OWEN to SUSAN OWEN, 5 March 1915[1]

'I know it's a – shabby, dingy little place,' he sobbed forth at last,
brokenly: 'not like – your cosy quarters – or Toad's beautiful hall – or
Badger's great house – but it was my own little home – and I was fond of
it – and I went away and forgot all about it – and then I smelt it
suddenly – on the road, when I called and you wouldn't listen, Rat'
KENNETH GRAHAME, *The Wind in the Willows*, 1908 – 'Dulce Domum'[2]

ONE famous Birkenhead resident, Nathaniel Hawthorne, admitted
that 'Liverpool, though not very delightful as a place of residence,
is a most convenient and admirable point to get away from'.[3] Owen did
escape, but not too far. In 1907, Tom Owen was promoted to assistant
superintendent and the Owens moved back to Shrewsbury. Shrewsbury
had become something of a railway town as a link between the
Midlands and the North, and with a grand neo-Tudor station, built in
1849 and expanded in 1855, and with a huge signal box the size of a
row of houses, it announced to the traveller that the railway was an
important part of the town's life. On a GWR railway map of the
period, Shrewsbury is like a squashed spider with six long lines

spreading out of it (three south, two north, one west) and another two lines nearby. The GWR owned the main line that ran down through Shrewsbury to places like Worcester, and, rather than the LNWR, it was the GWR, with its green locomotives and chocolate and cream carriages, that dominated the railway activity of the town.

Shrewsbury was already familiar to the Owens, since not only had they lived there before Birkenhead, Harold having been born there in Wilmot House, Canon Street, on 5 September 1897, but Tom Owen's parents had moved there from Nantwich, living at 2 Hawthorn Villas, Underdale Road, and it was to his parents' corner of the town that they now moved. Owen's paternal grandfather, a keen gardener and a believer in fresh air (his son, too, was a believer in 'Fresh air and manly sport'),[4] was less middle-class than Grandfather Shaw but the Underdale home was welcoming and Owen would pop round to his grandparents for tea until, in 1908, they moved to Torquay, where the air was even fresher.

Shrewsbury is a pretty, higgledy-piggledy place with lovely old buildings, steep Tudorish lanes, statues, views, the Market Square, parks, and, looping round the old town as a vast moat, the Severn. The writer Neville Cardus moved to Shrewsbury from Manchester in 1912 in order to be a cricket coach, and, as he left the station – Tom Owen's station – on a balmy evening, he found 'a lazy county town', a town of 'old timbered shops and chambers': 'To have lived at Shrewsbury in those days and known cricket there is to have lived in a heaven down here below.'[5] Owen praised Shrewsbury in his school exercise books, noting in 1908, for instance, in an uninspired essay on 'The River Severn' (for which he was given a mark of 18 out of 20), that 'the Severn is famous for its beauty', and that 'The Severn at Shrewsbury & for many miles up & down the stream affords excellent facilities for boating and fishing, & the fine scenery is much enjoyed by the visitors & residents'.[6] His character was partly defined by the differences between the places he grew up in – the difference between Oswestry and Birkenhead, and then the difference between Birkenhead and Shrewsbury.

Owen belonged to the less glamorous side of town, on the wrong side of the tracks, outside the loop of the Severn, beyond the railway lines towards the eastern edge of the town, but they were near Shrewsbury Abbey Church, where two of Tom's sisters were married, and their home was still in an attractive leafy location above the river meadows, very quiet, more rural than suburban, and only a pleasant walk away from the Free Library and Museum. This library was a three-century-old building that looked like a corner of Oxford; for most of its life it had been Shrewsbury School and still contained 'lockers and woodwork scrolled with the initials of generations of schoolboys'.[7] Charles Darwin, J. H. Reynolds (minor poet and dear friend of Keats), classicist John 'Demosthenes' Taylor, the poet Ambrose Philips, the hymn-writer Frederick William Faber, 'Prince of Romance', Stanley J. Weyman, Samuel Butler, author of *Erewhon* and *The Way of All Flesh*,[8] and many descendants of Baron Lewis Owen, had studied in the rooms where Owen was a regular visitor, and Owen, like them, could look out of the large windows across the town, taking in the castle, the spires of St Alkmund's and St Mary's and the hills beyond. Although he was a boarder, Darwin's family home was nearby and he could see it from those windows, and now the windows looked on to Darwin, the town's most famous son, after a statue of him was unveiled outside his old school in 1897. The top-floor schoolrooms, filled with light by the large windows, had become the Archaeological Museum and a room at right angles to this was the Natural History Museum. There were many portraits hanging on the walls of the building, depicting Shrewsbury worthies, some of them by famous artists. The library occupied several rooms, and the Reading Room was the old chapel, consecrated in 1617 – thus reading was treated as something sacred and transformative. Maybe that room, and the building generally, helped to foster Owen's deep love of books – in a letter of 1909, he refers to a morning at Shrewsbury Library and then to 'my "Library"' of books he owned at home.[9] It is to the credit of the Victorians that such a building should have become a possession of the entire town and had become a free museum and library dedicated to entertainment as well as education.

Perhaps the most interesting description of Shrewsbury at this time occurs in *The Bending of a Twig* (1906), a once well known story about Shrewsbury School. In that novel the schoolboy hero, Lycidas Marsh, visits the museum:

> he had begun to explore the Old Schools, raising their grey heights close by the railway station. Standing in the ancient rooms, he forgot all the trappings that make of them a town museum, and delighted to repeople them with the boys of centuries ago. He never tired of trying to discover how the rooms had been distributed. It seemed so impossible, that even thirty years back, the Schools had been confined in these cramped quarters! He liked to imagine the difference. Gradually he began to feel fond of these deserted courts, once thronged with boys, now loved by nobody, and of the two old figures, Polymathes and Philomathes, gazing sadly down upon the seedy patrons of the library. [...] When he had satisfied his budding soul, he would walk through the quiet stone-paved lane that leads to Palin's, the old tuck-shop famed in song, and there in the quaint-shaped old rooms would slake his hunger and conjure up yet more Salopians of other days. Usually, however, he found no lack of present-day Salopians.[10]

Owen wasn't fortunate enough to attend expensive Shrewsbury School, which had moved to less hallowed buildings on the other side of the river, and no doubt he looked with some envy at the boys in sixteenth-century Palin's, eating Shrewsbury Cakes or other treats while wearing their straw hats and dark serge suits, but nonetheless he trod in the footsteps of the famous Englishmen when he went to the old school building in order to read the books, inspect the natural history exhibits and admire Roman artefacts. The creeper-clad school educated him, and played its part in Owen's love for poetry, botany and the Roman Empire (all three of these loves would be found in poems like '1914').

His interest in the area's Roman heritage led him on many occasions five miles east of the town to the Roman remains at Uriconium (or

Viroconium), whence the artefacts at Shrewsbury's museum came after excavations in the nineteenth century. The Roman settlement of Uriconium was built in about AD 58 for the invasion of Wales, and later became a civilian city. In a poem about Uriconium, Owen describes the violence that has almost been forgotten – the Romans taking on the Welsh, and then the Saxons attacking and burning down the Roman city in about AD 400 – but he admires the arts and crafts of the violent past:

Plasters with Roman finger-marks impressed;
Bracelets, that from the warm Italian arm
    Might seem to be scarce cold;
And spears – the same that pushed the Cymry west –
Unblunted yet; with tools of forge and farm
Abandoned, as a man in sudden fear
Drops what he holds to help his swift career:
For sudden was Rome's flight, and wild the alarm.
The Saxon shock was like Vesuvius' qualm.

The museum was his muse. At Shrewsbury, Owen also read John Ruskin, the great Victorian who so elegantly celebrated the past and who seemed to like art more than people – it was said that Ruskin, like the Owen of 'Perversity', preferred smooth Grecian marbles to the occasionally hairy modern flesh of his beautiful wife, to such an extent that his wedding night was a disaster. Owen's teenage poetry was often antique and artificial, written in an old style with thee, thy, thou, dost, canst and yea. Indeed, one of the figures from the past who interested him was Thomas Chatterton, who wrote pseudo-archaic poetry and prose as a teenager in the eighteenth century. Owen wasn't just interested in history; he wanted to live in the past. Was the present so horrific that he had to turn away from it? Chatterton and Owen, like other lovers of the antique, came from fairly humble backgrounds but they also grew up in an environment where that love of the past could be stimulated and fed – Chatterton had the magnificent church of St Mary Redcliffe in Bristol, Owen had Shrewsbury.

Equally, Owen enjoyed walking out to the rustic old-world village of Uffington, where he could delight in the kind of rural Englishness that was about to disappear for ever more, and where, on Haughmond Hill, he admired the picturesque ruins of Haughmond Abbey and the view over Shrewsbury. His brother Harold has recalled the family's Sunday evening walks to Uffington church:

> The gradual approach to the tiny church through the mist-hung fields, the peaceful swishing sound that came from our quietly treading feet as we bent, but did not break, the yielding grasses; there was a modulation in all our voices which mysteriously orchestrated the sound of our unhurried walking. The air would be heavy with the scented richness of heavily breathing beasts. Wilfred's swallows (all swallows were Wilfred's because he liked them so much) would dart and plane around and between us, bats would circle our heads and never strike us, friendly blundering cockchafers would trundle out of nowhere and cannon playfully off our faces; as we neared the river we would hear the sucking pull and plop as cattle idled in the shallow mud-churned water, and across the river gleaming with friendly welcome we would see the dimly lighted windows of the little church.[11]

Many people would consider Owen fortunate to have been living in a such a beautiful corner of the country at a time when the motor car was still rare, horses ploughed the fields and only birds or shooting stars flew through the sky. Yet Owen also called Shrewsbury 'vile'[12] and dull, and in August 1909 he singled out Haughmond Hill and the museum as the only things he liked in Shrewsbury (when his mother was away). In his 'Roundel', a later poem about the Quarry, a public park in the town, Owen portrays the town as boring and lifeless, its residents as ignorant bumpkins. It is surprising that Owen remained so unenthusiastic about the town, and if he ever wrote poetry in praise of it that poetry doesn't survive. Perhaps Shrewsbury was a bit dull (there's a difference between beauty and excitement) – in 1890,

Baedeker's guide to Great Britain, giving the town's population as
just 26,480 (Liverpool's population was 552,425 and Birkenhead's
83,324), advised that 'Not more than half-a-day need be devoted to
Shrewsbury'.[13] During Owen's time there, the national press became
interested only when, during the early hours of 15 October 1907, an
express train left the rails at Shrewsbury, killing nineteen people and
injuring many more.[14] The newspapermen and photographers arrived
to capture the appalling wreckage, but once they and the debris had
gone, the town could return to its quiet ways and Tom Owen's work
on the railways quickly became undramatic once again. Shrewsbury
was also about as far from a major town or city as a small town in
England was likely to be. This was part of its charm, but possibly not
for a teenaged Wilfred Owen. In his poem about Uriconium in 1913
Owen seems to have enjoyed imagining a time before Shrewsbury
existed: the Shropshire of beautiful Italian jewellery, wolves, bears,
'men of shaggy hair', druids and Tuscan generals is an alternative to a
genteel Anglo-Saxon Shrewsbury of public-school boys, pampered
dogs and sombre churchgoing.

Perhaps when Owen rhymed 'pikel' with 'Michael' when describing
St Michael in one of his war poems, he was recalling the bell-jingles of
Shrewsbury: '"Three silver pikels," / say the bells of St. Michael's.'[15] Yet
Shrewsbury does not play a very noticeable part in Owen's extant poems.
Even 'Roundel' and 'Uriconium' are minor poems. This was an age in
which writers were seemingly keen to claim a corner of Britain as their
own territory – Brontë Country in Yorkshire, Tennyson Country in
Lincolnshire. Hardy Country was Dorset, D. H. Lawrence would claim
Nottinghamshire, Wordsworthshire was the Lake District, Hilaire
Belloc had Sussex, and so on. It was the time of the 'Struggle for Africa'
and the 'pole bagging' adventures of explorers, and writers planted their
flags too. As a poet from Birkenhead in Cheshire and two towns in
Shropshire, Owen could have claimed either county as his own, but they
never would become Owen country. There would be no Liverpool
poems; nothing like 'Penny Lane' and 'Strawberry Fields Forever'; no
poems about the Mersey. Another Great War poet, Ivor Gurney, would

be the one to celebrate the brown Severn in his poetry, not least in the collection *Severn and Somme*. And in 1896, with the publication of *A Shropshire Lad*, A. E. Housman, a Worcestershire man, had acquired Shropshire. Led there by Housman's poetry, E. M. Forster visited Shrewsbury in 1907 and found it 'unspoilt and alive: a city of vigor still adjusted to its beautiful frame. Poetry – or luck – in every inch of it.'[16] With Housman, and then E. M. Forster and P. G. Wodehouse, Shropshire was a special place, Arcadian, the land of blue remembered hills and Blandings Castle, but, unlike these literary visitors, Owen, the bona fide Shropshire lad, would not delineate the county in his writing. Owenshire would not have been Shropshire but abroad – first France and then Italy, the East, elsewhere. The crest he used as a fourteen-year-old could have been a badge for life: it combined a globe with a cross, and underneath ran the motto 'To Observe the World'.

The places of his childhood had little direct impact on his poems, but during these years Owen formed the most important relationship of his life, one that would have a significant impact on his poetry. The Owens lost their home, but Owen never lost his mother. Although he found it difficult to write successfully about Susan specifically, he was devoted to her, and her influence can be seen in his poetry, where mothers and children appear frequently. As Susan said after his death, 'Wilfred was always such a devoted son, our love for each other intense'.[17] As he admitted, 'I stand (yes and sit, lie, kneel & walk, too,) in need of some tangible caress from you [. . .] my affections are physical as well as abstract – intensely so'.[18] His childhood was very much his mother. Owen was solitary and bookish, and it is more likely that an enquiring, artistic boy will be very close to his mother if he grows up without a nanny, without a boarding-school education, without a beautiful home, and without the money for travel and an active social life, but with a hard-working father and a mother sufficiently cultured and sensitive to understand and entertain her child. Owen's relationship with his mother remained close, even when he was the teenager hiding away in his bedroom: Harold Owen observed that 'Wilfred had only one reliable relief from loneliness, the solace which my mother alone could give him'.[19] Those who knew Owen at this time referred to him as not only detached but also a 'cissy', 'mollycoddled' by Susan. As a teenager, he still had his mother peeling his apple at supper.[20] She helped to protect him from growing up.

Appropriately, when Owen's poethood was born at Broxton he was on holiday with his mother, and her only. It was there, Harold Owen says, 'among the ferns and bracken and the little hills, secure in the safety and understanding love that my mother wrapped about him with such tender ministration, that the poetry in Wilfred, with gentle pushings, without hurt, began to bud'.[21] Harold makes his brother's poethood sound like the offspring of an incestuous liaison in the bracken. Certainly, with Susan he could talk of his ardent hopes for a poet's life. As a boy he 'guessed that the fullest, largest liveable life was that of a Poet'.[22] Poetry from his teens shows an ambitious poet determined to learn his trade despite what he saw, at sixteen, as his 'lowliness, and lack of friends' (his Birkenhead friendship with Alec Paton had inevitably weakened).[23] Nonetheless, it would be fair to say that as a child Owen showed little extraordinary talent in any field. He was not Chatterton or Rimbaud, and, despite piano lessons, he was no Mozart. He doesn't seem to have had the mythically special, charismatic teacher who one day took him to one side and slipped him a slim volume of verse, awakening a genius that that teacher nurtured with books, money and attention; if anyone encouraged his artistic side then it was his mother. One school report said that 'His work is very fair but I expected rather a better place in the form; I think his abilities are excellent';[24] his writing at school was good but not remarkable. Owen's childhood was largely uneventful – like Philip Larkin in his poem 'I Remember, I Remember', he could have listed all the remarkable things that didn't happen. He was not considered a genius, no one saw the greatness in him, he had no life-changing friendships, he didn't have an unusual education; equally, he wasn't badly treated, he wasn't a street urchin or an exile or a runaway. He was loved, he was clothed, he was fed, he was moderately successful at school, he was a child: he spoke as a child, he understood as a child, he thought as a child.

By the time Owen reached his 18th birthday in 1911, he had a deepening interest in poetry, although his tastes, which were essentially Romantic, were not unusual – in particular, he was devoted to Keats. In an essay on 'Autumn' on 9 September 1907, Owen quoted from 'To Autumn', one of Keats's best-known poems, however ascribed the quotation to Sir Walter Scott and his teacher had to correct this error; however Owen soon knew Keats intimately. His poem 'Written in a Wood, September 1910' is about Keats, and 'Sonnet: Written at Teignmouth, on a Pilgrimage to Keats's House' was begun on 21 April 1911. He was interested in the man as much as the poetry, writing at Shrewsbury that:

> The poetry of Keats must have a peculiar charm to every reader, whether familiar with the story of the author or not, but when the circumstances of their composition are known one cannot fail to be doubly attracted by the rich effusions of the young beauty-lover.[25]

While on holiday at Torquay, Owen bought a biography of Keats and 'began this morning "with fear and trembling" to learn the details of his life': 'I sometimes feel in reading such books that I would give ten years of life to have been born a hundred years earlier (always providing that I have the same dear mother)'.[26] The unfinished poem from this holiday, 'Before Reading a Biography of Keats for the First Time', echoes Keats's 'On First Looking into Chapman's Homer', not least in its enthusiasm for reading. Keats's poetry offered him a world of dreams, seclusion, romance and escape, but, in its less exciting moments, the life chimed with his own. When Owen's mind was 'filled with cogitation and perplexities and despondencies' in 1911, he quoted a famous statement that Keats made at Teignmouth in 1818:

> 'The imagination of a boy is healthy, and the mature imagination of a man is healthy; but there is a space of life between in which the soul is in a ferment, the character undecided, the way of life uncertain, (yes!), and the ambition thick-sighted (yes indeed!)'[27]

At Teignmouth, in the same rainy, misty weather that Keats had known there, Owen went to Keats's house and 'gaped at it (regardless of people in the window who finally became quite alarmed, I fancy) – to my heart's content'.[28] The people at the house might have been alarmed, but visiting writers' 'homes and haunts' was far from uncommon: Owen can't have been the first to stare at that house. In 1892, one literary pilgrim observed that 'to trace the footsteps of the great and good, and to point out and describe the scenes which are indissolubly linked with their lives and writings, has become, in these later days, very fashionable'.[29] When he was in London later in 1911, Owen visited Keats's house in Hampstead, 'one of London's most holy spots'.[30] Owen was quite the conventional poetry fan of his time, Norfolk-jacketed with a slim volume in a buttoned-up pocket (which is how he was photographed in 1912), ever alert to literary associations and pained by 'the impossibility of seeing the departed hero'.[31] 'Sonnet: Written at Teignmouth, on a Pilgrimage to Keats's House' sits with innumerable amateur Edwardian poems of pilgrimage.

*

At the time of his pilgrimage to Teignmouth, Owen was a pupil-teacher in Shrewsbury. Outwardly, his life was a vision of normality – a typical young man somewhere near the middle of society, just slightly above the working classes. He had entered Shrewsbury Borough Technical School for the spring term in 1907 and trained as a pupil-teacher there: the Technical School was a pupil-teacher centre offering not only teaching experience in a school but also daily tuition at the centre rather than by the school head. Owen taught at Wyle Cop elementary school. Combining learning at the Technical School and teaching at Wyle Cop was not easy. One former pupil-teacher looked back at this time (of mornings spent teaching and the rest of the day studying) and said 'I have often wondered if anybody was ever as tired as I was then; I suppose I never had more than five hours' sleep in every twenty-four for more than two years'. It was hard work that pupil-teachers across the country were struggling with, fuelled by a

determination to elevate themselves socially and find a stable career.[32]
The pupil-teacher route allowed people from humble backgrounds to
rise in society, but only slightly. The elementary school teacher was not
well-paid, but he was not quite working-class.

Owen was living with his parents. In 1910, the family moved from
1 Cleveland Place, Underdale Road, Shrewsbury, to a house nearby on
Monkmoor Road, a modern orange-brick semi called 'Mahim'. Owen,
his family's 'Lone Wolf' or 'Old Wolf', sat in his attic bedroom at
Mahim and worked and dreamt and sulked and looked out at the coun-
tryside. His cry was a Garbo-esque 'I want to be alone'. Some of those
who knew Owen in his teens described how he was always at work in
his bedroom, and unsociable, detached,[33] 'disdainful, aloof, stand-
offish'.[34] The attic bedroom is traditionally the dreamer's room, a room
with fewer distractions, with its view of clouds and fields rather than
the street, and with the sound of birds rather than distant people – this
was a room for a young man who, we are told, felt superior to his envi-
ronment.[35] He could literally look down on his surroundings, on his
class, on his neighbours, and plan to escape them all.

The Owen family were classic examples of the lower middle
class. This was the class that J. B. Priestley (a year younger than Owen)
grew up in, and he has provided a detailed description of the world he
and Owen knew, saying that it probably supplied most cities and towns
'with about a quarter of their population': 'Most shopkeepers, office
workers, superior factory foremen, the less successful professional men,
teachers, craftsmen, commercial travellers ('salesmen' to us), owners
of small businesses, all were members of this class'. This class earned
anything from £150 to £500 a year, might employ some domestic
help, as the Owens did, and lived in a decent terrace or a semi.[36] Paying
a pound a week in rent, which was at the upper limit of what a man
of Tom Owen's income could afford, the Owens could be called
'comfortable'.

Within their lower-middle-class homes with their exotic or rustic
names in Shrewsbury or London or Oswestry or any town, men and
women struggled along with aching ambition and pride and a longing

for a better life (indicated in most cases by their willingness to pay for an education for their children). One of the best-loved comic novels of the period, *The Diary of a Nobody* (1892), captures this world, describing the lower-middle-class suburban life of the city clerk Mr Pooter and his family in The Laurels, Brickfield Terrace, Holloway, 'a nice six-roomed residence, not counting basement with a front breakfast-parlour': 'We were rather afraid of the noise of the trains at first, but the landlord said we should not notice them after a bit, and took £2 off the rent. He was certainly right; and beyond the cracking of the garden wall at the bottom, we have suffered no inconvenience'.[37] The twentieth century would be their century, and they would give it prime ministers, pop stars and great poets, but it is easy to laugh at the lower middle classes: they are at the heart of English social comedy of the last century or more, embarrassingly provincial with their Dunroamins or Mole Ends or Mahims, the garden gnome, the close, the semi, the serviette, local politics and the nicely kempt hedge. Owen's teenage letters have a Pooterish and Adrian-Moleish quality: 'Once again I am just too late to see a great personage'.[38] This comment to his mother, thanking her for his 19th-birthday present, speaks volumes:

> I am delighted with the colour of the slippers; nothing could be better – (unless it were a rather less dark colour; for by gaslight this looks not quite bright enough.) But they are distinctly large, and I think I shall ask for a smaller pair if you would be so very good; tho' it is hard for me to wait, you know.[39]

The lower middle classes are stereotypically slipper people, the boring people, the stiff-collared semi-educated aspirants who are obsessed with their own status, or who cannot afford to enjoy themselves lest they fail to get on (although they might aspire, 'if you would be so very good', to a decadently bright colour for their slippers). They are the products of 'Progress', that Victorian religion that Owen grew up believing in, and are laughed at for their gullibility or for their attempts at sophistication and self-improvement. Few writers want to be lower-middle-class:

many writers have wanted to be poor, and have dreamt of gypsies, tramps and whores, and many writers have wanted to be rich and posh, hoping to exchange their written words for the country estate or at least the privileged security of the upper-middle and middle-middle classes with their investments and their university degrees. But who wants to belong to the joyless, clueless class, the class that is neither one thing nor the other and is despised by those above and below?

Certainly, not all of the lower-middle-classes wanted to be lower-middle-class. Like many men of his social status, Tom Owen clung to a tale of family decline, and was proud to think of himself as a member of the fallen aristocracy, a man with 'Sirs' in his ancestry. But Tom Owen did not have a privileged upbringing. He had started his railway career aged fifteen as a clerk with the Cambrian Railways Company (probably in Oswestry), but in 1880, at the age of eighteen, decided to move to a clerkship in the headquarters of a rather more exotic company, the Great Indian Peninsula Railway (GIPR). He worked in Bombay for four years and this spell of his life, covering the years when a wealthier and better-educated man would have been at university, became the great adventure of his life when viewed from the grey normality of his later years. He would frequently recall his Indian days, although in a rather vague and unreliable manner, mixing truth with fiction. Equally, when he was in Bombay, he probably upgraded his own background, as many Englishmen in India did at the time. Precisely what Tom Owen did and saw amid the heat and dust of India is unclear, but the sea journey to Bombay on the SS *Benalder*, working as a 'boy', is attested to by the certificate of discharge, which would be venerated as a prized relic from his youth, rather like a degree certificate (he received 'Very Good' for 'Conduct' and 'Ability').[40] Tom Owen arrived at one of the great cities of the Empire, the city of palms and pearls, its greatness declared by buildings like the neoclassical Town Hall, the Gothic Bombay University, the High Victorian Elphinstone Circle and the ornate Victoria and Albert Museum – with, in front, its memorial tower dedicated to the Queen by Sir Albert Sassoon. At the landing-stage called Apollo Bunder, after a journey through the

Mediterranean and the Suez Canal, passengers from Britain would have seen the striking Royal Bombay Yacht Club, which had been built as recently as 1880. Almost exactly two years after Tom Owen, Rudyard Kipling arrived at Apollo Bunder in the city of his birth ('Of no mean city am I'),[41] and transferred to the railway, which would take him to Lahore. Bombay was a vast port, 'the gate of India', but the GIPR was equally important and in 1887, with its domed tower that resembles Tom Tower at Oxford University, and its statues, spires, gargoyles and turrets, the palatial and cathedralish Victoria Terminus, decorated by the art students of Kipling's father, would be opened as the grandest expression of this importance – 'it could make a persuasive claim to be truly the central building of the entire British Empire'.[42] Accordingly, the railway's British employees were treated well, and Bombay was a comfortable, healthy and modern place to live.

So, given his love of India and the career opportunities it offered him, one might wonder why Tom Owen chose to return to rainy, low-key Shropshire. Just like his time there, his decision to leave is shrouded in mystery, but it's possible that, like one of A. E. Housman's Shropshire men exiled in London or the Empire, he simply developed a longing for home. Certainly, Kipling would write about the loneliness of the Englishman in India. Perhaps, like rather less industrious eighteen-year-old gap-year travellers in India, Tom Owen 'found himself' and made plans for the future, and perhaps these plans involved marrying Susan Shaw, whom he might already have known from his time in Oswestry, but he returned seven years before he married her. Whatever the reason for his return, he clung to dreams of India, even as a sensible married man. 'Mahim', an unusual name in England, was the name of one of the islands of Bombay, taken from Tom Owen's Indian days. After Mahim was given to Charles II by the Portuguese, the British built a fort there, and it still stands by the beach. Kipling recalled Mahim in 'The Gipsy Trail': 'By a purple wave on an opal beach / In the hush of the Mahim woods'. The name fitted the suburban habit of naming an unexciting home after somewhere exotic – in the Highlands or the Mediterranean or the

Empire. The suburban house name represents dreams, memories, ambitions, disappointment, delusion. Here in 'Mahim', Tom looked through travel agents' catalogues, inspecting sea journeys he would never make.

Tom chose that name 'Mahim' of course, and Susan would show very little interest in her husband's time in India. She also seems to have been unaware of his alternative existence as 'the Captain': Tom used to like hanging around the docks in Birkenhead and even let himself become known to people down there as a sea captain, when he was no such thing, and he would take his sons to see the ships and sailors, bringing Indian sailors back to the family home for dinner on at least one occasion, like the captain of a ship doing his duty towards his crew. These sailors were a connection with Tom's own time of escape and reinvention, when he lived in India. Tom asked his sons to keep 'the Captain' a secret – later, his eldest son would show, in his poetry, an interest in secrets, informers, disguises and 'secret men who know their secret safe'.[43] Beyond seaside holidays in Aberdovey, Aberystwyth or Scarborough, Susan seems to have had little interest in the sea: it was to be seen and heard, but only from the pier, the beach or the promenade. To her family, Susan represented home, and she seems to have enjoyed her homemaking, even though she was often physically unable to do all she wished, as a result of a rather weak constitution. This was partly a consequence of their social position: Susan had to run the house, with minimal paid help, and there was no nanny or housekeeper. Owen did call his mother 'home (personified)'[44] in 1908, and ten years later he could still tell her that 'you are home'.[45]

In his teens and after, Owen showed some similarities to his father in so far as he looked for escape, although the closest he got to India was when reading the writer Rabindranath Tagore or when he imitated a 'salaamer' in baggy pyjamas and a turban made from a towel (a photograph of this impersonation was darkened to give him the appropriate skin tone).[46] Being as old as the cinema, which was arguably born in 1893, a few weeks after Owen, he had discovered escapist films:

That afternoon we also saw the 'Pictures'
The French boys always charm me, but the mixtures
Of Blood and Thunder Stories sometimes shock me.[47]

This was when he was seventeen. Almost as soon as cinemas arrived in England, Owen was paying a few pence in order to see 'wonderful Pictures (animated)'.[48] By 'animated' pictures he meant not necessarily cartoons, drawn on to the film – although these were shown from 1908 onwards – but 'Moving Pictures' generally. In August 1910, he saw *Buffalo-Hunting in Indo-China* in 'Animated Pictures' – this was one of a series of short French films about hunting around the world, magic casements opening on to exotic landscapes in Eastern Europe, Africa and Asia. The hunting series included films on falconry in Algeria, and wolf-hunting in Russia. In *Buffalo-Hunting in Indo-China*, one buffalo in particular is seen being shot in the kind of muddy, watery landscape that would later characterise the Western Front ('What passing-bells for these who die as cattle?').[49] Harold Owen, another keen cinemagoer, recalled that 'Sometimes Wilfred would glide silently down from his attic and quietly taking a place in the room would listen while my father drew us out about the films we had seen'.[50]

Wilfred followed his mother's tastes too by going to galleries, and sought out famous pictures in books and magazines, hungry for beauty and, like his father, far-off places. In September 1911, Owen stayed in Wimbledon and took the opportunity to visit London's galleries and museums. He would always be an admirer of London, excited by its range of cultural delights and by the sense of being somewhere necessary, the sense of sharing the streets with great men and important conversations. He went to the theatre and played the tourist, visiting the famous sights. At the National Gallery, he was entranced by the faces in the pictures, 'which have woven a spell over me', telling his mother, 'I must not begin to describe or to name even the pictures hanging there'.[51] He seems to have been more attracted to these faces than to those of the elegant gallery-haunting women, who used to come and go, talking of Michelangelo. He did report that at the Tate

Gallery a lady slipped over on the polished floor, but it was portraiture that thrilled him most of all. In 'Disabled', he would write that 'There was an artist silly for his face', and his poetry would provide some memorable faces, such as those 'Drooping tongues from jaws that slob their relish / Baring teeth that leer like skulls' teeth wicked'.[52] The wartime poem 'I Saw his Round Mouth's Crimson' is an eight-line portrait of a face.

Soon after his twenty-first birthday, Owen admitted that if he had been destined to be a painter, following the legendary lives of painters, he would in childhood have shown extraordinary talent. A surviving portrait sketch that he made of his brother Colin would infact suggest that Owen had little talent in that direction. Painting would be left to the other brother, Harold, who hoped to become a professional artist. In 1911, Owen told Harold that he was proud his brother had chosen art and was 'launched out upon its wide stream' (in 1913, Harold would launch himself on the wide seas, joining the Merchant Service and leaving that wide stream behind).[53] Owen launched himself upon poetry, arguing that painters must have studied poetry and that Keats was one such pictorial and 'Artist-souled' poet.[54] At the British Museum, he 'spent hours in subdued ecstasy' reading two letters by Keats as well as two books of manuscript poems that were open at 'The Eve of St Mark' and 'Hyperion'.[55] He studied Keats's corrections and handwriting closely: Owen was, as ever, the dedicated student of poetry, learning his trade, learning from the masters. He was now old enough for university, and in his visits to the British Museum, when many eighteen-year-olds would have been chasing after girls rather than Keats, he showed himself to be a budding scholar and a young man eager for a literary life.

CHAPTER 3

The Banned Word

And thou hast climbed the hill,
And gained the white brow of the Cumner range;
Turned once to watch, while thick the snowflakes fall,
The line of festal light in Christ Church hall –
Then sought thy straw in some sequestered grange.
MATTHEW ARNOLD, '*The Scholar-Gipsy*', 1853[1]

a University is not a birthplace of poets or of immortal authors
J. H. NEWMAN, *The Idea of a University*, 1852[2]

I N 1911 or 1912, Wilfred Owen could have been arriving at university
as the full cliché, tweedy with a tin trunk and a long scarf, talking to
a porter in an old gateway, ready for three years of beautiful buildings
and brilliant friends, a poet awaiting the glittering prizes. Rupert
Brooke went to Cambridge, Edward Thomas went to Oxford, Siegfried
Sassoon went to Cambridge, Edmund Blunden went to Oxford,
Robert Nichols went to Oxford, Robert Graves went to Oxford, Julian
Grenfell went to Oxford: most of the 'war poets' were Oxbridge prod-
ucts or Oxbridge-bound. Vera Brittain arrived at Oxford in 1914
hoping to 'begin to live'.[3] Wilfred Owen dearly wanted to go to Oxford.
In those years before the First World War, Oxford was in its Golden
Age, although a Golden Age sustained by wealth and inequality – the
angelic, golden-haired (and poorly educated) Prince of Wales arrived

as an undergraduate in 1912 as the crowning glory of this blithe and untroubled time. E. R. Dodds, a Professor of Greek who was born in the same year as Owen, went up in October 1912, and, 'in the last years of the Affluent Age', found Oxford 'absurd, delightful, totally irresponsible, and totally self-assured' – it was 'moulded on a way of life that appeared unshakeably preordained yet was about to vanish like the fabric of a dream'.[4] But Owen was denied the privilege of entering this secret garden. Harold Owen remembered his brother's 'passionate cries for three years at Oxford'.[5] The lack of Oxford actually made him positively angry, so in July 1913 Owen had explained that he hadn't been to Uriconium again, 'Perhaps because of those two Oxford Blues, whose colours are to me as red to a bull'.[6] On 25 July 1915 he would write to his cousin Leslie Gunston,

> Couldn't you divine why 'Oxford' is a banned word with me. Because it is one of my most terrible regrets. <u>I ought to be there</u>, not fuddling among the Vines. I ought to <u>have</u> <u>been</u> there, rather. Surely, you knew the cause of my 'flare'.[7]

By then, Leslie, the son of Susan's sister Emma, was in Oxford during his training as an architect, and enjoyed describing the university for Owen, also sending a postcard of New College. His spell there caused the flare of anger, exposing Owen's strong sense of entitlement to the university that had educated poets and was now entertaining Leslie.

The unrequited love is as much a part of one's life as the requited; in fact, it can be more powerful than the requited (as poets know). The road not taken was an important part of Owen's life – he felt regrets painfully and repeatedly, and he believed that Oxford would have helped his poetry. It is clear that Owen often thought of Oxford, even if it was a banned word, and he imagined himself as an undergraduate. Many writers have loved Oxford from outside, harbouring dreams of studying there despite lacking the money that could make that possible. As Owen had written at school, Keats's poetry is marvellous, 'especially when one remembers that Keats was born in a middling walk of Eng.

city life, and had neither a long period of schooling, nor a university training'[8] – a note that offers some hope for anyone who doesn't get to Oxford while simultaneously suggesting that a poet should have university and a proper schooling, but impoverished Keats was, like Owen, one of the greatest admirers of this city, and Keats's association with Oxford would have added to its attraction for Owen.

It was the 'Affluent Age', when, within the grey walls, money was married to medieval monasticism, and money was a problem for Owen. In 'To Poesy', written when he was about sixteen or seventeen, Owen says that he wants to learn to write poetry, which entails studying every writer, but 'I know this learning must be bought / With gold as well as toil, and gold I lack'. In 1912 the Warden of New College stated that for an undergraduate an allowance of £200 a year, excluding vacations but including a 'full part in games and social entertainments', was 'not an excessive amount'.[9] Not excessive perhaps, but it was about as large as Tom Owen's annual salary. There were, though, ways to get money: scholarships and bursaries were offered, and there were always poorer boys at Oxford who had got there through a mixture of luck, support, hard work and brilliance – indeed, an article on the Oxford under-graduate in the *Strand Magazine* in 1911 identified an increasing number of 'poorer men, with help and with utilitarian views, wishing to better their worldly prospects'.[10] By 1910 nearly 10 per cent were said to be from working-class or lower-middle class backgrounds, and according to New College's Warden in 1912, 'the number of the poor and struggling has increased':

Every College contains men who live with the greatest frugality and economy; some Colleges contain a very large number of such men, and all Colleges make it a point of conscience to keep considerable funds to assist men in their struggles. It would not be an exaggeration to say that any man of proved industry and ability coming to Oxford the gainer of a Scholarship or an Exhibition would be enabled to carry through his University course with the assistance which he could obtain from his College or elsewhere. County

Councils and other educational authorities often contribute largely, though not always judiciously, to enable deserving students to come to the Universities.[11]

But it was very hard to win one of the small number of scholarships and exhibitions, and Owen was neither an A1 scholar nor a mighty passer of examinations, 'those absurd old toll-gates'.[12] And Owen hadn't been to great schools, so any scholarship would have had to have been based on a great deal of self-education. Only the very brilliant could have overcome a lack of money and second-rate schooling. The few prominent Oxford men from working-class or lower-middle-class backgrounds had gone to famous schools.

There were also non-collegiate students, who needed less parental support because it was cheaper not to belong to a college. But Owen would not have wanted the lonely, anxious and half-fulfilled life of the non-collegiate students, and even so they tended to come from 'respectable' middle-class homes because non-collegiate study was still expensive. For any Oxford education Owen would have needed a scholarship or bursary of some kind: he considered begging money from a wealthier uncle, but the generosity of uncles seems to have been denied him. Moreover, even if he had had wealth, Owen would have had to acquire Greek. The thick-headed undergraduate, who drank and dined and rowed and roared his way through Oxford with little time for books, would have nevertheless have had to know Latin and Greek to an extent that Owen could not have matched. Although he was inclined towards the anti-Stratfordian insistence that Shakespeare must have had a university education, Owen, like Shakespeare, 'hadst small Latin, and less Greek'. Greek was still a compulsory part of the preliminary examination for any degree, and Owen hadn't learnt it (or had only the slightest acquaintance with it). Birkenhead School helped F. E. Smith to become 'a fox-hunting man who could swear elegantly in Greek', but Owen attended Birkenhead Institute;[13] Shrewsbury School employed eminent Greek scholars, but Shrewsbury Technical School, which gave Owen a good grounding in English and botany, was not a school for Greek.

Three years at Oxford between 1911 and 1914 would have given Owen time to write and discuss poetry in the comfort of a college. Whichever college he was at, he would have had a chance of meeting J. R. R. Tolkien, or Dorothy L. Sayers, or Sayers's friends Vera Brittain and Winifred Holtby. T. E. Lawrence was often away, but Oxford was still home and he had a post at Magdalen College. T. S. Eliot went up to Merton College in 1914. As his brother notes, Owen was aware that the lack of a university education left him outside literary society:

> Until a matter of months before he was killed, he did not, and was not able to meet people of literary importance, let alone mix freely amongst them. He knew well enough that three years at a University would have changed all this.[14]

Harold connects this lack of a university education to the fact that his brother was 'from a worldly point of view somewhat socially immature, really through lack of experience'.[15] Evelyn Waugh would later defend an Oxford education by claiming that 'Those who choose or are obliged to begin regular, remunerative, responsible work at the moment they leave school, particularly if they have had a fairly carefully tended adolescence, often show signs of a kind of arrested development'.[16] Wilfred Owen's boyishness could be ascribed to his swift movement from the comforts of his doting mother into the world of work. By his own admission, Owen was a boy in the autumn of 1911, still lovingly presenting to his mother 'my cheeks for the good-night kiss',[17] and he would later leave himself and others wondering whether he had ever grown up.

Instead of Oxford, Owen got another part of Oxfordshire, arriving at the village of Dunsden near Reading in October 1911 to work as lay assistant to the Rev. Herbert Wigan. For a bookish boy from a religious home, this had emerged as a natural and affordable step – he could help with parish work and be 'generally companionable to a lonely country-sequestered bachelor',[18] in return for board and lodging and pocket money, while continuing his studies. It was supposed to be a less exhausting option than teaching. Susan's sister's family, the Gunstons, lived near Reading and, from the Gunstons' vicar, Owen had been directed to Herbert Wigan.

This post offered Owen a taste of the affluence and civility that he had not known in Oswestry. It was the vicarage that really attracted him to the post. He hankered after a better, more beautiful world, and now he was wearing evening dress for dinner and having learned conversations of an evening, being 'very proper indeed',[19] living in a large vicarage with servants and books, and in a village that had literary and artistic associations. He was pleased to discover that Holman Hunt had lived nearby (Wigan met him) and that Mary Russell Mitford's *Our Village* (1832) describes the countryside near Reading. At Dunsden, Owen was given *Elizabeth Barrett Browning and Her Poetry* (1912),[20] and the book points out that *Sonnets from the Portuguese* was privately printed at Reading, and that Barrett Browning was friends with Mary Russell Mitford. He knew that in 1850 Tennyson had been married at Shiplake, three miles from Dunsden. Tennyson praised both the parish and the parson:

> Vicar of this pleasant spot
> Where it was my chance to marry,
> Happy, happy be your lot
> In the vicarage by the quarry.
> You were he that knit the knot!
>
> Sweetly, smoothly flow your life.
> Never parish feud perplex you,
> Tithe unpaid, or party strife,
> All things please you, nothing vex you,
> You have given me such a wife![21]

In *Three Men in a Boat* (1889), Jerome K. Jerome's story of a journey up the Thames from London to Oxford, Shiplake is described as 'a pretty village', and the river below 'very placid, hushed, and lonely [. . .]

It is a part of the river in which to dream of bygone days, and vanished forms and faces, and things that might have been, but are not, confound them.'[22]

Soon after arriving at Dunsden, Owen, always interested in the lives of writers and eager to follow in their footsteps, wrote a verse letter about the literary associations of the area – Shelley, who lived at Great Marlow and wrote poetry in his boat on the 'happy Thames'; Thomas Gray, whose 'Elegy in a Country Churchyard' belongs to Stoke Poges; Matthew Arnold, who loved Oxfordshire and Berkshire; and Tennyson, whose wedding took place 'small space away'.[23] The night before the wedding, Emily Sellwood stayed at a house called Holmwood, outside Shiplake, on the way to Dunsden, and later this house became the home of the parents of A. C. Swinburne – Owen owned Swinburne's *A Song of Italy*, which was partly written there. Owen might also have known of the Jane Austen associations: Austen's uncle having been vicar of Sonning at a time when that cross-county parish included Dunsden;[24] Austen's mother having hailed from Harpsden, a village down the road from Dunsden; and Austen herself having been at school in Reading.[25] Owen could not have known that this was also Orwell country. George Orwell, still simply Eric Blair then, was a nine-year-old schoolboy in 1912 when his family moved to Lower Shiplake (Shiplake and Dunsden are now in the same parish). Orwell's *Coming Up for Air* (1939) lovingly recalls this area: its protagonist, George Bowling, born in the same year as Owen, revisits the small Oxfordshire town of his happy childhood, a town that Orwell calls Lower Binfield – Binfield Heath was between Dunsden and Shiplake. Orwell's pre-war memories became Bowling's.

Owen's first letters home sound not so much like Bowling's memories as letters home by a fresher, describing the large and handsomely furnished bedroom, the staff who tidy his bedroom and bring his shaving water, his new companions, 'the wide luxurious chambers of the rich', his studies, and a lecture in 'Univ. College Hall' on Charles Lamb by Sir Walter Raleigh, Professor of English Literature at Oxford. Indeed, with 'an Oxford man',[26] Herbert Wigan, as his tutor, a man who had grown up within the Anglo-Catholic Oxford Movement, he was studying the Christian faith, following a path that so many Oxford men had taken since the university's creation. But he was also dealing with the Children's Service, the 'wretched hovels of this Parish', the 'crazy, evil-smelling huts of the poor',[27] old people who could not read, the poor educating him 'in the Book of Life', choirboys employed in farming, the Sunday School, and a flat tyre on the way to a Bible Society Meeting at Henley Town Hall. Pastoral matters and the practicalities of the vocation had no place in the Oxford education that the Anglican clergy received. And village life could not compare with the opportunities of a famous city. Mitford's *Our Village* (Owen owned a 1909 edition) begins by stating that a little village far in the country, a place of cottages, is a delightful place to live,[28] but Owen soon became dissatisfied with a strict vicarage of awful dinner and daytime silences and slaving away in a tiny, unremarkable village close to the vulgar redbrick modernity of Reading.[29] This was the world of *The Wind in the Willows* (1908), but Owen had very little opportunity for friendship, adventure and simply messing about in boats. Unlike Jerome's three men and a dog, he wasn't there to enjoy The Bull at 'fairy-like' Sonning[30] or the pleasant spirited company of men at Henley.

Dunsden must have seemed like a cruel parody of an Oxford education. He told his brother Harold, 'Yes, yes, as you so unpleasantly put it, perhaps I am decomposing in my wretched village. Why, why couldn't I have gone up to Oxford? Just think what I could have done with three years there!'[31] At Dunsden in December 1911, when he mentioned, in his verse letter, Matthew Arnold's hills nearby, he was referring to 'The Scholar-Gipsy' – Arnold's hero had had to leave Oxford because of poverty, and found magic, education and companionship elsewhere, Oxford being replaced by the gypsy community. That verse letter reveals a longing for education: Gray, a Cambridge don, offers 'golden teaching', 'Yet can I never sit low at his feet / And, questioning, a gracious answer meet'. Equally, Owen's verse letter confesses that he wants to befriend a young poet, 'To talk with him, and share his confidence'. And Oxford is mentioned frequently in

Owen's letters during 1912–13. When the Prince of Wales went up to Oxford in October 1912, Owen was dealing with the Harvest Festival, a ropey parish choir, a sick child called Edith Herridge, and the coal and clothing accounts. On 15 October 1912, Owen helped with the double funeral of a mother and her four-year-old daughter, which he described in the poem 'Deep Under Turfy Grass'. They had died in a terrible accident when the horses of their cart bolted and the cart hit a bank.

Like Shakespeare, Owen would only know Oxford as a place he passed through on journeys to and from home. Just as Shakespeare stayed at Oxford on his journeys between Stratford and London, Oxford would be the city the train stopped at during Owen's journeys between Shrewsbury and Dunsden. The GWR train from Paddington to Birmingham, where he could change for Shrewsbury, went through Reading and Oxford, and even the express train had five stops – Reading, Oxford, Banbury, Leamington, Warwick. His father's free train tickets for the GWR were the only way he could be sent off to Oxford. It's not even clear that Owen ever got off the train – the railway station might have been the closest he ever got to the university. Oxford was the dreaming spires seen, just about, behind shops and trees, from the railway on the edge of town. But maybe a mere glimpse was enough, or too much: presumably, at the GWR station, Owen saw undergraduates and dons on the platform and envied them.

Oxford was always beyond Owen's reach, no matter how close he got to it. But he sought replacements for the Oxford education that he never had. In 1911, he took the Matriculation exam for entry to London University, writing an English essay on 'The Ideal English King' and achieving a good pass overall yet nothing more, and the result sent him miserably to bed for a day but not to university. He complained rather bitterly that he had never had the chance to study properly for a scholarship because he had always been working along-side his studies – a lack of money seemed to have determined that he couldn't go to university. There had also been some mention of Liverpool University in September 1911, and while this would hardly have offered the ideal college life that he dreamt of, it would have been university; and others, such as F. E. Smith, whom Owen went to hear speak in the late spring of 1912, had used everyday Liverpool University as a stepping-stone to Oxbridge. The biographer Lytton Strachey found Liverpool's university intellectually and culturally malnourished in 1898 and quickly exchanged it for Trinity College, Cambridge.[32]

Nothing came of Liverpool but at Dunsden Owen got to know Reading University College, a small institution only a year older than he was,[33] having been founded by Christ Church, Oxford University, in 1892. Some of its buildings, such as Wantage Hall, mirrored the Tudor style of Christ Church, but Reading tended to specialise in rather modern disciplines such as Science and Agriculture (there was a College Farm and a Research Institute in Dairying), or indeed English Literature, which was a very new subject for English universities. The college embraced new ideas, whether they were the philosophy of Bergson or innovative treatments for the diseases of cattle.[34] Similarly, Reading was an old town that had become a place of modern industry, producing biscuits, beer, bulbs, bricks and the unpleasantly named Cocks's Sauce, a greedy town that gobbled up the countryside. (It is described in *Three Men in a Boat* as 'dismal, dirty Reading', which 'does its best to spoil and sully and make hideous as much of the river as it can reach'.)[35]

In 1912, enrolling in April, Owen studied botany and English there,[36] where he was 'a shy and not very happy boy rather obviously disappointed with his surroundings',[37] but was taken under the wings of two female academics, Edith Morley of the English Department, the first woman to obtain the title of professor at a British university,[38] and Mabel Rayner, BSc, the youngish botanist who loved poetry. Poetry and botany were natural companions, especially at a time when English poetry was still rooted in the countryside. Owen's interest in botany, which he had held throughout his years in Shrewsbury, had been stimulated by being in rural Dunsden, where he spoke to the choirboys about the local flora and wrote home about hedgerow flowers (one of his criticisms of the Rev. Wigan was that 'Large public parks laid out by legislature / Were his idea and cognisance of Nature').[39]

Sensing that he was lonely, Mabel Rayner befriended him and although they were never close he retained fond memories of her; she seems to have been, as he recorded when they first met, 'very nice indeed'[40] – she felt that her Irish and French ancestry appealed to his Celtic side. Edith Morley, on the other hand, was 'provocative, disturbing, aggressive, intransigent',[41] a gorgon-don to her male colleagues, but she had a Fabian suffragette's social conscience, having been converted to socialism by William Morris's *News from Nowhere*, and she worked on chivalry.[42] In these years immediately before the war, Owen studied under a woman who was an expert on Sir Philip Sidney, and wrote of his 'chivalry and love of adventure',[43] the 'gallant life of action',[44] military fame 'worthy of the land which gave him birth'.[45] Perhaps she was unfriendly towards her male colleagues because they were no Sidney, 'in the best sense a man of the world, a maker of history, not a pedant or a mere scholar'.[46]

Professor Morley had taken a liking to Owen (as an expert on Sidney, Shrewsbury School's greatest son, perhaps she enjoyed the fact that Owen came from Shrewsbury), and she remembered that with Owen 'We read Ruskin together and discussed his critical and art theories'.[47] Rather like Morley, John Ruskin combined medievalism with a form of socialism. W. G. Collingwood, a Liverpudlian who taught at Reading University College from 1905 to 1911, was Ruskin's friend and biographer, and had noticeably contributed to the atmosphere of the college. Rayner was friends with Collingwood and put Owen in touch with him. Unlike the author Arthur Ransome, Owen never had the opportunity to develop a close friendship with the kindly Collingwoods, but with Morley and Rayner Owen had some experience of Ruskin's influence and shared the Ruskinian interest in both the natural world and the world of books, both practicality and intellect. One day in May 1912, Rayner took him on an excursion into the countryside and then, over tea, talked to him of poetry. In July, he spent a merry evening with Mabel Rayner and another botany lecturer, when Mabel Rayner read Swinburne and Owen enthusiastically made the argument that Francis Bacon was Shakespeare (an argument famously promoted by the namesake of both Owen and Bacon, one Delia Salter Bacon). In Owen's head that summer, Shakespeare's *A Midsummer Night's Dream* became Bacon's *Midsummer Iced Cream*.[48]

Morley encouraged him to apply for a scholarship; but, alas, he failed the examination in 1913. He considered sitting for a scholarship again, although even if he succeeded he would have needed the support of his family, and that was by no means money that could be easily found. Fees were £20 per year and a hall of residence cost £32 to £42 and while a major scholarship was £65, a minor scholarship was only remission of fees.[49] In July or August 1913, when he was still desperate for the money for university, when 'those two Oxford Blues' at Uriconium made him wildly envious,[50] Owen wrote a sonnet about bounteous gardens, the poem expressing his sense of exclusion from those privileges of the wealthy:

> When late I viewed the gardens of rich men,
> Where throve my darling blossoms plenteously,
> With others whose rare glories dazed my ken,
> I was not teased with envious misery.
> Enough for me to see and recognize;
> Then bear away sweet names upon my tongue,
> Scents in my breath, and colours in my eyes.

Owen was not especially political, but the poem shows an attitude that is revealed again and again in his letters: he had no objection to wealth as long as he could benefit from it; he believed in elites, in exclusive institutions, as long as they accepted him.[51]

Nonetheless, over the years, Owen made some gestures towards favouring the university of life. In his copy of Keats he underlined the declaration 'O for a life of Sensations rather than of Thoughts!'[52] In 1912, he enjoyed George Borrow's *Lavengro*, in which Borrow chooses to become a wandering outsider, learning from the gypsies rather than being imprisoned behind a desk, deciding that it is better to be a tinker and his own master than to work as a scholar. Oxford represents the

stuffy world that Borrow leaves behind. We are told that 'Oxford' and
'orthodox' are synonymous,[53] and the 'Oxford-like manner' is boringly
urbane:

> All the publications which fell under my notice I treated in a gentle-
> manly and Oxford-like manner, no personalities – no vituperation
> – no shabby insinuations; decorum was the order of the day.
> Occasionally a word of admonition, but gently expressed, as an
> Oxford under-graduate might have expressed it, or master of arts.[54]

Owen could certainly complain about the artificiality and restrictions of
examinations, but Borrow's attitude was unlikely to have convinced
Owen, who could enjoy the book as fantasy, but knew how the rural
poor really lived; and he would have taken a university place at a shot
if the chance arose. He later wrote, '"What you want" said John
Bulman to me, "Is a course in the University of Life". I have taken that
Course, and my diplomas are sealed with many secret seals.'[55] But the
university of life was not what he wanted; it was what he got. Moreover,
he seemed to have the worst of worlds as neither merry tinker nor
learned scholar, but merely the studious servant.

Through the Dunsden days, Owen had been acquiring books,
building up a treasured collection as physical evidence of refinement,
and as the tools of the trade for an apprentice poet – nothing to rival a
university library, but a collection that came to represent his ambitions.
Some of Owen's books, such as Harold Begbie's *Broken Earthenware*
(1910), were quite recent, although the books he bought were usually
second-hand, Reading being a place for second-hand bookshops. He
found books in Reading and London, and through reading he escaped
Reading and Dunsden. Every acquisition was a step towards culture,
success, happiness, poetry. Some of the books are essentially textbooks,
such as Stopford Brooke's guide to English Literature, acquired in
March 1912, and a book called *An Introduction to Structural Botany*.
Others more directly reflect his passions. His delight in the literary
associations of places is seen in his copy of Sir Walter Scott's poem

Marmion in which he has written 'Among the Cheviots July 1912': the Cheviot hills stretch along the border between England and Scotland, in Walter Scott country, and *Marmion* is about the battle of Flodden Field, which took place at the foot of the Cheviots in 1513. Owen went to Flodden with a family friend Blanche Bulman, while he and his family were on holiday nearby, staying with the well-to-do Bulmans (Mrs Bulman knew Susan from Oswestry), and in a stiff breeze he walked about the battlefield imagining the battle and reading the poem. His copy of *Marmion* contains a sketch that he made of the battlefield. It's a little odd that a nineteen-year-old vicar's assistant was so rapt in the poem for a whole afternoon, and neglectful of the (engaged) young lady who accompanied him, because while many Victorians had enjoyed *Marmion*, they tended to do so as young boys who played with tin soldiers and wore toy swords.

Owen was roaming widely and eagerly among the Romantic poets. In September 1912 he bought W. M. Rossetti's biography of Keats, and was greatly moved by the description of the poet's death:

> I never guessed till now the frightful travail of his soul towards Death; never came so near laying hold of the ghastly horror of his mind at this time. Rossetti guided my groping hand right into the wound, and I touched, for one moment the incandescent Heart of Keats.[56]

Owen loved both the man Keats and his work. In February 1912, he bought a ten-shilling *Complete Keats* for three shillings and sixpence. Keats, his first love, was still first in his affections; and it *was* love, a form of teenage crush: in April 1913, he confessed to the odd fact that he was in love with a youth, and a dead one at that, rather than 'a real, live maid'.[57] He was light-heartedly confessing to a form of homosexuality, but only to love for those who could not hear him or respond to his advances: how wonderfully and innocently sexual that description of reading the Rossetti biography is, his 'groping' hand entering Keats and touching his burning heart. There was nothing illegal about being in love with a dead man, or entering a dead man;

indeed he wrote in a draft of a letter to his mother in April 1913 that 'I fear domestic criticism when I am in love with a real live woman' (it is not clear whether he means he has been in love with a woman or that he might be in love with one one day).[58] His love for Keats was the safest love of all.

Tennyson, himself deeply influenced by Keats, was another poet Owen was reading intensively. Tennyson's poetry seemed to fit in with Owen's life, complementing the slow passage of days at the Victorian vicarage. He read 'Ring out, wild bells' from *In Memoriam* on New Year's Eve 1911, and in April 1912 'I spent the whole of the morning in the garden – O magnificent environment wherein to read Tennyson!'.[59] He was, of course, well aware of Tennyson's marriage nearby, while the poem that might capture Owen's life most accurately is 'The Lady of Shalott'. The Lady of Shalott lived in isolation in her castle, weaving her magic web with colours gay and only seeing the rural world outside as reflections in a mirror: her predicament is taken as a representation of the life of writers, who live among books and dreams rather than reality. In early 1913 Owen referred to the Tennysonian painting *The Lady of Shalott* (1888, presented to the Tate 1894) by John William Waterhouse, although he disliked it because he thought the lady wasn't pretty enough – he contrasts her with the thrilling beauty in Val Prinsep's painting *The Goose Girl*, as if they are Page 3 pin-ups, which in a sense they were. The story of the Lady of Shalott would also have been evoked by Sonning, where Holman Hunt spent his last years. ('The village of Sonning is one of the prettiest in the Thames Valley, and no wonder Holman Hunt chose to live there'.)[60] First exhibited in 1905, five years before his death, *The Lady of Shalott* is arguably his greatest painting, and, being somewhat prettier, Holman's version is no doubt the Shalott painting that Owen preferred.

Owen became the kind of bookish teenager who was closer to dead writers than living people, and he saw the world and his own life through books. Herbert Wigan excited Owen with memories of travels in Italy, telling his parish assistant about how he 'read Romola in Florence overlooking Ponte Vecchia!!',[61] but the Rev. Wigan considered literature 'artificialized life', whereas Owen saw it as the 'Prime of life'.[62] To this extent, Wigan believed in the real world and Owen wanted the 'Shadows of the world'. But there was also in Owen, as in the Lady of Shalott, a desire to escape and see life (the Lady of Shalott's decision to look out of the window rather than into the mirror, and then her decision to venture outside into reality, quickly destroys her). He became half sick of shadows.

> When I am reading or studying, I long to be out, up and doing.
> When out, on holidays, I feel time wasted and crave for a book.[63]

This attitude suggests that he might not have been a thoroughly committed scholar at university, although he would have enjoyed some of the company.

Beneath his bookishness there was a longing for deep friendship with someone other than a dead writer; most people annoyed him but he wanted someone who could understand, and sympathise with, his personality. The one friend who is fleshed out in any detail in Owen's letters during the Dunsden period is his cousin Leslie Gunston. Owen spent happy hours with Leslie Gunston at Roman Silchester, and at the cinema in Reading, and Leslie himself had an interest in poetry. During their childhoods their friendship had been based around holidays: they would either visit each other's homes or take seaside holidays together – for instance, in 1918, Owen recalled Gicianto Ferrari, the 'Bird Man', an Italian he and Leslie encountered at a seaside holiday at Llandudno. Ferrari's little birds performed on the Promenade, pulling miniature coaches, doing circus tricks and firing tiny cannons. Now they could see each other more regularly because Leslie lived nearby, north of Reading at Kidmore End, where the little birds were less talented but where the Gunstons lived in middle-class comfort.

Nonetheless, Leslie wasn't always on hand, and a young man needs more than one friend. Owen once wrote to him asking for a letter because 'I've none to befriend me / When Dunsden immures'.[64] Indeed, Owen was looking for a Romantic friendship – possibly even a

romantic one – that Leslie doesn't seem to have offered, if only because
he was too familiar as a member of the family. By his own admission,
Owen suffered at home and at Dunsden from a lack of like-minded
company, such as he would have found at university, people he could
chat to about books or love, and during his time at Dunsden he wrote
a long poem about the Little Mermaid:

> A strange and lonely child seemed this Princess.
> Deep were the fathomings of her secret thought.
> Not that she shunned a sisterly caress;
> But, spoken to, faint-smiled, and answered naught.
> Loved she the silent deep? Nay, less and less
> She loved it! And as years new sameness brought,
> Its silence, its low stillness, its pale gloom,
> Weighed on her soul, and made sweet life a doom.

She changes from a mermaid into a young woman, having left home,
but she remains alone: 'Both day and night her lonely watch she kept /
Leaning above the milky, glistening foam'.[65]

Had he been in a town or city, Owen could have developed friend-
ships with young men his own age, but Dunsden offered few such
opportunities. He contented himself with the company of children –
just as Shelley had enjoyed playing with the pretty children of Marlow
nearby – and he did genuinely feel happier with them than with
Herbert Wigan:

> The weather last week was glorious; and one afternoon I half spent
> in a daisy-meadow, with the 'Fairy Bray', with another and (to me)
> more enchanting elf, being older and well-spoken, and with various
> insignificant brothers and sisters. We sought the Biggest Daisy, and
> the <u>Reddest</u> Daisy. My elf found them (oh yes, honestly!) <u>and</u> <u>I</u>
> found the Golden Age.[66]

The poem 'The Two Reflections' grew out of his days spent with village children:

> I seldom look into thy brown eyes, child,
> But I behold in them the deep, cool shade
> Of summer woods.

Inevitably, he found himself befriending someone he could only educate rather than converse with as an equal. A mysterious friendship developed at Dunsden with a schoolboy (born in 1899), Vivian Rampton, a promising youth of melancholy brown eyes and dropped aitches. 'We two were friends,' Owen wrote, sounding like Walt Whitman.[67] He called him his protégé and one of his favourite boys. A description in 1912, to Susan Owen, of the countryside of early March and a ramble with Rampton is wrapped up in fantasy and playfulness, and suggests that Owen wanted friendship, although it also suggests that at this time he had no serious attachment to Rampton:

> On Sat. I secretly met with Vivian at a stile and went a delicious ramble; lay in hawthorn glades, where antlered stags would come within a few yards of us. He read to me, and I told him tales. I took some figs of Mary's for him.[68]

Owen gave Rampton piano lessons and enjoyed his company. This friendship probably appeared to Herbert Wigan as inappropriate, and possibly was, although it is highly unlikely that it was sexual in any real way:

> But soon a heavier grief than this she had:
> Though loved as any fair young child might be,
> Though dear as many a lass to one same lad,
> She was not the devotion of his life;
> He never dreamed to take her as his wife.[69]

Perhaps it was one of those romantic friendships that were once associated with English adolescent boys, when they were almost men but might not see the friendship's sexual meaning.[70] The friendship, whatever it meant, played a part in the mutual frustration and incompatibility between Wigan and Owen.

Owen was, though, attracted to girls too, and this was not likely to be viewed favourably by Wigan either. Leslie Gunston, with whom Owen regularly discussed girls and with whom he later left the 'the key to many of my poems',[71] recalled that although Owen had a stronger but 'perfectly innocent' attraction to 'the beauty of boys' – 'The little boy Eros, as it were, held ascendancy over the woman Aphrodite' – he was 'far from being insensible to the beauty of women'.[72] On 9 January 1913, Owen wrote a sonnet that begins

> Daily I muse on her; I muse and fret;
> And take her little face between each hand;
> But spare her – even imagined – kisses yet.

As a young village girl, we assume, she cannot offer him the romance he seeks, but his poetry reveals an eagerness to fall in love. In January he also wrote a poem, presumably to the same girl, in which he is clearly attracted to her beauty, and has indeed, in a way, fallen in love: 'Only thy youth, fair child, thy beauty, joy, and youth, / Can give me all I want, heart-ease and rest'. He enjoys and needs her company, but there is no sense of a burning sexual passion:

> O Girl, a sole tear, shining on thy cheek for me
>   More strengthens me than glittering angel-ranks;
>
> Whose glory no eye sees; whose power is never felt,
>   Whose sinlessness supports no sinful head,
>
> Whose wondrous music never eased a human ear.
>   – Surely, because they are not, after all.[73]

The poems to this girl are wrapped up with a questioning of the Church and a feeling that love for beautiful people moves him more powerfully than the love for, or of, God.

In February 1913, Owen left Dunsden, in need of new company and a new environment. Leaving Dunsden gave him one aspect of the Oxford experience, 'my version of running away from College (Shelley, Coleridge)' – Shelley was at Oxford, Coleridge at Cambridge. And, in 1917, Owen would refer to Shelley as 'the greatest man Oxford ever turned out (turned out in the forcible sense, I mean)',[74] possibly recalling Dunsden. Shelley had left because he produced a pamphlet on *The Necessity of Atheism*. Owen left because he had had religious doubts – back in 1911, he had written, 'I am grappling as I never did before with the Problem of <u>Evolution</u>',[75] and if he could not form a conclusion back then, his reading and his botanical studies had pushed him towards the doubts that Darwin of Shrewsbury had conjured up for many Victorians, while the sight of poverty and death in the parish had made him only wonder, as many would do after 1914, why God allowed the innocent to suffer. And he had certainly become disillusioned with the Church of England, after dwelling with it at Dunsden. The worry had contributed to poor health – his mother later recalled that he 'came home very run down and was <u>very</u> ill with pneumonia'.[76] Like Shelley, though, he had also fallen out of favour with the powers that be, and the friendship with Vivian Rampton might have contributed to Wigan's desire to see Owen choose another parish or another career path.

Having turned down the chance to take up parish work at Bordesley in Birmingham (with a likeable clergyman who was a friend of a friend of Susan's), he returned to Shrewsbury in February 1913, where he was ill at home in Mahim during February and March. He was fortunate to have his mother there caring for him and feeding him up. When his brother Harold joined the Merchant Service on 13 March, and sailed for India, Owen was unemployed and directionless. He had his poetry but perhaps books could be blamed for this temporary downfall since he had slipped into overwork, too little exercise and a romantic longing

for friendship that had been fuelled by poetry. He went on holiday to
Torquay with his little brother Colin in 1913, and, although Keats was
still in his thoughts, he tried to escape from writing – he wrote to his
mother about 'the many books I am <u>not</u> reading, the merry faces I am
seeing' and how 'a pen is a dangerous thing to hold too long'.[77]
Nonetheless, in July 1913, Owen wrote his poem about Uriconium,
and the Roman city 'destroyed all at once about the year 584'[78] now
plays a part in Owen's recovery from his unhappiness:

> O ye who weep and call all your life too long
> And moan: Was ever sorrow like to mine?
>   Muse on the memories
> That sad sepulchral stones and ruins prolong.
> Here might men drink of wonder like strong wine
> And feel ephemeral troubles soothed and curbed.

So, free of Dunsden, denied university, his health restored, but in
need of an adventure, that summer Owen took a plunge that was as
exciting but somewhat less esteemed than going up to Oxford, moving
not to Bordesley or elsewhere for parish work, but, rather, to Bordeaux,
where he taught English at the Berlitz School. Like the Scholar-Gipsy,
one summer-morn he forsook his friends (not that he had many of
those), and went to join a foreign race and learn a new way of life. Yet
Owen continued to think that he might go to Oxford. He let it be
known in France that he would one day be an Oxford undergraduate,
so that an acquaintance out there would later report that 'he is giving
lessons in Bordeaux preparing for Oxford'.[79] It was either very naïve or
a lie. By then, Oxford was a closed door: at twenty-one, he still wanted
to go to university, but Oxford was not an option.

> She loosed the chain, and down she lay;
> The broad stream bore her far away,
>   The Lady of Shalott.[80]

CHAPTER 4

L'Homme du Monde

This perfect solitude of foreign lands!
To be, as if you had not been till then,
And were then, simply that you chose to be:
To spring up, not be brought forth from the ground,
Like grasshoppers at Athens, and skip thrice
Before a woman makes a pounce on you
And plants you in her hair! – possess, yourself,
A new world all alive with creatures new,
New sun, new moon, new flowers, new people
ELIZABETH BARRETT BROWNING, *Aurora Leigh*, 1856, Book VII[1]

Bordeaux est, sans contredit, la plus belle ville de France. Elle est un
peu en pente vers la Garonne.
STENDHAL, *Mémoires d'un Touriste* – Bordeaux, Monday 12 March 1838[2]

WILFRED Owen arrived in France in September 1913 in order to teach English at the Berlitz School. Through the autumn and winter in Bordeaux, when it was frequently wet, he worked long days in an elegant balconied building on the corner of the rue du Temple, above the glistening trams and umbrellas of the Cours de l'Intendance. The Berlitz language schools were found, and are still found, in most major European cities and teachers were required to converse only in the language they were teaching, not in the language of the students – the students were adults rather than children, and often needed English for their work. Nine years earlier, another writer had gone into exile by escaping to the Continent in order to teach at a Berlitz: James Joyce had hoped to teach at a Berlitz in Paris, left Ireland in October 1904 intending to teach at a Berlitz in Zurich, ended up at the Berlitz in Pola, then moved to the Berlitz at Trieste in 1905. He called Signor Berlitz a fool and an insatiable sponge.[3] Years later he adopted, and ridiculed, the question-and-answer 'Berlitz method' in the 'Ithaca' episode of *Ulysses* (1922), employing a series of questions and Joycean answers:[4]

> What possibility suggested itself?
> The possibility of exercising virile power of fascination in the most immediate future after an expensive repast in a private apart-ment in the company of an elegant courtesan, of corporal beauty, moderately mercenary, variously instructed, a lady by origin.[5]

Owen would employ the Berlitz method inappropriately, for a discussion of sex, in the poem 'Who is the God of Canongate?' during the war; and he had used the Berlitz method in a letter to his mother in October 1913, soon after arriving in Bordeaux:

> Why have I been silent?
> Because aweary.
> Why aweary?
> Because over-busy.
> Why overbusy?
> Because the English Miss is ill, and never started from England after all; nor ever will, but is sending another, who is to arrive <u>some time</u> next week.[6]

After 10 p.m. lessons, he usually walked the new English Miss back to the convent where she was staying, but she braved it alone on wet nights and in the rain he hurried down the narrow rue du Temple to his room in the rue de la Porte Dijeaux. When, thirteen years before, the painter Henri de Toulouse-Lautrec had spent a winter in Bordeaux, his badly lit studio was on the rue de la Porte Dijeaux, and after a day's work Lautrec moved on to the nearby Café de Bordeaux, the famous restaurant Chapon Fin, the opera and the ladies of the night (he was living in a brothel at 66 rue de Caudéran), spending evenings with 'Bacchus and Venus',[7] both of whom could be found on or near the rue de la Porte Dijeaux.[8] However, Wilfred Owen probably never accepted the kind offers of the many prostitutes who propositioned him (it was a port, after all), or spoke to them about the tiny, lisping Lautrec, so deformed and so memorably ugly: Owen's Bordeaux was not Lautrec's bawdy city, and not quite so *belle époque* – his was more a world of hard work, books, sobriety and Englishwomen living in convents. He went to cafés sometimes, but after a hard day's work he had little time (or money) for *la vie Bordelaise*, although, like the rain, its sound might have kept him awake or distracted him from his writing when he was in his lodgings at night. Probably one of the few things Owen and Lautrec shared was the weather: it had been horribly wet for Lautrec too, and he complained about the fog.

As winter advanced, the fog became a frequent visitor. Yet, despite the weather, the long hours and Owen's distance from his doting mother, Susan, it was, in an age of entente cordiale, a good time to be a Briton in France, and he was living a new life. Like Christopher Isherwood in *Goodbye to Berlin*, the short, dark-haired Englishman, clever and attractive, an aspiring writer abroad, teaching the English language and living in cheap lodgings, had chosen 'the break with the old life'.[9] Like Isherwood, he had chosen one of Europe's grandest cities. He told an old schoolfriend that he was lonely but 'Bordeaux is a very fine town, and is of all French cities the one that most resembles Paris'.[10] At the end of the Cours de l'Intendance, the Grand Théâtre stood proudly, all huge Corinthian columns and classical statues and *grande élégance*, probably the most famous building in the city and the subject of so many postcards (as well as pictures by Toulouse-Lautrec); a short walk round the corner, the bronze statue of Liberty crowned the

Monument des Girondins, which towered above the trees and houses. Owen sent a postcard of 'the fine monument' to his cousin Leslie Gunston soon after arriving in Bordeaux; a few yards from his lodgings was the classical archway, the Porte Dijeaux, erected in 1748 by the Marquis de Tourny, who, as Bordeaux's governor, introduced some of the city's finest 'royal' architecture. Much of the eighteenth- and nineteenth-century architecture, with its balconies and mascarons, is classical: it is a city of columns, statues and arches, appropriately enough, given Bordeaux's Roman origins and remains. Roman antiquities had been found on the rue du Temple and on the Cours de l'Intendance in the nineteenth century; and the Roman amphitheatre, the Palais Gallien, was a short walk from where Owen worked.

The artist Goya immortalised a Roman legacy, the bull-fighting, which was still popular in Owen's day. Famous for *The Disasters of War* and a form of monstrous Romanticism, Goya lived and died in a house on the other side of the road from the Berlitz School (his first nights in Bordeaux had been spent on the rue de la Porte Dijeaux). There were literary and artistic associations to almost any street. Near the Porte Dijeaux, Montesquieu had once lived. Bordeaux had even given England a medieval king, Richard II, who would, of course, become the subject of a play by Shakespeare, and was possibly related by marriage to Baron Lewis Owen, and in Bordeaux twenty-three-year-old poet Wilfrid Scawen Blunt fell in love with the famous Liverpudlian courtesan 'Skittles'. Victor Hugo, whom Owen admired ('I might babble of Victor Hugo,' he wrote),[11] in a well-known description of the city, had described it as a cross between Versailles and Antwerp. At the vast church of St Michel, Hugo had had a strange meeting with corpses, as if descending into Hell:

Suddenly, fixing my eyes on the wall, I saw that we were not alone.

Strange figures, standing upright with their backs to the wall, surrounded us on all sides. By the light of the lamp I got a confused glimpse of them across the fog which fills low and gloomy vaults.

Imagine a circle of terrifying faces, in the centre of which I was standing. The blackish and naked bodies were sunken and lost in the darkness; but I saw distinctly, starting out of the shadow, and leaning, as it were, somehow towards me, crowding one against another, a multitude of dismal or dreadful heads, which seemed to call on me with mouths wide open, but voiceless, and gazed on me from eyeless sockets.

What were these figures? Statues, of course. I took the lamp from the ringer's hands and drew near. They were corpses.[12]

According to another of Owen's favourite writers, Swinburne, this description of the charnel-house 'will now be for ever remembered by all students of his work as the subject of a realistic and tragic poem in prose which may be ranked among the greatest and most terrible triumphs of his imaginative and descriptive genius'.[13]

At every turn there was a wonderful church: St Michel, the cathedral, St Éloi, St Bruno, Ste Eulalie, St Seurin, St Louis, St Paul, St Pierre, Notre Dame. Every hidden square had an old church. Atop the tall Tour Pey-Berland, watching over everyone, stands the large golden Our Lady of Aquitaine, even more unignorable than the statue of Liberty at the Monument des Girondins. This was Owen's first meaningful experience of Roman Catholicism (he noted that English people don't have 'an inkling of what this people's religion consists of'),[14] and this faith, so different from his own rather spartan Protestantism, would have an influence on his later poetry. He lived among church bells, saints' days, funerals, crucifixes, processions, with a devout landlady and, on 1 November 1913, 'a concourse of some thirty miserables, who made offerings of music to the souls of the soldiers killed in 1870!'[15] He went to his first Catholic Mass in the draughty cathedral at Christmas. He attended Protestant services in France from time to time, but the Catholicism of Bordeaux, mostly experienced as a form of street theatre or when churches were quiet, made a change from Dunsden and Shrewsbury, and added to the ancient atmosphere of the city.

Yet Bordeaux was a modern city, too, at the forefront of change, with most of its 262,000 inhabitants connected to trade and industry. When a few days after Owen's arrival the French President, Poincaré, visited Bordeaux, travelling up the river in a torpedo-boat to be met by large cheering crowds in the heart of the city where Owen was one of the onlookers, the president praised this modern city's recent improvements. At 95 rue de la Porte Dijeaux, Owen happily found himself living as a lodger with, in the next room, a Frenchman who 'works for Pathé *Frères*, and has appeared himself in a film taken in Bordeaux'.[16] And soon after he arrived at the Berlitz, Owen was invited by one of his pupils to go motoring: perhaps this well-off pupil owned a powerful Georges Roy automobile manufactured in Bordeaux. But Owen was more interested in aeroplanes than in automobiles, having been greatly thrilled by seeing a plane for the first time in September 1912,[17] and now he had a plenty of planes to spot because Bordeaux had quickly become a centre for aviation. Indeed, in December 1913 an airman died near Bordeaux while attempting a non-stop flight from Paris to Bordeaux and back. In January 1914, Owen wrote home mentioning the imminent visit of Roland Garros, the famous pilot, and, in February, he watched flying that he found astounding.

Owen immersed himself in this city, and rather than playing the typical Englishman abroad, clinging to the ways of home, he went native, acquiring a plausible French accent and a taste for the French lifestyle. And yet in Bordeaux, despite all the dissimilarity, he thought of dull and dirty Birkenhead. In December 1913, Owen wrote home confessing that never in his life had he been 'so utterly towny as at this moment', not even in Willmer Road in Birkenhead 'in the old dark days'.[18] Like Henry James in 1882, he would have known that the appearance of Bordeaux, this handsome, opulent port 'with long rows of fine old eighteenth-century houses which overlook the yellow Garonne', 'makes the Anglo-Saxon tourist blush for the sordid waterfronts of Liverpool'.[19] Nonetheless, Owen wrote that although while he remembered Birkenhead he was close to tears, those tears were no longer of pain, memories having matured 'into Sweetness' after ten years.[20] After all, he was no longer there. One of his colleagues at the Berlitz, Miss Hewitt, the lady he often walked home in the evening, was from Liverpool or Birkenhead, and they got on well even though, as he noted, she was no great beauty. He might have been reluctant to reveal his family's fairly lowly status in Birkenhead, but they probably chatted about home. At times the Mersey's sailors also appeared in Bordeaux. Down by the waterside, among the Gallic voices and the accents from Spain, Italy, Africa, there was the occasional accent from his childhood. Owen mentioned one of these voices from the past when he wrote home, and he might have heard Liverpudlian voices trying a little French: *Mademoiselle, combien, belle, jolie, merci beaucoup.* Equally, as a child in Birkenhead he might have heard sailors from Bordeaux (no doubt they tried a little English, but, just in case, Liverpool produced French-language leaflets about syphilis). In Owen's time, the river in Bordeaux was still the city's workplace, busy with boats and ships from French ports and further off. 'I sometimes promenade along the docks, and see the ships of many lands,' he wrote.[21] Like Birkenhead, Bordeaux is a port that faces the river rather than the sea, but big ships were welcome.

With time passing, he was able to look fondly on the Birkenhead days, dark though they were. But to a young boy in Birkenhead, Owen or Malcolm Lowry or thousands of others, the ships of the Mersey conjured up dreams of escape and self-reinvention, a sense of the possibilities that travel offered. And now that he was abroad, Owen could recreate himself, while at the same time showing that he had something in common with his father, that railwayman who had hovered around Birkenhead docks pretending to be a sea captain. Owen lied through his teeth in pretending to French acquaintances that his father, a tailor's son and a railwayman, was a baronet, Sir Thomas Owen. Unconvincingly he claimed that his French friends had come to this conclusion and he had simply failed to correct them, but, nonetheless, he admitted to his father that he enjoyed this promotion in the class system.[22] Like his pretence in 1914 that he was on his way to Oxford, this was a childish fantasy worthy of the Great Gatsby, or of Frederick

Rolfe, the writer who styled himself 'Baron Corvo' (and in October 1913 died in Venice). A 'Baroness Orczy' (Mrs Montague Barstow) had written the Scarlet Pimpernel novels, which Owen enjoyed, and in those novels an English baronet behaves heroically across the Channel. Now Owen was Sir Percy Blakeney in reverse – Blakeney being a real baronet who took on another identity in France. Owen also read *The Prisoner of Zenda*, in which the English gent goes off to the Continent and quickly finds himself playing a king.

Many schoolboys in their first weeks at boarding school have elevated their parents' status, and the further away from home they are, the easier it is to lie. (At his Berlitz in Pola, Joyce had added a doctorate to his qualifications.) The sceptic might have wondered why the son of a baronet was teaching in a language school every hour God sends rather than studying at university, but the English aristocracy had long been known for their eccentricity. Remarkably, when Tom Owen visited his son in Bordeaux in October 1913 and was addressed as Sir Thomas Owen, he lived up to the lie quite readily, playing the part of the imaginary aristocrat with some confidence. But then, after all, Susan Owen had already given Owen the name Sir Wilfred Edward Salter-Owen, so Tom and his son were only following Susan's ambition. In fact, the baronet and his son got on together rather better than they did at their lower-middle-class Shrewsbury home: it was easier to put aside resentments, and a mutual feeling of disappointment – Tom wanting a manly son, Wilfred wanting a father of books and culture; each wanting the other to be more successful financially – in a situation where both father and son were 'significant people'. By adopting a mask they forgot their past. According to Harold Owen, this was the last time that Owen felt close to his father, and Harold remembered (possibly suspiciously clearly) Owen's later complaint:

> When I waved farewell to the make-believe 'Sir Thomas' on the hot, sun-baked quay-stones at Bordeaux, notwithstanding the false title, it was my real father I was saying goodbye to. . . . To that father, it seemed to me, I have said goodbye for ever.

Never again would his father be 'the person who dined with me in Bordeaux'.[23]

*

At their modest home in Shrewsbury, Tom not only lost the 'Sir' but also abstained from the wine that he had enjoyed when dining with his son in France. Bordeaux was 'a sacred city – dedicated to the worship of Bacchus'.[24] Wine, the biggest industry of the area, was a gift from the Romans. The vineyards could be seen from the city; thousands of bottles of wine departed from the quays. By 1914, Wilfred Owen was well acquainted with Bordeaux's most famous export, as he told his sister Mary, although sometimes he drank 'nothing but water':

> Strange is the change. – The first time I uncorked a Claret I was in a great funk. I am glad I was; but I'm not less glad that just at the moment of my third bodily-renewing, I have been able to fortify my tissue with real Bordeaux Red & White. I am conscious of at least an appearance of robustness in my face: for when shaving I have a tight round skin to deal with now.[25]

Wine could be justified as good for his health, and when he was a little ill in Bordeaux his doctor gave him a bottle of wine as a tonic, but Owen might not have swaggered in this way in a letter to his mother. He had already reassured her that, even in this city of wine, he was not betraying the essentially puritanical drinking habits of his evangelically Christian family. On 29 April 1914, he was probably telling the truth when he reassured his mother that 'Only in an <u>aesthetical</u> and <u>ideal</u>, or else in a <u>10 f-per-bottle</u> and Chateau-Yquem way, has Wine any seduction for me'.[26] Then, as now, Château d' Yquem was an expensive Bridesheady treat, a drink for baronets. When Owen arrived in September 1913, the warm weather was being kind to the vines in the Bordeaux area, the grapes ripened well and he would soon discover whether hopes for a good year had been fulfilled. We know that withdrawn and quiet Owen would become good fun after a couple of glasses of wine; but he assured his mother that, although he enjoyed the café culture, he was drinking non-alcoholic *sirops* in the cafés at night after work.

Susan had more than religious principles to make her afraid of drink. Her only brother, Edward Gough Shaw, had been a drinker and then he had disappeared abroad. It was his disappearance that led indirectly to the sale of Plas Wilmot, as the family needed a hard-working son to take over both their ironmongery business and their home. And now Susan's son had also gone abroad, to the drinker's paradise, but what might have worried her even more was his confession from Bordeaux on 24 May 1914 that he had the same personality as his wayward uncle. He described 'the Tragedy of Uncle Edward Shaw, torn up by the roots by a perverted appetite' – natures like his 'labouring for self-expression, produce Art' but 'rolling in retrogression produce Nothing or Crime'. Owen told his parents, 'you know that as Parents You have, of all the world, the least title to find fault with what I am'.[27] No wonder Susan Owen worried about her son being tempted by the demon drink in Bordeaux. Since the last news of Uncle Edward came in the year when Owen was born, it is as if Wilfred Edward was the replacement and return of Uncle Edward.

Susan's brother was the wild child: in a respectable, God-fearing family, he was the changeling, very different from his parents and siblings. He was, in fact, born over the border in Wales and it is as if the Welsh birth made him the clichéd wild, intemperate Celt among the thoroughly Anglo-Saxon Shaws. Another nephew, Harold Owen, explains: 'Edward, who down the years has become something of a legend and a rather romantic family skeleton, was indeed a delightful and likable boy, but irresponsible and much given to wild drinking parties and, I suspect, much attracted to the more light-hearted ladies'.[28] Edward was part Jack the Ripper, part Edward VII.

Edward Gough Shaw was born in 1864 at Llanforda, Denbighshire, and played football for Wales, although he was dropped in 1884 when it was decided that he was English. He played three internationals as a Welshman – one against Ireland in 1882, and, two years later, one against Scotland and another against Ireland. In that second game against

Ireland, in front of 2,000 spectators, he scored twice. It is the familiar story of the international sportsman, a talented goal-scorer, who quickly ends up drinking heavily, chasing women, tossing money away and acting recklessly. Indeed, in his famous poem 'Disabled' Owen describes the tragic consequences for the drunken, womanising Celtic footballer: 'It was after football, when he'd drunk a peg, / He thought he'd better join.' In his early twenties, Uncle Edward had inherited money and enjoyed it too much. He became a wanderer, unruly and rebellious. On at least one occasion, he enjoyed drunkenly firing a shotgun in the darkness outside Plas Wilmot. Eventually, in the late 1880s, he left Plas Wilmot and never came back. Owen never met his wild uncle.

Edward Shaw said he was running away to America, and America swallowed him up. At that time, America welcomed the poor, the unwanted, the hopeful: to those crossing the Atlantic, the Statue of Liberty offered the chance to make a fresh start. His story gave Owen much to think about:

> My Mother had an only brother once.
> Unto the midmost lands of that vast
>   continent went he.
> Messages were scarce, and twas not long
> E'er the dumb emblems of his voice
> Ceased, as might a singer gripped by
>   the sudden Death[29]

He was known to be in Denver, Colorado (in 'the midmost lands') in the year of Owen's birth. Denver in 1893 was an exciting place and a doomed place. It had spent twenty years as a boom town: in 1890 its population was twenty times what it had been in 1870, thanks to the rapid growth of silver mining. It was a city for chancers, dreamers, adventurers, speculators, desperados. It was vulgar, showy and raffish, the Las Vegas of its time. Indeed, it became famous as a city of sin – gambling, boozing and prostitution developed hand in hand with the mining, filling Denver with bawdy-houses, bars and casinos, while it

also became famous for crime and corruption under legendary charac-
ters like Soapy Sam. It was a city for 'Nothing or Crime'. In England,
Colorado also became associated with Ripper murders: at the time
there appeared a number of letters supposedly written by Jack the
Ripper, in one of which the Ripper claims to be a Colorado man. And
then the Colorado silver boom ended dramatically in 1893, plunging
Denver into a depression. If Uncle Edward was still there in 1893, he
was probably on the edge of an abyss. The fact that he had gone there
at all suggests that he liked 'the more light-hearted ladies', wanted the
life of glamour and needed money: Denver was a city where he could
get rich quick, and drunkenly tell barmaids about his many exploits. He
must surely have gone there because of the silver boom – as an investor
perhaps, as a criminal possibly, but probably seeking work above or
below ground at a mine. Years later, his nephew wrote in 'Miners': 'I
thought of all that worked dark pits'.

Given that Edward Shaw disappeared in the 1880s and was last heard
of in the 1890s, he was the family's little bit of 'Decadence', end-of-the-
century pleasure-seeking self-annihilation. It was the *fin de siècle*: the end
of an age – the progress of Victoria's reign, represented by Owen's father,
was being destroyed. In fact, this family tale shows how Victorian
progress created its own destruction: the self-control and religious faith
of Owen's grandfather, which was so vital to progress, led to his son's
rebellion, his 'retrogression'. Oscar Wilde caught the spirit of the times
in 1898 with the line 'Yet each man kills the thing he loves' – a line that
would echo in Owen's mind and appear in his poetry.[30] Men of the age,
labouring for self-expression, broke free from oppressive homes in order
to spend an allowance or inheritance on drink and sin, or escape to
America, like the alcoholic Birkenhead poet Richard Le Gallienne ('Oh,
witched by American bars').[31] Uncle Edward represents that feeling that
society was in decline, being eaten up by an evil within. It was the age of
Jekyll and Hyde (1886), which Owen would later read. Uncle Edward was
Hyde to the family's Jekyll. Whether, like Hyde and other *fin de siècle*
figures, Uncle Edward ended up killing himself, we cannot know, but he
probably did kill himself with drink and lust.

His nephew possessed at least an interest in self-destruction. His poetry from Dunsden talks of 'Annihilations of the Self, soul-suicides',[32] and how 'I long to drowse, and fall upon eternal sleep; / I want to sleep, but not to dream, and not to wake'.[33] In dejection, he had written at length about other men's suicides and their desire to 'loose / The heavy-weighted burden of their life / And make an end'.[34] This is his Keatsian self, half in love with death. The poet of Dunsden imagined that he could 'die away content, without regret',[35] and asked, 'Why have so many poets courted death?'.[36] His version of Hans Christian Andersen's 'The Little Mermaid' is a story of self-destruction too: first, by choosing to become human, she chooses the 'early grave, disease, / And void despairs' of mankind, humans having a far shorter lifespan than the mermaids, and then, heartbroken, she 'leapt into the sea: her grave' – 'The child hath cast herself away!' From Bordeaux at the end of 1913, Owen joked that he might go pole-hunting and that therefore he needed an anti-magnetic watch like that of Captain Oates. Earlier that year, news had reached Britain that Scott's expedition to the South Pole had ended with Oates going outside and Scott dying in his tent, both of them quickly becoming examples of modern chivalry and suicidal heroism. He referred in a letter to Oates's epitaph, which described 'a very gallant gentleman' who 'walked willingly to his death in a blizzard'.[37] But in Bordeaux Owen had 'health and happiness'.[38] He possessed his uncle's inclination towards escape and travel, but in Owen's case travel seems to have been more rewarding. Outside the family, he didn't have a friend in England, but exciting new friends and acquaintances drift through his letters during the first weeks of 1914: agreeable Michellet who had appeared in a book; the author who gave Owen a ticket to the Students' Ball in January; the youth he enjoyed aeroplanes with; 'the violin boy' (Owen's favourite music was the violin's); 'more desirable acquaintances, (Univ. Students)';[39] the young men he went to the carnival with. His carnival costume, in fine February weather, was a huge success: a scholar's gown on his back, a poet's laurel wreath on his head and in his hand the palm leaf, symbolising victory.

CHAPTER 5

Venus and Mars

les passions des hommes s'accordent à la violence du ciel
FRANÇOIS MAURIAC, *Génitrix*[1]

À l'ombre des jeunes filles en fleurs
MARCEL PROUST, title of second part of *À la recherche du temps perdu*[2]

IN Bordeaux in March 1914, it seemed to rain constantly; as in England, there had hardly been a wetter March. Rain soaked the sailors and dockers at the quays, and at the Place des Quinconces it ran down the statues of Montaigne, Montesquieu, Liberty, Eloquence, History, Bordeaux, Garonne, Dordogne, the Republic and Concord. Women moved about the streets as quickly as their long skirts would allow, and the benches favoured by young couples were left vacant. Against café awnings, the rain pattered so loudly that it almost drowned out the city's church bells, while at the vast Catholic cemetery the rain collected in the vases of dead flowers. Rain swelled the little pond in the Jardin Public, ready for the boys who pushed toy boats through the water there; rain encouraged commuters to decide against walking over the Pont de Pierre and opt instead for the comfort and shelter of the *gondoles bordelaises*, the little boats that ferried passengers across the River Garonne, leaving from the Chapeau-Rouge and weaving through the larger vessels towards the right bank; and rain encouraged the street-traders by the Grosse Cloche to dream of owning a shop. But Owen wrote home that 'the city of Bordeaux, as such, is very far from disagreeable!' and on days off 'I am (usually) wondrous happy'.[3] France appealed to him. It was in March 1914 that Owen described Bordeaux as 'an absolute change',[4] specifically a change from Shrewsbury, and to some extent – not least the 'Sir' for his father – he was hiding his childhood away, although he added that he himself had not changed absolutely.

On 18 March it was Owen's twenty-first birthday. He did a day's work but was given the evening off, and had dinner at the home of a new friend, Pierre Berthaud, a bright fourteen-year-old pupil from the school – Pierre's school-teacher parents made Owen very welcome, and good-natured Mrs Berthaud was especially kind to her boy's teacher. The Berthauds found Owen 'charming, a perfect fellow'.[5] This important birthday was a happy occasion, not least because Owen could not know what would happen to Europe in the summer. He later confessed that 'on my 21st Birthday, when I looked into the Future, I did not see the War coming [. . .] But if I had, I should certainly have borrowed sixpence and bundled over into Spain.' On one's twenty-first birthday, 'it is better to look forward than back, because that way one cannot see anything at all',[6] yet writing to his mother on 15 March he did look back over his childhood, right back to the day he was born:

> I would not <u>forget</u> so many things as I would fain remember and experience once more. There are not many individuals with whom I would change Personality if I could. And I know I have lived more than my twenty-one years, many more; and so have a start of most lives.
>
> I have yet to open the supreme present you made me on the day of my birth. I must not thank my Parents for any precious thing in my composition until I know it is there. I certainly have Hopes: the value of which is that of the cotton-wool enveloping the gold; but as my hopes are heavy on my soul, it is a good portent; there may be worth therein.[7]

There is self-confidence in this rather Delphic declaration, as if he feels that it won't be long until his talent reaches maturity. He had been, and would always be, a poet obsessed with growing up. Frequently, he mentions this transition from child to adult, but he could not quite decide whether, in his case, it had or had not yet occurred. He said that in 1911 he was a boy but by 1913 an old man, and yet he later revised that self-assessment, saying he didn't grow up until 1917.

It was in Bordeaux in the spring of 1914 that Owen told his mother that he wanted to try to become a great poet. His respect for poetry had only strengthened during the months in the city. One friend noted that there was something typically French about Owen:

> His residence in France may have deepened this attitude of respect,
> and almost awe, which had in it nothing of the Englishman's casual
> approach to books. To him they were all-important, while poetry
> was the very crown of life, and constituted its meaning.[8]

Owen was convinced that he had an artistic temperament and was afraid of what might happen if he failed to satisfy his need for self-expression. He needed time and space: he was worried that too much teaching was going to kill his poetry – in a school essay, written when he was fifteen, he had noted that Milton 'began the prosaic task of teaching, and for twenty years the poet sang no more'[9] – and, like other poets, he needed 'a large allowance of space between the poet and his father's door'.[10]

Given this Shelley-like commitment to escape and poetry, it is appropriate that for his twenty-first birthday he received from his family, at his request, the Oxford University Press edition of Shelley's *Complete Poetical Works*. Shelley, the son of a bona fide baronet, was a traveller-poet, quick to leave home behind, and now, although on a much smaller income, Owen was a traveller-poet too. Like Shelley, he wanted to see Italy (he was thinking of a move to Naples), but Bordeaux was a good substitute. Both men were sun worshippers – in his boat on the Thames, Shelley used to drift, 'his face upwards to the sunshine'.[11] Living at Dunsden in 1912, Owen had read a life of Shelley and was comforted by making comparisons between himself and the beautiful poet, noting that he and Shelley had similar temperaments and that when Shelley lived nearby in Marlow he, like Owen, would visit the sick and the poor. Owen was pleased to discover that the poet was a good man: 'I knew the lives of men who produced such marvellous verse could not be otherwise than lovely, and I am being confirmed in this continually.'[12] Like Ben Jonson in the dedicatory epistle to *Volpone* (1605), where he argues for 'the impossibility of any man's being the good poet, without first being a good man',[13] Owen still associated decent, kind behaviour with great poetry, and was as interested in the lives of the poets as in their work, taking a strongly biographical view, or at least favouring those poets who expressed themselves directly in their writing.

In asking for Shelley, Owen showed once again that his literary interests were focused more on dead writers than on his contemporaries. E. M. Forster's *Howards End* was published in 1910; Marcel Proust's *À la recherche du temps perdu* had begun with *Du côté de chez Swann* in 1913, the year of D. H. Lawrence's *Sons and Lovers* and Alain-Fournier's *Le Grand Meaulnes*; Joyce's *A Portrait of the Artist as a Young Man* was published in magazine form from 2 February 1914. One of Bordeaux's greatest sons, François Mauriac, published his first story, 'L'Enfant chargé de chaînes', in 1913. George Steiner has asked, 'Was 18 March 1914 the most extraordinary date in modern literature?' Not because it was Owen's twenty-first birthday, but because:

On that day, Fernando Antonio Nogueira Pessoa (1888–1935) took a sheet of paper, went to a tall chest of drawers in his room and began to write standing up, as he customarily did. 'I wrote 30-odd poems in a kind of trance whose nature I cannot define. It was the triumphant day of my life, and it would be impossible to experience such a one again.'[14]

Modern literature and Modernism had arrived, and while Modernism tended to position itself against Romanticism, Owen remained devotedly attached to his Keats and Shelley.

*

On 11 April 1914, Owen informed his parents that he was going into the countryside for a few days. At times, he would see the countryside as educational – literally, when studying botany – and his trip at Easter to some acquaintances, the Poitou family, at Castelnau-de-Médoc with his friend and pupil Raoul Lem, and Lem's parents, was to have an enlightening influence upon him. On Easter Morning, he met the Lems at the Gare du Médoc, in the north of the city up beyond the Chartrons district, and they set off by train to Margaux, 15½ miles away, before changing on to the branch line to Castelnau, a journey of a further 6 miles. They were met at the station by the ancient grandfather and his two granddaughters, Armande and Henriette Poitou. Armande had the more beautiful name but sixteen-year-old Henriette was the real stunner, a 'superb' girl – 'her beauty was of the stimulating, & quickly-effective kind'.[15] While the mother ('a broody hen')[16] and the emotional grandmother prepared dinner, the grandfather and the two girls, along with their handsome father, took Owen and the Lems into a flower-filled wood, where Owen presented a bunch of primroses, violets and marsh marigolds to Henriette. At the lunch table, her marvellous eyes kept turning to Wilfred ('exactly four times per minute').[17] Raoul had fallen for her and sulked for the rest of the day, which involved more bucolic walks in the woods beneath the oak leaves, the spring's blossom and the afternoon sun while cuckoos and daytime nightingales could be heard. In this idyll, they danced and walked arm in arm. Some bottles of vintage Médoc were enjoyed by the guests that evening, and then, listening to the nightingales, breathing the pine-scented air, and carrying sweet memories of the day, Owen found it hard to sleep. The trip transformed him, and when he returned to a hot and dusty Bordeaux everything felt 'far fairer' than it had.[18] He wrote 50 lines of poetry in as many minutes, and played spiritedly at the piano. Was he in love?

Alas, no – or if he was, he wouldn't tell his family. He told his sister that, unlike Raoul, he made no attempt to compliment Henriette on her loveliness. He was too old for her, and was proud to write home that he had resisted the temptation to take advantage of her 'young and ardent nature'.[19] He also pointed out that he had slept in the same room as Raoul. None of his extant poetry seems to be about Henriette and those 50 lines seem to have disappeared – although perhaps he thought of her when he wrote a poem called 'How do I love thee?', referring to captivating someone's 'fleet fancy' with 'pastoral attitudes in flowery pleasance' (exactly when Owen wrote this poem is unclear, but it was possibly 1917). Owen would see Henriette again, but after this romantic beginning there was no love story to follow; he told his mother, as well he might, that he didn't dance with Henriette one Sunday later in the month when he saw her again at a dance in Bordeaux, and 'I was less pleased with her than at first'.[20] He would also tell his mother that his future wife would have to be 'Beautiful', 'classically and romantically',[21] and it would seem that pretty Henriette didn't quite meet his high standards – a wife would have to satisfy at least 75 per cent of his sense of ideal beauty, he explained. We do not know how Henriette felt about Owen when she saw him there: were her eyes, which had been delightful in the countryside, still drawn to him? Did she leave disappointed, with those eyes inclined to shed a tear? Her sister Armande was staying in Bordeaux with the Lems for two weeks, having come back from Castelnau with Raoul, and managed to find a husband in that short time. Henriette might at least have hoped for a little romance, as any pretty teenage girl would, even on a Sunday. And if Owen was still known as the son of a baronet, he would have been a real catch. With a sigh, did she think back to when they danced in the woods beneath the blossom and the birdsong? Poor Henriette.

At Whitsun, the Lems took him out into the countryside again and Owen was subjected to a similar encounter with amorous young ladies; indeed, the most forward of them had been at that same dance in Bordeaux where Henriette waltzed ineffectually. How different the girls of France were from the girls in Shrewsbury and Birkenhead: his plain Scouse colleague Miss Hewitt does not seem to have made any advances at the Berlitz, even though she was in France, whereas when the Lems took him to a riverside village, he had four local girls after him. In the village, the friends of the Lems lived in the Town Hall, the Papa being Town Clerk. Unfortunately, with French girls Owen found it quite impossible to speak 'amorously and poetically for fear of being compromised':

> It is their own fault that they are watched and warded, as is proved by this incident. The *Jeunesse* consisting of two boys and four damosels were for a short time separated from the elders. And it was <u>not</u> I, who was just then engaged in a Botanical Investigation; nor yet Raoul; but one of the young ladies who suggested that now was the moment *pour s'embrasser*. I was so taken off my guard that I kissed the curly-head without so much as looking round; but I finished off the rest only with much pressure and bad grace! Clearly, it was a solemn and established custom, not a merry improvised lark![22]

Owen was writing to his sister Mary. Perhaps he is trying to flatter Mary by suggesting that English girls are more intelligent, but she might have been a little upset to read that her brother was having such larks while she was stuck at home as a drudge, physically weak and diminutive, already, as she turned nineteen, consigned to spinsterhood and to caring for her parents. Chasing and kissing boys was normal enough for girls, but it wasn't her fate; yet, given her caring and sweet-natured personality, she would nonetheless have been pleased to know that her brother was *gai* and *beau*.

Owen was unquestionably aware of his own attractiveness now: he was short but stylish, handsome and charming – 'My face is certainly satisfactory'.[23] At some point during his first months in France he acquired a moustache, which would become one of the most famous moustaches of the twentieth century, some way behind those of his contemporaries Chaplin and Hitler, but up there with those of, say, Harold Macmillan and H. G. Wells (when Owen met Wells he described the novelist's moustache as 'a brown sandbag').[24] He joined a long line of moustached poets, including Shakespeare, Donne, Hardy and Kipling, eschewing the clean-shaven look of a number of his literary idols such as Scott, Shelley, Keats, Wilde and Yeats, but holding back from the beard of Tennyson. Owen's father had a moustache too, but Owen opted for something rather more refined and cultured and less Victorian. In fact, Owen's moustache looked rather French – rather like that of Max Linder, the early film star, the French Chaplin, who was born near Bordeaux and studied at Bordeaux's Conservatoire. In July 1914, Owen went to a photographer's in Bordeaux and had his picture taken, noting 'The shadow quite spoils the chic effect of the moustache.'[25] In earlier photographs, taken in England, a moustache-less Owen looks much less mature and worldly-wise.

Another contrast is that in Bordeaux Owen had taken to wearing a bow tie, that moustache for the neck. With his boyish side-parting having turned into a centre-parting, which mirrored his dark and prominent eyebrows, the bow tie and the moustache gave his face striking horizontal emphasis and a kind of heightened symmetry. The bow tie, and knowing how to tie it, spoke of Owen's desire for a life of culture, study and civility. In Philip Larkin's novel *Jill* (1946), John Kemp, a freshman at university, buys a bow tie in an attempt to escape from his humdrum background and enter a new world of money and beauty; he wants to buy 'something he could wear to show his good humour' even though he doesn't have the money for an expensive new suit, and no doubt Owen's feelings were similar as he walked past the clothes shops of the Cours de l'Intendance and the Rue Sainte Catherine.[26]

The bow tie suited Owen, as did the bronzed skin he acquired in the spring and summer of 1914. He was pleased to tell his mother that his appearance and health had improved. He told her about the eyes that 'play upon me in the restaurant where I daily eat'.[27] Eyes focused on him – indeed, on his 'fine eyes'[28] – and, in return, he focused on eyes, which appear frequently in his poetry and letters. He sought 'an eye which takes all beauty in'.[29] In his poetry he is not only painterly but also interested in looking: one Bordeaux poem says 'let me look a long while in thine eyes, / For they are deeper than the depths of thought',[30] and his poetry is generally more visual than cerebral.

Owen had been looked at, but had he also known 'how slim / Girls' waists are'?[31] A man has the chance to do that when dancing, but Owen seems to have rarely, if ever, danced with a girl before he was twenty-one, and he may well have never kissed anyone. We should probably believe him when he tells his mother in February 1914 that he has not used any of Bordeaux's many prostitutes, whose gay outfits contrasted with the white blouses and long black skirts of the respectable women. Eyes played upon him in restaurants, but, along the Bordeaux streets at night, many slender hands were laid on his arm.[32] He informed his mother that he utterly detested these 'mercenaries', and it is hard to imagine him discovering how slim *their* waists were. But when at the same time he declared that 'All women, without exception, annoy me' (women rather than ladies?),[33] we should not conclude that he hadn't been attracted to women, or that he was not aware of their sexual power. A young man will often find the same woman annoying and alluring simultaneously, and he was also trying to reassure his mother that, there among the unblushing daughters of Gaul, he was behaving himself. Among the blushing schoolgirls of Dunsden, he had not been ignorant of their young beauty.

Around this time in Bordeaux he wrote a remarkable poem called 'Long Ages Past' (the fair copy is dated 31 October 1914) about a mad exotic beauty, 'the last fulfilment / Of all the wicked, and of all the beautiful', with a face 'fairer than a flower', who has such power over men, including the king, that she can commit murder. This poem has a connection with Owen's portrayal of women in his better-known war poetry, and the line 'And on thy brow the pallor of their death' would be echoed in 'Anthem for Doomed Youth' with 'The pallor of girls' brows shall be their pall'. Elsewhere, he would write of the dangers, not so much of women but of men's lust, something one has to learn to control. In 'Stunned by their Life's Explosion', he opts for poetry as a form of antidote to sexual desire:

Ah! pity these were told not that their thirsts
Are slaked nor by priest's wine nor lust's outbursts,
But Poesy. They, knowing Verse to be
God's soothest answer to all passion's plea,
And loving beauties writ and wrought of art,
Might yet have kept a whole and splendid heart.

Indeed, this poem may have been drafted in Bordeaux. But poetry had
been a substitute for love or sex for many years, ever since 'life's explo-
sion' of adolescence.

His teenage years in Shrewsbury had not been rebellious or social,
as he whiled away the hours in his attic bedroom. In his copy of the
biography of Shelley, he highlighted in pencil the remark that Shelley
'passed among his schoolfellows as a strange and unsocial being' as if
aware of its applicability to himself.[34] And then, from 1911 until 1913,
Owen was living in a vicarage in a very small village. His poetry before
Bordeaux is the poetry of detachment. If he socialises in his poetry then
it is with the dead, whether the Romans in 'Uriconium' or Keats in
'Written in a Wood, September 1910' and 'Sonnet Written at
Teignmouth, on a Pilgrimage to Keats's House' or Chatterton, who
died at seventeen in the most famous literary attic, a death depicted by
Henry Wallis in 1856 in a painting Owen would have seen at the Tate
in 1911 – 'But Death is not the end: / No death for such as thou,
O Chatterton!'.[35] Or, in his isolation, Owen addresses poetry itself –
'Speak to me, Poesy! Give me on this height / The one true message of
thy thousand oracles!'[36]

Later, he would decide that 'a garret on the Continent seems my
only hope, that is to say if even this can be managed'[37] – the garret
being the romantic, grown-up version of the attic. To go to a foreign
country where you know no one is to isolate yourself once again, yet
Owen had neither a garret nor an attic in France, and in fact acquired
more of a social life. Or, at least, although he had little time for leisure
he was eager for more and enjoyed the spare time he had, going to
cafés, the cinema and the music-halls, meeting interesting young

people, visiting parks and beautiful churches. 'Leisure here would be so much more precious than in Shrewsbury,' he wrote in May.[38] He was also attracted to Bordeaux University as a place of congenial company. On 10 May 1914 he could inform his sister that he had 'half a dozen students of Bordeaux University with whom I might become intimate'.[39] Wanting to study, he suspected that 1914 – or possibly 1915 – would be his last chance, since he was already older than most undergraduates. He was teaching young men from the university and at least one student from Bordeaux's Conservatoire. Bordeaux's university was founded in 1441, although it was really a nineteenth-century university and rather more modern than Oxford; a Toulouse-Lautrec picture of the Students' Ball makes it look positively avant-garde. In June 1914, Owen was considering taking a diploma at Bordeaux University, but the summer's events soon made that impossible – by September, he was complaining that 'The Minister for War is in the University where I ought to be having my Courses'.[40]

By 1915, he was able to write that he preferred the city to the 'secret deserts', 'Society' to 'Nature': 'I thought I could / Be quit of men, live independently' but now he has a passion for 'Crowds surging; racket of traffic; market row'.[41] Those crowds surging were probably those of the animated assemblage he encountered at Bordeaux on Bastille Day, 14 July 1914. A very large crowd gathered for the impressive fireworks in the Place des Quinconces and then a ferocious storm broke, sending what seemed to be most of Bordeaux hurrying back home: 'The noise of hundreds of thousands of feet and voices surging back into the town was a noise not to be forgotten'.[42] That crowd reminded him, appropriately enough, of Dickens's French Revolution novel, *A Tale of Two Cities*, whose crowds owed something to Thomas Carlyle's *The French Revolution*, which Owen owned.[43] But his description of Bastille Day, written a fortnight after the assassination of the Archduke Franz Ferdinand, also suggests the war that was only about a fortnight away: a great thunderstorm combining with fireworks to produce something like a bombardment on the Western Front. Owen complained about 'a pandemonium of thunder claps' going on through the night until six in the morning and disrupting his sleep, while on the Western Front he would one day complain about 'offensive' skies that 'shriek all night with flights of shells'.[44] Nonetheless, for most of July the main story in the French newspapers was the Madame Caillaux scandal, not the 'European crisis', and very few expected war.[45] Madame Caillaux, wife of the Foreign Minister, was accused of shooting a newspaper editor who had been persecuting her husband. After an encounter with a German in December 1913, Owen had said that 'I should have welcomed a war with Germany',[46] but in his letters from 1914 the first reference to the fast-approaching war occurs on the evening of 29 July, the day after Austria-Hungary declared war on Serbia.

*

In England in July, a familiar way of life went on, everyone seemingly unaware that these were the last few days of an England that would be lost for ever. Henley Regatta began on Wednesday 1 July, only a cycle ride from Dunsden. In the wonderful weather of that Wednesday and Thursday, the *haut monde* were out in force, colourfully clothed and celebrating their leisured lives. Meanwhile, the Royal Agricultural Society's Show was taking place in Shrewsbury, right in front of Mahim in fact, and Owen compared it with the Bastille Day celebrations in Bordeaux, noting that Shrewsbury's crowds were surely nothing compared with the 'the mass standing in the Place des Quinconces last night'.[47] Owen's parents let a room in their home to one of the crowd, but Susan Owen had wanted her eldest son to return from France for the show. On 11 June he wrote, 'Don't expect me for the Show' because 'There's nothing for me in it'. He evidently wasn't attracted by the butter-making competitions, the bottled fruits, the Welsh mountain sheep, the shire horses, the Berkshire pigs, the Hereford cattle, the dog show or the many other delights. Owen was looking forward to a sophisticated summer in France. But on Friday 3 July, despite an unfortunate turn in the weather, Shrewsbury's crowds were unusually large because on that day King George V made a day excursion from London to the show. Perhaps it was a more cut-price or provincial crowd than the Season-goers at Henley, but everyone wore their best and endeavoured to look as fine as any debutante or Eton swell.

The Warwick Bioscope Company filmed the King's visit in some detail, giving us a wonderful portrait of Owen's Shrewsbury and of a pre-war England that would soon be gone. This was still an age of horses, and motor cars were assigned minor roles in the drama of the King's visit. However, at the beginning and the end of that day the steam train was centre-stage so Tom Owen, a Tory royalist, could play his part, and can perhaps be glimpsed in the entrance to Shrewsbury Station in the film. The King, newly arrived from London, steps from the station into a carriage pulled by four white horses, and as he journeys along the town's crowded streets, beneath Union flags and windows filled with people, he is met with craning of necks and doffing of top hats. Black-clad as if at a funeral, and with a few clean handkerchiefs waved, they seem to be saying goodbye to an era. Children are held up for a proper look by fathers who would soon be holding guns. Many men are in uniform already, but they represent tradition rather than war. Periwigs and tricornes are bowed, and white-bloused women in shop doorways stand respectfully as antiquated figures file down a commercial street, captured by modernity's new toy, the film camera. The people are almost as excited by this as they are by the King. There's another recent invention, Boy Scouts (Owen's little brother Colin was one of the Shrewsbury Boy Scouts), as well as choirboys, mortarboards, bowler hats, boaters, prim schoolmistresses, smartly dressed postmen, soldiers with swords, pretty nurses, puffed-out bobbies, every English stereotype. The King too was a very English king, the apotheosis of the English country gentleman; he himself was exhibiting 42 animals in the livestock sections. He inspects a line of elderly veterans as if they are cattle on show. Bulls plod slowly, a sign says 'Shorthorn', handsome horses are paraded. It all suggests the security and regularity of rural life; and, as the King leaves, there are many smiles from a jostling, merry crowd of young men who follow the King's carriage past the camera.

If England had been threatened by the murder of the Archduke Franz Ferdinand on 28 June, it seemed unaware of the danger. Skies were grey but there were no discernible clouds of war on the horizon; as in France, no shadow was cast by the murder in Sarajevo. On 30 June, indignation and deep concern was expressed by the Prime Minister, who described the assassination as one of those crimes that make us despair of the progress of mankind, but there is no sense that on 3 July, the day of the Archduke's funeral, King George V felt personally threatened by what happened in Sarajevo. One suffragette was removed from the station by the police as a precaution, but the Shrewsbury crowd behaved impeccably. At the civic ceremony in the Square, the King referred to war and peace:

> You have recalled the history of Shrewsbury, once the scene of many famous battles memorable in the annals of our country, and now in these happier and quieter days a thriving centre of peaceful pursuits and the home of a great public school.[48]

Cadets, shop assistants, farm boys, lads in the parcel office, chaps in the choir – even the horses at the show – would soon be drawn into the war, but they offered no threat or protest. Those girls waving handkerchiefs in a street gay with bunting would soon be waving off brothers and lovers. The King would come to represent that generation of parents – fathers especially – who sent their sons to war and made so many widows. Owen's parents belonged to the same generation as the King: Tom was born in 1862, King George in 1865, Susan and Queen Mary in 1867; the royals' first child, the future Edward VIII, was born a year after Wilfred Owen.

The King would soon be spending four years inspecting not prize bulls and veterans of the Crimea, but rows of freshly recruited soldiers (no older than his own sons), all to die as cattle. Later, deep in the war, just weeks before soldiers became 'cattle' in 'Anthem for Doomed Youth', Owen would report that 'The King is said to be coming here next week – coming to see how his thin bullocks are fattening'.[49] The King's visit reminded him of the show in 1914, the soldiers became bullocks, the parade ground the show, and the Royal Agricultural

Society thus contributed to one of the most famous poems of the century. Although Owen would also write a poem called 'The Show', it is not about that show of July 1914. 'The show' had become a soldier's term for battle and while the poem does deal with the land and 'creatures', the land is mire and those creatures are doomed soldiers. In 'The Show', Owen produces something akin to the work of Goya, another of Bordeaux's adopted sons. If there was any thought of the Shrewsbury Show, the poem does not show it. And, at the Shrewsbury Show, if anyone thought of impending battles, they did not show it either.

CHAPTER 6

The Valleys Shadowful

High are the peaks, the valleys shadowful,
Swarthy the rocks, the narrows wonderful.
ANON., *The Song of Roland*, ll. 814–15[1]

La ville des baisers, Bagnère, aux vents du soir
Livre sa nudité de nymphe et de baigneuse.
LAURENT TAILHADE, '*Épigramme*', ll. 5–6[2]

A town can tell its story through its railway stations. Tom Owen's
Shrewsbury Station was 'the Gateway to Wales', fortified with battle-
ments: Shrewsbury was a border town, and, as the King said, a town of
battles. By contrast, the Gare St Jean at Bordeaux is one of the more luxu-
rious stations in France, a château for *le chemin de fer*, suited to vineyards
and the city's eighteenth-century prime, and its rail shed sits on classical
columns, like those of the Grand Théâtre. Wilfred Owen arrived here
early on the morning of 30 July with plenty of time to take in the marbled
and wood-panelled rooms, as well as the commuters who were coming
and going, talking of war, brandishing *La Petite Gironde* or *La France*. He
enjoyed stations – they were educational. Once, back in 1908, he had
written a 'Description of a Railway Station at a busy Time of Day':

The first striking impression on entering one of our large stations at
a busy time is the number of people crowding the platform & jostling

and hurrying to and fro apparently in the greatest confusion. It is said that a certain philosopher used to moralise upon life from a position where he could command a view of many people; & perhaps there could be no better place for this than a railway station; – here all classes & conditions resort & every conceivable type may be seen, & here their excitable or calm self-possessed natures are manifested.[3]

A large map on the wall above the ticket office showed the routes through southern France, and all the evocative and mysterious stations along the map's red lines. His route would take him through Lamothe, Ychoux, Laluque, Dax, Lacq, Artix, Pau, and Tarbes. Owen was going down to the Pyrenees.

He was going to spend a month and a half as a tutor to the Léger family. They were escaping from the furious heat of a Bordeaux summer, which drove the wealthier residents up into the mountains. Bordeaux can be wet and foggy in the winter but in summer it goes to the other extreme. (François Mauriac thought that the extremes of the city's weather contributed to the moods and passions of the residents, who never seemed to act moderately.) The Légers had invited Owen to their villa in the mountains for the second half of the summer because Madame Léger, an elegant Parisian businesswoman, needed to learn English before October. Monsieur and Madame Léger also had a daughter of eleven, Nénette, who would appreciate his company. In time, it would become clear that Madame Léger had an eye for Owen, but he had more of an eye for Nénette – a chaste eye perhaps:

> So back I drew tiptoe from that Princess,
> Because it was too soon, and not my part,
> To start voluptuous pulses in her heart,
> And kiss her to the world of Consciousness.[4]

At Dunsden he had written about the Little Mermaid, and Nénette was like the mermaid at the start of the fairy tale, when she is a young girl living beneath the sea, ignorant of life at the surface:

And of the youngest's utter loveliness,
I rest content to wake a wistful guess.

Her skin is delicate and freshly clear
As petals of wild rose; and in her eyes,
As in the stillness of an evening mere,
All heaven's purple concentrated lies.

So when the First World War began – Germany declaring war on France on 3 August, and Britain entering into war with Germany on 4 August – Owen was in France with Nénette, 'for whom I draw, play the piano, make boats, act comedy, invent stories, play hide-and-seek, bury dolls, etc.'[5]

The train to the Pyrenees left at 7.30 a.m. and Owen had, for company part of the way, a pupil of his and that pupil's sister and cousin. Owen enjoyed the countryside beyond the window and was excited to see the flat southern fields and then the mountains, which rose up without warning with startling abruptness. As a schoolboy, he had written a piece called 'Description of a journey from Constantinople to Merv' (his teacher gave it 10/10), in which 'a soft wind was stirring the palm-trees when we saw in the hazy distance our destination',[6] and although this wasn't Merv, it was the nearest he would come to that beautiful train journey, for the Pyrenees offered the exotic mix of palm trees, soft wind and hazy views of mountains. In his Pyrenean poem 'From My Diary, July 1914', he describes 'Stirs / Of leaflets', 'Leaves / Murmuring' and 'Braiding / Of floating flames across the mountain brow'. When he eventually arrived at Bagnères-de-Bigorre, a town 1,800 feet above sea level, he found, waiting for him, a donkey-*charrette*, Monsieur Léger and Nénette. Their villa, the Villa Lorenzo, attractive but almost vulgar, architecturally an appropriate combination of French and Spanish, nestled on a hillside outside Bagnères-de-Bigorre, a short walk or donkey ride away from the town. Owen found that 'A few yards from my door a brook keeps up the "noise of a hidden stream, that to the sleeping woods all night, singeth a gentle song"', misquoting Coleridge's 'The Rime of the Ancient Mariner'.[7] As the guidebooks pointed out, the many rivulets of the River Adour produced a gay brattling merriness of sound.

The town of Bagnères-de-Bigorre had long been known for its healing springs. It was said that Venus was kept beautiful by bathing in the waters of Bagnères, and the Romans had built baths and a temple of Diana there. Montaigne, one of Bordeaux's greatest sons, had visited, as had Rossini and Flaubert, and so had many English tourists – the English Church, Holy Trinity, was built in 1859 and there was also an English doctor. It wasn't a large town, with a resident population of under 10,000 Bigourdians, but it received about 30,000 visitors a year. In the nineteenth century it had become a modern health resort, but older buildings remained, such as the medieval church of St Vincent. There were more than 50 springs, and 30 of these were available for use, where visitors could try a number of treatments and different kinds of water. The ailments that could be treated were various:

> The saline sources of Bigorre suit exhausted temperaments, nervous women suffering from green-sickness or worn out by the excitement of fashionable life. This spot invites delicate or languid constitutions, or such as have been unduly stimulated by moral impressions or excesses of the nervous system. Everything here tends to rest these worn-out organisations, to calm nervous agitation, to refresh mind and body, and even to console the heart when it is inaccessible to the gentle beauties of nature. The graduated use of these unctuous, tonic, and slightly stimulating waters dissipates vapours, drives away spleen, this cruel disorder of the soul, by re-invigorating the digestive powers and bracing up the bowels.[8]

Owen would soon recognise that the place was strengthening him and improving his looks: he responded not so much to the water as to the sunshine, the air, the people and the prettiness.

The guidebooks agreed that it was a remarkably elegant and attractive town, with its neat, Spanish-looking, whitewashed houses, its gardens, its modern facilities, its wonderful views of the mountains, including the 10,000-foot Pic de Midi, and its beautiful women. Unlike other spa towns and health resorts, Bagnères tended to attract the glamorous pleasure-seekers more than the desperate invalids: this was not quite *The Magic Mountain*, Thomas Mann's novel about the victims of tuberculosis in an Alpine sanatorium before and into the First World War. The waters of Bagnères had welcomed Venus, and now the town received thousands of modern-day Venuses, keen to be cured of minor 'feminine ailments' or simply happy to enjoy the promenades, plays, concerts, balls and shops, 'worn out by the excitement of fashionable life' but eager to enjoy a Pyrenean version of the fashionable life of Paris or London or Bordeaux, in a mean summer temperature of 64°F and surrounded by misty mountain scenery. At the Casino, the focal point of the town, built a decade before Owen was born, there was, in addition to the swimming baths, a ballroom, a smoking room, a theatre, an assembly room, a concert room and a restaurant. Cards and billiards could be played there; concerts were given daily. There were many expensive hotels, the opulent Hôtel de Paris the most expensive of all. The whole town existed for comfort and pleasure.

Some people would have found Bagnères un-Pyrenean or inauthentic, but, living up on a hillside out of sight of the town, Owen could experience the primitive spirit of the Pyrenees while having easy access to the urban glamour. In *Hills and the Sea*, which would become a favourite book of Owen's in 1915, Hilaire Belloc's travels in the High Pyrenees take him 'far from every sort of derivative and secondary thing and close to all things primary',[9] and Owen was able to experience this 'primary' world too. Bordeaux was a big change from England, and Bagnères-de-Bigorre was a big change from both – indeed, a magical transformation had happened. Owen wrote of 'Lives / Wakening with wonder in the Pyrenees'.[10] His life was now 'a lived-out book'.[11] Despite the modernity of Bagnères, he had entered into a land of fairies, knights, sprites and visions. The local people had held on to a belief in witches and fairies, and the mountains boasted fairy grottoes. Within living memory, a woman had been burned as a witch in the

Pyrenees. And in the Pyrenees, Roland, the perfect knight of the *Chanson de Roland, Orlando furioso, Orlando innamorato* and other poems, died a heroic death in battle, at Roncevaux (Roncesvalles) 'upon a border strange'[12] in 778:

> Rollant regards the barren mountain-sides;
> Dead men of France, he sees so many lie,
> And weeps for them as fits a gentle knight[13]

Roland was associated with the church of Saint-Seurin in Bordeaux.[14] Later, Owen would call the *Chanson de Roland* quite as delightful as Chaucer, and posthumously become the dedicatee of C. K. Scott Moncrieff's translation, which Owen had encouraged him to write.

Here in the Pyrenees, Owen found 'The Sleeping Beauty', Nénette:

> Sojourning through a southern realm in youth,
> I came upon a house by happy chance
> Where bode a marvellous Beauty. There, romance
> Flew faerily until I lit on truth –
> For lo! the fair Child slumbered.

Sleeping Beauty was one of the lived-out books: his poem adapts the story of Sleeping Beauty so that the fair Child isn't woken. Burne-Jones had done something similar with the famous *Briar Rose* series: 'I want it to stop with the Princess asleep and to tell no more,' he wrote, 'to leave all the awakening afterwards to the invention and imagination of people and tell them no more.'[15] But the sleep in Owen's poem is childhood and to awake is to leave that fairyland and enter sexual consciousness. And here in the Pyrenees he returned to his own childhood's more magical moments:

> Instead of dew, descended on the moors
> The ether – of the high celestial floor
> Over the boscage of the foreign hills

Floated the fullness of the merry moon.
And there a little while, I fell immune
Unto the harrass of these latter years
For I so repassed into my life's arrears.
Even the weeks at Broxton, by the Hill
Where first I felt my boyhood fill
With uncontainable fancies and strange movements . . .[16]

Even more than the gentle hills of Broxton in Cheshire, the mighty Pyrenees were mysterious and otherworldly. More importantly, Owen was living near Lourdes where the Virgin Mary, the *Dame blanche*, once spoke to fourteen-year-old Bernadette Soubirous. She had a total of eighteen visions in 1858, and while the springs at Bagnères-de-Bigorre were secular and worldly, the spring at Lourdes was holy and miraculous, because St Bernadette had found it at the grotto, while eating mud and scraping at the ground in religious ecstasy. On 6 August 1914, Owen sent his mother a postcard of 'Bagnères-de-Bigorre, Route de Bagnères à Lourdes'.[17] Before he left Bordeaux he had joked with his mother about his imminent proximity to Lourdes: 'Don't expect the seaside to work miracles in a fortnight. T'aint as if you were going to <u>Lourdes</u>, hem!'[18] By 1914, Lourdes, with all its hotels and different accents (including Liverpool's), was a major pilgrimage site, giving half a million communions a year and providing many miracles, and, as the Baedeker guide noted, 'the torch-light procession, about 8pm, presents a fairy-like scene. (Beware of pickpockets.)'[19] Lourdes usually received 120,000 visitors in four weeks between 15 August and 15 September, which included three days of 'national pilgrimage' in August. Hilaire Belloc, declared in 1914 that 'from the year 1904, about Easter time, I have had no doubt that here the best influence there is for men (I mean that of our Blessed Lady) is active':

It is my advice especially to those who have no devotion or faith, but whose minds are none the less free and who have the means and the leisure, to go to Lourdes and see what they shall see. It is much

the greatest experience in travel they are likely to have in the modern
world.[20]

Owen was so near in the summer of 1914 that it is hard to believe
that he didn't go to Lourdes. Lourdes and Bagnères-de-Bigorre are in
separate valleys, and the main road between them went via Tarbes, but
there was a smaller road from Lourdes over the edge of the valley that
joined the main road about four miles from Bagnères-de-Bigorre;
as the crow flies, the two towns are about ten miles apart. A motor
omnibus ran from Lourdes to Bagnères, making a 13½-mile journey.

Bordeaux had introduced Owen to the charms of Roman
Catholicism. He had grown up in a household where Catholics were
viewed with suspicion, but he visited churches in Bordeaux and in May
1914 'fell, only for a few minutes, it is true, under the spell of the
Catholic Religion'.[21] Protestants might view Catholicism as a form of
black magic, a casting of spells, but Owen was genuinely attracted to
the art of religion, praising the priests' chanting, which spoke to the
soul as sweetly as the nightingale. How often he fell under the spell
again, and for how long, will never be known, but he would have been
reluctant to tell his Low Church Protestant family if the spell had
worked for more than a few minutes. He read books by Catholic
apologists, and the poem that begins 'The city lights along the water-
side' is evidence of a Catholic tendency that persisted deep into the war:
it was revised at some time between October 1917 and January 1918
but drafted earlier, probably in 1914:

> The city lights along the waterside
> Kindled serene as blessèd candleshine.
> The fires of western heaven, far and wide,
> Rose like the reredos of a mighty shrine.
> Slow swung the odorous trees from side to side,
> Like censers, twining twilight mist for fume;
> And on the mountain, that high altar-tomb,
> The sun stood full of wine, blood-sanctified.

Soft, soft as angels mounting starry stairs
The smoke upclomb to space; the while a wind
Sung like an organ voicing many prayers.
I, sliding beads, mine errors to rescind,
Of slowly slipping tears, heard God, who cares,
Ineffable God, give pardon that I sinned.

This portrait of a Catholic city was possibly created under the influence
of Elizabeth Barrett Browning's *Aurora Leigh* (1856), a book that
Owen was especially fond of. Aurora, the daughter of an Italian mother
and an English father, returns to Italy in Book VII and we are provided
with a once-famous description of Florence. The start of Owen's poem
echoes Browning's 'The city lies along the ample vale, / Cathedral,
tower and palace, piazza and street';[22] and Owen's sun on the mountain
'full of wine, blood-sanctified' is close to Browning's description of the
hills around Florence:

The Vallombrosan mountains opposite,
Which sunrise fills as full as crystal cups
Turned red to the brim because their wine is red.[23]

On the other hand, the 'angels mounting starry stairs' would seem to
be in Venice. Angels mounting starry stairs are a much-photographed
feature of St Mark's Square: at the top of the façade of St Mark's
Basilica, directly above the main entrance and the four bronze horses,
St Mark stands, and on steps up to him are the angels walking above a
pattern of stars in a blue sky.[24]

Whether Owen is pretending to be a Catholic in that poem, or
playing with an idea, or exhibiting a rather deeper feeling, other poems
of his have a Catholic flavour too. It is sometimes suggested that Owen
had lost his religious faith by 1914, but this would not seem to be the
case: he had lost his faith in his Low Church evangelical background, but
not in Christianity – not quite. He had lost faith in the Rev. Herbert

Wigan, but Wigan had moved against his own family's Anglo-Catholicism and the Roman tendencies of his youth – 'when he died, a biretta and signed portrait of Leo XIII were found buried beneath a mountain of evangelical divinity'[25] – into a much lower form of Anglicanism, and perhaps Owen would have been happier in a High Church vicarage. It cannot be said that Owen became a Roman Catholic, but he was certainly increasingly at ease with its ways.

The Légers, though, do not seem to have taken much interest in religion. They were modern, sophisticated and pleasure-seeking. Looking back, Owen saw the Pyrenees days as 'amazing pleasure',[26] and even more special after the hard labour of the Berlitz School. Monsieur Léger was an actor and knew how to enjoy himself, and, although over fifty, was, according to Owen, 'still a boy'.[27] He had led a glamorous life, and Owen seems to have enjoyed his company; for instance, he impressed Owen by having known Elizabeth Barrett Browning (who died in 1861). Owen would always be attracted to people with money, social status and famous friends – but no more than most people, perhaps. Through the Légers, he met the kind of people he had never socialised with in England – it is not clear whether he was still lying about his family's social position, but he was probably not entirely frank and, like so many people on holiday, could exaggerate a little. He had uncles who were reasonably well off, but now he was in another world – one that combined money with culture and sophistica-tion (by contrast, one comfortable uncle of Owen's was a tinplate broker and another sold pork). The Légers' friends included a marvel-lous violinist, actors and academics, and, more importantly for Owen, famous beauties and famous poets.

Madame Léger herself had been a beauty, and photographs would suggest that she was still easy on the eye – she was much younger than her husband, and, like the quintessential Frenchwoman, she was thin, wonderfully elegant, with luxuriant hair, fine clothes and 'shapely features', and, even though many Frenchwomen were already forsaking cosmetics as a patriotic wartime gesture, she wore perfect make-up every day. There's a photograph of Owen and *la belle Léger* at the

Casino in Bagnères, 'the town of kisses',[28] sitting close to each other, their arms touching. How beautiful and happy Owen and his employer look: he the dashing gent (sporting, for the first time in photographs, his famous moustache) and she in an elegant, pale, layered and pleated afternoon dress with large cuffs and a rosette, probably the best-looking lady in the crowd, certainly the most eye-catching. St Bernadette had found her *Dame blanche* a few miles away, and now Owen had his. She has a nose rather like that of Madame Gautreau, the notorious pale-skinned beauty, an American in Paris, whose nose was immortalised in John Singer Sargent's *Madame X* in 1884.[29] It is characteristic of her that she is sitting in the front row, but this might have been because her husband was speaking on the stage. In a photograph of the Villa Lorenzo taken from about a hundred yards away, she might be the shapely Venus striking a pose on the steps.

How different she was from Owen's mother, who invariably wore black, having a rather puritanical approach to clothes and a moral objection to make-up. And how his mother must have wondered about Madame Léger. Owen was quick to point out that Madame Léger was a respectable, educated, well-born businesswoman, allaying his mother's suspicion that she was an actress (actresses being little better than the mercenaries prowling Bordeaux's streets). He said he could not find her '*belle*' or 'pretty', but later admitted that when fully made up she looked 'a surpassingly fair and dangerous woman';[30] and he also admitted that she found him attractive, that he found her 'a most amiable hostess'[31] and she 'has even confided to me that she doesn't love her husband excessively'. She told him that 'she could do whatever she liked with her men friends'.[32] This all sounds so clichéd, so familiar, a situation ripe for adultery – the bald, elderly husband, his attractive young wife and the handsome tutor, and a holiday resort where sex could be had discreetly, away from the eyes of Bordeaux (a little surprisingly, both Lourdes and Bagnères-de-Bigorre had many prostitutes at this time, because of the tourist trade). Mme Léger even asked Owen to accompany her to Canada in the spring: her husband would not be going with her, and she would pay for everything. This offer made Owen's 'heart bound',[33] but we must accept his clear statement to his mother regarding Madame Léger:

> I am conscious that she has a considerable liking for me, both in a physical and intellectual sense. She is now equally conscious that the former liking is not reciprocated – not one little bit – and continues to like me for my mind's nature. If it were not so, – I should hop it, immejit.[34]

Years later, a French scholar learnt, 'I think from Owen's mother', that:

> he was acting as tutor to some French child, and that the mother, being sentimentally idle, fell for the young Englishman. No doubt he resisted temptation, but his mother seemed to bear a grudge against the French vamp. In any case, he probably acquired some experience at her hands in practical fields.[35]

Experience at Madame's hands is a possibility, but Owen may have been honest when he told his mother that he was more interested in beautiful Nénette. Indeed, his interest in the young girl feels a little wrong to a modern observer because he does come close to behaving towards her as if she is a lover: although he says in 'The Sleeping Beauty' that he must not 'start voluptuous pulses in her heart, / And kiss her to the world of Consciousness', the mere fact that he writes about her in that way is a little odd, and he tells his mother that he strokes her hair, and she strokes his, and she comes to him for 'kisses and hugs'.[36] Owen also noted playfully that Nénette's dreams, which she recited to him at breakfast, were 'as shocking as could be'.[37] One can accept the innocence or harmlessness of this, while at the same time being reminded of Nabokov's *Lolita*, the story of a cultured man in love with a selfish twelve-year-old 'nymphet': Owen tells his mother that the fair girl has a 'magnificent physique';[38] he tells his sister that Nénette has 'a very pretty Body', 'has the devil in her eyes', and is 'coquette in matters of dress and is sensitive to my least remark in this respect'.[39] Somewhere Nabokov is smiling. Owen certainly found youngish girls attractive, having written poetry about another 'fair child' at Dunsden, and later writing, at twenty-four, about 'some charming dancing by a girl of 13 or 14',[40] and about a dozen teenage girls who danced and sang and who had adorable slender bare legs; he waved and blew kisses.[41] And so he wrote of Nénette that 'this child naturally occupies a good deal of room in my thoughts; but I am – alas or happily, who shall say? – too old to be in love'.[42] This might not have been *The Magic Mountain* but maybe it was Mann's *Death in Venice*, in which a writer acquires a dangerous obsession with a child when they are both on holiday.

Owen was too old to be in love with her perhaps, but at that time – at all times, indeed, but at that time especially – falling in love with a schoolgirl was not unknown, and had its artistic associations. When Owen speaks of her exquisite dancing and says she resembles a ballet dancer, one might be reminded of the ballet girls of Degas, such as the sculpture *Little Dancer of Fourteen Years* (1881). Degas and other artists of his time fixed their gaze on adolescent girls – in Degas's *A Young Girl Reading on the Floor* (c.1889), the admiring eyes could be those of a tutor. In the 1880s, the novelist Wilkie Collins pretended that he was married to an eleven-year-old girl: he called her Mrs Collins and a 'sly little hussy'; he told her that 'With all your faults, I love and adore you'.[43] A *fin-de-siècle* poet, Ernest Dowson, courted eleven-year-old Adelaide Foltinowicz; and Owen knew all about John Ruskin falling in love with nine-year-old Rose La Touche, 'Dear St Crumpet'.[44] Owen also discovered, and chose to inform his mother, that Madame Léger was proposed to when she was fourteen and got married when she was seventeen and a half.

Owen thought back to his days in Dunsden, where he had known the boy Vivian Rampton. He wrote about him at Bagnères in August 1914: 'would it / Be better never to have looked on him?'[45] Rampton 'suffered that grand, crucial change / The inalterable change, from boy to man'. The change is also 'secret', 'sad' and 'critical'.[46] These thoughts could have been evoked by Owen's attraction to Nénette, who may in fact have had a more substantial impact on his poetry. She is the girl in 'The Sleeping Beauty' and 'From My Diary'. 'Song of Songs' of 1917 echoes 'From My Diary, July 1914', and in it we may well have a portrait of Nénette:

> Sing me at dawn but only with your laugh:
>   Like sprightly Spring that laugheth into leaf;
>   Like Love, that cannot flute for smiling at Life.

> Sing to me only with your speech all day,
>   As voluble leaflets do. Let viols die.
>   The least word of your lips is melody.

On 20 August 1914, he said of Nénette that 'Her voice is a continual music'.[47] Owen had translated Nénette into music:

> I translated Nénette by the marvellous 'Rustle of Spring' of Sinding: and I maintain the likeness to be perfect. The grace of the whole, the absence of any melancholy, the pretty rippling triviality of the greater portion; and the sometime sinking into a rich, rich abundance of life and earnestness – that is Nénette.[48]

In 'Song of Songs', the loved one is likened not just to music but to 'Spring that laugheth into leaf' and 'voluble leaflets'.

Another poem that has a number of similarities to 'From My Diary' is 'Impromptu', written in Bordeaux in 1915. Nénette could be the 'Child' of the poem: he says, 'Child, let me fully see and know those eyes! / Their fire is like the wrath of shaken rubies', praising these eyes for 12 lines. Owen had been much taken with Nénette's eyes, saying 'her chief feature is her eyes [. . .] richly fringed with lashes [. . .] they become extraordinarily alive'.[49] In 'The Sleeping Beauty', she is 'keen of glance'. In that poem she is the 'Child'; indeed, she is 'the fair Child', and the Child in 'Impromptu' is addressed as 'fair love'.

Nénette represented purity and happiness, and the ideal childhood. Owen had never known girls like her when he was a child. Falling for her, he fell for that childhood he never had; and she offered an escape from the unattractive realities of adulthood. Nénette grew up to be a writer and translator. When she translated D. H. Lawrence's *The Rainbow* into French, as *L'arc-en-ciel* (1939), she may have remembered her summer with Wilfred – the novel was written through 1913–15 (in August 1914 a version called 'The Wedding Ring' was returned to Lawrence by the publishers Methuen). The character Anna in *The Rainbow* encounters Skrebensky, 'her mother's friend', the first person who 'affected her as a real living person, whom she regarded as having definite existence':

> When Anna was about ten years old, she went with her mother to spend a few days with the Baron Skrebensky. [. . .] Anna was very much impressed by him. [. . .] She thought him a very wonderful person. She was shy of him, she liked him to talk to her. She felt a sense of freedom near him. [. . .] She had recognised the Baron Skrebensky as a real person, he had had some regard for her. But when she did not see him any more, he faded and became a memory. But as a memory he was always alive to her.[50]

The oddest aspect of Owen's relationship with Nénette is that Madame Léger was playing a part too, making it quite a triangle as she spoke to Nénette about Owen and almost encouraged Nénette to see him as a boyfriend:

> I consider I have an important rôle to play, for Madame has announced to her daughter that she desires her to marry (at 19) an Englishman, ten years older than herself, who is to be intelligent and *beau*. So I am a sort of sample.[51]

Owen was ten years older than Nénette. Despite this remarkable confession, Madame Léger said that she refrained from praising Owen excessively when Nénette was gushing about him because she didn't want to put any ideas into her daughter's head, 'and I don't want her to suffer any chagrin when you leave!'[52] This is similar to Owen saying that he didn't want to 'start voluptuous pulses in her heart'. Owen added that his continual presence had had an effect on Nénette that her mother perceived with alarm – both mother and daughter had fallen for him. Was Madame Léger using her daughter as a tool in her own seduction of the tutor? Or, most disturbingly, did she see her daughter as a rival? Was Owen kissing and stroking Nénette in order to make Madame Léger jealous? The three of them seem to have created a weird muddle of flirtation, '*Coquetterie*', flattery, playfulness, vanity, happiness, beauty and innocence. Living with his two beautiful admirers, the sexually naïve provincial youth was in an unusual position, and with Madame Léger he seems to have shown a degree of restraint that many other poets, and most twenty-one-year-old men, would have found impossible.

In this land of pleasure, Owen had another admirer too – one who was rather less beautiful. Laurent Tailhade was a fifty-nine-year-old poet, well known but not necessarily admired for his subversive opinions and his bohemianism. T. S. Eliot's journal *The Egoist* provided a perceptive portrait of him in 1918:

> There is more knowledge than judgment, and the wit is rather dangerous. On the whole, M. Tailhade is an average Parisian intellect, but he can make amends for his faults on occasion. Constantly verve and journalistic brilliance have the better of meditation. Laurent Tailhade would have shone in the times of journalism's glory. Nowadays he falls between two stools. He is too good a journalist to be successful in the Press, and not quite good enough an intellect to hold a place of eminence in the world of letters. His mistake is to have an opinion on everything – a Parisian weakness – and a man without vision cannot have an opinion on everything, and if he be gifted with vision even this will only help him to realize his shortcomings. Yet no one can wish for a more valuable gift.[53]

Tailhade was known as a lady's man – money 'is a pleasure that one tosses like flower-petals beneath the feet of lovely women'[54] – but he was probably bisexual, and his poetry runs the gamut of sexual possibilities, from chivalric romance with elegant ladies,[55] to 'Facing the Prospect of an Imminent Dose of Syphilis', to sexual antics with young choirboys, and his interests may have included Owen. When the photograph of Owen and Madame Léger was taken at the Casino in Bagnères, they were there for a lecture by Tailhade, who was from the area originally (he was born at Tarbes), and he was invited to lunch at the Villa Lorenzo and then invited to live there. He agreed, and was also happy to encourage an aspiring poet, which is what Owen was now presenting himself as.

Having accused both Madame and Mademoiselle Léger of being coquettish, Owen seems to have played the coquette towards the elderly poet, happy to dine with him, to visit his hotel and to express admiration while at the same time chuckling to his mother about Tailhade's affectionate response: Tailhade 'received me like a lover', 'he quite slobbered over me' and, squeezing his hand many times, sitting him down on a sofa, pressed Owen's head against his shoulder.[56] Tailhade found Owen's eyes very lovely and said that Owen had the neck of a statue, much to Owen's amusement, although he reassured his mother that Tailhade was interested in his beautiful soul rather than his beautiful body. If Owen's mother worried about her son sharing a roof with Madame and Mademoiselle Léger, she must have been even more anxious about him living with Tailhade. Owen admitted to Susan that Tailhade is 'one of the wickedest satirists, and cruellest enemies that have ever used the French language as a lash', but reassured her that he's also 'a charming old gentleman'.[57] Tailhade addressed him as 'My very dear friend', 'My dear Wilfred' – 'Wilfred, I embrace you very affectionately,' he wrote.[58] He did try to move into the villa but kept having to leave because of ill health, so he had little chance to press Owen's head against his shoulder again before Owen's stay ended, although an amusing photograph was taken in September at the villa – Owen and Tailhade hold a book together and the elderly, overweight Frenchman has his other hand on Owen's shoulder; Owen has not put an arm round Tailhade and looks rather less comfortable than he was when sitting next to Madame Léger. But he clearly enjoyed playing the poet and was undoubtedly excited to be friends with a man he saw as a great French poet. He gave Tailhade his fountain pen, which Tailhade treasured, seemingly aware of its phallic symbolism – he was given 'the daily pleasure of holding in my hand such an intimate object which belonged to you for a long time'.[59]

Tailhade was a name not only for his role in poetry, but also for his involvement in politics. After an anarchist attack at the Chamber of Deputies in Paris, Tailhade had suggested that the fine gesture was more important than the victims. There was some poetic justice then in 1894 when Tailhade was himself the victim of an anarchist's bomb. He was dining by the window at a Parisian restaurant when an explosion blinded him in one eye. As an anarchist-sympathiser, Tailhade did not receive all the sympathy a victim of terrorism might expect, and the incident was rendered slightly comical by the fact that not only was the lone victim an anarchist (and, if the bomber was Félix Fénéon, someone the bomber knew and admired), but that the bomb was hidden in a pot-plant and thus was absurdly worthy of the Scarlet Pimpernel, with the fuse running up its stem to where it was lit by a cigarette. So if Tailhade looked at Owen in the way that certain French women did, desirously and possessively, then he did so with only one eye – and if his eye had a twinkle in it, then it was probably the eye made of glass. He was known to surprise dinner guests by removing his glass eye at the dinner table, which must have been a sight worth seeing at the Villa Lorenzo. He was a ridiculous, unattractive and pitiable figure, not a man whom Owen was likely to be seduced by, and had no significant influence on Owen's poetry, but Owen's 'Ballad of the Morose Afternoon' is a translation of a Tailhade poem, and he was an extraordinary famous man, another example of how far away Shrewsbury was.

Meanwhile, similarly far away in the distance, the war went on. The men of the Pyrenees had swiftly left in order to fight and a healthy man like Owen was viewed with suspicion, either as a Frenchman avoiding his responsibilities or as a German spy. The departure of the young men had left the town to women, old men and the unfit (including some wounded from the war). But nowhere in France could have been further from the horrors of war: Owen was at the southern end of the country while the fighting took place in Belgium, and he was in a remote villa with a family – and a child especially – who were most unsoldierly, although Nénette enjoyed talking about the war. This suited Owen, who admitted on 28 August that 'The war affects me less than it ought':

> But I can do no service to anybody by agitating for news or making dole over the slaughter. On the contrary I adopt the perfect English custom of dealing with an offender: a Frenchman duels with him: an Englishman ignores him. I feel my own life all the more precious and more dear in the presence of this deflowering of Europe.[60]

He was writing poetry about the deflowering (or not) of Nénette rather than the deflowering of Europe. In the same letter he showed how Darwin influenced his perception of the war. As a teenager in Shrewsbury, he had walked past the Darwin statue every time he went to the Free Library and the museum; he shared Darwin's interest in botany; and Darwin had undermined his faith – evangelicals suffered most from the discoveries of the nineteenth century because they relied so heavily on the Bible, eschewing 'Romish' ritual and tradition – but now he attempted to apply Darwinian Natural Selection to current events. Darwin had famously argued at the very end of *On the Origin of Species* that 'from the war of nature, from famine and death, the most exalted object which we are capable of conceiving, namely, the produc- tion of the higher animals, directly follows',[61] whereas Owen tried to understand not the war of nature but a specific war:

> While it is true that the guns will effect a little useful weeding, I am furious with chagrin to think that the Minds which were to have excelled the civilization of ten thousand years, are being annihilated – and bodies, the product of aeons of Natural Selection, melted down to pay for political statues. I regret the mortality of the English regulars

less than that of the French, Belgian, or even Russian or German armies: because the former are all Tommy Atkins, poor fellows, while the continental armies are inclusive of the finest brains and temperaments of the land. There is no exception made but for the diseased, the imbecile, and the criminal.[62]

In a school essay called 'My Native Country', written in Shrewsbury on 30 September 1907, Owen had said of England that 'each generation has been better than the one before it',[63] but now this progress seemed at risk. In '1914', drafted towards the end of that year, he wrote that:

> The foul tornado, centred at Berlin,
> Is over all the width of Europe whirled,
> Rending the sails of progress. Rent or furled
> Are all Art's ensigns. Verse wails. Now begin
> Famines of thought and feeling.

Since Owen's birth, progress had given the world the aeroplane, the Zeppelin, ragtime, the Boy Scouts, the cinema, the radio, the electric vacuum cleaner, the electric washing machine, the crossword puzzle, the helicopter, stainless steel, the Nobel Prizes, the Special Theory of Relativity, the quantum theory, the Old Age Pensions Act, the National Insurance Act, the Parliament Act. But where was Europe heading now?

Yet if Owen wanted to save his own fine brain and temperament, and head to safety, then he was in fact on the very edge of peace: Spain, which remained neutral, was only a few miles away, sharing the Pyrenees with France. Spain would contribute nothing to the war, not even 1918's mass-slaughterous Spanish flu, which came from America. As he would recall, 'In August 1914, when the moon was red, I used to go up at night to a hill-top, and look at Spain. I still do that in dreams.'[64] Owen could have 'bundled over into Spain'.[65] He could have found refuge in a Spanish inn, like that of Belloc's famous 'Tarantella',

And the tedding and the spreading
Of the straw for a bedding,
And the fleas that tease in the High Pyrenees,
And the wine that tasted of the tar?[66]

How different his life would have been then: the war could have been
lived out in the sunlight that warmed whitewashed walls, cobbled
squares and black-clad matrons, or in the shade of the cool colonnade
with a glass of Rioja or a lemonade. And years later, in the army, he
suggested that he should have made this move – or, at least, he should
have done so before the war began: once the war had begun he would
have been running away rather more dishonourably, and it would have
been a little more difficult, and even at this point Owen had no idea
that the war would become years of slaughter. He even showed some
interest in fighting, saying that 'After all my years of playing soldiers,
and then of reading History, I have almost a mania to be in the East,
to see fighting, and to serve',[67] although this was to his little brother, a
patriotic Boy Scout to whom he couldn't be as honest as he was to his
mother. Owen was more interested in poetry and happiness than in
war, and on his hilltop in the Pyrenees he must have been tempted to
slip over quietly. At least one person who knew him was under the
impression that Owen, a black-haired little man, had 'dark Iberian
blood' (certainly, Wales has long had many people of Spanish descent),
and perhaps this story came from Owen himself.[68] Owen took an
interest in Spanish poetry and had been trying to learn Spanish in
Bordeaux. The perfect place to learn Spanish would have been in
Spain, 'the safest spot in Europe'.[69]

CHAPTER 7

Mist' Howin's Honied Slumber

The fortnight at Venice passed quickly and sweetly – perhaps too
sweetly; I was drowning in honey, stingless.
EVELYN WAUGH, *Brideshead Revisited*, Book One, Chapter 4[1]

I am reasonably happy, which is all one can expect in this rotten world.
It was raining on the day we left Bordeaux. A sad day; not a happy
departure; haunting memories; vague regrets; still vaguer hopes. I doubt
the future. For indeed – I ask myself – why should one trust it? And also
why be sad? A little illusion, many dreams, a rare flash of happiness then
disillusionment, a little anger and much pain, and then the end – peace!
That is the programme and we shall be seeing this tragicomedy to the
finish. One must be resigned.
JOSEPH CONRAD to MARGUERITE PORADOWSKA, 15 May 1890[2]

W ILFRED Owen returned to Bordeaux in the middle of September
1914, when it was the time of the grape harvest. The country-
side had lost many of the men who would normally have picked the
grapes, but nonetheless the vineyards would have been home to an
army of grape-pickers. The crop was smaller this year, but 1914 was a
vintage year for Bordeaux. The train from the Pyrenees ran briefly past
the vineyards, through the Sauternes wine country – Sauternes is home
to the high-quality, sweet and pricey Château d'Yquem wine that

Owen favoured. Perhaps he recalled a phrase that he had used years before, at Dunsden: 'Adieu paniers, vendanges sont faites' – farewell baskets, the vine-harvests are done.[3] The phrase was from a seventeenth-century song that is used at the end of a play about Parisians venturing out into the countryside for a pastoral late summer, helping out with the grape harvest, enjoying the landscape, falling in love. But the summer and the harvest had to end one day, and Owen and the Parisian Légers returned to the city.

Temporarily, Owen moved in with the Légers at 12 rue Blanc-Dutrouilh. Bordeaux had been transformed while he was away: mobilisation took place on 2 August, which meant that the theatres, music halls and cinemas were closed, men left for the army, and cars and horses were requisitioned. A boys' school became a war hospital for the troops, and, as the numbers of wounded quickly increased, the soldiers arrived with stories of how the German army was moving through Belgium towards France, inflicting heavy losses on French and British forces. Then on 3 September the government moved to Bordeaux, which was much further from the fighting than Paris. Thousands (Owen suggested 50,000) arrived in the city from Paris, including the poet and playwright Paul Claudel. Private houses, theatres and public buildings became government offices: the university became the War Ministry, a school became the Finance Ministry, the law courts became the Justice Ministry, the Grand Théâtre the Fine Arts Ministry and the Alhambra theatre became the National Assembly. The newcomers also took over the streets and the Jardin Public, with their Parisian *chic* and their *savoir faire*: 'In certain streets pass a dream of fair women',[4] Owen, recalling Tennyson, told his brother, who, being a sailor, had fewer beauties for his eyes to feast upon. Well-dressed Madame Léger had some competition.

On 23 September, Owen described seeing wounded soldiers, both German and French, in the temporary hospital in the boys' school. His letter to his brother Harold included drawings to illustrate his descriptions of the wounds: 'One poor devil had his shin-bone crushed by a gun-carriage-wheel, and the doctor had to twist it about and push it

like a piston to get out the pus'.[5] Out of the letter stares a face with
weary, melancholy eyes and a hole in his forehead. Owen said he was
not much upset and was living in an admirable fashion, eyeing up the
newcomers, making good use of a requisitioned motor car that a friend
had use of, and continuing to live in some luxury, with plenty of time
on his hands since he was no longer slaving away in the Berlitz. He was
staying with the Légers in a handsome four-storey town house in a
sought-after location – at one end of the street was the Jardin Public,
and at the other the Place des Quinconces. And yet he felt he would
have to return to Britain – for financial more than patriotic reasons.
At the end of September, he applied for a temporary job as a French
master in Birkenhead. It is a little surprising that he considered
returning to Birkenhead, where he had been mostly unhappy and was
repulsed by its ugliness. Only a fortnight later, he admitted that 'I never
see in France any scabby-haired, mud-stockinged arabs, hoarse of voice
and hard of eye, such as breed in Liverpool muds'.[6] Moreover, the
Mersey hadn't been a good place for poets; as Owen noted in March
1912, it was in Liverpool in 1888 that 'Matthew Arnold [. . .] fell down
dead – from heart failure'.[7] Arnold's old friend, A. H. Clough, declared
that 'Liverpool is a dismal place'.[8] For a year and a half, from 1879 to
1881, the poet Gerard Manley Hopkins was a priest in the rat-and-
brothel-infested slums of Liverpool, 'face to face with the deepest
poverty and misery', and hated 'this horrible place': 'it used to disgust
me to see the pavement regularly starred with the spit of the workmen
going to their work'; more importantly, 'Liverpool is of all places the
most museless'.[9]

Nothing came of this application to Birkenhead, and Owen stayed
in Bordeaux. But it is worth wondering whether Owen had any kind of
Liverpudlian accent at this point. Had he entirely removed this indica-
tion of his origins? As a child he would have been strongly encouraged
never to speak with a Scouse accent: one day, the Scouse voice would
become fashionable, and middle-class John Lennon would adopt one,
but in Owen's day it was a barrier to success. That other Birkenhead
boy, the thrusting F. E. Smith, is said to have arrived at Oxford

sounding like Gracie Fields, but swiftly acquired the voice of the Establishment. When Owen walked Miss Hewitt home in the evening, did she hear the Mersey in his voice? But would the French ever have spotted that he didn't speak like a baronet? His French accent may well have been more upper-class than his English accent. There is no recording of Owen's voice – there are recordings of earlier writers like Tennyson and Browning, but Owen's voice has been lost for ever, along with those of others, such as D. H. Lawrence. Owen's has been called a 'well-proportioned' voice, possessing a 'soft modulation, even-toned, but with a warmth in it',[10] which may or may not suggest the lack of a Liverpudlian accent. A Mary Ragge, who knew the Owen family in Shrewsbury, said that Owen had no provincial accent and was well spoken, but a posher friend found him 'perceptibly provincial', an odd remark that suggests that Owen's voice was a little bit regional: it was 'a pleasantly modulated voice',[11] which might be a way of describing a slight regional accent. Indeed, Owen has also, believably, been described as having a grammar-school accent, which would have been an accent that aspired towards the public-school RP accent yet still retained its local origins.

When in one poem he rhymes 'Stair' with 'there' and 'blare' we would assume that he doesn't intend the words to be pronounced with the Scouse accent of his childhood, which would have pronounced 'fair' as 'fur', 'stair' as 'stir'. There are some interesting possibilities, though: in one sonnet from 1917, the last six lines end with 'bird's', 'hair', 'words', 'aware', 'uncurled', 'world', and in a Scouse accent they could all rhyme; yet the sonnet form requires that 'hair' shouldn't rhyme with 'bird's', which does suggest that Owen didn't write with any hint of a Liverpudlian accent (in Birkenhead today, 'word' would be pronounced 'waird', but in Owen's day this pronunciation was probably only found among the Liverpool Irish). Yet it is clear that Owen was closely atten-tive to vowel sounds – noting at one point that in Birkenhead a 'Cecil' became 'Cicil' – and Owen certainly disliked the Mersey sound, as his brother Harold discovered in 1913:

As I was closing his bedroom door, he called out to me to remind me how atrocious my English still was, and barked at me that if – when we met again – he found that I had the slightest trace of a Liverpool accent, he would disown relationship for ever. I did not answer him back, but went on down the stairs to join my father and Colin, who was to come with us to see the ship.[12]

Owen could say of a seagoing 'donkey-man' in Bordeaux that he had 'a delightful Liverpool brogue', but only because, as Owen admitted, Liverpool and Birkenhead had been left far behind.[13] The accent was delightful because it was now foreign, and very far from his own voice. It is possible that Owen had a touch of a rustic Shropshire in his speech. John Betjeman and John Piper used to do a comic Shropshire accent 'full of flat vowels and hard "g's" – "swimmingg" and "sing-gingg"',[14] which gives a different dimension to 'I heard the singing of your wings' retreat' in 'To Eros' and 'Singing of summer, scything through' the hay' in 'From My Diary, July 1914', or the 'passing-bells' in 'Anthem for Doomed Youth'. The g sounds are characteristic of the Scouse accent too, as it happens. But then Owen was described as having a 'rather velvety voice' with 'soft consonants'.[15]

He also worried about his vowel sounds when speaking French: his dislike of regional accents extended to France. He was anxious that he might acquire 'the ugly accent of working-class (not peasant) *Bordelais*'.[16] He wanted to acquire a classic French accent, like Monsieur Léger's. Owen knew that a proper accent opened doors, but there is more than pragmatism to his obsession with his voice: Owen attempts to perfect his voice in the way that he was trying to perfect his poetry, in the way that he was also concerned about his appearance – his dislike of regional accents might not be very acceptable today when Liverpudlian voices are commonly heard on the BBC, but Owen wanted what he saw as perfection. Earlier in 1914 he wrote to his sister Mary, 'I now realise that *I* must have had an abominable accent; for tho' I have made radical alterations in my pronunciation since being here, I am still a long way from perfection'.[17] Owen associated a good accent with a good education – he wanted to be educated, and therefore wanted to have the right accent in both French and English. His argument to his sister and then his mother was that he had been badly taught in England, where most teachers of French had, he thought, an execrable accent: 'I consider it a scandal that such teachers as taught me French should be allowed in Schools'.[18]

On the rue Blanc-Dutrouilh, a badly taught French accent, a working-class Bordelais accent, a Liverpudlian accent or a Shropshire accent would all have been recognised because one of the neighbours was the British Consul, A. L. S. Rowley, who lived at number 18, and Owen got to know him, possibly with the assistance of Madame Léger. Rowley was from an upper-class family (the Rowleys had a great talent for naming their children aristocratically – Arthur Langford Sholto Rowley was the son of Hercules Langford Boyle Rowley and in 1952 inherited the title of Baron Langford of Summerhill from one Clotworthy Wellington Thomas Edward Rowley). He would have spotted the lie if Owen was still pretending to be the son of a baronet, but Owen may nonetheless have exaggerated his background some- what, because Rowley and his consulate would find some prestigious pupils for Owen. When Owen had moved out of the rue Blanc- Dutrouilh, and was living at 31 rue Desfourniels in the autumn of 1914, Rowley helped him to become tutor to the Viscount de Maud'huy, and the 'ridiculously English' sister of the Vice-Consul ('a genuine well-bred Englishman')[19] helped him to become tutor to the nephews of Miss Anne de la Touche. Bobbie and Johnny de la Touche were 'English thoroughbreds'[20] and pupils at Downside, the expensive Catholic public school at the Benedictine Downside Abbey in Somerset. They also had literary status because they were related to the Rose La Touche with whom John Ruskin was obsessed when she was a young girl and he was easily old enough to be her father. The de la Touche name was rather magical for Owen, who had admired Ruskin for many years, and befriending the boys would be a way of following in another writer's footsteps.

It was only three years since Owen was a pupil-teacher in an elementary school in a poor corner of Shrewsbury – there had been no viscounts or thoroughbreds at Wyle Cop School, and it is unlikely that any of the undernourished pupils there were, like the de la Touche boys, nephews of the Baronne de Bock and nephews of the governess to the princesses of the Belgian royal family, or related to the girl Ruskin didn't quite marry. The boys at Wyle Cop spoke with an un-regal, un-literary commonness: 'Hall the skule his 'aving er oliday, so Mist' Howin wunna ave is sums & stuff what 'e learns us wiv hon Fursdee same as hother times.'[21] The training at Shrewsbury Technical School for Mr Owen ('Mist' Howin') was hardly a background fit for his new pupils and presumably this was not the training that had got him his position with the Viscount and the de la Touches. The Légers had been instrumental in introducing Owen to the right people, by giving him a way out of the Berlitz, and he was pretending that he was off to Oxford soon. The war also played its part, because the boys were unable to return to Downside due to the German threat in the Channel. The war was creating 'temporary gentlemen' by commissioning so many men who would not have been officers in peacetime, and here was Owen, a temporary gentleman in Bordeaux, pushed up the class ladder by a war he was avoiding. Perhaps he pretended, too, that he had been at Shrewsbury School, a public school superior to Downside, rather than Shrewsbury Technical School (the word 'Technical' made a lot of difference). While there is a very important distinction between being educated *at* Shrewsbury and *in* Shrewsbury, Owen might have allowed some slippage in his prepositions. Indeed, he had, in a way, been educated at Shrewsbury School, having been a regular visitor to the library and museum in the old school buildings.

Now he was living on the rue Desfourniels, and travelling out to the de la Touche boys in Mérignac, on the western edge of Bordeaux, and to the Viscount's fourth-floor room in Bordeaux. His role with the flighty nineteen-year-old Viscount was as much one of supervisor as tutor, and given that the Viscount was the nephew of a famous general serving in the war, Owen came close to being a secret agent in this position. Rowley appointed Owen no doubt hoping that Owen would pass on any useful information (Britain needed to spy on its allies as well as its enemies) and, more importantly, help to keep the Viscount out of trouble since there was much paranoia about German agents either honey-trapping or blackmailing influential figures who might be inclined towards scandalous behaviour. In 1917, Owen wrote 'The Fates', which features both the femme fatale and the informer disguised as a servant:

> They watch me, those informers to the Fates
> Called Fortune, Chance, Necessity, and Death;
> Time, in disguise as one who serves and waits,
> Eternity as girls of fragrant breath.
> I know them. Men and Boys are in their pay,
> And those I hold my trustiest friends may prove
> Agents of Theirs to take me if I stray
> From fatal ordinance.

He wrote that 'here I have so many sources of information', one of whom was the Viscount.[22]

Owen also had pupils who came to his own well-appointed room. The rue Desfourniels was a little to the south-west of the centre, beyond the cathedral and the hospital, and it was another nice place to live, but not quite as chic as the rue Blanc-Dutrouilh (the nearby rue de Pessac was known for its brothels). Number 31 looked rather like the Légers' house but it curved round a corner into the rue de Belfort so that Owen's two tall windows faced in different directions. He wanted to attract high-class pupils so he was renting a large, expensive room, with a little dressing room attached, and it contained some fine furniture. Owen was beginning to take an interest in antiques, partly because he was regularly exposed to expensive possessions in the homes of his well-to-do friends: he could tell that his Louis XV bureau was genuine and that one of his wardrobes was also Louis XV while the other was

Louis XVI. His landlady treated him very well: her son was fighting in the war while this Englishman was reading in an armchair in front of his marble fireplace, or admiring himself in one of several mirrors, but neither she nor any of the pupils seem to have objected to Owen's failure to return home to fight. The journey across the Channel would certainly have had its dangers, but English tourists still regularly travelled to southern France and Owen could have found a way home if he had wanted to. Clearly, Owen was now reluctant to return because he had found enough work as a tutor to be able to stay, and although he wouldn't quite have admitted it, he wasn't sufficiently keen to give up his handsome room, his exciting friends and his well-bred pupils in order to see his mother, whom he genuinely missed, if that would mean having to join the forces: 'as for losing any modicum of desire to get home . . . what possessed you (to speak plainly) to pen that imagination???'[23] By the end of 1914, 1,186,337 British men had voluntarily joined up, but his axiom was 'my life is worth more than my death to Englishmen'.[24] His 'fight' and 'struggle' would be literary.[25]

So he journeyed no further than Mérignac. The journey to Mérignac would have taken him past the huge Catholic cemetery, with its innumerable remarkable sepulchral buildings, lined up like bathing huts at the seaside, where elderly women could be seen sweeping, lighting candles, changing flowers, and praying. Owen had once complained that his landlady on the rue de la Porte Dijeaux had disappeared to the cemetery for a large part of the day to tend the dead 'and left the living to fend for itself',[26] but the man who wrote 'The City Lights Along the Waterside' and 'Anthem for Doomed Youth' would have been intrigued by this cemetery, and no doubt the rows of graves pricked his conscience. Nonetheless, he enjoyed Mérignac, as if he was on holiday, especially once he had moved there to live with the de la Touches in their home as tutor and friend, happy among the trees and sparrows, which he did just before Christmas 1914. Like the holidaymaker, he sent a series of picture postcards from Mérignac: pictures of 'Mérignac, Place de Capeyron', 'Entrée du Chateau Foucastel', 'Entrée du Bourg', 'Vue générale du Domaine Beau-Désert', 'Hôtel de Ville', and 'L'Église'.

But most of all he enjoyed the company of the de la Touches and their friends: he became very close to the family, almost as an adopted brother to the boys, with whom he played like a child.

If the sight of wounded men in Bordeaux troubled him, he was slow to act on his conscience, failing to make definite plans for returning to England. In February 1915, Owen attended a concert for the wounded at the temporary hospital in the boys' school: was he there for the wounded or for the music? He was pleased to report that the great Lucienne Bréval sang, only for six minutes but beautifully; and Bréval was visiting the famous actress Sarah Bernhardt, now hospitalised in Bordeaux, having had a leg amputated. Owen seems to have been more interested in seventy-year-old Bernhardt, whom he had seen in the film *Queen Bess* in 1912, than in the average wounded soldier in the temporary hospital. But then that imperious actress was still a symbol of France: the pre-war beauty had represented *la belle France* of that time, and now, disabled but strong and determined, she represented wartime France and went one-legged to the trenches to spur on the troops. Could Owen show the same courage and determination?

*

Owen made a flying visit to England in May 1915, having been commissioned by a Monsieur Peyronnet, a scent manufacturer, one of his former pupils, to represent him at the British Industries Fair. This allowed Owen to return to childhood again, by journeying to Shrewsbury to see his mother, and, before leaving London, by fulfilling a desire to see the Mile End Road, in which he had not set foot since he was five years old when his uncle, an East End doctor, had worked there: it was dark, but he remembered where his uncle's practice was and the name 'Dr Loughrey' was still up on red-lit glass above the door. Returning to France, he thought much of Hilaire Belloc on the Channel – Anglo-French writer Hilaire Belloc was obsessed with both sailing and walking, and Owen had read his *Hills and the Sea* (1906), possibly under the influence of the de la Touches, who would have known the name, since Belloc's sons also went to Downside.[27] Much of *Hills and the Sea* is about the Pyrenees. Belloc appealed to Owen as a poet who was also a man of action; even, for a while, a soldier. Perhaps, too, Belloc, like the de la Touches, appealed to him as a Roman Catholic.

Owen was soon back in Bordeaux, but he wasn't going to be able to play like a child forever. He had to consider a career. Rowley suggested that Owen become a consul (on £600 per year) at a time when these positions were usually occupied by men from much more privileged backgrounds. Owen was deluding himself when writing home to his mother about this career option – 'This must be considered' – since he knew that the career required 'a coach' (that is, a pricey personal tutor), 'a sojourn in Spain (for another language)' and 'a "Tea-Party Examination" with the Foreign Secretary or one such'.[28] He was still away with the fairies of the Pyrenees. It could not have happened without a generous benefactor, and one must wonder about the likelihood of that sojourn in Spain during a time of war. No doubt Owen was wondering about the war too, cunningly planning belatedly to take himself over the Pyrenees into a neutral country.

With military service increasingly unavoidable for a healthy young man like Owen, he began to wonder about crossing more mountains and entering Italy. He had already fancied going to Italy to teach, and had dreamt of getting back to nature 'on the Côte d'Azur, or at Sorrento and Amalfi, by the blue Italian Seas',[29] but soon after Italy joined the war on the French and British side on 20 May 1915, ten months after the start of the war, Wilfred Owen was considering entering the Italian military. Such was his desire to go home. If he had to do his bit, he would serve in northern Italy. And the man who as a boy had dressed up in the uniform of a hussar (a cavalryman) wanted to serve on horseback. In July 1915 he declared, 'I seriously should like to join the Italian Cavalry; for reasons both aesthetic and practical',[30] and was quite taken with this dream: 'Now if I could make it a real, live adventure, a real, old adventure, by flinging myself into Italy . . . ?'[31] On the evening of 20 May, had not rabble-rouser and poet Gabriele d'Annunzio announced to the feverish crowds in Rome that 'In each of us burns the youthful spirit of the two twin Horsemen who guard the Quirinale', and that 'They will descend tonight and water their horses in the Tiber, beneath the Aventine Hill, before riding towards the Isonzo that we shall turn red with barbarian blood'?[32] Fighting for a country other than one's own was not unknown – a youngish, smallish petit bourgeois chap with a moustache and artistic ambitions, one Adolf Hitler, was Austrian but fought for Germany (due to 'bureaucratic oversight').[33] Owen could have become another Sir John Hawkwood, the medieval knight from Essex who made his name and fortune fighting for Florence and was immortalised, as a hero on horseback, by a Paolo Uccello fresco in Florence's cathedral.[34] According to a contemporary, Hawkwood became 'regenerated more strongly and more healthful in fiber and body under the moderating sky of Italy'.[35]

The Italian cavalry offered Owen, in his mind, a chivalric, poetic war – a war for individuals rather than the mass; a war without machines; a war with heroes; a war where it is sweet and decorous to die for your country. He would fight an old war, one of those that he pretended to fight when a child. On 18 August 1914, D. H. Lawrence had written a newspaper article in which he recalled talking to an Italian army officer who had argued that the Italian soldier 'was the finest soldier in the world at a rush' but that the Italians weren't suited to modern warfare:

'Well,' I said, 'that is because they cannot feel themselves parts of a machine. They have all the old natural courage, when one rushes at one's enemy. But it is unnatural to them to lie still under machine-fire. It is unnatural to anybody. War with machines, and the machine predominant, is too unnatural for an Italian. It is a wicked thing, a machine, and your Italians are too naturally good. They will do anything to get away from it. Let us see our enemy and go for him. But we cannot endure this taking death out of machines, and giving death out of machines, our blood cold, without any enemy to rise against.'[36]

Lawrence had first lived in Italy in 1912 and 1913, finding it 'lovely as a dream'[37] – his wife recalled that 'Italy was a happy revelation for him'.[38] Italy was the destination that the cultured Englishman treasured above all others. The Victorians had taken the Romantics' love of Italy and turned it into a craze, and the Edwardians had flocked there, as E. M. Forster would show in *A Room With a View* (1908) and *Where Angels Fear to Tread* (1905), where Italy is the enchanting, liberating romantic alternative to staid, repressed, suburban England. (Thomas Mann offered a German version of this myth of Italy in 1912 in *Death in Venice*.) As Lawrence declared from Italy in 1913, 'here it is so free' and 'The tightness of England is horrid'.[39] Owen's heroes went to Italy and fell in love with its buildings, its people, its climate, its landscapes – Ruskin did, and Byron, Keats, Shelley, Tennyson, the Brownings – and now he could fulfil the dream while at the same time playing the dashing, Byronic cavalryman. The writers of Italy had created Italy for him: it was a city made out of books. He wanted to take Shelley's advice in *Adonais*: 'Go thou to Rome, – at once the Paradise, / The grave, the city, and the wilderness'.

Owen's book collection, a slowly acquired representation of his hunger for art and beauty, included a number of works about Italian or Roman matters: not just Romantic and Victorian poetry (Keats, Shelley, Browning et al., and Swinburne's *A Song of Italy*) but also *Plutarch's Life of Julius Caesar*, George Eliot's *Romola*, A. S. Wilkins's *Classical Antiquities. II. Roman Antiquities*, and Bulwer-Lytton's *The Last Days of Pompeii*. When Owen later referred to 'low sly lives / Before the fauns' in 'Miners' and to 'Sly fauns' in 'Sweet is your Antique Body', he was probably recalling 'The Evening Hymn of the Hours' near the beginning of *The Last Days of Pompeii* (1834):

The Fauns were slily peeping; –
   The Fauns, the prying Fauns –
   The arch, the laughing Fauns –
The Fauns were slily peeping![40]

Italy features in several of Owen's poems. He mentions Verona in 'Golden Hair':

> Not Petrarch wore such coronals, nor Laura,
> Nor e'vn his orange-trees by old Verona

Some of Owen's poems are Italian or Petrarchan sonnets. In his poetry we can see the influence of Roman poetry and also later Italian poetry, such as Dante's. Owen had seen Henry Holiday's *Dante and Beatrice* (1883) and Dante Gabriel Rossetti's *Dante's Dream* (1871) at the Walker Gallery in Liverpool during the Birkenhead days, and Dante was probably a poet he first encountered at school. Owen owned *The Vision of Hell, Purgatory, and Paradise of Dante Alighieri*, a translation by H. F. Cary. Virgil's *Aeneid* was referred to quite clearly in the poem 'Arms and the Boy'.[41] The Latin title of his poem 'Apologia Pro Poemate Meo' was originally incorrect ('Apologia Pro Poema Mea'), yet Owen had studied Latin enthusiastically, and he greatly admired the Roman Empire, although not naïvely. During the war that distant world seemed more civilised than the present:

> For after Spring had bloomed in early Greece,
> And Summer blazed her glory out with Rome,
> An Autumn softly fell, a harvest home,
> A slow grand age, and rich with all increase.
> But now, for us, wild Winter, and the need
> Of sowings for new Spring, and blood for seed.

With its Darwinian sense of progress, its botanical imagery, and its interest in Rome, this poem, '1914', could be said to have grown out of the museum at Shrewsbury. The hope is that Rome would come again.

Yet Owen never did visit Italy. Owen's concern about joining the French or Italian army was that when the war finished he might not be allowed to leave and, as a volunteer, would have to serve his term, which might be several years, even in peacetime. Neither was Owen much of a horseman: at thirteen this Don Quixote rode a donkey. A friend had been impressed by his ability to ride a horse on New Brighton beach as a child, and there's a photograph of Owen on a pony at Scarborough, but he admitted that he couldn't really ride. He was using the war as wish-fulfilment rather than considering what he could realistically offer. The young man who pretended he was a baronet's son could imagine himself as a horse-riding gent. He was only from a horsey background in the literary sense that he had long been intimate with the knights of *Marmion* and the Round Table, and it wasn't the cavalry that the Italians needed when, since their border with Austria-Hungary was mostly mountainous, they were facing a war of snow, ice and avalanches, climbing some of Europe's tallest peaks, hauling artillery by hand, and even skiing, with few opportunities for cavalry charges. There was also pressure from home: Susan Owen was opposed to him joining the Italian army, ostensibly because she thought he wouldn't be accepted but more likely because she wanted him to come home and train in his own country. Nonetheless, like Oxford, Italy played a major part in Owen's life even though he never managed to go there. (His brother did, briefly, and Owen was excited by the prospect of writing to him at an Italian Port.)

In Bordeaux, through June, July and August, Owen enjoyed the summer, writing 'I'm fairly settled down to Exile, work, heat, and the rest of it':[42]

> I pity you your bad weather. Here bad weather is impossible, for if it rains the nights are deliciously cool, and if the sun opens out like the mouth of a seven times heated furnace I am not incommoded. This kind of blazing heat stuns one pleasantly, like strong music.[43]

He now had an especially beautiful room, lofty, upmarket, balconied and high-ceilinged, with fine furniture, a marble mantelpiece and a view of the cathedral. Here he read Flaubert, and then went for walks in the 'don't-care-a-hang weather',[44] or sat in cafés drinking coffee and chatting with friends. At Preignac one day he was dancing with the country maids. At Mérignac, he played with the boys, and, when roaming the woods at Mérignac, the heather reminded him of Broxton in Cheshire, just as, in the previous summer, the Pyrenees had reminded him of Broxton.

He later wrote a poem about the de la Touche boys, expressing the desire to remain in childhood where, as on the beach, everything is soft and nothing can hurt:

> We cannot help but fall;
> What matter? Why, it will not hurt at all,
> Our youth is supple, and the world is sand.

The poem echoes the start of William Blake's 'Auguries of Innocence', 'To see a world in a grain of sand', and echoes, too, the famous lines at the end of another poem about innocence (and its loss), *Paradise Lost*: 'They hand in hand, with wandering steps and slow, / Through Eden took their solitary way'. Owen and the children 'try / To go forever children, hand in hand'. What the poem seems to hint at is a refusal to fall in the sense of the Fall of Man – a refusal to grow up – but this was also a time when the dead soldiers were 'the fallen' and Owen captures his reluctance to leave the de la Touches for the forces. This poem was a recollection of the local Atlantic beaches of the Côte d'Argent, and most likely the world of sand that is the Dune du Pilat, the largest sand dune in Europe, over 100 metres high, down which one can scamper or slide to the sea. In late July, he wrote, 'It will be pleasant to round off the "Mérignac Period" of my time with a week or so of nothing but "Ragging"', and planned to go on some excursions with the boys.[45] In August, he was also very keen to go further afield, to the beautiful city of Rouen, which was traditionally the centre of the popular cult of his near-namesake St Ouen (pronounced like 'Rouen'), who had been bishop there (on one occasion Owen styled himself 'Wilpher d'Oen').[46] In St Julian's at Shrewsbury, he had on many Sundays sat looking at the chancel's medieval stained glass brought from Rouen during the French Revolution.

The summer and his time in France would not last for ever, and he had to make the most of this moment of grace. One Sunday in August he had a pleasant two hours with 'a poor apprentice-tailor, formerly door-keeper' of the Berlitz School: they laughed about the old days, and 'he said many quaint things, and we rescued the boats of the little boys around the pond in the *Jardin Public*, and I earned a momentary place in the garden of boyhood, whence I am now so long banished, and that afternoon was generally very happy'.[47] Owen probably recalled the Jardin Public in the lines beginning 'I know the music', which were written in 1917: he refers to 'The warbling drawl of flutes and shepherds' reeds', and a statue he knew well was Henri-Charles Maniglier's *Berger jouant de la flûte* (Shepherd playing the flute), which was and is in the park right next to the circular pond where the boys launched their little boats. In 1917, he would also write 'Disabled':

> Through the park
> Voices of boys rang saddening like a hymn,
> Voices of play and pleasure after day,
> Till gathering sleep had mothered them from him.

At Birkenhead, he had played with paper boats with his friend Alec Paton, and when he was tiny his father had made him a toy boat with real care and precision; Owen had had a sailor suit to match, as the French boys would have had. His brother Harold was serving in the navy, but Owen preferred the garden of boyhood. Owen had argued that playing toy soldiers as a boy gave him a hunger to serve in the army, but now playing boats beside the piping shepherd was a moment of escape from the conflict.

He was determined to enjoy the summer, but could not quite forget the war – 'I only feel <u>traitorously</u> idle: if not to England then to France'.[48] As time passed it was increasingly likely that he would have to join up, as a result of both internal and external pressure, although friends in France were keen for him to stay. Through the summer he made enquiries and dithered and planned, and gave mixed messages, seeming, at last, quite keen to fight, but also unenthusiastic: 'I am already quaking at the idea of Parade; and yawning with the boredom of it. [. . .] It will be painful now to quit Bordeaux!!'[49] He also hints at a reluctance to be put in the position where Germans he knew in Bordeaux would be his enemies because, while he hadn't got on with all of the Germans he met, he had no hatred of the German race. He wrote in August 1915 that 'I hear through a Swiss that many of the Germans I knew here are still alive, fighting in the Vosges'.[50]

He knew that there was only one genuine career, that of poetry: 'I found only one Field in which I could work willingly [. . .] There is one title I prize, one clear call audible, one Sphere where I may influence for Truth, one workshop whence I may send forth Beauty, one mode of living entirely congenial to me'.[51] But if he had poetry then perhaps the army would be bearable. At the end of the summer, by which time two and a quarter million men had volunteered in Britain but five million men of military age had not yet joined the forces, Owen returned to his mother country: he was still slightly undecided about his plans, but it was now likely that he would join the Artists' Rifles, which trained cultured chaps for commissions as officers. He had seen a recruitment announcement about the Artists' Rifles when he was in London for Peyronnet. Bordeaux had made Owen officer material, not least by allowing him to improve his French – commissions were offered to men who had been teaching on the Continent, 'gentlemen returning from abroad',[52] but was Owen now a gentleman? The army was increasingly taking officers from the lower middle classes. And with conscription becoming likely, it was better to answer the call of duty by volunteering, rather than by compulsion.

Owen left Bordeaux in the middle of September. The train, crossed the river, giving him, from the bridge, one last striking view of the city spread out like a picture, with the spires of the left bank above the masts of the curving river that glided at its own sweet will. It was a year since his return from the Pyrenees and again it was the time of the grape-harvest as the train ran out into the countryside. Even more than in the previous September, this harvest was hit by the lack of workers. Château d'Yquem, indeed, had become a war hospital. And rain, mildew and humidity had damaged the grapes so that the wine this year would be far worse than in 1914. (It was a wonderful year for German wine, though.) Enjoying the combination of heat and rain, Owen had nevertheless commented that in that weather 'the vines will be spoilt'.[53]

Adieu paniers, vendanges sont faites.

CHAPTER 8

Mother and Fatherland

Without your Letters I should give in. <u>What</u> <u>to</u> I know not, but I 'sorter'
feel I should 'give up the unequal contest!' – without a definite object for
carrying on. And that object is not my Motherland, which is a good
land, nor my Mother tongue, which is a dear language, but for my
Mother, of whom I am not worthy to be called
<u>The Son</u> x x x
WILFRED OWEN, 4 April 1917[1]

On the whole, I am fortunate to be where I am, and happy sometimes,
as when I think it is a life pleasing to you & Father and the Fatherland.
WILFRED OWEN, 18 March 1916[2]

I N London in late October or early November 1915, Owen wrote a
train poem, 'It was a Navy Boy', where there's a brief encounter
between the poet and the navy boy in 'my compartment of the train'. It
is an intriguing poem because it brings together the railway, where his
father worked, and a sailor, which is what his father wanted to be. Owen
says 'I am no "sir"', possibly recalling the invention of 'Sir' Thomas
Owen, and yet it isn't a poem about his father – the poem could have
become an analysis of a father–son relationship, but in fact it is about a
mother–son relationship. A father isn't mentioned, but the poem ends
with devotion to the mother. Tom Owen was not at the front of his

son's mind; letters home from Bordeaux and London are to Susan, not
Tom. The father slips into the background, and, looking at the letters,
we see that Wilfred was his mother's son. The two Owen men looked
alike, as they knew, but Wilfred was not going to be his father's boy: for
years, they had not been close, and on Guy Fawkes Night 1917, Owen
said that 'I can't get sociable with my Father without going back on
myself over ten years of thought',[3] suggesting that there had been a
parting of the ways when Owen became a teenager, bookish and
'unmanly', and unlike his father. If they had in common a taste for
escape and make-believe, that only took them away from each other
rather than bringing them together (apart from during Tom's visit to
Bordeaux in 1913).

'Father issues' lie behind the work of many poets – Shelley,
Tennyson, Plath, Larkin, even Shakespeare – but in Owen's case it
would seem that his father didn't beat him (and didn't hit Susan),
he didn't go bankrupt, he didn't burn his son's books, he didn't
force him to play football, he didn't send him to a brutal boarding
school, he didn't turn him out on to the street at fourteen, he didn't
disinherit him, he didn't sexually abuse him. What he did was worry
about his teenage son, suspecting that he was too much of a mummy's
boy, and too bookish: Harold Owen recalled his father's 'petulant
upbraiding of Wilfred for his obsessional preoccupation with books'
and his mother's attempts to protect her son 'so that they seemed to be
aligned together to oppose my father'.[4] Tom Owen was not a great
admirer of poetry, although he did write a poem, a series of limericks
really, about his family during the war. This is how he describes
himself:

There was an old man of Shrewsbury,
'Volunteer' in the just cause against Jerry;
But, too old for the fray,
He at home had to stay
In the sleepy old town of Shrewsbury.

And this is how he describes Wilfred:

> There was a young man in the Army
> Who on poetry went slightly 'barmy',
> His odes on the War
> Were more telling by far
> Than all the proud boasts of the Army.

Tom Owen shows here some respect for his son's work, and a desire to understand this poetry lark, but he didn't really want a stay-indoors poet for a son. He wanted – like most fathers – a son in his own image, but one a little more successful and a little richer. Tom had urged Wilfred to lead a manly life and he became uneasy about his son's refusal to be 'normal': his message was 'More exercise, my boy', 'Play games, play games, play games', 'Fresh air and manly sport', 'Manly sport, manly sport'.[5] It was Tom's second son who did become a manly sailor. (Indeed, if 'It was a Navy Boy' is a conversation with a member of the family then it may have been a conversation with Harold.)

Tom Owen's enthusiasm for sport and manliness became an enthusiasm for doing one's bit in the war. To his son, he represented Britain and the conflict – looking at photographs of Tom Owen with his big moustache, you can see Kitchener pointing and saying 'Your Country Needs You'. This face of Kitchener haunted thousands of men, tugging at their conscience, scaring them into action – and some, including Owen, were also haunted by the father. So Owen would write, 'Admire at least my soldierly braggadoccio to Father',[6] and in 'S.I.W.' the father is like his own:

> Patting goodbye, doubtless they told the lad
> He'd always show the Hun a brave man's face;
> Father would sooner him dead than in disgrace, –
> Was proud to see him going, aye, and glad.

Owen decided that in order to be a poet he would have to keep his father at arm's length.

Yet he did join the army in October 1915. But the focal point of 'It was a Navy Boy' is the mother, and the poet suggests that his own attitude to the war has been changed by the revelation that the boy is serving in order to support his mother, fighting for the mother before the Motherland. Around this time, Owen wrote another poem about mothers, 'Whereas Most Women Live'. In 1916 he would write 'A New Heaven', celebrating mothers, and in early 1917 he would write 'Happiness' and dedicate it to his mother. 'Happiness' is a poem about the child and the sadness of ceasing to be one: 'The former happiness is unreturning'. In the drafts, he had written,

> Happy are they who see not past the scope
> Of mother-arms. I loosed them, broke the bond.
> Not one day happy have I gone beyond.

Owen wrote 'BAD' alongside these lines and also crossed out 'a Mother's boy',[7] but he was beginning to accept himself as a mummy's boy, a boy who is happiest in his mother's arms. Mothers appear frequently in his wartime poems, although the mother is usually an unnamed or unidentified mother rather than Susan specifically (at times in his drafts, he is unsure whether to say 'Mother' or 'mother'). The war, and Owen's unsuccessful romantic life – anyhow limited by joining the army – might have driven him into a position where his mother was reconfirmed as the centre of his attention. She had always been important to him, but she became more important at this time, from the point when he entered the army. He was in effect choosing to love an unreal figure – a woman he hardly saw, a woman who existed in his imagination and in her letters. She was the object of his affections, instead of other women, but she was also pure and angelic. His mother became a representative of the ideal, secure home life, an 'other' place to escape to in thought and only occasionally in person. In a letter, he could omit his father and reconstruct his family home. Owen's mother came to represent the childhood idyll, and was home personified. With his mother he built a Motherland of peace to stand against the Fatherland of war.

It would be easy to reach, as many have done, for Freudian and pseudo-Freudian terminology in order to categorise Owen as 'Oedipal', trapped in his 'mother-fixation', a psychoneurotic unable to detach his sexual impulses from his mother.[8] Canon Herbert Roland Bate, who knew Owen in the army, describes in his memoirs Owen loving his mother with the devotion of a lover, and refers to the seeds of an Oedipus complex.[9] After all, Owen does enjoy telling his mother that she is 'very very beautiful'.[10] He also admitted during the war that for a man of his age he was unusual in holding his mother as the person he loved above all; but 'I believe it will always be so with me, always'.[11] Susan was a good person, and they had always been close, but she was recreated as the personification of home, childhood, peace and poetry as an alternative to war and sex. (She performed some of the symbolic function that Nénette had performed.)

It was inevitable that the mother, as an ideal, would become more important to soldiers at a time of such horror and slaughter. The war made soldiers long for home and mother, in a way that they had not done before the war: Owen wrote that the favourite song of the men was 'The Roses round the door / Makes me love Mother more'.[12] A cult of the mother developed in the press, the theatre, the music halls. And 'Mother' was often the last desperate word of the dying soldier infantilised by a Western Front bullet, as one veteran, Harry Patch, recalled:

> I came across a Cornishman, ripped from shoulder to waist with shrapnel, his stomach on the ground beside him in a pool of blood. As I got to him he said, 'Shoot me,' he was beyond all human aid. Before we could even draw a revolver he had died. He just said 'Mother.' I will never forget it.[13]

Other writers often turned to their mothers – in thought at least – as an escape from times of difficulty and sorrow. Through poverty, unhappiness and ill health, D. H. Lawrence clung to his mother Lydia, and his relationship with her was reflected in *Sons and Lovers*. Several other war poets were also devoted to their mothers. 'And so when I remember you / I think of all things rich and true', Siegfried Sassoon wrote in 'To My Mother', in lines that sound like verse from a cheap greetings card.[14] Equally, reading about writers' lives, Owen had seen that a loving mother might be necessary for literary success. He wrote, on 24 July 1912, that:

> I found on reading Mr. Collingwood's *Ruskin* that Ruskin (my King John the Second) used to write elaborate (or at least full) letters to his anxious parents every single day, when he was once in one part of Switzerland and they in another; and that a remissness in this respect – say of three days would put Mama in a rare flutter.[15]

In his copy of *Sir Walter Scott* by Richard H. Hutton, Owen highlighted the sentence 'Sir Walter records many evidences of the tenderness of his mother's nature, and he returned warmly her affection for himself'.[16] In his copy of a biography of Byron by John Galt, for instance, he would have read about Byron's great love for his mother, whose indulgence of him impaired his manliness but formed the poet. The mother can even be the spirit of poetry, and the reason for the poems.

*

Wilfred Owen joined the 28th Battalion of the London Regiment (Artists' Rifles) on 21 October 1915 at Duke's Road, opposite the Athenian caryatids of St Pancras Church. The terracotta relief above the doorway to the headquarters depicted the heads of Mars and Minerva, and Duke's Road was a noble enough context in which to take the king's shilling. He was willing to serve in the Territorial Force for the term of four years, and took the official oath: 'I Wilfred Edward Salter Owen swear by Almighty God, that I will be faithful and bear true Allegiance to His Majesty King George the Fifth, His Heirs, and Successors, and that I will, as in duty bound, honestly and faithfully defend His Majesty, His Heirs, and Successors, in Person, Crown, and Dignity against all enemies, according to the conditions of my service.'[17] The Medical Inspection Report described his height as 5 feet 5 inches, and his chest

as 36 ½ inches when fully expanded, his vision as perfect and his phys-
ical development as fair. Some records give Owen's height as an inch or
half an inch taller than that of 5 feet 5 (which was also, for instance, the
height of Lawrence of Arabia), but he was officially two inches taller
than the minimum height. Although, at first, Kitchener's recruits had
had to be 5 feet 6, on 5 November 1914, after three months of the war,
the height requirement had been reduced to 'normal standard' for
infantry of the line (5 feet 3 inches; with a chest measurement of 36 ½
inches). So, for a year now, Owen had been regulation army material,
and could possibly even have squeaked in in August 1914.

Owen may have pleased his father by finally joining the military,
taking the manly path or at least letting the army try to make him
manly, but by joining the Artists' Rifles he could excite his mother's
artistic ambitions for her son – the Artists' Rifles' name seemed to
combine his father's ambitions with his mother's. It was indeed, as the
comically oxymoronic name would suggest, a corps for artists, espe-
cially when it was created in 1859, and had for decades evoked amusing
thoughts of soldiers brandishing paintbrushes, polishing their boots
with oil paint, and sleeping under a painter's canvas – a comicalness
that only heightened the tragedy of the Artists in the First World War,
where 2003 of its members were killed. Owen excitedly told his mother
that the Victorian painters Lord Leighton and John Everett Millais
had belonged to the Artists' Rifles when it was a territorial battalion (in
October 1915 it became an Officer Training Corps). The Artists had
originally had their headquarters at Burlington House, home of the
Royal Academy, where their First World War memorial now is. And
as a new recruit in October 1915 Owen found himself training in a
rather artistic district of London: he was living in Tavistock Square in
Bloomsbury, a large square of brown-brick houses with a rusticated
white ground floor, where, as he told his mother, Dickens had lived;
this was where Dickens wrote about the London fog and mud at the
beginning of *Bleak House*, as if London was like the no-man's-land of
the First World War. Today, Tavistock Square is known not for Owen
or Dickens but for peace: in the London bombings of 7 July 2005, an

eighteen-year-old suicide bomber killed himself and thirteen others there, and it is now the site of the national memorial for the four London bombings. It was already, however, a 'peace square', with a statue of Mahatma Gandhi, a memorial to conscientious objectors – 'To All Those Who Have Established and Are Maintaining The Right to Refuse to Kill' – a cherry tree planted in memory of Hiroshima, and a field maple planted to mark the United Nations' International Year of Peace in 1986.

He was near the University of London and the British Museum, and would march past them or perform drill outside them, and even then the boarding houses and flats of Bloomsbury contained a large proportion of London's writers and intellectuals. Although this was before the Bloomsbury Group came into bloom, Lytton Strachey already lived in the area and Virginia Woolf had been a Bloomsbury resident until her marriage in 1912 (Tavistock Square contains a bust of Woolf, who moved there in 1924). And, since Owen was regularly doing drill in Cartwright Gardens, a short walk away, on the other side of Woburn Place, and since the headquarters at Duke's Road were just round the corner from Woburn Buildings, he would on many occasions have walked past the flat of one of his literary heroes, W. B. Yeats, who might have dreamt of Sligo but between 1896 and 1919 was frequently at 18 Woburn Buildings, working by candlelight beneath the death mask of Dante and engravings by Blake. If passers-by glanced up at a big window above a cobbler's shop, looking out on to a trafficless raised flagged pavement, they could often see Yeats walking and talking in his living room. Bow-fronted, narrow, atmospheric Woburn Buildings is one of the more Dickensian corners of London, where a hungry orphan might have been found peering into a shop window. It was built in 1822 by Thomas Cubitt, who built Tavistock Square. It is pretty, but Yeats was, he confessed, tied to London by the need of a woman friend, and he was in London in October and November 1915 while Owen was there too. However, Owen seems to have missed this opportunity to encounter a literary great, or, at least, he never mentioned it to anyone. Perhaps he saw a tall shadowy figure at a window and thought nothing more of it as he tramped to or from Cartwright Gardens or Duke's Road in his new army overcoat. But it was probably around this time that Owen started reading Yeats with devotion.

Similarly, Owen could have seen D. H. Lawrence, Ezra Pound and T. S. Eliot in London at this time, on the streets or in the underground, but, as unknown figures, they were just faces in the crowd. D. H. Lawrence was trying to initiate 'a new movement for real life and real freedom' from 1 Byron Villas in the Vale of Health, Hampstead, where in November autumn leaves were burned on Hampstead Heath 'and the leaves are like soldiers'.[18] Owen was one of the soldiers on the autumnal Heath – Keats's Heath – as Bate recalled:

On Fridays came the weekly route-march. Led by the regimental band we went past Lords' Cricket Ground, along Finchley Road to Swiss Cottage, and up to Hampstead Heath. Girls waved to us and threw us cigarettes and sweets. On the Heath we did field-exercises, and afterwards were dismissed so that we could refresh ourselves at Jack Straw's Castle before we returned to our billets in our own time.[19]

On the Heath, Owen wrote in 1912, 'I walk with spirits, and the voice / Of men long dead is busy in my ear'.[20]

Lawrence and John Middleton Murry had also taken a room at Fisher Street near the British Museum in order to hold public meetings against the war, the 'great consuming fire'.[21] Lawrence was declaring, too, that 'We must rid ourselves of this ponderous incubus of falsehood, this massive London, with its streets of nullity: we must, with one accord and in purity of spirit, pull it down and build up a beautiful thing'.[22] Pound could have been seen leaving or entering Yeats's flat, and his electric-shock hairdo was not exactly inconspicuous, but in Bloomsbury he would not have been extraordinary, while Eliot, who had fantasised about giving up the English language and trying to write in French in Paris, was being very ordinary, teaching in High Wycombe, although he tried to spend as much time as possible in

London. ('I love to be in London, especially as I begin to know more people there. I want to know all sorts of people – political and social as well as literary and philosophical'.)[23] These roads not taken – Yeats, Lawrence, Pound, Eliot – remind us that Owen was *modern* but took a different road from Modernism.

Yet the army for Owen was hardly avant-garde. Joining the Artists' Rifles was like a return to school: a return to uniforms, boredom, discipline, classes, physical education ('We lost in the Match with Eton'),[24] rules, short hair and polished boots, a lack of privacy, restricted freedom, the Sergeant-Major as the teacher bawling at his 'lovely boys'. On 29 October 1915, Owen admitted, 'I never felt devotion, and not much respect, for any authority or individual in this world since I left the 3rd form of the [Birkenhead] Institute; but I am beginning again under these fellows'.[25] He showed none of the affection for his schooldays that other men of his generation would, but he had an enormous interest in school, and he dearly wished that he had been at a great public school. The Artists' Rifles was the nearest he had come to achieving that dream. It offered some grandeur in that all of his fellow soldiers were 'officer material', some were public-school men, and the Artists considered themselves one of the better battalions. The public schools had their own Officers' Training Corps, so that some of the Artists were already used to marching and saluting, and treated the army as merely an extension of what they had known for years at school. Owen, however, had not had military training before, apart from his hours spent as a little boy dressed up in the military uniform his mother had made for him, and his games of toy soldiers in Birkenhead.

The Second World War poet, Keith Douglas, described himself in the third person in terms that would apply to Owen: 'As a child he was a militarist, and like many of his warlike elders, built up heroic opinions upon little information [. . .] As you would expect, he played with lead soldiers, and toy artillery.'[26] Two photographs show a very young Owen playing in a military uniform. Indeed, Owen liked Sir Walter Scott's remark that 'you will find me a rattle-skulled, half-lawyer, half-sportsman, through whose head a regiment of horse has been exercising since he was five years old'.[27] On 10 August 1914, possibly recalling that Scott remark, he had announced that he had almost a mania to fight after all his years of playing soldiers. Later in the war, he wrote about those 'children ardent for some desperate glory',[28] and, recalling his own childhood games, would express 'the philosophy of many soldiers':

> I suppose
> Little I'd ever teach a son, but hitting,
> Shooting, war, hunting, all the arts of hurting.
> Well, that's what I learnt[29]

In 1915, Owen's tastes could still be rather schoolboyish. In early November, he told his mother that he had seen *The Scarlet Pimpernel* at the Strand Theatre. Owen enjoyed it, as did the public (it had been running for a decade), but it had terrible reviews in the press, who considered it all very childish and trivial. The Scarlet Pimpernel performed his heroics in France using cunning disguises and an assumed name. It was a world away from the Front, even though, by joining the army, every soldier had taken on a new identity (Owen himself spoke of 'my transformation into a Soldier'),[30] but no doubt *The Scarlet Pimpernel* reminded Owen of the Bordeaux years, and it offered escape for families whose own men were serving in France in rather less dashing circumstances. Owen was less impressed by the latest Scarlet Pimpernel novel, *El Dorado*, which wasn't very readable, but he had recently read it nonetheless. He could have been reading Ford Madox Ford's *The Good Soldier*, Virginia Woolf's *The Voyage Out*, or D. H. Lawrence's *The Rainbow* (all 1915), but he still enjoyed popular fiction and always would – he could fill his precious spare time by reading adventure novels, tales of the well-to-do and derring-do. In this he was not alone: in fact, twentieth-century British poetry would be dominated by men who liked their fiction easy and exciting – men like Dylan Thomas, W. H. Auden, John Betjeman and Philip Larkin. In the Artists' Rifles, it appears that Owen even tried, unsuccessfully, to write stories for *The Boy's Own Paper*, which placed a strong emphasis on the 'great public schools', and its schoolboy readership discovered tales of boarding-school life as well as tales of adventure in the Empire.

His taste in poetry was more sophisticated and elevated though, and, still obsessed with writers' homes and haunts, he probably took the opportunity to hunt for London spots associated with the great poets. For *The Boy's Own Paper*, he tried to write a story about searching for Shelley's house (presumably 15 Poland Street, Soho, a short walk away). He also discovered that near Tavistock Square there was the Poetry Bookshop, run by the influential poet Harold Monro. So, although Owen probably missed the opportunity to meet Yeats and Pound, he would have heard about them from Monro. Yeats gave a reading at the bookshop on 3 July 1913, six months after it had opened, and would give a second reading in April 1916. Owen soon took a room right opposite the bookshop, eager to be near the heart of poetry, and had he stayed there for long enough he would no doubt have encountered a number of leading poets of the day, but in mid November, after only a few days, he was moved out to the edge of London, Hare Hall near Romford, to a large military that occupied a country estate.

That winter, as in the previous two winters, Yeats and Pound retreated to a country cottage, Stone Cottage, in Sussex, where they strove towards a more modern poetry and practised duelling (Yeats supposedly 'envied those poets who had experienced the reality of war'),[31] while Owen, in a hut at Hare Hall in Essex, was learning how to kill and striving to find time for reading and writing. Had he only known it, luck had presented him with the chance to develop a literary friendship with an older poet, a friendship that might have paralleled and rivalled that of Pound and Yeats, for Edward Thomas was also at the camp with the Artists' Rifles, commenting that it 'is excellent but on the dullest flattest piece of a beautiful piece of country'.[32] But if they met they seem not to have known each other as poets, and Thomas was hiding his literariness, saying 'I read less than any man in the hut'.[33] Neither man makes any reference to the other in his correspondence, and it is probably another of those missed chances that a life collects. Owen did buy Thomas's book on Keats in 1916, but there is no other suggestion that he knew Thomas as a writer, although he probably knew him as a soldier: Thomas was teaching recruits at the camp and Owen was in all likelihood one of his pupils. For Thomas, who had once wanted to be an Oxford don, teaching map-reading was the nearest he would get to fulfilling that ambition. While at the Artists' Rifles headquarters on Handel Street in London that autumn, he had run map-reading exercises on Hampstead Heath, which Owen might have taken part in: 'I help to look over men's work & take a squad of 20 or so out on Hampstead Heath to take bearings & sketch a map on the spot etc.'[34] By December, Thomas was a map instructor at Hare Hall teaching 'a five days course, five days on end with a platoon of 50 men beginning (as far as possible) at the point where they left off at October in town,'[35] and his men learnt 'the elements of map-reading, field sketching, the use of compass and protractor, and making a map on the ground with and without the compass'.[36] He wrote of his luck and guilt on 20 December 1915:

So I may continue in this safe job, only too safe, with only too good company. I shouldn't mind being a great deal less comfortable. In fact I should be easier if I were less comfortable.[37]

At the end of January, Thomas felt 'dissatisfied with the work I do and more conscious of my failure to teach. Certainly we don't teach them as much as we should.'[38] Owen had his maps course during that month, finding it intensive, grumbling about spending his daytime outdoors with notebooks and compasses, and spending his evenings with maps. Thomas may have been characteristically dissatisfied, but he was perfect for the job, since he had spent his life escaping into the countryside, and had written books like *The Icknield Way*, *The South Country*, *The Heart of England*.

As poets Owen and Thomas are complementary rather than similar – Thomas wrote a number of poems at Hare Hall, and some of them clearly describe his time there (for instance, '"Home"', 'Rain', 'As the Team's Head-Brass'), whereas there are no extant Owen poems that can be confidently be said to have been written at Hare Hall; on the other hand, Thomas didn't write any poems at or about the Western Front before he was killed on 9 April 1917. The two men had also lived very different lives – Thomas had had the public-school and Oxford education that Owen envied and was married with three children – but the two of them nevertheless had enough in common to have had some things to talk about. Perhaps for both men the most remarkable month of their lives so far was August 1914, which Thomas spent on holiday in the countryside far away from the war, and both men would remember this month in their poetry as a time of beauty, leisure and friendship. Later, Owen acquired Walter de la Mare's *Motley and Other Poems* (1918), which happens to include 'To E.T.: 1917', written in memory of Thomas following his death at the Front, but there is no reason to think that Owen connected this E.T. with a fellow soldier at Hare Hall.

Camps like Hare Hall were the ultimate expression of the 'Back to the Land' movement, sending middle-class, mostly towny men into the countryside to live a simple outdoor life of action, free from the desk and all the bourgeois encumbrances of the modern world. For Edward Thomas, it was a continuation of the life he had chosen when at the start of the century he had left his native London for rural Kent and then rural Hampshire. He was one of many who had felt that a return to nature would bring happiness. It had become fashionable among writers and artists to seek the peasant's life, and the Artists' Rifles included among its number the simple-lifers, bohemians and neo-pagans of pre-war England who had enjoyed cooking their own dinner near a flimsy tent or a tiny boat, had bought rustic pottery and dressed in brown corduroy and tweed, had, like Rupert Brooke, gone skinnydipping at the first opportunity, had convinced themselves that tankards of home-made cider were better than college wines, had lusted after dairymaids and their own Highland Marys, and had played at being gypsies like Toad in *The Wind in the Willows*, a book that captured this Edwardian spirit.

Owen, though, would have been happier with Toad Hall, or Hare Hall itself – a Palladian country house of 1769, designed by John Paine, with its colonnades, Tuscan porch, giant portico, pediment and oval staircase – rather than a bleak hut. He loved the countryside and had read George Borrow's *Lavengro*, with its celebration of gypsy life, but he was less committed to this way of living than many of his contemporaries were. Country life should be comfortable. Owen liked fine French wines and *objets d'art*. At Dunsden before the war, he had enjoyed visiting Crowsley Park with its gardens, hawthorns and a deer park where antlered stags would wander up to visitors, and Earley Court, where he met a bishop and took tea in the 'immense' billiard room. He had also lapped up the generosity of the grand estates near Bordeaux, especially his favourite, Château du Parc ('I am invited to go and play tennis at the Chateau on the first fine day!!').[39] In contrast, he spent Christmas 1915 in a hut at Hare Hall with his fellow cadets.

At Hare Hall, officers occupied the house, huts colonised the green acres, and army boots and tyres turned the grass to mud alongside tall trees that had looked down on many decades of horses and flowers and courting and hunting. As with so many country estates, the First World War ended a way of life. Other estates, like Evelyn Waugh's Brideshead, survived until the next war, only to suffer the indignities and vandalism of occupation by the army. Brideshead suffers in the way that Hare Hall suffered, with the house bashed about and the huts 'from which rose the rattle and chatter and whistling and catcalls, all the zoo-noises of the battalion beginning a new day': 'Hullo, someone seems to have been making a beast of himself here; destructive beggars, soldiers are!'[40]

So Owen sought out home comforts, which were to some extent provided by a local family called Williams, including four children, two boys and two girls, who enjoyed entertaining soldiers – he found that their home rather recreated the happy atmosphere of Mahim. Similarly, there was hospitality and an evening of music at the genteel home of a family called Harper. He was also keen on getting back to 'the luxury of breathing LONDON',[41] and with Liverpool Street Station being only a dozen miles away, it was barely out of sight. In the poem 'A Palinode', probably composed in October 1915, he declares a new preference for the city rather than the countryside:

> Some little while ago, I had a mood
> When what we know as 'Nature' seemed to me
> So sympathetic, ample, sweet, and good
> That I preferred it to Society.

But 'The City now / Holds all my passion'. He even managed to stay at the Poetry Bookshop for a few days at the end of February and the start of March, and showed some of his poems to Harold Monro. Monro made some positive remarks and encouraged Owen to be 'modern'.

When Owen returned to Romford, he was no longer in Hare Hall hut but sharing a large house. He was in Essex through the rain of December, then the snow of February, until spring arrived. By 18 March, when he became 23, the weather had changed, the snow had melted, the sun had become warm, the birds in the Essex trees were nesting and waking the soldiers early. In May 1916, he sent his mother a picture postcard of Venice. The message on this card didn't refer to Venice, but it was surely a response to the Austrian threat to that precious city. Owen would have imagined going there one day, and yet it must have seemed at this moment that Venice would be ruined before he had the chance to see it. His postcard was postmarked 19 May 1916, and on 17 May *The Times* had reported that the Austrians had carried out a general attack on the Italian front in the Trentino ('Big Austrian Attack. Italian Defeat Claimed'). Venice itself was under threat. The following day, the newspapers carried the official communiqué from Vienna on 17 May, which reported various successes, including an attack on Venice by 'A strong squadron of our military and naval aeroplanes early yesterday morning and the night before'.[42]

During 1916, Owen was keen to join the Royal Flying Corps (which became the RAF). He had been enamoured with flying since he was a teenager and there was something rather boyish – Peter-Panish – about his desire to fly, a desire for freedom and adventure, a desire to never grow up. Orville Wright made the first flight when Owen was ten years old; Owen was fifteen at the time of the first flight in Britain, and nineteen when, seeing for the first time an aeroplane in the sky, he was impressed by 'the calm, yellow sunset sky, and the planes gliding smoother than wings'.[43] He then watched some astounding flying in Bordeaux (using the new word 'Aerobatics'),[44] and became convinced that flying should be his occupation not only for the duration of the war but also in the peacetime years that would follow a British victory. The aeroplane was the most modern of inventions but it took Owen back to flight in the classical world – winged Eros became the subject of two of his poems ('To Eros' and 'To the Bitter Sweet-Heart'), and Owen cited Perseus (who had a winged horse), Icarus, Mercury and Hermes when he tried to convince his mother that flying was the thing for him:

By Hermes, I will fly. Though I have sat alone, twittering, like even as it were a sparrow upon the housetop, I will yet swoop over Wrekin with the strength of a thousand Eagles, and all you shall see me light upon the Racecourse, and marvelling behold the pinion of Hermes, who is called Mercury, upon my cap.

Then I shall publish my ode on the Swift.

If I fall, I shall fall mightily. I shall be with Perseus and Icarus, whom I loved; and not with Fritz, whom I did not hate. To battle with the Super-Zeppelin, when he comes, this would be chivalry more than Arthur dreamed of.

Zeppelin, the giant dragon, the child-slayer, I would happily die in any adventure against him. . . .[45]

In 'The Swift', written and rewritten between 1912 and 1917, man and bird are compared:

O Swift! If thou art master of the air
Who taught thee! Not the joy of flying
But of thy brood: their throttles' crying
Stung thee to skill whereof men yet despair!

And yet Owen had also been thrilled by the aerobatics of magnificent men in their flying machines. Was there, in Owen's delight in flight, a hint of that Merionethshire spirit of the mountain Owens, those fore-fathers who had been at home with heights and had spent lifetimes looking down on to passes and valleys? Both of Owen's brothers shared his love of flying and would get to fly: Harold trained at the Royal Naval Air Station in 1916 and Colin joined the RAF in 1918. Owen himself had a seemingly successful interview in London with a major at the RFC HQ, and at times in 1916 it looked as though he was going to succeed in transferring to the Royal Flying Corps. But in the end Owen never was accepted and never did take to the skies.

With the Royal Flying Corps, there was the prospect of going to Egypt and he was greatly excited by this; a large part of the attraction of flying was that it would take him to Cairo. Egypt rivalled Italy in Owen's affections: in Bordeaux on 13 November 1914, he wrote in delight that he had just come into contact with a medical student, Antonio, who belonged equally to the two countries that interested him most, as an Italian educated in Egypt – 'when he speaks, with hands on heart and eyes upturned of "his Country" it is Egypt he means'.[46] Soon after the start of the war, Owen had announced that he was desperate to serve in the East, and had told Laurent Tailhade of his desire to 'go off to Egypt and "ancient India"'.[47] In the drafts of the war poem 'The End' he refers to the 'eternal Nile'. But he never made it to Egypt, any more than he became a pilot or saw Italy or went up to Oxford. Only a few months from the end of the war, he was still saying 'Really I would like most to go to Egypt or Italy'.[48] His interest in Egypt was centred around antiquities, as was the case with scholar-soldier Lawrence of Arabia, who, in December 1914, joined Cairo's General Staff and on 15 December took up residence at the Grand

Continental Hotel. D. H. Lawrence reported in a letter in September 1914 that in the Egyptian sculpture at the British Museum he saw 'what we are after [. . .] the tremendous *non-human* quality of life'.[49] Owen had visited the Egyptian Rooms in the British Museum, and in 1913, in an unfinished, much-corrected poem called 'Scene: Con Val-Escent Stage of New Monia', Owen referred to digging or exploring in Cairo. In 'Uriconium', he says that 'The dust, that fell unnoted as a dew, / Wrapped the dead city's face like mummy-cloth', and during the war he returned to the 'mummy-case' when describing a bandaged soldier in 'A Terre'.

For the Victorians and Edwardians, many suffering from 'Egyptomania', Egypt represented pleasure, luxury – even sin. So Hadjetian Cigarettes of Cairo used a 1911 poster depicting a practically naked beauty, an art nouveau Cleopatra, smoking what would seem to be a post-coital cigarette (she is wearing a wedding ring, though).[50] In Bulwer-Lytton's *The Last Days of Pompeii*, we are told that 'The Egyptians, from the earliest time, were devoted to the joys of sense', and Arbaces, who inherited 'their appetite for sensuality', was 'the solitary lord of a crowded harem'.[51] Now, for some, Egypt was associated not with Cleopatra and the harem, but with homosexuality. Some men who dreamt of Egypt dreamt of Arab boys, and visited this permissive land for the fulfilment of desires, far from the British eyes of the law and the family, even though Egypt was essentially a British colony. For E. M. Forster, Egypt became the place for the first sexual exploration of his homosexuality, in Alexandria in 1916 at the age of thirty-seven. It would be impossible to say for certain that Egypt (or Italian-Egyptian Antonio) had any such attraction for Owen, but, increasingly, as the war progressed, he manages to offer us evidence of what is often interpreted as his homosexuality, or perhaps bisexuality would be more accurate. Nonetheless, despite what some might think, a moustache and Egyptian cigarettes do not a homosexual make, and it's difficult to imagine Owen behaving like Forster, 'parting with Respectability' with a random soldier on a beach[52] and writing to a friend about 'hundreds of young men' who 'go about bare chested and bare legged, the blue of their linen shorts and the pale mauve of their shirts accenting the brown splendour of their bodies. Forster added that 'down by the sea many of them spend half their days naked and unrebuked'.[53]

*

In England in May, when the camp was surrounded by nightingales and the may blossom was out, Owen's time in Essex came to an end: he found himself joining neither Egyptians nor aviators, but Lancastrians. He had applied for a commission (temporary for the period of the war), the application form stating that he was of pure European descent and that his chest size had increased by 1½ inches as a result of the six months of training. As early as January he had been recommended for the Manchester Regiment, and after a spell of leave he joined the 3rd/5th Manchester Regiment as a 2nd Lieutenant in June, after a total of 227 days in the Artists' Rifles. This was something of a disappointment to Owen because he had no desire to be associated with industrial Lancashire, which he had already experienced in his childhood. When he was in the Artists' Rifles awaiting a commission, twice he was offered the chance to become an officer in a Lancashire regiment and he turned both offers down: 'I said NO! with a loud voice'.[54] He didn't consider himself sufficiently prepared, but he was also far from keen to join the Lancastrians. Even in the Manchesters he found himself commanding men he had difficulty liking. He described soldiers from Lancashire as rather rough, and said that the 'Lancashire Mill Hands' were 'weeds, why, Weeds':[55]

> The generality of men are hard-handed, hard-headed miners, dogged, loutish, ugly. (But I would trust them to advance under fire and to hold their trench;) blond, coarse, ungainly, strong, 'unfatigueable', unlovely, Lancashire soldiers, Saxons to the bone.[56]

Owen himself could have been called something of a weed, given his size, but if they were 'Saxons to the bone' they were very different from this Celtic Owen.

The Manchester Regiment, founded in 1881, had a good reputation for soldiering, having won two Victoria Crosses in the Boer War and then further VCs already in the current war, but it was not as glamorous as those regiments of the other well-known officer-poets of the First World War: Brooke was in the Royal Naval Division, Siegfried Sassoon and Robert Graves were in the Royal Welch Fusiliers, Charles Hamilton Sorley in the Suffolk Regiment, Edward Thomas in the Royal Garrison Artillery, Edmund Blunden in the Royal Sussex Regiment, Robert Nichols in the Royal Field Artillery, Julian Grenfell in the Royal Dragoons. Owen was so unhappy with his regiment that he made more than one attempt to move into another less northern berth.

In the Manchester Regiment, he might not have been entirely satisfied with his military lot, but he had the excitement of living as a military gentleman (a temporary gentleman). He enjoyed the officer's privileges and the uniform, acquiring the dashing riding crop of the landed gentry and of his beloved cavalry rather than the usual cane – in a photograph of the officers of the 5th (Reserve) Battalion in July 1916, he's the junior man, the new boy, sitting at the feet of his seniors, but his riding crop is conspicuous among the schoolmasterly canes. Having left teaching behind, he would not have wanted a cane, even if, given his height, the riding crop must have made him look like a jockey. He knew that the officer is a work of art, who must be beautiful because he commands his men through his appearance as well as his actions. He also had a servant now, not quite a gentleman's personal gentleman like Jeeves (whom P. G. Wodehouse introduced to the world in 1915) – indeed, Owen's servant was a rather doddery old man – but 'My servant has nothing else to do but serve, so that is satisfactory'.[57]

Owen was quite aware of the beautiful side of war and shared this understanding with many of his poetic heroes – in his copy of *Sir Walter Scott*, he had picked out the statement that 'the pomp and circumstance of war gives, for a time, a very poignant and pleasing sensation'.[58] Owen had delighted in Scott's *Marmion* as a teenager, and he hadn't lost his love for Scott's chivalric world where battle is poetic:

in August, Owen had an hour to wait at Tamworth Station, so he went in search of Lord Marmion, 'my old friend' (Owen always enjoyed socialising with the well-to-do) because Marmion was Lord of Tamworth. Tamworth Castle was made magical by poetry and 'a low, glamorous Moon' – 'to see any strange place by a vague moon, for an hour, is better than a week's stay there', Owen declared, presumably recalling Scott's famous lines about Melrose:

> If thou would'st view fair Melrose aright,
> Go visit it by the pale moonlight;
> For the gay beams of lightsome day
> Gild, but to flout, the ruins grey.[59]

Owen spent the summer at Witley, Aldershot and Mytchett, three camps near Guildford, training for battle, mostly in 'musketry'. This area was not so very far from Dunsden, but it was a different kind of landscape and, when he could find the time, he enjoyed exploring alone. He found Guildford very charming and it reminded him of Shrewsbury a little. One day of perfect June weather he cycled there for tea and contentedly sat in an old bay window on the pretty High Street for an hour. Equally, the countryside had 'some lovely bits of road, field, cottage, and street'.[60] On another visit, he went to Thorpe's bookshop on the High Street and watched the punts and canoes on the little river. In Guildford, or when cycling along the Surrey lanes, Owen was in an attractive and familiar version of England: teashops, stiff bicycles, old houses, flowers, silence. He was in a picture postcard, or a Rupert Brooke poem. He owned a 1916 impression of Brooke's *1914 and Other Poems*, which had been such a popular book since Brooke's death in April 1915. Brooke asked, at the end of 'The Old Vicarage, Grantchester', 'is there honey still for tea?', and in 'The Soldier' he provided one of the most famous celebrations of England:

> If I should die, think only this of me:
> That there's some corner of a foreign field

That is for ever England. There shall be
In that rich earth a richer dust concealed;
A dust whom England bore, shaped, made aware,
Gave, once, her flowers to love, her ways to roam,
A body of England's, breathing English air,
Washed by the rivers, blest by suns of home.

And think, this heart, all evil shed away,
A pulse in the eternal mind, no less
Gives somewhere back the thoughts by England given;
Her sights and sounds; dreams happy as her day;
And laughter, learnt of friends; and gentleness,
In hearts at peace, under an English heaven.[61]

Perhaps Owen would not have been happy living in Guildford, but now he was the visitor and, happily, the only people he needed to talk to were the staff in shops. But even in this England, Owen could not forget the war. Brooke's 'The Soldier' is a war poem that hides the war behind the pretty countryside, and Owen's response to Brooke came in 'An Imperial Elegy', a poem written between September 1915 and early summer 1916, and most probably in 1916 after Owen had joined the Manchesters:

Not one corner of a foreign field
But a span as wide as Europe;
An appearance of a titan's grave,
And the length thereof a thousand miles,
It crossed all Europe like a mystic road,
Or as the Spirits' Pathway lieth on the night.
And I heard a voice crying
This is the Path of Glory.

Owen's copy of *1914 and Other Poems* contains a photograph of Brooke's grave that Owen would seem to have kept from a magazine,

but whereas Brooke's poem focuses on the prettified death of one
soldier, Owen's poetry takes on the horrific deaths of so many. The
poem could be interpreted as Owen's objection to the implicit imperi-
alism of Brooke's desire to turn a corner of a foreign field into another
piece of England, and he certainly brings to the war a perspective that
is more European than English, but it is at the same time a poem that
grows out of England and out of English poetry, its first line coming
from Brooke and its last from Thomas Gray's 'Elegy Written in a
Country Churchyard' (1751):

> The boast of heraldry, the pomp of pow'r,
> And all that beauty, all that wealth e'er gave,
> Awaits alike th' inevitable hour.
> The paths of glory lead but to the grave.[62]

That churchyard was about thirty miles from Guildford. Perhaps we
should interpret the 'voice crying' as Gray speaking in response to
Brooke. In 1914, Owen had described a boy 'snatching a fearful joy',[63]
referring to another Gray poem, 'Ode on a Distant Prospect of Eton
College' (1747), a moving portrait of boyhood and of the longing to be
young again, whence that voice heard in 'An Imperial Elegy' might
derive: 'They hear a voice in every wind, / And snatch a fearful joy'.[64]
At Dunsden, Owen had described Gray's 'majestic utterance', his
'mighty chant', his 'golden teaching' – Gray 'speaks / Strong things
with sweetness', as would Owen as a war poet. Owen's complex person-
ality can be seen in the image of the author of this poem sitting alone
in a teashop in a 2nd Lieutenant's uniform, sipping tea and admiring
the quiet old street through latticed glass.

Even in Surrey, life wasn't all bike rides, tea and flowers. For
instance, at camp Owen was practising bomb-throwing with real live
Mills grenades. Cecil Day Lewis, the future Poet Laureate and editor of
Owen's poetry, was a schoolboy living at Witley at the time, while his
father was an army chaplain, and he recalled an incident at the Witley
camp in the summer of 1916: 'one day my father, returning to the

cottage, told us in hushed tones that an instructor had been killed at the bombing range, throwing himself bodily on a Mills bomb which was knocked from a pupil's hand by the parados of the trench as his arm swung back to throw it'.[65] Owen's summer married danger with Arcadia. Very few of his poems have survived from this year of training, but 'Storm', a poem dated October 1916, captures the paradoxical atmosphere, referring to 'brilliant danger' and speaking of beauty that is hidden by gloom, but this is a poem about a beautiful man or boy. It might be a homosexual love poem in which Owen confesses his love for a nameless someone, possibly a soldier, but this puzzling poem could also be about a number of other things, and its power lies in its mysteriousness. The poem even says 'Glorious will shine the opening of my heart', which suggests that Owen was remembering the Roman Catholicism of France, where the sacred heart of Jesus or Mary, exposed and emitting beams of light, was a common image.

'Storm' may have been written in Oswestry, where Owen was born. He returned there in the early autumn, possibly for the first time since he had left at the age of four. From Witley in September 1916 he began a letter with 'OSWESTRY!!!': 'This is a good war today: just heard that we go to the Oswestry Camp next week.' The news left him winking at the ceiling. He suggested that his mother should join him in Oswestry and she presumably did, because the letters to her provide no description of the town and the old home. They would have gone back to Plas Wilmot – Owen was always a great one for visiting writers' homes and haunts, and here he had the chance to make a literary pilgrimage to his own birthplace. This was a time when there was a craze for visiting writers' birthplaces, and the author of a book called *Some Literary Landmarks for Pilgrims on Wheels* lamented, 'What a pity it is that babies who are to become famous should not always be born in picturesque surroundings!',[66] but Owen's native surroundings would satisfy the pilgrim, either then or now. There was a simple feeling that a fine home helped to make a fine writer, a feeling that Owen tended to share, and one that Plas Wilmot would suit.

To his mother, Oswestry was where she had been happiest and her favourite child understood how painful the departure from there had been for her. Harold Owen, who was born a few months after the family left Plas Wilmot (born in September 1897, he may have been conceived there), provides a story that comes close to being the ejection from the Garden of Eden. Oswestry was more Susan Owen's Eden than Wilfred's – she's the one who felt the sadness of the last night in the old home, with the empty shelves, the blank walls, the memories drifting about like ghosts – but Owen seems to have acquired from her the sense that they had come down in the world and had been treated unfairly. As if to emphasise the contrast between what the family left and where they went, Owen visited Birkenhead in October too. He spent 40 minutes there during a train journey, but Birkenhead revisited was not a happy experience and it was then that he told his mother that he couldn't think how they ever survived the place.

Plas Wilmot must have had a part to play in Owen's character in so far as he carried within himself a strong class-consciousness, mixing together a feeling that he had been hard done by, a sense of his own superiority, compassion for the poor, admiration for the upper classes and a powerful determination to achieve fame and fortune whilst pretending that fame and fortune were not important to him (poets are above such things). His desire to become a poet came as much from a desire for status and fame as from a desire to write poetry, but he also hankered after the life of rural seclusion, which Plas Wilmot also repre-sented. Owen's life was in a way, and in his mother's eyes, an attempt to recover Plas Wilmot. In 1911, Owen described a dream 'which I almost think has been cherished from my earliest remembrance, that of my sweet Mother, in a delightful garden, passing a bland old age among her greenhouses, and in a small carriage drawn by an ambling pad-pony'.[67]

But there is no poem about Oswestry. Perhaps Owen felt that A. E. Housman had already said it all. Only that summer, in August 1916, Owen had bought Housman's *A Shropshire Lad*, a little book that includes some of the most famous poems of longing:

1 A Victorian gathering at Plas Wilmot, *c.*1895. Wilfred sits on his mother's lap next to his grandfather. The children on the front row are Wilfred's Gunston cousins; and Susan's sister, Emma Gunston, stands at the back next to the servants. Photograph probably taken by John Gunston.

2 Wilfred Owen, dressed for heroism: in 'Arms and the Boy', he wrote, 'Let the boy try along this bayonet-blade / How cold steel is, and keen with hunger of blood'.

3 My subject is War: 'Lend him to stroke these blind, blunt bullet-leads, / Which long to nuzzle in the hearts of lads' ('Arms and the Boy').

4 A postcard of the Woodside landing stage at Birkenhead: this ferry terminal was next-door to the station where Owen's father worked. On the other side of the Mersey, there are the sooty spires and chimneys of Edwardian Liverpool.

5 'I seriously should like to join the Italian Cavalry': Wilfred, Mary, Tom, Colin, Harold and Susan at Scarborough.

6 A postcard of Wroxeter, Uriconium (Viriconium). Owen was happy 'midst the crumbling battlements of Viriconium', but the ruins also made him think of destruction, death and Hell.

Wroxeter, Uriconium.

7 A postcard of Dunsden Vicarage, Reading: 'Really, I am even more charmed with the Vicarage than ever'.

8 A postcard of Dunsden Vicarage, Reading: 'The house is even larger than I ever thought – two staircases – and quite a labyrinth of passages upstairs'. The vicarage was a more impressive building than Dunsden's church.

9 Owen posing at Dunsden, probably in 1912. He might look like a university student, but at Dunsden he read 'the Book of Life'.

10 A postcard of the Cours de l'Intendance, photographed from the end that joins the Place de la Comédie and looking up towards the Place Gambetta. The Berlitz School was on the left-hand side of the street. The Grand Théâtre is in the Place de la Comédie, a short walk from the river.

11 A postcard of the Porte Dijeaux from the Place Gambetta. Owen lived in the Rue de la Porte Dijeaux: his front door was 'on the left, a few yards through the "Gate"'.

12 The Casino at Bagnères-de-Bigorre, August 1914: Owen sits in the front row with Madame Léger on his left; and, next to her, her face hidden by a hat, sits her daughter Nénette.

13 A postcard of 'Bordeaux. – La Terrasse du Jardin public': 'we rescued the boats of the little boys around the pond in the *Jardin Public*, and I earned a momentary place in the garden of boyhood, whence I am now so long banished'.

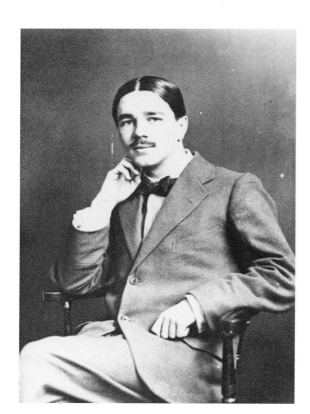

14 The young poet, now sporting a moustache. Photograph probably taken by John Gunston, *c.*1915.

15 'So, pack up your troubles in your old kit-bag / And smile, smile, smile': Owen as the smiling Tommy, in the Artists' Rifles. Photograph taken in 1915 or 1916, probably by John Gunston.

16 'The face of Wilfred Owen, moustached and with centre-parted hair, looks out at us eternally from 1916' (Philip Larkin). Wilfred Owen in the uniform of a second lieutenant of the Manchester Regiment, photographed by John Gunston.

17 'There was something at once clear-cut and fluid about the features, and the figure had the elegant compactness of a small boy's together with the robuster development of the young man's. This union of opposites was, I fancy, characteristic of his whole personality, and may perhaps explain his power of inspiring affection in men and women alike' (Frank Nicholson). Photograph taken by John Gunston in 1916.

18 'Tennyson, it seems, was always a great child. So should I have been, but for Beaumont Hamel': some letters of the village's name remain on the ruined railway station, but Beaumont Hamel, France, has become another Uriconium. An official photograph, probably taken by John Warwick Brooke.

19 An official photograph of soldiers crossing the River Ancre. The Ancre joins the Somme at Corbie. Owen's 'At a Calvary near the Ancre' recalls the Western Front of early 1917.

20 A trench message dog with members of the Manchester Regiment, including a young soldier shading his eyes at the back. Owen had described the men of the regiment as 'hard-handed, hard-headed miners, dogged, loutish, ugly'. Photographed by John Warwick Brooke in 1918.

21 A wartime postcard showing the survival of the Virgin Mary after the destruction of a church: 'Madone intacte après le bombardement de l'Eglise'. In 'Le Christianisme', Owen wrote that 'the church Christ was hit and buried / Under its rubbish and its rubble' but 'One Virgin still immaculate / Smiles on for war to flatter her'.

22 'In this war He too lost a limb': a victim of the Western Front, Christ hangs above mud and war graves in 1916. A war time postcard.

23 Craiglockhart Hydropathic. The Hydro became Craiglockhart War Hospital and then a convent and part of a university. Photographed by George Washington Wilson.

24 Ottoline Morrell, Dorothy Brett and Siegfried Sassoon in 1917. Sassoon encouraged Owen to visit Lady Ottoline Morrell at Garsington Manor, her home near Oxford. Morrell was attracted to Sassoon, and thought of him as a twin brother and an angel; but by the end of the war she was finding him coarse, cruel and vain. Taken by an unknown photographer.

25 John Duncan, *The Coming of Bride*, 1917. Owen greatly admired this picture of a Celtic spring, writing 'I have been made very sad by the extreme beauty of the eyelids of one of his Faces'.

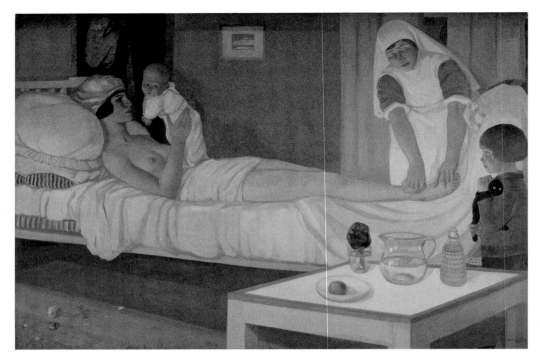

26 Cecile Walton, *Romance - Cecile Walton, 1891–1956 (With her children Edward and Gavril)*, 1920. Describing Owen after meeting him in 1917, Walton said that he was a 'very young boy'.

27 Eric Robertson, *Miss Maidie and Miss Elsie Scott* (1915). Maidie Gray before her marriage, depicted with her sister. Both sisters gushed all over Owen in the summer of 1917. The painter of this moody portrait, married their friend Cecile Walton in 1914, having been introduced to her by John Duncan.

28 Wilfred Owen with Arthur Newboult in 1917. Owen said to Arthur that 'From off your face, into the winds of winter, / The sun-brown and the summer-gold are blowing' ('Winter Song').

29 An Edwardian postcard depicting Edinburgh's Princes Street within a copy of *The Scotsman*. Owen's 'Six O'Clock in Princes Street' is about a newspaper-seller.

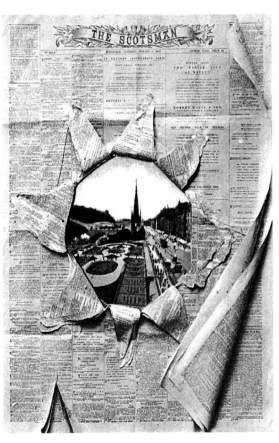

30 Robert Ross with Violet Bonham Carter, photographed by Ottoline Morrell in 1917. When Ross died in 1918, *The Times* commented that 'friendship was the chief business of his life'.

31 'I sit in the middle of my five-windowed turret, and look down upon the sea': the large, white, turreted Clarence Gardens Hotel looks out across Scarborough's North Bay.

32 Edward Stanley Mercer, *Charles Kenneth Scott-Moncrieff, 1889–1930. Translator of Proust.* Owen's friend is in the uniform of the King's Own Scottish Borderers. In Scott Moncrieff's translation of Proust, Mme Cottard says that the most important thing about a portrait 'is that it should be like, and a pleasant likeness, if you know what I mean'.

33 Wilfred Owen's friend Philip Bainbrigge, between Cyril Alington and Malcolm White, at Shrewsbury School in 1915, hatless in a low deckchair. In 1918 he had some idle hours with Owen. He was killed in action but wanted to be remembered as a schoolmaster who enjoyed 'lying naked in the sun'.

34 A postcard of Harrow School c.1914: Owen associated Harrow with 'heights of thought, heights of friendship, heights of riches, heights of jinks', and described a Harrow boy as 'the best piece of Nation left in England'.

35 A postcard of Fountains Abbey. During his time at Ripon in 1918, Owen found that 'adventuring on Fountains Abbey by chance did me a world of good'. He also enjoyed Fountains Hall, the house near the Abbey ruins.

36 Wilfred Owen at Hastings in August 1918. The last portrait photograph of him, it was made for Susan Owen from a photograph of Wilfred, Susan and Colin together, and, in it, he has acquired the appearance of a disembodied spirit.

37 Mahim, Monkmoor Road, Shrewsbury: 'we heard the dread news there on Nov 11th/18'. Photograph probably taken by John Gunston.

Into my heart an air that kills
From yon far country blows:
What are those blue remembered hills,
What spires, what farms are those?

That is the land of lost content,
I see it shining plain,
The happy highways where I went
And cannot come again.[68]

Housman's poetry would influence a number of Owen's poems about the war, including 'Disabled', 'Anthem for Doomed Youth' and 'The Send-Off'. Robert Lowell said that 'One feels Housman foresaw the Somme',[69] and Housman can be heard behind war poems by, among others, Siegfried Sassoon, Rupert Brooke, C. H. Sorley and Edward Thomas. *A Shropshire Lad* sold relatively slowly when it was published in 1896, but the Housman craze developed until, according to the poet Robert Nichols, in 1914 'Housman was in every pocket'[70] (but not in Owen's, it would seem) and that craze was fuelled by the war. *A Shropshire Lad* even crossed the Atlantic, where the novelist William Faulkner was an admirer, and in his novel *Soldiers' Pay* (1926), a wounded pilot carries a copy of *A Shropshire Lad*.

Reading Housman, Owen, a real Shropshire lad, must have been taken back to his childhood:

High the vanes of Shrewsbury gleam
Islanded in Severn stream;
The bridges from the steepled crest
Cross the water east and west.

The flag of morn in conqueror's state
Enters at the English gate:
The vanquished eve, as night prevails,
Bleeds upon the road to Wales.[71]

In July, Owen had described his little brother as 'the only chap I really
care for: the Shropshire Lad',[72] which shows that he knew Housman's
poetry slightly before he bought the book, and that he connected the
book with his own background. And *A Shropshire Lad* was published at
a time when Owen was living in Oswestry. Indeed, Owen made a small
number of markings in his copy and these suggest that he saw the
poems as fragments of his own biography. A few lines are highlighted
in the margin, including four lines from a poem called 'March', in
which the month of his birth is a time of creation and new beginnings
in Shropshire:

> The boys are up the woods with day
> To fetch the daffodils away,
> And home at noonday from the hills
> They bring no dearth of daffodils.[73]

He marked lines in the previous poem too, lines that capture not only
his father's railway station but also, in describing the prison that was
next door, the sense of imprisonment and frustration that Owen felt in
Shrewsbury as a teenager:

> They hang us now in Shrewsbury jail:
>   The whistles blow forlorn,
> And trains all night groan on the rail
>   To men that die at morn.
>
> There sleeps in Shrewsbury jail to-night,
>   Or wakes, as may betide,
> A better lad, if things went right,
>   Than most that sleep outside.[74]

This is one of five poems highlighted in the list of contents, out of the
sixty-three poems in total, and he marks specific lines in only three
poems. If Owen read these poems soon after buying them, then the

markings he made express a sense at that time that death was imminent as, amid much contemplation of where he would be posted, the training progressed towards a conclusion. Reading *A Shropshire Lad* in 1916, Owen, still hoping to go to Egypt with the Flying Corps, underlined two lines about Shropshire soldiers fighting and dying overseas: 'And the Nile spills his overflow / Beside the Severn's dead'.[75] In early November, when he was in Southport after nearly a month at Oswestry, he tried for a draft to Egypt, hoping to exchange the cold sands of Lancashire for the Flying School in Cairo, but by the end of the month, by which time he was further up the coast in Fleetwood in charge of a firing party, this draft was washed out and a rumour of a draft to India went unfulfilled.

He enjoyed Fleetwood, a town of beaches and fishwives, and so did his men. He watched over his lads, picking out 'the Smart "laads"' from the uncouth and ungainly,[76] and he always had an eye for the younger, innocent lads, who seemed to need more protection: he knew who those underage were, and was happier with 'lads' more than 'men'. Yet if Owen was a Shropshire Lad, the soldiers in the lower ranks were not always capable of mirroring Housman's poetry, being urban rather than rural, not as hardy or handsome as 'men from the barn and the forge and the mill and the fold', and unlikely to go to see the cherry hung with snow. Owen was, however, determined to do his duty and serve all his men – he might not have felt any great desire to serve his King, but he would serve the Lancashire weeds, the King's malnourished, ill-educated subjects from the industrial North, and he would attempt to protect them in France. For France was now soon to be their destination. Owen was given embarkation leave prior to a journey across the Channel to the Western Front.

Am I getting fed up with England?[77]

CHAPTER 9

The Octopus

It was of course dark, too dark, and the ground was not mud, not sloppy
mud, but an octopus of sucking clay, 3, 4, and 5 feet deep, relieved only
by craters full of water. Men have been known to drown in them. Many
stuck in the mud & only got on by leaving their waders, equipment, and
in some cases their clothes.
WILFRED OWEN to SUSAN OWEN, 16 January 1917[1]

Praise the Lord upon earth: ye dragons, and all deeps;
Fire and hail, snow and vapours: wind and storm, fulfilling his word.
PSALM 148, *v.* 7–8

A T the very end of 1916, after seeing his family at Christmas,
Wilfred Owen arrived in France, having narrowly escaped a rail
accident on his way to Folkestone and then having crossed the Channel
from there. His arrival in France gave him some of the excitement that
he had experienced when he arrived there in 1913. Unlike most soldiers,
he was able to speak to the locals, and he was barely a foreigner.
Returning to France in 1915, he had written that it took just three hours
for everything to cease to feel foreign. At the large camp at Étaples, he
was 'in perfect spirits' now, and possessed 'a fine heroic feeling'.[2] He was
in the camp of a Sir Percy Cunynghame, who, Owen noted, had bagged
for his mess the Duke of Connaught's chef.[3] In such aristocratic condi-
tions, rainy though it was, he could imagine the fine heroism of the past.

Now attached to the 2nd Manchesters, he took the train and joined them at Halloy near the Somme, the river that had been rolling along pacifically enough for many centuries but is now only ever associated with slaughter. This was not Bordeaux or Roncevaux, and he was soon 'let down, gently, into the real thing, Mud'.[4] Mud got everywhere: 'I am perfectly well and strong, but unthinkably dirty and squalid'.[5] They moved to Bertrancourt, and as he got deeper into a landscape of ruins and mud, not washing and trying to keep out the water, his appearance changed:

> I am not allowed to send a sketch, but you must know I am transformed now, wearing a steel helmet, buff jerkin of leather, rubber-waders up to the hips, & gauntlets. But for the rifle, we are exactly like Cromwellian Troopers. The waders are of course indispensable. In $2\frac{1}{2}$ miles of trench which I waded yesterday there was not one inch of dry ground. There is a mean depth of 2 feet of water.[6]

He was more Roundhead than Cavalier now. As one soldier wrote,

> We had been brought up on the history of the Boer War and patriotism and heroics and everything, and we thought the war was going to be over before we could get there. However, in about half a minute all that had gone. I wondered what the devil I'd got into because it was nothing but mud and filth and all the chaps who were already there, well, they looked like tramps, all plastered with filth and dirt, and unshaven.[7]

Owen would later write about soldiers 'Bent double, like old beggars under sacks, / Knock-kneed, coughing like hags'.[8]

He was soon not just at the Front, but, as he put it, in front of the Front. In early 1917, a series of small attacks by the British in the Somme region, in January and February, were diversions intended to suggest a major attack in the area in the spring. It was these attacks that became Owen's first experience of fighting, rather than one of the great attacks, of thousands of men going over the top all at once all along the line, that – largely because of the first day of the Somme – have become our idea of war in the trenches. Owen entered No Man's Land near Beaumont Hamel, and on 16 January wrote to his mother with his survivor's report:

> My dug-out held 25 men tight packed. Water filled it to a depth of 1 or 2 feet, leaving say 4 feet of air.
>
> One entrance had been blown in & blocked.
>
> So far, the other remained.
>
> The Germans knew we were staying there and decided we shouldn't.
>
> Those fifty hours were the agony of my happy life.[9]

In this letter he told his mother that he could see no excuse for deceiving her. His work would be increasingly driven by a need to tell the truth. His war poetry would become the survivor's sorrowful recollection and recreation of what happened, and it would record his growing love and respect for his men. From censoring their letters, he knew something of their own responses to the trenches. In several cases, the poems he began later in the year are near to the letters written in the first moments of respite. So he told his mother, 'I kept my own sentries half way down the stairs during the more terrific bombardment' but 'one lad was blown down and, I am afraid, blinded'.[10] 'The Sentry' would describe how:

>   thud! flump! thud! down the steep steps came thumping
> And sploshing in the flood, deluging muck,
> The sentry's body; then his rifle, handles
> Of old Boche bombs, and mud in ruck on ruck.
> We dredged it up, for dead, until he whined,
> 'O sir – my eyes, – I'm blind, – I'm blind, – I'm blind.'

The poem also describes 'one who would have drowned himself for good'. Owen told his mother that 'I nearly broke down and let myself drown in the water'.[11] But he resisted that impulse towards self-destruction that his uncle Edward had displayed. It was his duty to survive, and, as a survivor, speak for the dead.

So far in life Owen had already had some experience of war and death. It would be wrong to suggest that he was so naïve that he ever thought, even as a boy, that war is not horrific. Owen is frequently portrayed as some kind of fool who had thought war all flowers and japes until he arrived at the Western Front, and was so shocked and angered by the reality that he became a great poet. Yet Owen knew about war and death – he had ministered to the sick and dying in Dunsden, he had been in military training for over a year, and even in Bordeaux he had seen wounded soldiers. He had been living in Birkenhead when many wounded soldiers returned to the Mersey ports from the Boer War. Some children might have believed that it is pleasant and exciting to die for one's country but Owen did not, and that was one reason why he had put off joining up. And not going to the Front until there had been two and a half years of trench warfare, he was less likely to be unprepared for what this modern war was like. The 'Never such innocence again' myth of men marching off in the sunshine of 1914 into a war that they could never have been prepared for could not apply to Owen. But just because he had been prepared for war did not mean that he would like it, and of course he was horrified and angered. It's also true that the Front was still a shock. The war was worse than he could have envisaged: no one could really quite know and feel the Western Front without being there. 'We are wretched beyond my previous imagination,' he wrote, on 19 January.[12] Indeed, while history was repeating itself, this was also a war like no other before. The actual experience of war was shockingly different from reading about it; to be aware that one's own death is close is different from seeing wounded soldiers; to experience battle is different from any amount of military training.

War in the trenches is ugly. Death is death, but perhaps it can become sweet and decorous in some contexts. Owen had grown up intensely aware of the visual beauty of war – the knights of *Marmion*, muscular lads, uniforms, green landscapes, Rome. He had wanted to join the Italian cavalry because he would be beautiful on horseback in an Italian landscape. If a poet must die let him die in a poetic place. If he had ever fancied death, if he had ever been attracted to the early deaths of Keats and Shelley, he had not dreamt of dying in a landscape like the Western Front's. Keats died a horrible, slow, coughing death, one that Owen had been deeply moved by when reading about it as a teenager, but he died in Rome, unlike the men coughing like hags in sludge, corpses and chlorine gas. Beautiful Shelley had drowned beautifully in Italy, unlike the soldier drowning in 'Dulce et Decorum Est', which was written later in 1917:

Gas! Gas! Quick, boys! – An ecstasy of fumbling,
Fitting the clumsy helmets just in time;
But someone still was yelling out and stumbling,
And flound'ring like a man in fire or lime . . .
Dim, through the misty panes and thick green light,
As under a green sea, I saw him drowning.

In all my dreams, before my helpless sight,
He plunges at me, guttering, choking, drowning.

If in some smothering dreams you too could pace
Behind the wagon that we flung him in,
And watch the white eyes writhing in his face,
His hanging face, like a devil's sick of sin;
If you could hear, at every jolt, the blood
Come gargling from the froth-corrupted lungs,
Obscene as cancer, bitter as the cud
Of vile, incurable sores on innocent tongues, –

My friend, you would not tell with such high zest
To children ardent for some desperate glory,
The old Lie: Dulce et decorum est
Pro patria mori.

He quotes a line of Latin from the poet Horace, 'It is sweet and meet to die for one's country'. During the war, the line was described as 'the best-known line of war poetry in all the world',[13] and it was used in various contexts before and during the war, but Owen may well have seen *The Boy's Own Paper*'s poem 'Dulce et Decorum Est' by M. F. Laurie. Laurie's poem of 20 lines is about 'A boy – just a schoolboy, who wanted to fight for his country, / Wanted, if need be, to die for her, – yet his years were too few, / Only sixteen – but his heart was the heart of a soldier', and ends:

Glorious death to die, falling for God and their Country!
    Honour be theirs – we mourn them with proud, heartfelt tears.
May their *dying* teach you to *live* – it may be obscurely,
    But truly and purely; fighting for God through the years.[14]

Owen's 'Dulce et Decorum Est' is not in fact a poem that accurately captures his own attitude to the war, and there was always something Horatian or *Boy's Own Paper* about his outlook, but his powerful poem, a cinematic portrait of the trenches, is rightly famous. Although there was always a form of continuity with his pre-trenches life and writing, the shock of January and February 1917 changed Owen and his poetry, and in extreme cases like 'Dulce et Decorum Est', Owen would seem to be rejecting some of the tastes and attitudes of his recent past.

On 19 January, he wrote to his mother of 'GAS', capitalised as in 'Dulce et Decorum Est', but he was now a long way back in a ruined village.[15] There was then no letter until he wrote on 4 February that since his last letter he had had another strong dose of the advanced front line, and wrote about the lack of beauty:

I suppose I can endure cold, and fatigue, and the face-to-face death, as well as another; but extra for me there is the universal pervasion of <u>Ugliness</u>. Hideous landscapes, vile noises, foul language and nothing but foul, even from one's own mouth (for all are devil ridden), everything unnatural, broken, blasted; the distortion of the dead, whose unburiable bodies sit outside the dug-outs all day, all night, the most execrable sights on earth. In poetry we call them the most glorious. But to sit with them all day, all night . . .[16]

He had spent his life striving for beauty, and sometimes he had found it; he wanted to write beautiful poetry; he had disliked the dirty lace curtains of Birkenhead, the impoverished lives of villagers at Dunsden and, during training, some of the roughness of the Lancastrian recruits. The poet suffers more, he held, because he is more sensitive to beauty. He felt that he was unlike the majority. Did Oscar Wilde suffer more in prison because he had the aesthete's hatred of ugliness? And is a poet born or made? Perhaps Owen was more sensitive to beauty because he had lived in Bordeaux, where the buildings contributed to his aesthetic sensibility, and because he had devoted his time to reading beautiful poetry. Shrewsbury, the Pyrenees, paintings, they too had had an improving effect, but he was now suffering for that improvement. Perhaps if he had always lived in Birkenhead he would not have been so horrified by the ugliness of the trenches. Rough Lancashire lads might have coped more easily on the Western Front, having grown up in bookless homes in industrial towns among devil-ridden mouths; but Owen's swearing was produced by the Western Front. Here was the Keatsian 'chameleon poet', devil-ridden. The feeling in Owen's letters at this time is not that the poet was made by the war but that the poet had to survive it – it could only harm the poet, body and soul.

It was the heart of winter. As *The Times* reported at the start of February, 'When icicles hang by the wall and in all other kinds of likely and unlikely places; when the fields and hills are a dreary expanse of limitless white, the skies like steel, and the roads as hard as iron and as slippery as skating rinks; when the thermometer resolutely sticks at a point only a few degrees above zero [Fahrenheit] – when, in fact, the weather is as arctic as it has now been for the last three weeks all over France, life in the trenches and the cantonments behind them is not altogether an agreeable experience.'[17] The severe winter not only offered frostbite and death from exposure but also an increased likelihood of being killed by a shell:

> It made things almost impossible, because a shell bursting a quarter of a mile away could kill you. Now usually if you were in luck a shell could burst within a few yards of you and if your number wasn't on it you were all right. But at that time these shells they just hit this solid ice and they scattered.[18]

Owen soon experienced the near-death state that he later described in 'Exposure' (written a year later):

> Our brains ache, in the merciless iced east winds that knive us . . .
> Wearied we keep awake because the night is silent . . .
> Low, drooping flares confuse our memory of the salient . . .
> Worried by silence, sentries whisper, curious, nervous,
>   But nothing happens.

He wrote to his mother on 4 February saying that it was impossible to stand up or even crawl about because they were behind only a little ridge screening them from the Germans' periscope. The first line of Owen's poem alludes to Keats's 'Ode to a Nightingale', but the poem also seems to recall and evoke the vast empty, lonely landscapes endured by polar explorers and mountaineers. 'We were marooned on a frozen desert,' he told his mother.[19]

Before the war, Owen had been interested in mountaineering and polar exploration, giving his friend Alec Paton *The English at the North Pole* for Christmas in 1906; founding the AGBS (Astronomical, Geological, and Botanical Society) with his cousins in 1907 with a desire to pursue mountain-climbing (the noblest of noble sports), a desire for exploration of certain glacial regions, and finding polar exploration alluring. 'Exposure' is the nearest he would get to describing the trials of a Captain Oates or Scott. Like polar explorers, the men of 'Exposure' turn to thoughts of home in an attempt to try to keep themselves alive. Owen told his mother that thoughts of her kept him warm. In 'Exposure', Owen and his companions, like Scott and his men in the tent in the blizzard, are powerlessly waiting for death finally to arrive: 'Pale flakes with fingering stealth come feeling for our faces'. Scott famously wrote that 'Had we lived, I should have had a tale to tell of the hardihood, endurance, and courage of my companions which would have stirred the heart of every Englishman'. In an attempt to encourage hardihood, endurance and courage in the soldiers, Herbert Ponting's film footage of Scott's expedition was shown on the Western Front. But Owen soon lost the fine heroic feeling and 'Exposure', written a year after the events it describes, is not concerned with courage and heroism. This is war and the pity of war:

> Tonight, this frost will fasten on this mud and us,
> Shrivelling many hands, puckering foreheads crisp.
> The burying-party, picks and shovels in shaking grasp,
> Pause over half-known faces. All their eyes are ice,
>   But nothing happens.

'Exposure' speaks of how 'love of God seems dying', a remark that encompasses two equally believable meanings, namely that God's love for man was disappearing and that man's love for God was too. Often, when describing the war, Owen turns to his religious upbringing: the first encounter with mud was a form of baptism; the Front was like the Slough of Despond of John Bunyan's *The Pilgrim's Progress* (the book Tom Owen gave to Susan in 1904), Dante's *Purgatorio*, the Bible's Sodom and Gomorrah, Babylon, and, above all, Hell. The Hell he had been brought up to fear had now been encountered; again, in that sense the Western Front was familiar even if it was new. It was a cold, wet hell. And, inevitably, he would rhyme 'Hell' with 'shell'.[20] But he also turned to his childhood interest in astronomy when describing No Man's Land: 'No Man's Land under snow is like the face of the moon chaotic, crater-ridden, uninhabitable, awful, the abode of madness.'[21] Like the moon this was a new territory, and familiar France had become strange. In 'The Show' he would describe 'a sad land, weak with sweats of dearth, / Grey, cratered like the moon with hollow woe'. As a child he would have leapt at the chance to see the moon up close.

Even cricket provided an image for describing soldiers crossing No Man's Land towards the German trenches: 'we carried on like a crowd moving off a cricket-field'.[22] Owen's childhood provided a way of understanding the experience. He had been interested in ancient wars and battles, and disasters such as Pompeii, for many years. He had been excited by the events of 24 August AD 79 when Pompeii was destroyed by Vesuvius's torrents of burning mud, the smoke, the poisonous mephitic gases, and the rain of stones of different sizes; now he experienced at first hand the mud, the poison gas, the artillery shells, bullets and shrapnel. And even though Owen might seem to reject antiquity in 'Dulce et Decorum Est', his mind kept returning to the ancient world in his wartime letters and his poetry. A bandaged soldier might look like a mummy, and chariots and hecatombs creep into his descriptions: the museums of his childhood had come to life (and death). The archaeological approach to the war is found in the first lines of an unfinished, untitled poem:

As bronze may be much beautified
By lying in the dark damp soil,
So men who fade in dust of warfare fade
Fairer, and sorrow blooms their soul.

He knew about digging and soil. Indeed, his mind must have been sent back to the appearance of the archaeological sites he had haunted as a teenager, since they had in effect been transformed into the mud, ruins and trenches of the Western Front – in photos depicting Uriconium or Silchester before the war, the sites look like a benign Western Front, a series of trenches dug into the earth. His trench poem had been 'Uriconium', which grew out of the archaeological trenches and associated these trenches with the grave, and now the trenches and graves of France were to produce another kind of poetry, grave and trenchant.

*

For three weeks in February, Owen had some respite while he underwent training at the Advanced Horse Transport Depot behind the line at Abbeville, which he had studied in books a decade before. He also noted excitedly that he had been on a 'gallant' ride near the battlefield of Crécy, another site that he had once upon a time learnt all about.[23] At Crécy in the Hundred Years War, on 26 August 1346, the greatly outnumbered Englishmen of Edward III heroically defeated a French cavalry charge, showing that archery and infantry could overcome knights on horseback. These weeks at the Advanced Horse Transport Depot, nearly six centuries later, were made pleasant not only by the location but also by the opportunity to work with horses and to come as close as he would come to playing the knight in shining armour or being in the Italian cavalry:

> I have just come in from driving G.S. Wagons with 4 horses. This hour's work is about all we do in the morning, and this afternoon we are driving out to a Horse Hospital. I tell you, these days are the best I've ever had in the army.[24]

'Dulce et Decorum Est' has its wagon, presumably horse-drawn, and that poem from later in 1917 seems to reject the glory of war, yet at Abbeville he was still able to appreciate chivalry.

But he was soon back with the 2nd Battalion of the Manchester Regiment, and soon in a good warm dug-out, decorated with French postcards, picturing 'embraces, medals, roses and mistletoe!',[25] and then in a less cosy billet as the severe weather returned. In mid March, a few days short of his 24th birthday, Owen suffered a nasty case of concussion from a fall in the darkness. A medical report recorded that in

March 1917 he fell down a well at Bouchoir, and was momentarily stunned. Owen called it 'a kind of well, only about 15 ft.', and then revised this to 'a shell-hole in a floor, laying open a deep cellar'.[26] It was an accident that was later echoed in arguably his greatest poem:

> It seemed that out of battle I escaped
> Down some profound dull tunnel, long since scooped
> Through granites which titanic wars had groined.[27]

He was hit on the back of his head when he fell, but his head wasn't fractured or cut open and the hurt was slow to materialise:

> I felt nothing more than a headache, for 3 days; and went up to the front in the usual way – or nearly the usual way, for I felt too weak to wrestle with the mud, and sneaked along the top, snapping my fingers at a clumsy sniper. When I got back I developed a high fever, vomited strenuously, and long, and was seized with muscular pains.[28]

He spent his birthday in a hospital bed at Gailly, although it was not until the evening that he realised it was his birthday, and he was out of action for three weeks, resting in hospital. In itself this fall might not have been serious when compared with the injuries that other men were receiving, but one might wonder whether it had any lasting effect on Owen's head. He received three weeks' treatment but in May he admitted that he was still suffering from the headaches traceable to his concussion. More importantly, there has long been a feeling that creativity can be intensified by brain injuries. For instance, it has been suggested that the rapid and remarkable change in the work of the painter Augustus John – a development from conventional talent into passionate originality – stemmed from hitting his head on a rock while swimming at Tenby as a young man. There is a condition called 'acquired savant syndrome', which would apply to the more extreme cases: following a head injury and concussion, the injured person acquires a new or greater talent for something. A musician with the

syndrome has said that 'It's as if my knock on the head unlocked some-
thing latent, or enabled me to use some part of my brain I simply
couldn't access before'.[29] Could Owen's development as a poet during
1917 be ascribed to this bang on the head? Like John's, Owen's work
acquired a greater passion and vigour (even when dealing with death
and paralysis), becoming disinhibited and self-confident: some would,
of course, ascribe that improvement to the shock of experiencing the
Western Front, and Owen himself said as much, treating January 1917
as a watershed, but a more specific and physical instance of shock
might also have played its part. This might be as simplistic as the
suggestion that great art is created by madness, and we should note
Augustus John's response to his own swimming accident:

> and thus was born the myth of my *genius*, due, it seemed clear, solely
> to the bang on the head I had incurred while bathing. This, it was
> thought, had released hidden and unsuspected springs . . . It was all
> nonsense of course; I was in no way changed.[30]

But then Owen's injury was in some ways more severe: unlike Owen,
John had not been stunned or received concussion. Owen hit the back
of his head, whereas the cases of acquired savant syndrome tend to be
associated with damage to the front (especially front-left) of the brain,
but damage to the left temporal lobe is still a possibility. The injury in
Bouchoir did at the very least set Owen thinking about identity,
memory and the grave. On 23 March he drafted 'With an Identity
Disc', which he sent to his brother Colin as evidence that he had not
become 'clean mad and translated by my knock on the head' and that
'my old form of madness has in no way changed'.[31] The poem considers
how his death might be 'memoried'.

At the same time, he was considering how he would live if he
survived the war. On 21 March he wrote to his sister Mary saying that
he amused himself with drawing plans for country houses and bunga-
lows that he could one day live in (alone). By 24 March, he had decided
to live in a cottage in Kent, Surrey or Sussex where he could write and

keep pigs. He would have cheap hired labour. Appropriately, pigs are mud-loving creatures, and by now he was, of course, quite accustomed to mud. So it was perhaps not the greatest change from the war, but it was the abruptest possible change from his flying ambitions of 1916 and from eighteen months earlier, when he had declared that 'The City now / Holds all my passion'. One senses that in his hospital bed he was looking back as much as forward: drawing a picture of his dream home is something a young boy would do. On holiday at a muddy Welsh farm in August 1905, he had drawn a picture of a Dutch barn in a letter to his mother, and wrote excitedly about some wee piglets, drawing the nine little piglets with their mother – in this picture, the sow looks like a dog and the little piglets look like mice.

Owen had soon recovered enough to return to his men. On 9 April, the day Edward Thomas was killed at Arras, Owen wrote to his brother Colin asking whether he wanted any souvenirs and saying he had already taken a German banknote for him and the name-patch out of a coat. For himself, Owen had taken a German pilot's bloodstained handkerchief as a touching souvenir. He was a little behind the line, but was preparing to go back to the Front, and it was not long before he was in the wars again. On 12 April he returned to the Front at Savy Wood near St Quentin and was there for twelve days. During that time he was blown up by a shell explosion while he was asleep. Owen's letter to his mother on 25 April provides more detail, and shows how Owen was still determined to tell his mother the truth, however distressing. He describes how, a fortnight before, he had been rushed up into the Line, and for twelve days he didn't wash his face, or take his boots off or sleep a deep sleep, and he was stuck in holes waiting to be blown out by a shell:

> I think the worst incident was one wet night when we lay up against a railway embankment. A big shell lit on the top of the bank, just 2 yards from my head. Before I awoke, I was blown in the air right away from the bank! I passed most of the following days in a railway Cutting, in a hole just big enough to lie in, and covered with corrugated iron.

My brother officer of B Coy, 2/Lt Gaukroger lay opposite in a
similar hole. But he was covered with earth, and no relief will ever
relieve him.[32]

On 1 May, he was observed to be shaky and tremulous, his conduct
and manner were peculiar, and his memory was confused. He acquired
a stammer, one that echoed what he would soon describe as 'the stut-
tering rifles' rapid rattle'.[33] Owen was sent to the No. 41 Stationary
Hospital at Gailly where he was under observation and treatment by
Captain Brown RAMC, Neurological Specialist, for a month. His time
in hospital seems to have been recalled in the poem 'Conscious':

> His fingers wake, and flutter; up the bed.
> His eyes come open with a pull of will,
> Helped by the yellow mayflowers by his head.
> The blind-cord drawls across the window-sill . . .
> What a smooth floor the ward has! What a rug!
> Who is that talking somewhere out of sight?
> Three flies are creeping round the shiny jug . . .
> 'Nurse! Doctor!' – 'Yes, all right, all right.'
>
> But sudden evening blurs and fogs the air.
> There seems no time to want a drink of water.
> Nurse looks so far away. And here and there
> Music and roses burst through crimson slaughter.
> He can't remember where he saw blue sky . . .
> The trench is narrower. Cold, he's cold; yet hot –
> And there's no light to see the voices by . . .
> There is no time to ask . . . he knows not what.

In his letters from hospital, Owen mentioned 'great blue bowls of
yellow Mayflower',[34] and the flies all around and about the beds.
Although presumably a description of a fellow patient, the poem
captures something like the state that Owen was in. His mind was

often still at the Front, present and past being merged together, memories returning unwanted, and he was struggling to be in control of his consciousness. These confused conditions come from a traumatic experience more than any physical consequence of fighting. Earlier he had had the bang on the head, and no doubt this played a part, but now the shock was more internal. He told his sister that it was not the explosives or the fighting that made him shaky but the horror of being stuck in a hole near the remains of Gaukroger.

*

We see in Owen's time in France in the early months of 1917, the emergence of a bitterly negative attitude towards both the British government and its keenest supporters, including the Church of England. In a letter of mid May 1917, Owen portrays himself as a true Christian:

> I am more and more Christian as I walk the unchristian ways of Christendom. Already I have comprehended a light which never will filter into the dogma of any national church: namely that one of Christ's essential commands was: Passivity at any price! Suffer dishonour and disgrace; but never resort to arms. Be bullied, be outraged, be killed; but do not kill.[35]

This remark shows Owen's proximity to Shelley, whose 'Essay on Christianity' has been described by William Sharp as 'a reverent recognition of the character, mission, and teaching of Christ, and an impassioned reprobation of dogmatic Christianity'.[36]

Owen couldn't understand how clergymen from 'his Grace of Canterbury' and the bishops downwards – and the King as head of the Church – could reconcile Christianity with support for the war, especially when the war no longer seemed to be simply a war of defence. Congregations were also guilty: Owen could only conclude that there must be far fewer Christians than churchgoers. 'Pure Christianity will not fit in with pure patriotism,' he added. Christ speaks in many languages, including German. The chaplain who used the Union Jack as an altar cloth throughout the war is just one example of how Christianity was hijacked by patriotism.[37] Owen's position was not an entirely uncommon one among those who had been to the Front: a nurse wrote, 'I wish those people who write so glibly about this being a holy war and the orators who talk so much about going on no matter how long the war lasts and what it may mean, could see a case – to say nothing of ten cases – of mustard gas in its early stages – could see the poor things burnt and blistered all over with great mustard-coloured suppurating blisters, with blind eyes [. . .] fighting for breath, with voices a mere whisper, saying that their throats are closing and they know they will choke'.[38] The Papacy would soon reject any notion that this was a holy war, in words that echo Owen's own. On 1 August, Pope Benedict XV, speaking 'in the name of the Divine Redeemer, the Prince of Peace',[39] called for a cessation of hostilities:

> Shall, then, the civilized world be nought but a field of death? And shall Europe, so glorious and flourishing, rush, as though driven by universal madness, towards the abyss, and lend her hand to her own suicide?[40]

The Pope hoped to see 'ended at the earliest moment the terrible struggle that appears increasingly a useless massacre'.[41] While Owen was angered by religious men who said it was good to be in Hell, there were, too, religious men who sought to end that Hell.

In his letters and poetry, Owen also now sees a great difference between God and Jesus, between the Old Testament and the New. This attitude would be expressed later in the year in the poem 'Soldier's Dream', where Jesus the pacifist ends the war:

> I dreamed kind Jesus fouled the big-gun gears;
> And caused a permanent stoppage in all bolts;
> And buckled with a smile Mausers and Colts;
> And rusted every bayonet with His tears.

And God the warmonger starts the war again. God is the father and can represent those fathers, like Owen's own, who are enthusiastic about the war, as if war itself is good, and send their sons off to die. God, of course, sent his son to die on the cross, and seems to ignore any pleas for compassion; as Owen would write in 'A Tear Song', 'God for his glittering world / Seeketh our tears' and 'God hath no ears'.

In May 1917, Owen wrote that 'Christ is literally in no man's land'.[42] For him and other soldiers, the statues of the crucified Christ, which were everywhere in rural France, came to represent the soldiers of all nations, even those of non-Catholic or strongly anti-Catholic backgrounds such as Owen's own; and these statues were themselves bashed about, dismembered, blown to smithereens in the fighting. The wounded statues also came to represent the violent rejection of Christianity by the governments, generals and clergymen who prolonged this holy war. Recalling his months in France in early 1917, 'At a Calvary Near the Ancre' he uses a battered statue of Christ ('One ever hangs where shelled roads part'), and ends with the statement that 'they who love the greater love / Lay down their life; they do not hate'. In May 1917, quoting John 15:13, he wrote, 'Greater love hath no man than this, that a man lay down his life – for a friend' (a principle he returned to in a poem called 'Greater Love').[43] In 'Le Christianisme', another poem that derives from his experiences in early 1917, the statues of the Virgin and the saints may represent the true Christianity that has been forgotten or brutally treated:

So the church Christ was hit and buried
    Under its rubbish and its rubble.
In cellars, packed-up saints lie serried,
    Well out of hearing of our trouble.

One Virgin still immaculate
    Smiles on for war to flatter her.
She's halo'd with an old tin hat,
    But a piece of hell will batter her.

The immaculate conception of the Virgin was strongly associated with Lourdes, where, less than four years after the dogma was formally established by the Papacy, St Bernadette saw the white lady who, when asked her name, smiled and said 'I am the Immaculate Conception'. The statue at the grotto carries the words 'Que Soy Era Immaculada Councepciou'.[44] Owen's statue may in fact have been a statue of Our Lady of Lourdes, the ruined building thereby serving as the Pyrenean grotto. But Owen isn't trying to suggest, as Hilaire Belloc did, that this was a war between Catholic civilisation and the pagan barbarism of Germany: Owen had sent Leslie Gunston a postcard of 'Arras Cathedral in flames' in August 1915, no doubt because he was trying to persuade himself and his cousin to do their bit in the face of these German atrocities – atrocities against art as much as against Christianity – yet we see in the poem that the 'piece of hell' is not necessarily German. Owen admired Belloc greatly and was reading him in France[45] but he couldn't quite accept bellicose Belloc's view of either the war or Catholicism, saying in March 1917 that he 'went into the great Gothic Church, and listened under the nave, as Belloc says, for the voice of the Middle Ages' but all he could hear was a priest with 'a voice very much beyond the middle age'.[46]

There was a 'St. John in bathing costume looking ruefully at another saint in a gold dressing-gown'.[47] Here Owen is possibly recalling W. J. Locke, a now forgotten but once very popular novelist, whom he was reading in 1917 ('You took me for a saint in a dressing-gown').[48] But, although he might still possess a Protestant's suspicion of Catholic icons, what we see here too in 'Le Christianisme' is his continuing and heightened devotion to the mother, the suffering mother; a devotion that inhabits every letter to his own. If he speaks of her in religious terms in his letters, calling her an angel and connecting her to the Virgin Mary, it is not just grand praise – she was something to believe in. Susan Owen did all she could for the family, and as he says at the end of 'A New Heaven', 'our own mothers' tears shall heal us whole'. Fathers might send sons to war, but mothers are still immaculate: 'By your love, O Mother, O Home, I am protected from Fatigue of life and the keen spiritual Cold':[49] he confessed that without her letters he would give in. He thanked her for her 'gracious truths'.[50]

> Remember, O Most Gracious Virgin Mary,
> that never was it known that anyone who fled to Thy protection,
> implored Thy help or sought Thine intercession,
> was left unaided.[51]

The connection between Owen's mother and the divine motherhood of the Virgin Mary is seen too in the drafts of 'Happiness', which he started in Abbeville in February 1917. In this celebration of childhood, he says he was 'Harboured in heaven'[52] with 'happiness our Mother gave us'[53] but 'Have I not wrought too sick and sorrowful wrongs / For Her hand's pardoning?'[54] He considers using the capitalised 'Mother' and 'Her' in order to give Her divine status.

*

Owen could, in his imagination, elevate his own status too, imagining himself as King Arthur. On 9 May, he made a visit to the village of Corbie near Amiens, travelling there down the Somme Canal from Gailly in a steam-tug in hot May sunshine. He described the journey for his mother the following day:

> The scenery was such as I never saw or dreamed of since I read the *Faerie Queene*. Just as in the Winter when I woke up lying on the burning cold snow I fancied I must have died & been pitch-forked into the Wrong Place, so, yesterday, it was not more difficult to imagine that my dusky barge was wending up to Avalon, and the peace of Arthur, and where Lancelot heals him of his grievous wound. But the Saxon is not broken, as we could very well hear last night.[55]

In Owen's imagination, the Western Front became the borderland battleground between Celts and Saxons, rather like Shropshire, in fact.

This journey inspired the poem 'Hospital Barge', which was written in December 1917.

Owen might not have had a grievous Arthurian wound but he caught trench fever and had a temperature of 102.9. His nerves, though, were the greater problem. It was decided by the doctors that Owen had neurasthenia attributed to shock from a shell explosion – this was shell-shock, and he was eventually sent home. He was transferred to No. 1 General Hospital at Étretat, and then on 16 June he travelled from Le Havre to Southampton, and thence to the Welsh Hospital at Netley in Hampshire, a collection of huts erected and maintained by voluntary contributions from Wales ('It is pleasant to be among the Welsh').[56] The proceedings of a Medical Board assembled at the Welsh Hospital at Netley on 25 June 1917 record that:

> There is little abnormality to be observed but he seems to be of a highly strung temperement [*sic*]. He has slept well while here. He leaves Hospital to-day transferred to Craig Lockart [*sic*] War Hospital, Edinburgh for special observation and treatment.[57]

He was declared unfit for General Service for six months, unfit for Home Service for three months, and unfit for light duty at home for three months. So he was to have three months at Craiglockhart. The report incorrectly gives his home, 'Mahim', as 'Malsin': *malsain* is French for 'unhealthy'.

CHAPTER 10

Brock's Folk

There's night and day, brother, both sweet things; sun, moon, and stars, brother, all sweet things; there's likewise a wind on the heath. Life is very sweet, brother; who would wish to die?
GEORGE BORROW, *Lavengro*, Chapter xxv[1]

Though here there are some patients very seriously ill, the fear and horror of madness that I used to have has already lessened a great deal. And though here you continually hear terrible cries and howls like beasts in a menagerie, in spite of that people get to know each other very well and help each other when their attacks come on.
VINCENT VAN GOGH, May 1889[2]

ON the morning of Monday 25 June, Wilfred Owen left Netley and took the train to London. Arriving after lunchtime, he had an afternoon as a gentleman of leisure, shopping and gallery-going, spending his officer's pay. Even at Dunsden, he had rarely had the time or the money to pop up to Town for an afternoon of self-indulgence. Nonetheless, his description of his afternoon in London shows that, had he so wished, he could have written the kind of very English social comedy, revolving around class, clothes, cream teas, chatter and curates, that would be mastered by his fellow Oswestrian, the novelist Barbara Pym (born in Oswestry in 1913, she was, like Owen, the grandchild of a successful Oswestry ironmonger, which must be the perfect background for a study of the class system):

> I had tea at the Shamrock Tea Rooms, perhaps the most eminently respectable exclusive and secluded in Town. There was the usual deaf old lady and her Companion holding forth upon the new curate. I happen to know that a few stories higher in the same building is an Opium Den. I have not investigated. But I know. That's London. I met few faces I knew. But Strolling down New Bond Street, I ran into the last person on earth or under the earth that I wished to meet: Major, now Colonel, Dempster, of the 2nd Battalion. We stopped, of course, and he pretended to be very affable and cordial. Yet I know a more thorough-bred Snob does not exist – even in the imagination of Thackeray.[3]

Lieutenant-Colonel J. F. Dempster, who had taken charge of the 2nd Manchesters, might have been a horrid old snob, but, like the proper English gent, quite the Burlington Bertie, Owen happily had time to amble down to the shops of the West End, all a long way from Shrewsbury and Birkenhead. He had himself measured for new trousers at Pope and Bradley's (specialists in dress clothes) and bought a new hat at Peter Robinson's (Experts in the World of Fashion). He seems to have rather enjoyed his uniform, both as a symbol of his new gentlemanly status and simply as clothes to buy and try on and have cleaned and ironed and look handsome in. Perhaps this was a family matter, since his paternal grandfather was a tailor, although not the Mayfair kind: buying clothes was a form of self-improvement, and we can see the pleasure taken in them by a young man who had a shoemaker great-grandfather and a tailor grandfather. His life could be told as a wardrobe of clothes – the sailor suit, the home-made Hussar's uniform, a straw hat (subject of a dream he found most distressing in 1909),[4] the rather Freudian slippers of 1912, the Norfolk jacket, the de rigueur evening suit at Dunsden, the teacher's gown, the bow tie, French fashions ('Monsieur Dubo through the intervention of some friend, can get stuffs <u>at Tailor's Prices</u> from Paris, and in fact a fine selection of Spring-Summer Patterns is in my room at present'),[5] the cadet's uniform, the officer's uniform, and all the life-and-death fussing about socks and gloves and coats in the freezing trenches. His wartime letters are like a wardrobe of clothes, as are his poems – 'his ghastly suit of grey, / Legless, sewn short at elbow'; 'hardness of indifference, like a glove'; 'Glory I cast away, as bridegrooms do / Their splendid garments'.[6]

Wearing the new hat and a new collar, he boarded the sleeper train to Edinburgh, taking a corner seat. His mother's maiden name, Shaw, can be a Scottish name – the Irish playwright Bernard Shaw, whom Owen took an interest in, was descended from Highland Shaws – and in the Lowlands 'shaw' means 'a small wood'; nonetheless, any Scottishness was a long way back and Owen was a foreigner to Scotland, a country he had known only at its border. In the train, he read some Israel Zangwill, an author who appealed to Owen's belief that 'the Jews are a delightful people, at home';[7] although it might have been another beloved people he was reading about, because if Zangwill mostly wrote about Jewish life, he also wrote *Italian Fantasies* (1910), which, by tackling Dante, Byron, Venice, and so on, would have attracted Italy-loving Owen. When he arrived in Edinburgh, he found that Craiglockhart War Hospital was a taste of Italy too, an ashlar Italianate Victorian pseudo-palazzo that had been a hydro, a health farm before the war, offering health-improving water treatments amid the hilly Midlothian landscape (Craiglockhart was at the green edge of Edinburgh). Its 160 officers were all suffering in different degrees from shell shock.

The area had its literary connections. The Hydro had been advertised with a quotation from *Marmion* describing the view from the hills around it. But the strongest literary association was with Robert Louis Stevenson, and, although Stevenson had died in 1894, Owen was thrilled to be in the country of RLS. Stevenson, an Edinburgh man, holidayed in the countryside near Craiglockhart: at Colinton, where Stevenson's grandfather lived and every sight and sound had conspired

'to feed a romantic imagination',[8] Owen met one of Stevenson's child-
hood friends; and he also got to know Lord Guthrie who lived nearby
in Stevenson's holiday home, Swanston Cottage, on the lower slopes of
the Pentland Hills. While at Craiglockhart, Owen read *St. Ives*,
Stevenson's war novel, where Swanston Cottage is described as 'a little
quaint place of many rough-cast gables and grey roofs' and a bit like 'a
rambling infinitesimal cathedral'.[9] The poet Ivor Gurney, who arrived
at another Edinburgh war hospital on 23 September 1917, was excited
by the Stevenson associations too: 'There are many memories round
this city, but the dearest to me are those of R. L. S., that friend of
Everyman.'[10] Stevenson was not only a friend of Everyman but an
example, like Keats, of the connection between ill health and literary
creativity – Keats and Stevenson conjured up realms of gold, not
despite sickness but somehow because of it, in response to it, out of it.

It was not until later in the year that Owen read *The Strange Case
of Dr Jekyll and Mr. Hyde* but that novel, although set in London,
would have been an appropriate novel in Craiglockhart, which
seemed like a scholarly and gentlemanly place by day but at night was
filled with monstrous screams as, in nightmares, the men were sent
back to the Front. In 'Mental Cases', Owen would describe men
driven mad by murderous memories: 'Memory fingers in their hair of
murders, / Multitudinous murders they once witnessed'. Memories
plagued those men who had experienced the war, especially at night
when a man was at his most defenceless. But at first, in a Scottish
summer of long days and little night, the light kept Owen awake at
night, perhaps mercifully. On 1 July Owen described how he had
noticed that it never grew quite dark all night, with daylight glim-
mering through his window at two in the morning. Unable to sleep, he
read W. J. Locke, possibly *The Morals of Marcus Ordeyne* (better than
Thomas Hardy, according to Owen), a breezy romantic novel about a
wealthy historian and an uneducated eighteen-year-old girl who has
escaped from a harem: 'I have never experienced such an odd sensation
in my life as a touch of Carlotta's fresh young arms upon my face and
the perfume of spring violets that emanated from her person. [. . .] She

has a child's engaging way of rubbing herself up against one when she wants to be particularly ingratiating.'[11] It is also a war novel in so far as one of the characters dies in the Boer War: '"*Dulce et decorum est*. He died for his country," said I.'[12]

'Dulce et Decorum Est' (drafted at Craiglockhart in October) is the best-known description of Owen's dreams, where the speaker describes how a man was caught in a gas attack, and how 'In all my dreams, before my helpless sight, / He plunges at me, guttering, choking, drowning': 'some smothering dreams' would stop the addressee from telling the 'old Lie'. All the 'ing' words, 15 in 28 lines, serve to emphasise that the trenches are still very much in the present, returning uninvited and unwelcomed at night. At Craiglockhart, Owen had horrible dreams, often memories of the Front, but also those of a more civilian character, featuring shocking incidents like motor accidents. Owen was keen to point out that he had not 'had a "breakdown"' – 'I am simply <u>avoiding</u> one'[13] – and he had had nightmares before joining the forces, but breakdowns and madness haunted the hospital.

The significance of the hospital's location next to a mental hospital was not lost on the officers of Craiglockhart, nor on the locals who saw that the officers had to wear blue armbands at all times and concluded that the armbands indicated insanity. There was also a rumour that the men were victims of venereal disease. Many people disagreed with the idea of sending these shirkers on holiday rather than punishing them, but the officers were treated well, on the whole, by those inside and outside the hospital. It was indeed something of a holiday camp, and Owen called it a holiday in a letter to his father (a remark intended to annoy the old man perhaps) even if the weather was mostly terrible. Lieutenant J. H. Butlin, one of the patients who was there when Owen arrived, shows us the leisurely daily life:

It is a magnificent hydro standing in palatial grounds fitted with all the comforts that man's ingenuity can contrive. Swimming, baths, billiards, gardening, bowls, tennis, fret-work etc are some of the hobbies one is expected to take up. Personally I am thinking of writing a book: provided one is in by six o'clock and conforms to a few simple rules life is a complete and glorious loaf. [. . .] Can you imagine me, my dear Basil, getting up and taking a swim before breakfast? Doing a little gardening and poultry farming after breakfast? Fretwork and photography after lunch? Viewing natural scenery after tea? Reading and writing after dinner and then to bed?[14]

Butlin played bridge every day, and, weather permitting, tennis; there was also golf. It was something of a Butlin's holiday camp. For the day Owen arrived, Butlin's diary simply says 'Fine. Tennis in morning. Tea in Edinburgh. Slight rain after tea.'[15]

Owen was fortunate to be put in the care of a doctor whose interests and methods chimed so well with his own. A Scotsman born in 1879, the son of a poet and a farmer, Arthur Brock was a scholar interested in legends, history and folklore – 'Somewhat of a crank' – and he was a man of the great outdoors, which even his appearance seemed to suggest: he was 'Very tall, thin, hunched up shoulders, big blue hands, very chilly looking, with a long peaked nose', and his high-pitched squeaky voice was 'suggestive of Arctic regions'.[16] One who knew him recorded the doctor's attitude to the patients at Craiglockhart:

Full of energy. Pushed his patients out of bed in the dark cold mornings and marched them out for a walk before breakfast. Rumour has it that they bolted themselves into lavatories and bath-rooms, but he was wise to that. One officer boasted that if he lay flat under his bed, so that the untidy bed clothes hid him, as if he were an early riser, he escaped.[17]

Brock believed in 'ergotherapy', 'the cure by functioning' – a belief that men could return to normal through working,[18] although the work was usually a form of leisure, with the soldiers making full use of the Hydro's facilities. He sought the true employment of leisure – he didn't want anyone simply 'killing time' – believing that shell-shock patients were no longer part of normal life and needed to be reconnected with it. This could mean visiting Edinburgh's urban poor or teaching in a local school or joining the Camera Club, but essentially Brock's treatments were a form of primitivism or neo-paganism: he felt that modern life generally is damaging – the war was just an intensified version of the life that was already causing mental ill-health in the years before 1914. Underlying his work there was a belief in traditional ways of life ('Primitive peoples know better'),[19] and a preference for the countryside rather than the city: 'Are not these horrors of war the last and culminating terms in a series that begins in the infernos of our industrialized cities?'[20] He held that 'Our civilization has become a purely urban one; the city has forgotten the countryside from which it sprang'.[21] The city disconnects men from normal life, as do modern inventions like the cinema, a feeling shared by another Craiglockhart doctor, W. H. R. Rivers, an anthropologist drawn to 'primitive' cultures, who considered it much better for soldiers to play golf 'than to be perpetually immured in a picture house, or to parade Princes Street for the gratification of their own vanity'.[22] Brock's bracing morning walks were a way both of taking exercise and of getting back to the land; as he said, 'let us give Nature a chance'.[23] Even the names Brock and Rivers were suitably rural. The featureless, blasted Western Front, dominated by the machine gun, artillery and barbed wire, was the visual representation of the death of the countryside. Men were encouraged to work on local farms or grow vegetables in the Hydro grounds; there was a chicken-run under the trees; even 'imaginative work' should be 'an organic outgrowth from life'.[24] This was a nature cure, a Romantic belief in the countryside, an attitude found in the literary world (Wordsworthian, Ruskinian) transformed into psychiatry; it was akin to the 'Back to the Land' movements and circles of Owen's time, all in their way blaming the modern world for unhappiness and ill health.

Activities at Craiglockhart were expected to be practical and useful, as if in some primitive community – in July, Owen reported that he spent a morning beating out a plate of copper into a bowl. Owen was also keenly involved in the Field Club. In July, he contributed a report on the creation of the Field Club to *The Hydra*, the Craiglockhart magazine:

> The following office-bearers were elected: – President, Capt. Brock; secretary, Mr. Chase. Recruits are wanted. Don't wait to be pushed. 'The wind's on the heath.' [. . .] 'Our broodings over the face of the earth, and the firmament, and the waters under the earth, will be quite primitive – without form, but, we hope, not void.'[25]

'The wind's on the heath' was an allusion to a famous passage celebrating the simple life in *Lavengro*, the book by George Borrow that Owen had read a few years previously, the story of an educated man who gets back to the primitive way of things by joining the gypsies. The passage in Borrow's book declares, 'Life is very sweet, brother; who would wish to die?', which could be taken as a response to Horace's 'Dulce et decorum est pro patria mori'. Borrow was another of the literary associations of the place, having lived in Edinburgh Castle because his father was in the army, and his time in Edinburgh is described in *Lavengro* with a characteristic eye for the natural world: 'It was a beautiful Sunday evening, the rays of the descending sun were reflected redly from the grey walls of the castle, and from the black rocks on which it was founded.'[26] Indeed, Brock encouraged the officers to learn about the history, geography and culture of the local area, and again there was in this a belief in local communities, working with the land, tradition and folk culture. In a sense, he wanted to make the men a little Scottish. This worked with Owen, in that when he wrote his well-known poem 'Disabled' about a Scottish soldier disabled by the war, he not only showed his sense of connection with Edinburgh – Owen may even have seen the physically damaged soldier as a version of his psychologically damaged self – but he adopted a mildly Scottish voice, as if writing in a refined Craiglockhartian accent: 'Aye, that was it, to please the giddy jilts / He asked to join'. 'Disabled' is, equally, a poem worthy of Scottish Presbyterianism, in that lying, drinking, vanity, games and womanising are all punished: if the soldier hadn't been a sinner he wouldn't have been punished with disability. The poem is suggested by a letter in which Owen claims, in a rather Keatsian moment, that 'I am whatever and whoever I see while going down to Edinburgh on the tram: greengrocer, policeman, shopping lady, errand boy, paper-boy, blind man, crippled Tommy, bank-clerk, carter, all of these in half an hour'.[27] Keats argued that the poet has no identity, and is continually informing and filling some other body. Yeats, too, held that a poet must assume the mask of some other self. Owen becomes Edinburgh, and while, elsewhere in his writing, the window can be a barrier, here it helps to make him part of Edinburgh, and the people he sees are Scottish.

From an early stage in his career, Brock had been interested in national identity and belonging, themes that were emphasised by studying in Vienna and Berlin: 'To what extent should one become a German when one goes to Germany?'[28] The emphasis was on 'home', a word that had acquired extra significance during the war. The war, like modern life, took men away from home, which meant not just a house but an organic community, the individual's natural and proper environment. Brock was interested in Scotland's Brownies, benevolent creatures from folklore who haunted houses and did the housework, and he was interested too in similar genii and house spirits in other countries. The belief in community stretched to believing in the traditional family. In his book *Health and Conduct*, Brock discusses the gradual break-up of real home life before the war and the growing disharmony between mother and child, emphasising the need to regain harmony and end this modern dissociation between the child and its parents. Equally, modern life damaged men by not allowing them to become adults. He saw the ordinary progress of the individual's life appeared to halt, and that he ceased to grow up or even fell back into childhood,[29] and believed this childishness of his patients was caused partly by pre-war life, and partly by the war. The screaming patients at night in Craiglockhart were men infantilised, crying for their mothers or for the nurse as mother-substitute, afraid of the dark, even wetting the bed.

Although Brock complained about regression – the modern man's feeling that he is safer when tied to his mother's apron-strings, the desire to seek refuge in the past – his own beliefs too were essentially regressive, turning to a traditional way of life and a close connection with the land, which had, of course, been his own upbringing as a farm boy, and he was trying to send the men back to his own Scottish childhood. Indeed, Craiglockhart could be seen as the return to childhood on a grand scale – not just because of the shell shock but also because of the treatments. Even model boats were made in a workshop for sailing competitions on Craiglockhart Pond, where a Model Yacht Regatta took Owen back to his childhood and he thought how his father would have liked to compete. No doubt it evoked memories of the Jardin Public too, where in the garden of boyhood he happily rescued the boats of the little boys around the pond. At Craiglockhart in August, the schooner *Mystery* was a popular winner in front of enthusiastic supporters. In this garden of boyhood, 'this abode of bliss',[30] R. L. S, the schoolboy's favourite, was the presiding genius. There was also a ban on sex. J. H. Butlin landed himself in trouble when he brought his girlfriend back to the hospital one evening: the commanding officer, finding them on a quiet bench, accused him of breaking the rules. 'I learned afterwards that a few minutes before he found me, he came upon an officer who had brought up some harlot from Edinboro and was in the act of copulation with her.'[31] The next day, he went to the officer's room like a naughty boy called to the headmaster's study. Certainly, there was a boarding-school atmosphere (as with thirteen-year-old boys, the emphasis on exercise was an attempt to manage sexual energy as well as shell shock).

It was also an atmosphere filled with legends and fairy tales. Brock was a classicist who frequently turned to myths and legends for guidance and exempla, and he also took a deep interest in Celtic or Scandinavian fairy tales and folklore. This too was an aspect of the regime that appealed to Owen. Given that one of Brock's obsessions was the '*Genius Loci* – the soul of the place'[32] as embodied by the Brownie, the Kobold, the Kelpie, and similar guardian spirits, we can

see Brock's influence in Owen's use of the spirits of places in three
poems over the next six months: 'Who is the god of Canongate?'
('*Where is thy shrine, then, little god?*'), Princes Street's 'Pale rain-flawed
phantom of the place' and 'the ghost of Shadwell Stair' ('I am the
shadow [. . .] I watch always').[33] Owen had long been interested in
sprites and fairies, as he had shown in 'A New Heaven', and he had
once turned two of Hans Christian Andersen's tales into poetry.
Indeed, in one of Owen's most Craiglockhartian poems, 'Disabled',
there is an echo of one of Andersen's tales 'The Little Mermaid', as if
Brock's fairy tales haunted Edinburgh; RLS, too, had seen Edinburgh
as a 'lamplit, vicious fairy land'. The disabled soldier (something of a
spirit of the place) remembers the park 'When glow-lamps budded in
the light blue trees' and in the mermaid's garden beneath the sea, which
is itself like a municipal park with carpet-bedding, there are 'fiery red
and deep blue trees, the fruit of which shone like gold [. . .] Everything
was bathed in a wondrous blue light down there; you might more
readily have supposed yourself to be high up in the air, with only the
sky above and below you, than that you were at the bottom of the
ocean.'[34] The mermaid's world beneath the sea before she goes to the
surface corresponds to the soldier's Edinburgh before he went to war;
the loss of his legs becomes a grim reversal of her equally tragic loss of
her tail in return for legs. Both 'Disabled' and Owen's earlier poem
'The Little Mermaid' are poems about growing up and yet, in the act
of growing, remaining infantilised for ever, never to know married life:

> Tonight he noticed how the women's eyes
> Passed from him to the strong men that were whole.
> How cold and late it is! Why don't they come
> And put him into bed? Why don't they come?

The park is a place for children.[35]

Similarly, Owen wrote, at Brock's urging, the poem 'The Wrestlers'
about Heracles (Hercules) and Antaeas (Antaeus), where the emphasis
on youth is seen in Hylas, Heracles's young page who doesn't

necessarily even feature in the story but becomes the hero in Owen's version of the ancient tale, because, although a figure of peace and love, it is he who tells Heracles how to defeat Antaeas: 'Antaeus deriving strength from his Mother Earth nearly licked old Herk',[36] but Heracles realised that he could defeat Antaeus by lifting him off the ground:

> If thou could'st lift the man in air – enough.
> His feet suck secret virtue of the earth.
> Lift him, and buckle him to thy breast, and win.

Brock wrote, in an article for *The Hydra* entitled 'Antaeus, or Back to the Land': 'Now surely every officer who comes to Craiglockhart recognises that, in a way, he is himself Antaeus who has been taken from his Mother Earth and well-nigh crushed to death by the war giant or military machine.' Brock argued that Antaeus 'typifies the occupation cure at Craiglockhart' and his story is 'the justification of our activities'.[37]

Owen got to know, through a friend of a friend, the Edinburgh artist John Duncan, an associate member of the Royal Scottish Academy who lived in Edinburgh at St Bernard's Crescent and who like Brock, had been a friend and follower of Patrick Geddes, the Scottish academic and social reformer. Owen owned *St Columba: A Study of Social Inheritance and Spiritual Development* by Victor Branford, published by 'Patrick Geddes and Colleagues', and the frontispiece is 'St Columba on the Hill of Angels from a drawing by Mr John Duncan, A.R.S.A.' Duncan specialised in legends and fairy tales, especially Celtic subjects such as *The Awakening of Cuchulain, The Riders of the Sidhe, St Bride, Tristan and Isolde* and *The Children of Lir*. Children were a recurring element of his work: Duncan had married in 1912, aged forty-five, and had two daughters, Bunty, born in 1913, and Vivian, born in 1915. Duncan himself said, 'I have a great opportunity of grace in my dear and talented children for which I can never be too grateful':

> They point the way for me to a truer and better art than any I have
> ever known or so it seems to me. So far they have no false standards

of taste and feeling, but respect and react spontaneously to the love-liest things. We in our long artistic education have accepted many a false standard, at first often with modesty and self distrust we have allowed a hypocrisy and bit by bit we have perverted ourselves. To regain the spontaneity and simplicity to become little children is to enter into the Kingdom of Art.'[38]

Characteristically, it was a child that Owen was drawn to when he visited Duncan, and we can also see that Owen was thinking about beauty, realism and the role of art:

The best visit I made was to John Duncan: a pretty great artist [. . .] He is 'one of the ones' in the Academy; but didn't sell his picture this year. It is a thing of many beauties. I have been made very sad by the extreme beauty of the eyelids of one of his Faces. But he used no model for her. It is a sad thought that Nature can't grow a face as old Duncan can. [. . .] I got so comfortable at Duncan's.[39]

The painting is called *The Coming of Bride*. The painting portrays the ancient Scottish folk-tale about the arrival of spring. On 15 March 1917 Duncan recorded in his notebook that this painting should repre-sent 'freshness and spontaneity and life and joy'.[40] Then, on 20 March he noted that 'the colour if it does not sing, at least chirps [. . .] I might at last succeed in making the colour sing'.[41] Originally, in the winter and spring of 1917, the picture was called 'Spring Song' and Duncan may still have referred to it by this name when he showed it to Owen, who had himself been one of the March-born. Owen wrote a poem called 'Winter Song' at Craiglockhart in October.

Not only did Duncan paint pictures of Scottish folklore, tales and legends, he also lived the life of the 'Celtic Twilight', believing in fairies and magic. Duncan was a member of the Edinburgh Theosophical Society, saw visions and heard fairy music. He lived apart, dwelling in his own mind. He believed in reincarnation too. The film-maker Donald Cammell, whose family knew Duncan, showed an early gift for drawing and possessed so clear an idea of perspective that Duncan maintained it proved that Cammell had learnt the skill in a previous incarnation. It is characteristic of Duncan that he married a woman who had, he believed, found the Holy Grail in a well at Glastonbury. Another insight into Duncan is offered by a letter he sent to D'Arcy Wentworth Thompson congratulating him on his knighthood in 1937:

> You will pardon an artist (as I aspire to be) for saying that in looking at all the faces in todays [sic] Scotsman I think that of Professor Darcy [sic] Thompson the best embodiment of the title – most fitting to the part – the face of a gallant knight chevalier of the Ideal.[42]

Duncan was attracted to the world of King Arthur, producing a painting called *Merlin and the Fairy Queen*, and his *The Taking of Excalibur* of 1897 depicts Merlin rowing the boat that carries Arthur to the sword. Duncan was more at home with King Arthur and the Celtic Twilight than with the twentieth century; although tied closely to Edinburgh, he didn't paint pictures of Edinburgh, or of Dundee, the city where he was born in 1866. His Scotland was a mystical, half-real wild domain, more Outer Hebrides than Edinburgh's New Town.

Yet Duncan also represented one of the tastes of Edinburgh at the time – a taste that Brock had himself become addicted to. The Celtic atmosphere of Edinburgh was no doubt a little artificial, and it has been noted that Scotland's Celtic Twilight produced no one to match W. B. Yeats or J. M. Synge, but it was potent and pervasive. Rather than an isolated anomaly, Craiglockhart was to some extent representative of the city. Indeed, a decade earlier the Celtic Twilight had captured the writer Joyce Cary when he studied in Edinburgh, living near Duncan in St Bernard's Crescent:

> Impressed with Celtic crosses, runic writings, wandering bards (or at least an old man who played the Celtic harp and sang the old songs in pubs for pennies), and the dramatic sight of the ancient

castle itself and Holyrood Palace, Joyce began to use a monogram of
Celtic design to sign his drawings; he designed a costume for
himself, that of a Celtic demon with horned helmet and fur cloak,
to wear to a student masquerade ball, and he wrote some abomi-
nable poetry, half cavalier and half rotten Rossetti.[43]

Wilfred Owen loved the Celtic Twilight, but his poetry at
Craiglockhart was neither half cavalier nor half rotten Rossetti, and
far from abominable. He wrote poetry like 'Dulce et Decorum Est',
'Disabled' and 'Inspection':

'The world is washing out its stains,' he said.
'It doesn't like our cheeks so red:
Young blood's its great objection.
But when we're duly white-washed, being dead,
The race will bear Field Marshal God's inspection.'

He also began 'The Sentry', his poem of slime, shells, dug-outs,
whizz-bangs, corpses, muck and blood. And yet much of the poetry
at Craiglockhart has some similarity to the world of Duncan.
Understandably, he did not always want to recall the war – he says in
'The Sentry', 'I try not to remember these things now'. He wrote about
a medievalish world of knights in his 'Ballad of Lady Yolande' and
'The Ballad of Many Thorns'; his poetry echoes Tennyson, Keats and
Yeats; he attempted poetry about Perseus; he wrote about Heracles;
there's twilight, there's the dawn and there's a touch of Scotland – 'The
birds fifed on before, shrill-piping pipers, / Right down to town' in
'The Promisers'. Whether or not it is a response to *The Coming of
Bride*, 'Winter Song', when compared with 'Inspection', seems to speak
in a different voice:

From off your face, into the winds of winter,
The sun-brown and the summer-gold are blowing;
But they shall gleam again with spiritual glinter,

When paler beauty on your brows falls snowing,
And through those snows my looks shall be soft-going.

*

Nowadays there seems to be something like Nazism in Brock's emphasis on roots, the homeland, the soil, the group rather than the individual, 'belonging', 'struggle', the past, native culture, paganism, classicism, the folk, and work – half in jest, Owen called Craiglockhart 'this excellent Concentration Camp'[44] – and as it happens an Arthur Bruck and a Wilfred von Oven would play significant parts in the Third Reich;[45] or, alternatively, there is in Brock something of Lord Summerisle from the film *The Wicker Man*;[46] but, as Brock made clear, war was the enemy and the regime was unaggressive (beyond Brock pushing patients out of bed for early morning country walks), and Owen responded well to Brock's ideas. This Back to the Land spirit was combined with the comforts of the Hydro and Edinburgh, so there was none of the muddy discomfort of the Front or even Hare Hall. Equally, characters like Brock and Duncan could appeal to the Romantic side of Owen's nature, which delighted in early Yeats and in King Arthur. Owen was able to see Edinburgh as a magical uninhabited space of rocks and ruins:

It is worthy of mention that we have been in mist for 3 days: a gloriously luminous mist at times. I saw Holyrood on Sunday Afternoon (being alone on Salisbury Crags), a floating mirage in gold mist. A sight familiar enough in dreams and poems, but which I never thought possible in these islands. It was the picture <u>of</u> a picture; if you understand. I don't.[47]

In Owen's Birkenhead days, Liverpool's Walker Gallery, which he visited, possessed Daguerre's Romantic *The Ruins of Holyrood Chapel*, while with the gloriously luminous mist he was recalling Coleridge's 'Dejection: An Ode': 'This light, this glory, this fair luminous mist, / This beautiful and beauty-making power'.

Owen might have been in dejection at times, remembering the war, but he enjoyed Craiglockhart, where the nightmares abated, and so did his stammer. It did him good to be active, and, at a time when the natural reaction to trauma would have been to hide away like a wounded animal, he benefited from company. Owen remained rather solitary by inclination but Craiglockhart forced him to be part of a community.

Rather than seeing the place as a hospital or a loony-bin, Owen called it his 'free-and-easy Oxford' (indeed, the building has since become a university). In May 1917, before arriving at Craiglockhart, he wrote that he had met 'a Trinity College (Oxford) boy';[48] now he had his own chance to experience collegiate life, but one where scholarly pedantry was eschewed. He gave a talk on botany entitled 'Do Plants Think?' in which he referred to Oxford and pedantic academics, and once more mentioned Oxford's expulsion of Shelley.[49] Not going to university might have been the making of Wilfred Owen, and it is possible to argue that if he had gone to university he would not have written his war poetry – could the varsity man have written 'Dulce et Decorum Est'? – and free-and-easy Craiglockhart would not have sent Shelley down. Arthur Brock, educated at Edinburgh University, played the role of a tutor, and it was Brock who believed that 'our work must be constructive and productive, not merely critical and academic'.[50] More than a conventional university, Craiglockhart was close to the 'Bardic College' that, later in the century, the poet W. H. Auden would imagine as the ideal place for the training of poets. This is what he proposed:

1. In addition to English, at least one ancient language, probably Greek or Hebrew, and two modern languages.
2. Thousands of lines of poetry in these languages to be learnt by heart.
3. Instruction in prosody, rhetoric and comparative philology.
4. The only critical exercise would be the writing of pastiche and parody. All critical writing, other than historical or textual, would be banned from the college library.

5. Courses in mathematics, natural history, geology, meteorology, archaeology, mythology, liturgies and cooking.
6. Every student would be expected to take personal charge of a domestic animal and a garden plot.[51]

These principles were as good as met by Craiglockhart. For instance, Owen was not only taking an interest in Ancient Greek, but also trying to learn German, a curious choice in wartime, perhaps, but he had fancied learning the language before the war. Pastiche and parody played a significant part in his writing at this time, including a jokey contribution to *The Hydra*, his 'Extracte from the Chronicles of Wilfred de Salope, Knight', describing hospital life in medievalish language. Like Auden, who had a lifelong love of the sciences, Owen was quite capable of combining an artistic sensibility with scientific pursuits like the Field Club's botany; neither poet felt the need to take sides. He was learning poetry, yet probably not thousands of lines by heart, but he also had to learn lines for the stage. In early August he was given the role of Mr Wallcomb in Craiglockhart's production of *Lucky Durham*, an Edwardian comedy that gave Owen the chance to tread the boards for the first time (although he had long been a manner of performer, and as a child he used to pretend to be a clergyman, conducting services in the sitting room). Theatricals were popular at Craiglockhart and Owen had a long-standing interest in plays, both the highbrow and the low; neither was he averse to playing a part, trying out new identities. He described Edinburgh Castle as having 'the appearance of a huge canvas scenic device',[52] as if just living in Edinburgh was a performance. He tried to write a play of his own, although it no longer exists and doesn't seem to have been a very serious enterprise – he was playing at being a playwright.

Owen even took on the editorship of the magazine *The Hydra* (for six issues from 21 July) when Brock encouraged him to become involved in its production. The magazine was not a very physical activity – although Owen did see swimming as the secret of his productivity as the editor, because a swim 'never fails to give me a Greek feeling of energy and elemental life'[53] – but the magazine was a way for Brock to make his ideas known, and it placed an emphasis on the local environment and fostered a sense of community while also recording all the activities that were taking place. 'Back to the land' was a refrain in *The Hydra* under Owen, but by publishing poetry and fiction it gave him a chance to present Craiglockhart as a nest of singing birds. Through its production Owen got to know other officers of a literary bent. The most significant was a Scotsman, Lieutenant J. B. Salmond of the 7th Fife Battalion of the Black Watch, one of the most dashing and heroic of Scottish regiments, himself a sportsman, like the young soldier in 'Disabled', although, unlike that Scotsman, he was also a university graduate and a man of letters. Salmond attended 500-year-old St Andrews University before following his father into journalism, working for the *Daily Mail* and *The Boy's Own Paper* – his writing was very much of the derring-do type with 'gallant men of action',[54] games and the military a speciality. With Owen he discussed 'many mighty things and men'.[55] He was a man who could cry 'Play up, play up, and play the game'.[56] Salmond was also something of a poet, and would later write his own war poem using 'Noble and sweet to die for Fatherland' (a translation of 'Dulce et decorum est pro patria mori') but without disapproval or doubt.

At Craiglockhart one morning in mid August, Owen went round to the room of another poet, who later recalled his first meeting with Wilfred Owen:

A favourable first impression was made by the fact that he had under his arm several copies of *The Old Huntsman*. He had come, he said, hoping that I would be so gracious as to inscribe them for himself and some of his friends. He spoke with a slight stammer, which was no unusual thing in that neurosis-pervaded hospital. My leisurely, commentative method of inscribing the books enabled him to feel more at home with me. He had a charming honest smile, and his manners – he stood at my elbow rather as though conferring with a superior officer – were modest and ingratiating.

He gave me the names of his friends first. When it came to his own
I found myself writing one that has since gained a notable place on
the roll of English poets – Wilfred Owen.[57]

Owen reported that the sun blazed into his room 'making his purple
dressing suit of a brilliance'.[58] He had a soft spot for imperial purple
and if he makes the moment sound like a painting it is indeed worthy
of one, just as there are paintings depicting the moments when Robert
Burns met Sir Walter Scott, and Dante met Beatrice; for this was
Siegfried Sassoon of the Royal Welch Fusiliers, who had arrived at
Craiglockhart on 23 July. *The Old Huntsman and Other Poems* had been
published on 3 May, and among the poems in the collection were
'Golgotha', 'Arms and the Man', 'Died of Wounds' and 'The Death-Bed'
– 'The Death-Bed' was one of eight poems from the collection that
were also included in *Georgian Poetry 1916-17* (1917), and Owen called
it 'a piece of perfect art'.[59] But it was the following collection, *Counter-
Attack and Other Poems*, a year later, that contained the really angry
poems that Sassoon is now known for – 'The General', 'Glory of
Women', 'The Fathers', 'Suicide in the Trenches' – and in that collec-
tion Sassoon's 'Survivors', dated October 1917, described Craiglockhart:

No doubt they'll soon get well; the shock and strain
  Have caused their stammering, disconnected talk.
Of course they're 'longing to go out again,' –
  These boys with old, scared faces, learning to walk.
They'll soon forget their haunted nights; their cowed
  Subjection to the ghosts of friends who died, –
Their dreams that drip with murder; and they'll be proud
  Of glorious war that shatter'd all their pride . . .
Men who went out to battle, grim and glad;
Children, with eyes that hate you, broken and mad.[60]

He arrived at Craiglockhart having made his name less as a poet
than as a public protestor against the war, a refusenik who was discussed

in Parliament and sent to Craiglockhart as an alternative to a military prison. 'A Soldier's Declaration' had been written in June and published in July:

> I am making this statement as an act of wilful defiance of military authority, because I believe that the War is being deliberately prolonged by those who have the power to end it:I am a soldier, convinced that I am acting on behalf of soldiers. I believe that this War, upon which I entered as a war of defence and liberation, has now become a war of aggression and conquest. I believe that the purposes for which I and my fellow-soldiers entered upon this War should have been so clearly stated as to have made it impossible for them to be changed without our knowledge, and that, had this been done, the objects which actuated us would now be attainable by negotiation.
>
> I have seen and endured the sufferings of the troops, and I can no longer be a party to prolonging those sufferings for ends which I believe to be evil and unjust.
>
> I am not protesting against the military conduct of the War, but against the political errors and insincerities for which the fighting men are being sacrificed.
>
> On behalf of those who are suffering now, I make this protest against the deception which is being practised on them. Also I believe that I may help to destroy the callous complacence with which the majority of those at home regard the continuance of the agonies which they do not share, and which they have not sufficient imagination to realise.[61]

Rather like Clint Eastwood throwing his police badge into the water at the end of *Dirty Harry*, Sassoon had, apparently, thrown away into the mouth of the Mersey, as an angry gesture, his Military Cross (not, as was sometimes believed, the medal itself, but the MC ribbon on his uniform).[62]

It was to Sassoon that Owen showed his poetry. 'Anthem for Doomed Youth', especially, has come to be an illustration of their friendship. Sassoon helped with the title, suggesting 'Doomed', which

Owen used, although the latter also resisted Sassoon's corrections, and we see in the poem not Sassoon's voice but Owen's growth into poetic maturity. Sassoon pointed out later that any emendations he recommended were made hastily in uncongenial surroundings and he only saw the poem in something close to its final form; also that it was 'the first occasion on which I was able to hail him as my equal'.[63] Written in September, 'Anthem for Doomed Youth' is one of Owen's most famous poems, and a poem that shows the full emergence of a voice that, like Sassoon's declaration, speaks for those who suffered at the Front:

> What passing-bells for these who die as cattle?
> 　– Only the monstrous anger of the guns.
> 　Only the stuttering rifles' rapid rattle
> Can patter out their hasty orisons.
> No mockeries now for them; no prayers nor bells;
> 　Nor any voice of mourning save the choirs, –
> The shrill, demented choirs of wailing shells;
> 　And bugles calling for them from sad shires.
>
> What candles may be held to speed them all?
> 　Not in the hands of boys but in their eyes
> Shall shine the holy glimmers of goodbyes.
> 　The pallor of girls' brows shall be their pall;
> Their flowers the tenderness of patient minds,
> And each slow dusk a drawing-down of blinds.

So often quoted and anthologised, so often studied at school, so often treated as a straightforward cry against the war, this is in fact no such thing, nor is it a rejection of Christianity. It has a Catholic air, which owes something to France and to Owen's time in Bordeaux (a draft uses 'priest words' and 'requiem') – those 'passing-bells' belong to Roman Catholicism, where they are sounded after death in order to encourage prayers for the soul of the dead person, and also, contrary to the usual interpretations of the poem, sounded while a person is dying. And while it is not straightforwardly a rejection of the Church of England, it does reflect Owen's thoughts about the contrast between evangelical Christianity and Catholicism, such as this remark from May 1917:

> The evangelicals have fled from a few Candles, discreet incense, serene altars, mysterious music, harmonious ritual to powerful electric-lighting, overheated atmosphere, palm-tree platforms, grand pianos, loud and animated music, extempore ritual; but I cannot see that they are any nearer to the Kingdom.[64]

The poem argues that the dead deserve the full attention of the Church, ceremonial and lavish. The pity for the soldiers is there, the sorrow at the slaughter, but this is not a declaration against the war – unlike Sassoons's declaration, it could not be paraphrased as 'Finished with the War'. Ultimately, the poem's concern is religious and aesthetic: it asks for beauty, it asks for bells, orisons, choirs, prayers, candles and flowers. The lives of the men in uniform are worthy of beauty. Just because there is a war on, we must mourn properly, and still sing.

The Prime Minister David Lloyd George, had made a similar argument a year earlier, in August 1917, as Minister for War, when he addressed the National Eisteddfod at Aberystwyth with a much-publicised speech, in which he dismissed the argument that the Eisteddfod should not be held during wartime:

> Why should we not sing during war? Why, especially, should we not sing at this stage of the War? The blinds of Britain are not down yet, nor are they likely to be. The honour of Britain is not dead, her might is not broken, her destiny is not fulfilled, her ideals are not shattered by her enemies. She is more than alive; she is more potent, she is greater than she ever was. Her dominions are wider, her influence is deeper, her purpose is more exalted than ever. Why should

her children not sing? I know war means suffering, war means sorrow. Darkness has fallen on many a devoted household, but it has been ordained that the best singer amongst the birds of Britain should give its song in the night, and according to legend that sweet song is one of triumph over pain.[65]

This speech seems to have influenced Owen's poem, especially the poem's last line. Owen took an interest in Lloyd George, and his father was a great admirer of the Prime Minister, partly because Lloyd George was Welsh. Owen was referring to Lloyd George when he reported in January 1917 that 'if there is any power whom the Soldiery execrate more than another it is that of our distinguished countryman'.[66]

CHAPTER 11

Modern People

Yet 'the world is a pleasant place'
I can hear your voice repeat,
While the sun shone in your face
Last summer in Princes Street.
EDWIN MUIR, 'For Ann Scott-Moncrieff, 1914–1943'[1]

I spoke; and at once the Crusaders have multiplied to infinity. Villages
and towns are now deserted. You will scarcely find one man for every
seven women. Everywhere you see widows whose husbands are still alive.
ST BERNARD of CLAIRVAUX[2]

THROUGH the late summer of 1917, Owen's friendship with
Sassoon developed, with Sassoon providing advice to the junior
poet – Sassoon was the senior man not only in their poetic careers but
also in age, class, education, height and military experience. He referred
to Owen as 'my little friend', 'an interesting little chap', 'perceptibly
provincial'.[3] Born in 1886, Sassoon had attended Marlborough College
and Clare College; Cambridge; he had a private income from his
wealthy family; he had acquired influential and literary friends at an
early age, including Edmund Gosse and Edward Marsh; and at the
Front he had shown incredible bravery, being recommended for the
Victoria Cross. In other ways they were kindred spirits, in terms, for
instance, of their need for subtitude; and they were both close to their

mothers (Sassoon had not known his father very well before he died in 1895). Owen told his mother that he and Sassoon 'have followed parallel trenches all our lives, and have more friends in common, authors I mean, than most people can boast of in a lifetime'.[4] Owen would describe Sassoon as the dearest of all friends. He underwent no Damascene conversion at Craiglockhart, but meeting Sassoon was certainly an important moment in his life.

He was strong enough to resist some of Sassoon's guidance, but 'The Dead-Beat' was written 'in Sassoon's style' and was begun on 22 August – it employs Sassoonish bluntness and his anger at injustice, and shows Owen's desire to capture the speech of the common soldier and the true trench experience:

He dropped, – more sullenly than wearily,
Lay stupid like a cod, heavy like meat,
And none of us could kick him to his feet;
– Just blinked at my revolver, blearily;
– Didn't appear to know a war was on,
Or see the blasted trench at which he stared.
'I'll do 'em in,' he whined. 'If this hand's spared,
I'll murder them, I will.'

That is how the poem begins, and it ends with 'Next day I heard the Doc's well-whiskied laugh: / "That scum you sent last night soon died. Hooray!"' Owen's 'Conscious' is similar to 'The Death-Bed' in *The Old Huntsman*; 'The Next War' begins with lines by Sassoon as an epigraph; 'Wild with All Regrets' is dedicated to Sassoon. Other poems were less Sassoonish and Sassoon's greatest influence was probably the confidence and excitement that he gave to Owen, who worshipped his fellow poet and had found the kind of literary friendship that he had hoped to find at Oxford. However, Owen was undoubtedly encouraged to adopt a greater realism and directness. Sassoon admitted that 'My only claimable influence was that I stimulated him towards writing with compassionate and challenging realism. [. . .] My encouragement was opportune, and I can claim to have given him a lively incentive'.[5] Realism and directness was to be found in Sassoon's recent poetry, but also, as Sassoon saw after the war, in Owen's letters to his mother from the Front before he met Sassoon. Owen's letters achieve Matthew Arnold's aim for literature, that it should see the object in itself as it really is, seeing war with warts and all, refusing to jack war up to a romantic or heroic level.

Faced with the relationship between Sassoon and Owen, we might not call it homosexual, but it would be appropriate to think of D. H. Lawrence's contemporaneous remarks about male friendship:

> Not something homosexual, surely? Indeed, you have misunder-stood me – besides this term is so imbedded in its own period. I do not belong to a world where that word has meaning. Comradeship perhaps? No, not that – too much love about it – no, not even in the Calamus sense, not comradeship – not manly love. Then what Nietzsche describes – the friend in whom the world standeth complete, a capsule of the good – the creating friend, who hath always a complete world to bestow. Well, in a way. That means in my words, choose as your friend the man who has centre.

'I believe tremendously in friendship between man and man, a pledging of men to each other inviolably.'[6] Sassoon could not insist too strongly that the relationship was '<u>ideal</u>', that they were 'brother poets': 'It was natural, unimpeded friendship and artistic collaboration.'[7] Sassoon and Owen – or the schoolboy's elision, Owenansassoon – have been treated as one of the great partnerships of the modern age, something to rival Lennon and McCartney, Burgess and Maclean, Fred and Ginger, Edward Thomas and Robert Frost, Ezra Pound and T. S. Eliot. Indeed, the nineteenth-century poets Owen wanted to emulate often came in pairs: Wordsworth and Coleridge, Keats and Shelley, Byron and Shelley, Arnold and Clough, the Brownings. Nor would it be inap-propriate to liken them to Laurel and Hardy or Morecambe and Wise, for Sassoon recalled Owen's sense of humour, noting 'We were never solemn with one another'.[8] Owen, though, preferred a Renaissance example, seeing Sassoon as Don Quixote and himself as the famous Spaniard's servant, Sancho Panza, a perceptive comparison given that Cervantes's comic romance laughs at chivalry and Quixote's mind has been disordered by chivalric romances, a scenario not a million miles from Craiglockhart and poems like 'Dulce et Decorum Est'. Of course, partnerships are not always what they seem. Owen had no intention of being a 'sort of sub. SS',[9] and neither is ambitious Sancho Panza a sort of miniature version of his master; in fact, he is often shown to be cleverer and more worldly-wise than Quixote. Owen was already a poet when he met Sassoon, and Owen's poetry remains his own. Sassoon was keen to point out that he hadn't turned Owen into a war poet. And, for his part, Sassoon once admitted to finding Owen 'embarrassing'.[10]

Looking at a poem so Sassoonish as 'The Dead-Beat', one can see other influences at work too: even Charlie Chaplin, the little tramp, haunts the poem. On 21 August Owen paid his second visit to Sassoon, and the following day wrote that 'The Dead-Beat' was written after leaving Sassoon. On 22 August, Owen also reported seeing 'Ch. Chaplin again'. A 'dead-beat' is a tramp or good-for-nothing. Owen had already pointed out that he was a Chaplin fan. Owen had professed to be unimpressed with this 'mechanical entertainment',[11] but, like millions of others, he fell for Chaplin's tramp down on his luck. Films were shown to the enthusiastic crowd at Craiglockhart, despite the misgivings of Brock and Rivers, and Chaplin films were advertised in *The Hydra*. In the draft of 'Disabled', the Scotsman was a cinema-goer: 'Ah! he was looked at when he used to stand / Each evening outside cinemas'.[12] Brock had complained that the cinema was a distraction from reality, offering 'brighter prospects by far than the real world', and considered the escapism of melodramas especially harmful to the shell-shocked soldier,[13] but Chaplin appealed to soldiers in a different way, offering them one of life's sufferers. Indeed, the unspoken nature of silent films seemed to capture the muted, withdrawn nature of Craiglockhart patients, including an untalkative, occasionally stuttering, Owen.

Some lines of the original version were adapted into eight lines that appeared in *The Hydra* on 1 September 1917. These may constitute the first poem (by a major poet) to mention Chaplin:

Who cares the Kaiser frowns imperially?
The exempted shriek at Charlie Chaplin's smirk.
The *Mirror* shows how Tommy smiles at work.
And if girls sigh, they sigh ethereally,
And wish the Push would get on less funereally.
Old Bill enlarges on his little jokes.
Punch is still grinning at the Derby blokes.
And Belloc prophecies of last year, serially.[14]

Having been through the thick of it, Owen was now eager to criticise the Home Front, and complain that those at home had little idea of what the war entailed. Even his beloved Belloc had blotted his copybook by holding forth belligerently on a war he was watching from afar. No doubt Owen had been discussing Belloc with Sassoon, who wrote on 21 June that:

A long statement of the war-aims etc by Belloc in *Land and Water* leaves me quite unconvinced. He argues from the point of view of British rectitude; and it is that which I am questioning. Worst of all, he argues on the assumption that 'the next few months' will bring a military decision; he has done this since 1915, so one cannot put much faith in him.[15]

*

In Edinburgh, through a fellow Craiglockhartian called Charles Mayes, who was another of Brock's patients and had been at the hospital since March, Owen got to know not just modern films but also modern people:

Mayes introduced me to some 'modern' people, and I went there yesterday afternoon: – two men and their wives, who share a big house in a fine Georgian Crescent in Edinburgh.

The ladies wear short hair and decorative gowns, and think themselves artistic. But yesterday they had to mind their babies, which being self-centred, unmannerly blobs of one to three years bored me utterly.

The drawing room was worth seeing with its black carpetless floor, white walls, solitary superb picture, grand piano, Empire sofa and so on.

I think they are genuine people – the more so because they adore their progeny than because they profess to admire my poetry.[16]

This was Leonard and Maidie Gray, and Francis (known by his middle name, Eric) and Maria Steinthal, although Eric was mostly away serving in the army, and the two young couples lived at 21 St Bernard's Crescent, the Georgian crescent where John Duncan also lived – or, rather, it was two crescents opposite each other, creating an eye-shaped square that isn't square, with an eyelet-like islet of garden in the middle. Owen would soon be writing about a perfect little dinner at the Grays', an evening of 'extraordinary fellowship in All the Arts'.[17] This was artistic Edinburgh, a Scottish equivalent of Bloomsbury, a Scottish bohemia, even though some of the buildings were remarkably grand.

Maria (née Zimmern) was German, but the German-sounding Steinthals, of Frankfurt-ancestry, were from Yorkshire, which is where Martin, one of the babies Owen encountered, had been born in 1916, and it was in the large Yorkshire home, designed by Norman Shaw, of Eric's well-to-do artistically inclined parents that G. K. Chesterton often met Father John O'Connor, the inspiration for the fictional detective Father Brown.[18] Chesterton, a close friend of the Steinthals, had written a masque for them in 1904:

Upon this place in after time shall stand
A splendid house that shall be called St John's.
This glade of which I am king, this Yorkshire vale
Of this hereafter Steinthal shall be King
Here, on this barren glade on which we tread,
Steinthal shall have a garden[19]

As in the Pyrenees, Owen was entering a glamorous, cultured world that he had not known as a child, and by now he had more confidence and status when moving in these rarefied circles. He could boast to his mother that Eric Steinthal had been to Oxford, and it would have been through the Steinthals that Owen managed to get hold of some original drawings by Chesterton for the November *Hydra*. Maria Steinthal was herself an artist and was keen to use Owen as a model. As Owen would write in 'Disabled', 'There was an artist silly for his face, / For it was younger than his youth, last year'.

The resulting picture has not survived but Maidie (Mary) Gray (née Scott) and her sister Elsie, whom Owen also got to know, had proved to be more successful models – they are the subject of a beautiful portrait by Eric Robertson, which had been exhibited at the Royal Scottish Academy in 1915. Maidie also appears in Robertson's *The Daughters of Beauty*, which was exhibited at the RSA in 1917 and depicts an array of women gathered together near St Bernard's Crescent. Robertson was serving with an ambulance unit in the war by this time, but Owen met his wife Cecile Walton – another of the beauties in *The Daughters of Beauty* – who was the daughter of a Glasgow School painter, an excellent artist herself and one of the St Bernard's Crescent circle, having lived at number 21 before the Grays. This group of modern people would play a significant part in Owen's Edinburgh life; according to Leonard's younger brother, Cecil, this group and their friends constituted 'the few intelligent people who lived in Edinburgh – for however lovely a city she may be, and no one admires her more than I, the inhabitants are, for the most part – or were in my youth, at least – the most provincial, puritanical, Philistine community on the face of the earth'.[20] Cecil himself was sojourning in Cornwall that summer, where his neighbour and close friend was D. H. Lawrence, who, with his German wife and anti-war sentiments, 'was also in flight from a hostile and unsympathetic world'.[21]

Like the Lawrences, the Steinthals faced difficulties because of their German connections, and these modern people of Edinburgh shared, too, some of Owen's feelings about the war, as can be seen in Cecile Walton's letter to Sassoon on 18 August 1917:

As admirers of your writing we find it obvious from your poems that your present attitude of mind is the result of a perfectly clear evolution of thought and certainly not the result of any physical shock from which you may suffer. This must be plain to any sensitive mind even though it is not in sympathy – as we are – with your position.

The fact that you have proved that those who have courage in the field are capable of Pacifism, while convincing many, will still leave untouched those whom no logical proof on earth will turn from this aggressive passion and who therefore attribute your views to mental strain.[22]

And yet this was a circle of friends that didn't include Sassoon himself: he was referred to by the circle but not known personally. In fact, it was a very feminine group – Owen also befriended Maidie's mother, and Maria's mother-in-law – and it was the effusive but sincere young women that he would become especially close to, women who belonged to the happier Edinburgh of 'Disabled':

About this time Town used to swing so gay
When glow-lamps budded in the light blue trees,
And girls glanced lovelier as the air grew dim, –
In the old times, before he threw away his knees.
Now he will never feel again how slim
Girls' waists are, or how warm their subtle hands.

This was a dramatic change from the men's world of Craiglockhart and the trenches. If Hercules and Antaeus was the story of Craiglockhart, then St Bernard's Crescent might have been that of Hylas and the Nymphs, the story of Hercules's companion who was abducted by the beautiful water nymphs and fell in love with them.

Both Maidie and Elsie took a shine to Owen. One day in October, Elsie gave Owen a 'tête-à-tête dinner', becoming 'very personal during the meal'. Describing the dinner to his mother, Owen was keen to point out that nothing happened, rather ungallantly saying that Elsie was 'some four feet high'.[23] Owen had more time for Maidie, the more beautiful of the sisters, describing her as really witty, and she had already fallen in love with him. She gushed over him and gave him presents, and talked about him excitedly to her friends. On one occasion, the friends went for dinner at the luxurious Caledonian Hotel, a place of marble and gold and deep-pile carpets, where, from the high ceiling in the dining room, the electric chandeliers picked out dashing officers with beautiful ladies. It was there that Maidie, with a certain amount of fuss, passed a note to Cecile saying that Cecile must be nice to Owen, 'a dear a real dear'. No doubt he was and she was nice to him, because the dinner went swimmingly while Maidie grew confessional. Owen was charming, even if his conversation was based on 'Oh rather' and 'I should just think so'.[24] He is unlikely to have been thoroughly relaxed in the company of a beautiful stranger in such a ceremonial context. Owen eventually had to return to Craiglockhart, and other members of the party wandered home alongside the river:

> It was a long way round to St Bernards [sic] Crescent but it gave Maidie ample opportunity to embark upon a most remarkable story concerning her intense but purely spiritual passion for the young officer Owen, and of his intense but respectful passion for her. Maidie was in tears by this time with her nose buried in the early Victorian bouquet which Cecile had given her earlier in the evening: 'did Mr Nicholson understand her did Owen understand', sobbed Maidie. 'She had the best husband in the world the very best but well – you see Leonard and Maria are in love with each other'. It is 'all quite spiritual theres [sic] no sex about it', Maidie went on, 'all emotion – but Owen is so charming you can't help loving him don't you love him Mr Nicholson? don't you Cecile'. And so Maidie whimpered on.[25]

Back at St Bernard's Crescent, Cecile Walton took off all her clothes, put on a scanty Egyptian outfit that she had created for herself, and danced rather revealingly to the gramophone; thereby providing a live performance of the 'pagan brazenness rather than parlour propriety' that the art of Walton and Robertson became known for.[26] That evening their friend Frank Nicholson, a librarian who gave Owen some German lessons, saw more of Cecile Walton than he might have expected to.

The group were very 'modern' in their sexual behaviour – not only were Maidie and Leonard unfaithful, but Eric Robertson and Cecile were too; Eric Robertson in particular being known as something of an immoralist.[27] Leonard seems to have taken an interest in both Maria and Cecile. Number 21 St Bernard's Crescent was quite the bohemian household:

> Maria, who was staying with the Grays while her husband was away in the army, came down from the upper floor to talk to Cecile. Maidie had already written to Cecile to say that she simply loved Maria and while she, Maidie, did all the house-keeping, Maria went out to work; and Maria and Leonard were deeply in love which made 'everything comfy'. Cecile, having now met Maria, was not at all sure about this and when she discovered that Maidie had two young army officers vying for her affection, she concluded that all Maidie wanted was for Leonard and Maria to give her a good excuse for a 'little nonsense' with the officers.[28]

Not long after, Eric Steinthal returned on leave and moved his wife and child into a hotel, leaving Maidie in tears. Walton had also 'received a ridiculous letter from Leonard Gray asking her to spend a weekend with him in the country' and 'wondered whether it might be that Maidie wanted to take her precious Owen away and Leonard was not keen to be left out on a limb'.[29] Owen's rather chaste love poem 'Spells and Incantation', with its focus on jewels, may possibly be addressed to Maidie – in September he reported that he had a jolly afternoon with Mrs Gray, who wore weird clothes and some priceless rings, and they rummaged over a delightful old curiosity shop, but there's no need to conclude that Owen had an affair with Maidie, although there was clearly a flirtatious intimacy between them. Maidie was an emotional, rather sensitive creature, the type that could fall in love easily, and Owen was wary of visiting her if they would be in the house alone, but her relationship with Owen was significant for them both, and he would stay in touch with her after leaving Craiglockhart. Although this was another 'Affair Léger', in this case he could stay friends with his admirer. Ultimately, Maidie saw 'her precious Owen'[30] as essentially sexless, like a child. To Eric Robertson, Cecile Walton described the twenty-four-year-old as a 'very young boy'.[31]

Owen found time to enjoy the company of children while he was at Craiglockhart. He spent some happy hours teaching at an Edinburgh school, called Tynecastle School, and, near Craiglockhart, was blessed with 'the conviviality' of children at Colinton:

Someday, I must tell how we sang, shouted, whistled and danced through the dark lanes through Colinton; and how we laughed till the meteors showered around us, and we fell calm under the winter stars. And some of us saw the pathway of the spirits for the first time.[32]

He got to know the Newboult family of Leith too, who knew his mother, and befriended the Newboult children, taking young Arthur Newboult to Edinburgh Zoo, and buying him his first penknife. Arthur is the subject of the poem 'Winter Song':

The browns, the olives, and the yellows died,
And were swept up to heaven; where they glowed
Each dawn and set of sun till Christmastide.
And when the land lay pale for them, pale-snowed,
Fell back, and down the snow-drifts flamed and flowed.

From off your face, into the winds of winter,
The sun-brown and the summer-gold are blowing;

But they shall gleam again with spiritual glinter,
When paler beauty on your brows falls snowing,
And through those snows my looks shall be soft-going.

Arthur's fourteen-year-old sister Mary (the age that Nenette Léger
would have been by then) also acquired Owen as a friend: 'It was just
wonderful for me to find someone like Wilfred to be interested in a
raw, awkward schoolgirl such as I was'.[33] Owen read his poetry to her,
in a voice she found beautiful, and he helped her with her English
homework, bringing the classic authors to life for her – Owen was still
in love with the great writers as people as much as for their writing.
Mary Newboult noted that his ability to convey to her the personalities
of the writers came from a deep interest in, and compassion for, other
people.

*

With Maidie Gray Owen got to see not just the Caledonian Hotel but
also 'Lower Edinburgh', going slum-visiting into some of the worst
areas of poverty in Britain:

> We were by then mingling with a crowd following a poor (sober)
> woman who was being arrested. Tomaso was out, but we found a
> suitable object of compassion in his (unmistakably Italian) boy who
> had impaled his leg on a railing-spike. We did not inspect the leg.
> The smell of carbolic was strong enough under the clothes.[34]

This was almost certainly the Grassmarket, where the Italian commu-
nity lived – a corner of the Old Town that had been impoverished for
centuries and had absorbed many Italian immigrants from the 1880s
onwards. It was a world that Muriel Spark (born in Edinburgh in 1918)
later described in *The Prime of Miss Jean Brodie*: 'the reeking network of
slums which the Old Town constituted'. Like Jean Brodie and Sandy
Stranger, Maidie Gray and Owen ventured into the slums, peering at

the squalor of the Canongate, the Grassmarket, the Lawnmarket, 'names which betokened a misty region of crime and desperation'.[35] Looking back on her friendship with Owen, Maidie recalled that the two of them often visited the Italians in the slums, 'where again, despite his silence, gentle gravity, and reserve, Wilfred was adored – there is no other word for it'.[36] She saw that 'The bond which drew us together was an intense pity for suffering humanity – a need to alleviate it, wherever possible, and an inability to shirk the sharing of it, even when this seemed useless'; and that this was 'the keynote of Wilfred's character; indeed it was, simply, Wilfred'.[37] He shared her acute sensitiveness, tenderness and sympathy, and expressed these qualities with a reticent playfulness.

The pursuit of suitable objects of compassion by Owen and the kind-hearted Maidie Gray seems to have helped to produce 'Six O'Clock in Princes Street':

> In twos and threes, they have not far to roam,
>   Crowds that thread eastward, gay of eyes;
> Those seek no further than their quiet home,
>   Wives, walking westward, slow and wise.
>
> Neither should I go fooling over clouds,
>   Following gleams unsafe, untrue,
> And tiring after beauty through star-crowds,
>   Dared I go side by side with you;
>
> Or be you in the gutter where you stand,
>   Pale rain-flawed phantom of the place,
> With news of all the nations in your hand,
>   And all their sorrows in your face.

Brock held that 'It is when our heads are high in the clouds of unpracticality, our feet clean off the earth, that the Hercules of war will overcome us',[38] but this poem is not so much about getting back to the land as about connecting with the downtrodden fauna of a city street.

Edinburgh's Princes Street is one of the great streets of Europe, admired by Owen and millions of other people over the years, and the Caledonian Hotel is at one end. Statues, gardens, the Scott Monument, St John's Church and neoclassical galleries adorned one side, while Mammon owned the other: there, on the ground floor, shops wore snow-white awnings. In Stevenson's *St Ives*, the hero can see Princes Street from his imprisonment in Edinburgh Castle:

> my eye (even while I thought) kept following the movement of the passengers on Princes Street, as they passed briskly to and fro – met, greeted, and bowed to each other – or entered and left the shops, which are in that quarter, and, for a town of the Britannic provinces, particularly fine.[39]

With Mrs Gray, one of the wives heading westward in his poem – St Bernard's Crescent being at the west end of the New Town – Owen sought out poverty, taking gifts of food, but he was troubled by the reserve and nervousness that Maidie and her friends noticed in him, a characteristic reserve that had been intensified by his recent trench experiences. Owen was probably recalling Oscar Wilde's line that 'We are all in the gutter, but some of us are looking at the stars'.[40] 'Six O'Clock in Princes Street' represents the clash between the well-off St Bernard's Crescent crowd and the poor they tried to help, and in doing so captures a social conscience and a sense of guilt. He was no longer in Hell, and had acquired wealthy, glamorous friends, while others still suffered every day and as a way of life. This guilt would feed into his later poems. Appropriately, he would later give Maidie Gray an original manuscript of 'Miners', a poem of compassion for poor unfortunate lads at home and abroad.

Along with the guilt there was a fear of his own capacity for cowardice. To many people in the forces and at home, having 'bad nerves' or being nervous was frequently held to be the same as a loss of nerve; being 'highly strung' to be the same as cowardly. 'Neurasthenia' and 'shell shock' were to many just euphemisms for cowardice, mere tricks for saving officers from disgrace and punishment. Lord Moran, a sensitive and highly able doctor who won the MC at the Somme, argued that once the name shell shock was coined there was an escape route for the man who was afraid:

> The pressure of opinion in the battalion – the idea stronger than fear – was eased by giving fear a respectable name. When the social slur was removed and the military risks were abolished the weaklings may have decided in cold blood to malinger, or perhaps when an alternative was held out the suggestion of safety was too much for their feeble will. The resolve to stay with the battalion had been weakened, the conscience was relaxed, the path out of danger was made easy.[41]

Owen's father seems to have worried about whether his son had lost his nerve, and showed some reluctance to visit his son at Edinburgh, whereas Susan did visit him there. A number of Owen's war poems take on courage and cowardice, especially in relation to the Home Front, as in 'The Dead-Beat' with its thought that 'his pluck's all gone, / Dreaming of all the valiant, that *aren't* dead'. In 'Six O'Clock in Princes Street' Owen accuses himself of cowardice – not on the battlefield but at home. He should 'dare' to go side by side with the urchin; and that this might be daring in the context of a war is somewhat absurd, like T. S. Eliot's 'Do I dare to eat a peach?' in 'The Love Song of J. Alfred Prufrock', which was published in 1917, but in fact courage was needed for even a stroll down Princes Street, as a contribution to *The Hydra* by 'An Inmate' reveals:

> Now if I walk in Princes Street,
> Or smile at friends I chance to meet,
> Or, perhaps, a joke with laughter greet
> I'm stared at.[42]

The officers stuck out because they had to wear blue armbands at all times, but the stares were also likely to suggest that cowardly men skiving off fighting at the Front should not be enjoying themselves in Edinburgh.

The men of Craiglockhart also had to find the courage to confront the war they had fought in on the Home Front. Owen's desire to befriend the newspaper-seller in 'Six O'Clock in Princes Street', and his slum-visiting, go hand in hand with his determination to recollect and record the trenches. 'Following gleams' is an allusion to a Tennyson poem about Merlin; tiring after beauty and fooling over clouds suggest a head-in-the-clouds detachment from life and a refusal to see its horrors; the newspaper-seller, while not directly connected to the war, is carrying news of the conflict in his hand and his own poverty and sorrow etched on his face. In the gutter, he stands in for the soldier in the trenches. The public's seeming indifference to the poor fellow mirrors their apparent indifference to what the private soldier has had to endure.

In the drafts of 'Six O'Clock in Princes Street', the poem was more clearly about a desire to confront the reality of the war. Owen observed that the people of Edinburgh knew the war as simply 'handsome men in kilts', 'sugarless tea', 'Gas-driven busses [sic]' and 'a chalking of the pavement'.[43] The Edinburgh resident was unable truly to know what the war was like, partly because Edinburgh was so many miles further from the Western Front. London was prey to Zeppelin raids (one began the night Owen's train left for Edinburgh), and while Edinburgh experienced some too, with Haymarket, the Grassmarket and Leith being attacked, they were not such a threat, and on the south coast of England soldiers' families and girlfriends could sometimes hear the artillery in France. Even in London, the vibrations were felt at the most intense moments of shelling, shaking David Lloyd George himself. Later, in London and elsewhere in England, Owen would feel the same frustration at the lack of understanding.

Owen's war poetry is characterised by his ability to focus not on the stars but on those in the gutter, not on the glory of the martial ideal but on those in the trench or the war hospital. He does not seem to have been keen to discuss the trenches with the St Bernard's Crescent circle – not least because they themselves had loved ones out there. They weren't the naïvely bellicose women whom both Owen and Sassoon would be angered by – women who drove men off to fight – and they didn't need to have any illusions broken. But Frank Nicholson has recorded that, man-to-man, Owen was a little more forthcoming about the war:

> he took me with him to have afternoon tea in a café, and this is the incident that stands out most clearly in my memory of him. It was really the only occasion on which he had an opportunity of speaking freely to me, and it was then that I got a hint of the effect that the horrors he had seen and heard of at the Front had made upon him. He did not enlarge upon them, but they were obviously always in his thoughts, and he wished that an obtuse world should be made sensible of them. With this object he was collecting a set of photographs exhibiting the ravages of war upon the men who took part in it – mutilations, wounds, surgical operations, and the like. He had some of these photographs with him, and I remember that he put his hand to his breast-pocket to show me them, but suddenly thought better of it and refrained. No doubt he felt that the sight of them would be painful to me, and perhaps also that such methods of propaganda were superfluous in my case.[44]

These photographs may have been Owen's poems, which he referred to as photographs because of their directness and realism, but they could also have been actual photos (which no longer exist and no one actually recalled seeing). Kodak, for instance, was advertising a cheap, small camera called the Vest Pocket Autographic Kodak ('The Soldier's Kodak')[45] and Kodak's Brownies were even cheaper, so it would not have been impossible for Owen to acquire photographs of the dead and wounded, especially if they were taken in Britain. In *The Hydra*, an advert offered 'Everything for the Photographer', and the Craiglockhart

Camera Club was very active. Other men were known to have such photographs. It is even possible that Owen used the photographs for inspiration. So the poem 'Smile, Smile, Smile' is about photography and 'the sunk-eyed wounded'.

The poet who delighted in childish play and was at home in the past became, at the same time, the poet known for his ability to record in harrowing detail the horrors of the war. In hospital at Gailly, he had read Elizabeth Barrett Browning's *Aurora Leigh*, her long poem about Italy and 'those old days of Shropshire', where she informs us that:

> Nay, if there's room for poets in this world
> A little overgrown (I think there is),
> Their sole work is to represent the age,
> Their age, not Charlemagne's – this live, throbbing age,
> That brawls, cheats, maddens, calculates, aspires,
> And spends more passion, more heroic heat,
> Betwixt the mirrors of its drawing-rooms,
> Than Roland with his knights at Roncesvalles.
> To flinch from modern varnish, coat or flounce,
> Cry out for togas and the picturesque,
> Is fatal – foolish too. King Arthur's self
> Was commonplace to Lady Guinevere;
> And Camelot to minstrels seemed as flat
> As Fleet Street to our poets.

Yet Owen retained the romantic head-in-clouds side of himself; in 'Six O'Clock in Princes Street' the realism and the romanticism seemed to exist simultaneously. It isn't quite true that the Western Front turned Owen into an angry poet of verbal documentary – not every poem from Craiglockhart, or later, is like 'Dulce et Decorum Est'. He greatly admired a painting called *Avatar* by Henry Lintott, another resident of St Bernard's Crescent and a friend of the Grays. *Avatar* is a war painting, but not the equivalent of Owen's photographs or 'Dulce et Decorum Est': Lintott's painting uses the knight in shining armour that we would associate with Tennyson, aestheticism and the Celtic Twilight and he is being carried into heaven by attendant spirits. 'Avatar' can be used generally to mean quintessence, embodiment or archetype: the knight represents all dead soldiers, or the painting is itself the embodiment of the war. It is remarkable that on 2 October Owen told his mother about visiting Lintott, 'an excellent gentleman';[46] and the first manuscript of 'Dulce et Decorum Est' is dated 8 October; it was probably the next day that he sent it to his mother; and on 14 October he told Susan Owen that a couple of days earlier he had been to see the Lintotts again – 'Lintott has reason to be proud of his work'.[47]

CHAPTER 12

The Ghost and Graves

LA VAROLE Will your lordship venture so soon to expose
yourself to the weather?
LORD FOPPINGTON Sir, I will venture as soon as I can to
expose myself to the ladies.
LA VAROLE I wish your lordship would please to keep house a
little longer; I'm afraid your honour does not well consider your
wound.
RICHARD BRINSLEY SHERIDAN, *A Trip to Scarborough*, 1777[1]

I'm Burlington Bertie
I rise at ten thirty and saunter along like a toff,
I walk down the Strand with my gloves on my hand,
Then I walk down again with them off.
W. F. HARGREAVES, '*Burlington Bertie from Bow*', 1915[2]

WHEN Wilfred Owen appeared before the Medical Board at the
end of October 1917 he was deemed to be unfit for General
Service 'permanently', unfit for a garrison or labour battalion abroad
'permanently', and unfit for Home Service for 'four months', but fit for
'Light duty of a clerical nature' and was given three weeks' leave.[3]
Sassoon was keen for Owen to spend some of his leave at Garsington
Manor near Oxford, where the generous and comical hostess was Lady
Ottoline Morrell, who invited to her home writers, intellectuals and

artists, the great and the pseudo-great. One guest, D. H. Lawrence, had seen Garsington as a moribund England:

> When I drive across this country, with autumn falling and rustling to pieces, I am so sad, for my country, for this great wave of civilization, 2,000 years, which is now collapsing, that it is hard to live. So much beauty and pathos of old things passing away and no new things coming: this house – it is England – my God, it breaks my soul – their England.[4]

Lawrence depicted arty Garsington in the as-yet-unpublished novel *Women in Love*, where Ottoline Morrell is the ridiculous Hermione Roddice, superficial, vulgar, sinister. Owen was undoubtly susceptible to old things, to country houses and to Oxford, but he ultimately decided not to go. Certainly, Owen and his poetry have never sat easily within Modernism and the avant-garde. And it is quite clear too that Owen had no desire to be an ersatz version of his friend Sassoon, or one of Sassoon's little discoveries. He didn't know that Sassoon had recently sent Ottoline Morrell *The Hydra*, saying of Owen's 'Song of Songs', a little cattily, that 'The man who wrote this brings me quantities & I have to say kind things. He will improve, I think!'[5] It is perhaps for the best that Owen ultimately chose not to go to Garsington because he would no doubt have been treated as a quaint new toy, and at Garsington he might have come under the influence of either some of the more pretentious examples of literary pond life, or the loud pacifism of the house – a political and confrontational pacifism that could have led Owen into serious trouble. It was Ottoline Morrell and the Garsington crowd who had helped to push Sassoon into his famous protest, and, not having Sassoon's background, contacts or reputation for bravery, Owen would not have been treated as leniently by the authorities as his friend was.

Instead he made a short visit to his parents in early November. His mother was thankfully no Ottoline Morrell. From Shrewsbury he admitted to Sassoon on 5 November that he was getting along with his

mother but unable to be sociable with his father (the letter describes
Sassoon as 'father-confessor').[6] In that same letter Owen announced
that he was 'getting Colvin's new *Life of Keats*, no price advertised, but
damn it, I'm to enjoy my Leave!',[7] and after making a flying visit to
London, he visited his cousin Leslie Gunston in Winchester, the city
where Keats had lived and had written 'To Autumn'. On Sunday
11 November, the day of the year that twelve months later would see
the end of the war and then for ever more be associated with remem-
brance, having taken in a Sunday concert at the Queen's Hall in
London, excited by London, Owen headed to the station, arriving at
Winchester at 8.30 p.m. Leslie was carrying out his war work at a
YMCA at nearby Hazeley Down, so there were no home comforts and
Owen slept there on a camp bed.

Owen served coffee to the men in the YMCA on the Monday
morning before lunching at Winchester, where he spent the afternoon
in the cathedral with Leslie. Keats, of course, knew the cathedral,
writing in 1819 that:

> I take a walk every day for an hour before dinner and this is gener-
> ally my walk. I go out at the back gate across one street, into the
> Cathedral yard, along a paved path, past the beautiful front of
> the Cathedral, turn to the left under a stone doorway – then I am
> on the other side of the building – which leaving behind me I pass
> on through two college-like squares seemingly built for the dwelling
> place of Deans and Prebendaries – garnished with grass and shaded
> with trees. Then I pass through one of the old city gates and then
> you are in College Street.[8]

Owen had once dreamt of being buried in Westminster Abbey, but
Winchester Cathedral is the Abbey's rival as England's Valhalla: it is
a house of God but also the symbolic home of what Lawrence had
called the 'beauty and pathos of old things'. On 12 November, as the
autumn sunlight moved along the south side of the cathedral picking
out the stained glass of one window then the next, Owen had for

company the ghosts of Egbert of Wessex, King Alfred, St Swithun, King Cnut, King Harthacnut, William Rufus, William of Wykeham, William of Waynflete, Izaak Walton, Bishop Gardiner (who died in the same year as Baron Lewis Owen), Cardinal Beaufort, and various knights, schoolmasters, soldiers. A nineteenth-century memorial to the 97th The Earl of Ulster's Regiment is a reminder that many officers and soldiers were 'killed in the trenches' before the First World War. Jane Austen died at Winchester in 1817, a century before Owen's visit, and was buried at the north side of the cathedral nave. Did Owen think of his own grave and of his own hopes for literary immortality?

Owen's poem 'A Tear Song', a poem about a chorister, in which Owen states that 'God for his glittering world, / Seeketh our tears',[9] might have been inspired by Winchester Cathedral and was drafted between November and January. The opening lines seem to capture Winchester, the longest church in England, 560 feet from east to west, the nave itself being a vast 250 feet long:

> Out of the endless nave
>   Chorus tremendous,
> While the gruff organ gave
>   Sponses stupendous.

The poem describes God's 'casket', possibly recalling the caskets of the cathedral, and even the poem's reference to Robin Hood and his merry men is not inappropriate, given that this cathedral is a remnant of Merry England.

Owen's visit to Winchester also produced 'Asleep', which was written on 14 November. Owen reported that it came from the Winchester downs, as he crossed their long backs, and he could almost see the dead lying about in the downs' hollows.[10] These downs of southern England had been loved by the Edwardians: walker-writers such as Edward Thomas and Hilaire Belloc described in affectionate detail their journeys through the downlands. Belloc's *The Old Road* (1904) describes a long walk to Winchester, and there's a remarkable passage in *The Four Men* (1912) in which Belloc contemplates death and immortality among the South Downs in November, on the Day of the Dead:

> I knew as this affection urged me that verse alone would satisfy something at least of that irremediable desire. I lay down therefore at full length upon the short grass which the sheep also love, and taking out a little stump of pencil that I had, and tearing off the back of a letter, I held my words prepared.
>   [. . .]
> 'He does not die' (I wrote) 'that can bequeath
> Some influence to the land he knows,
> Or dares, persistent, interwreath
> Love permanent with the wild hedgerows;
>   He does not die, but still remains
>   Substantiate with his darling plains.[11]

But rather than celebrating this English landscape, Owen fills it with the dead – just as Sassoon, hallucinating, saw corpses lying about on the pavements in London.[12] At the Front, he had found a tendency among the soldiers to call No Man's Land 'England';[13] now, England became No Man's Land. Consequently, he wrote a poem about a soldier in the trenches who was shot while sleeping. As Belloc hoped, this soldier becomes part of the landscape, but only by rotting into the mud.

At the end of his time in Winchester, where he had sat among the illustrious dead, contemplating Heaven and immortality, Owen wrote his 21-line poem, which ends as follows:

> Whether his deeper sleep lie shaded by the shaking
> Of great wings, and the thoughts that hung the stars,
> High-pillowed on calm pillows of God's making,
> Above these clouds, these rains, these sleets of lead,
> And these winds' scimitars,
> – Or whether yet his thin and sodden head

Confuses more and more with the low mould,
His hair being one with the grey grass
Of finished fields, and wire-scrags rusty-old,
Who knows? Who hopes? Who troubles? Let it pass!
He sleeps. He sleeps less tremulous, less cold,
Than we who wake, and waking say Alas!

At the cathedral, Owen had seen large war memorials that made use of angels and offered the idea that men who died fighting for Queen Victoria now lay shaded by the shaking of great wings and the thoughts that hung the stars, high-pillowed on calm pillows of God's making. A prominent memorial to those Hampshiremen who fell in the Boer War is topped with caring angels; another memorial shows a massive, risqué angel protecting two dashing upper-class Victorian officers. Even more unignorable is the pompous monument to Bishop Samuel Wilberforce, the Victorian enemy of evolution, who, in death, rests on an ample pillow, his bed held up by angels and his head shaded by an angel with generous wings.

A walk among the autumnal fields around Winchester had given Keats 'To Autumn' – in Keats's poem, autumn can be seen 'on a half-reaped furrow sound asleep' – and a walk into Winchester from Hazeley Down gave Owen 'Asleep'. In the second half of 'Asleep' we can also see the influence of another poet with a Winchester connection, William Collins (1721–59), a scholar at Winchester College, an ambitious, depressive graveyard poet who wrote about war. Owen owned two editions of the poems of Collins. 'Asleep' is haunted by Collins's best-known poem, a 12-line war poem, 'Ode, Written in the beginning of the Year 1746', which is usually known by the first four words of the first line, 'How sleep the Brave':

How sleep the Brave, who sink to Rest,
By all their Country's Wishes blest!
When *Spring*, with dewy Fingers cold,
Returns to deck their hallow'd Mold,

She there shall dress a sweeter Sod,
Than *Fancy*'s Feet have ever trod.

By Fairy Hands their Knell is rung,
By Forms unseen their Dirge is sung;
There *Honour* comes, a Pilgrim grey,
To bless the Turf that wraps their Clay,
And *Freedom* shall a-while repair,
To dwell, a weeping Hermit there![14]

The similarities between the two poems are many: the euphemistic sleep of death; the rhyme of mould/old/cold in Owen's poem recalling the rhyme of 'cold' and 'Mold'; 'low mould' echoing 'hallow'd Mold'; Collins's 'Sod' and Owen's 'sodden'; 'a Pilgrim grey, / To bless the Turf' and 'the grey grass / Of finished fields'; even the exclamation mark at the end of both poems. When they wrote these poems, Owen and Collins were the same age.[15]

*

Owen returned to Shrewsbury for a few more days until the end of his leave, before reporting to Scarborough on 20 November. He was not expecting to be going back to the Front again: 'I <u>think</u> I am marked Permanent Home Service'.[16] His quarters were the turreted Clarence Gardens Hotel on the town's North Bay, the quieter and more refined of Scarborough's two beaches. Between the two beaches, there were rows of boarding houses and holiday homes, with their pastoral, exotic or aspirational names. Scarborough was a major holiday resort and a place of play. Its cricket festival had in peacetime been held on North Marine Road at a ground that was only a six-hit away from the Clarence Gardens Hotel: great cricketers like Gilbert Jessop, who joined the Manchester Regiment, and Wilfred Rhodes, once the most famous of all Wilfreds, had played there.

Owen had holidayed in Scarborough as a child, and had himself played cricket in the town: on 2 December 1917, he wrote to his mother saying, 'Did I tell you the Hotel stands on the edge of the North Cliff; just where we played cricket once?'[17] (What could be more English than Scarborough and cricket?) His father was a cricketer and, wanting his son to be manly and play games, had encouraged him to take up cricket, for which Owen had shown some talent before he rejected games in favour of poetry (but cricketing poets are legion; Sassoon, for one, was a cricketer). He did return to cricket: crossing No Man's Land towards the German trenches, he likened it to leaving a cricket field, and later, when the weather improved, Owen did become a boy again, playing some cricket at Scarborough with fellow soldiers.[18] Owen would also make return visits to South Sands, the busier, more garish side of town: a photograph shows him sitting seriously on a South Sands pony in 1905, which was as close as he ever got to being the cavalryman he had hoped to be. He also visited a second cousin, May, who had lived in Scarborough when Owen was a child, and who had a close relationship with Susan and Tom, whom she often visited when the children were young. For some time, she ran a private school in Scarborough, with no qualifications but some success. And in this town from his childhood, Owen now read Henri Barbusse's war novel *Under Fire* (1917):

There he played, on the golden or ruddy ground; played – even – at soldiers. The eager joy of wielding a wooden saber flushed the cheeks now sunken and seamed. He opens his eyes, looks about him, shakes his head, and falls upon regret for the days when glory and war to him were pure, lofty, and sunny things.

The man puts his hand over his eyes, to retain the vision within. Nowadays, it is different.[19]

Scarborough was a town more associated with the pleasures of summer than the pain of war, and yet in December 1914 its South Bay had come under attack from three cruisers of the German battle fleet. This audacious attack did more damage than a Zeppelin raid could have achieved, and boldly brought the war to the Home Front. Holes were left in shops, boarding houses, the Grand Hotel, the ruined castle and, as the British press were keen to point out, in churches. Even without German cruisers, Scarborough was a scary town in the off-season, as one resident noted: 'At Scarborough in the winter the incessant roar of the sea, the salt spray that stung the face far inland, the bitter cries of wheeling and pouncing gulls, the attitudes of the bare trees, caught, as it were, in the very act of flight, all seemed designed to create and maintain an atmosphere of power, tension and of actual terror.'[20] In the churchyard, above the town, there sleeps one of those three weird sisters, the Brontës: Anne Brontë died at Scarborough and was buried there in 1849. Even higher above the town is the castle, an eerie Norman eyrie, which sits atop the high ground that separates the South Bay from the North Bay – a promontory that Brontë described as 'the semi-circular barrier of craggy cliffs surmounted by green swelling hills'.[21] All seaside resorts in the off-season are depressing, lonely, boring, ghost-ridden, as cold sea winds rattle the sash-window panes of silent boarding houses, the sea moans loudly as if dying with the year, and frost makes wild patterns on the windows of locked shops. It seems particularly inappropriate and cruel that a place dedicated to summer should be invaded by winter, but Scarborough must have been an extreme case, given its craggy, remote and exposed northern location.

Owen developed his own sad seaside life in Scarborough, where his fellow officers, who were unhappy with his cold aloofness, called him 'the ghost'. One fellow officer, H. R. Bate, remembered Owen at Scarborough, suffering from 'colossal conceit or pathological shyness', self-enclosed, silent and solemn: he 'deliberately shunned all contact with his comrades'.[22] The Clarence Gardens Hotel itself was a somewhat lonely place, standing as it does like an isolated castle high above the beach, horribly exposed to the fierce winds and storms that came in from the North Sea and haunted by the sea's unsettling roars, as if bravely protecting the tall boarding houses that are a little further away from the sea and run along the road that rises to the real castle. The castle-like qualities of the architecture of the hotel were limited to the white fairy-tale turret and the sheer bulk of the building, but it had become a military base when, being a comfortable berth, it was taken over by the army officers of the Manchesters (the soldiers were stationed at a barracks outside the town). Not that Owen's duties were very martial at Scarborough; he took a hotelier's role in this town of hoteliers. He became a 'Major Domo' who ran the hotel as an officers' mess, issuing the orders to cleaners and cooks. In 'A Terre', written at Scarborough, a severely wounded soldier feels that a lifetime of domestic drudgery as a servant would have been better than his own slow death, dying of war 'like any old disease':

> Here in this mummy-case, you know, I've thought
> How well I might have swept his floors for ever.
> I'd ask no nights off when the bustle's over,
> Enjoying so the dirt. Who's prejudiced
> Against a grimed hand when his own's quite dust,
> Less live than specks that in the sun-shafts turn,
> Less warm than dust that mixes with arms' tan?

For Owen, grateful not to be wrapped in bandages, the hotel was, all the same, a kind of 'mummy-case', because he had become his Mummy, complaining to her like a harried housewife that 'The C.O. is a terrible old "Regular", and I am in mortal terror lest one day his bath-water should be cold, or his plates too hot.'[23] And Owen was the Lady of Shalott, trapped inside with her feminine pursuits while outside the men went by, living the tougher life: 'You should hear me rate the Charwoman for leaving the Lavatory-Basins unclean. [. . .] I do no parades, but have not yet allowed myself any free time for walks.'[24]

Nonetheless, even when he was hidden away in his hotel, there was a view to see and sigh after:

> Went to the most atrocious bad play [. . .] there were a dozen girls who danced & sang by way of Interlude; & they being only 14 to 18 had adorable slender bare legs, nude as you could wish. What's more

some of them came outside the Hotel next day. I waved and blew
kisses from the window, but didn't speak to them.[25]

There's something of the saucy seaside postcard here, a variation on the
'A Fine View' postcards of the time, in which cheeky chaps at the seafront
enjoy the ladies' slender legs (Which view do you like best? . . . The back
view is absolutely grand . . . The prettiest view on the promenade.)
Higher up the hotel, in his moments of freedom, Owen had a wonderful
view from his five-windowed room in the turret. This view could easily
compete with the view of the cathedral in Bordeaux, or of the mountains
in the Pyrenees. In one direction the verdant coastline, which included
the terraced Clarence Gardens, and straight in front of his room was the
sea, which, even on the clearest days, seemed to be endless. During
the summer, he had told his mother to forget herself and her problems in
the presence of the sea, as if the water could wash away troubles. Now, in
December, using the sea, he announced that 'The tugs have left me; I feel
the great swelling of the open sea taking my galleon',[26] as he produced
some of his best poetry. From high up in his room, soon after arriving at
the hotel, he wrote 'The Show', a poem in which he looks down from on
high – he sees the Western Front rather than Scarborough, and the poem
was influenced by Barbusse's *Under Fire*, but the poem captures the expe-
rience of looking down on to the beach and Clarence Gardens and seeing
tiny people coming and going. The poem begins, 'My soul looked down
from a vague height, with Death, / As unremembering how I rose or
why'. The Scarborough sea view in rough late autumn suited the passage
from *Under Fire* that must have influenced Owen's poem:

And there amid the baleful glimmers of the storm, below the dark
disorder of the clouds that extend and unfurl over the earth like evil
spirits, they seem to see a great livid plain unrolled, which to their
seeing is made of mud and water, while figures appear and fast fix
themselves to the surface of it, all blinded and borne down with
filth, like the dreadful castaways of shipwreck. And it seems to them
that these are soldiers.[27]

Owen took every opportunity to hide away and write in his room, and he told Sassoon that the poem was written in two hours of leisure on 26 November and then completed when he got up early the next morning. Although he was sociable enough with 'Coz. May' in December, he had acquired a reputation for being remote and self-absorbed. The boy she had known, who hid away in his attic bedroom in Shrewsbury, was now a man who hid away in his high bedroom in Scarborough. The words contemporaries used to describe the teenager at Shrewsbury are the same as those H. R. Bate used to describe the Scarborough officer: one who knew him at Shrewsbury had noted the detachment that Bate later observed[28] and while Bate remembered 'a positive attitude of aloof superiority[29] [. . .] his aloofness, his self-enclosed withdrawn solitariness', a fellow pupil at the Technical School called him 'disdainful, aloof, stand-offish'.[30] Colleagues at Scarborough called him 'the ghost'; Owen's family had called him Lone Wolf.[31] In his teens and now at Scarborough, his shyness combined with a faint dislike of most of those who surrounded him. Owen had shown in Bordeaux and Edinburgh that he could be sociable in the right company: after Craiglockhart and St Bernard's Crescent, his fellow officers were somewhat disappointing ('There is no one here whose mind is Truth, or whose body Keats's synonym for Truth'),[32] and, faced with the opportunity to chat or play cards with them, Owen chose, instead, poetry, preferring to be, in the words of Philip Larkin, 'Under a lamp, hearing the noise of wind, / And looking out to see the moon thinned / To an air-sharpened blade'.[33] As a result, this Emily Dickinson of Clarence Gardens became a rather mysterious figure to his colleagues. There's an Agatha Christie novel that revolves around a Mr Owen whom no one knows ('He hadn't got it clear who this fellow Owen was [. . .] there was some mystery about Owen [. . .] I am quite certain that I have never met, or become friendly with, anyone of the name of Owen') and, with the initials U. N., his name becomes 'by a slight stretch of fancy UNKNOWN!'[34] W. E. Owen remained a Mr Unknown too.

However, Owen returned to Edinburgh to visit his friends in December: Maidie Gray had written begging him to go up to see them all, and that decided it. When he dropped in on Craiglockhart there were still many men he knew, and they feared that he had come back relapsed. Revisiting Tynecastle School, he and the boys once again enjoyed H. W. Longfellow's *The Song of Hiawatha*, one of his favourite books[35] – 'That is not a book: it is a dream'.[36] Remarkably, he must also have recalled lines from Longfellow's poem when that December he wrote 'Hospital Barge', the poem about the Somme Canal and King Arthur. He had once used the lines in an essay when he himself was a schoolboy: in 1908, he had written a piece on 'The River Severn' (for which he was given a mark of 18 out of 20), and, in order to describe his river, he quoted lines about another:

Down the river came the Strong Man,
In his birch canoe came Kwasind,
Floating slowly down the current
Of the sluggish Taquamenaw,
Very languid with the weather,
Very sleepy with the silence.[37]

This is Kwasind's journey to death. 'Hospital Barge' begins,

Budging the sluggard ripples of the Somme,
A barge round old Cérisy slowly slewed.
Softly her engines down the current screwed,
And chuckled softly with contented hum,
Till fairy tinklings struck their croonings dumb.

The sonnet goes on to recall Arthur's journey to Avalon.

Owen also returned to another Arthur, Arthur Newboult, and it was probably at this point that he wrote a second poem about his young friend:

Sweet is your antique body, not yet young.
Beauty withheld from youth that looks for youth.
Fair only for your father. Dear among

Masters in art. To all men else uncouth
Save me; who know your smile comes very old,
Learnt of the happy dead that laughed with gods;
For earlier suns than ours have lent you gold,
Sly fauns and trees have given you jigs and nods.

But soon your heart, hot-beating like a bird's,
Shall slow down. Youth shall lop your hair,
And you must learn wry meanings in our words.
Your smile shall dull, because too keen aware;
And when for hopes your hand shall be uncurled,
Your eyes shall close, being opened to the world.

In a photograph of Owen in uniform in 1917, he sits with the boy Arthur. Aloof and shy though Owen was, he desired company. And friendship with a child was one way of escaping from the world, remaining detached from his peers while at the same time achieving friendship. Arthur is a valued friend because his eyes are not yet 'opened to the world'. Much of his poetry that was written at this time came from these conflicting impulses – for instance, in 'Apologia Pro Poemate Meo', he says 'I have made fellowships' but love is 'wound with war's hard wire whose stakes are strong', which is a remarkable image for how Owen wanted love yet 'shunned all contact' and was 'self-enclosed'; in 'My Shy Hand' (drafted in August and revised at Scarborough), 'My shy hand shades a hermitage apart, – / O large enough for thee, and thy brief hours'.

Escape, friendship, and the paradoxical situation of wanting both were expressed in Owen's greatest poem, 'Strange Meeting', composed in the early months of 1918 – 'I am the enemy you killed, my friend'. The poem begins with a Dante-like descent into the underworld:

It seemed that out of battle I escaped
Down some profound dull tunnel, long since scooped
Through granites which titanic wars had groined.

Yet also there encumbered sleepers groaned,
Too fast in thought or death to be bestirred.
Then, as I probed them, one sprang up, and stared
With piteous recognition in fixed eyes,
Lifting distressful hands, as if to bless.
And by his smile, I knew that sullen hall, –
By his dead smile I knew we stood in Hell.

Perhaps that profound dull tunnel recalls the railways of Owen's father, but Dante's visit to Hell is mirrored by Owen's descent. Hell had certainly been an unforgettable part of Owen's Protestant upbringing, but there's also something Catholic about the poem. The German 'Strange friend' he encounters, a man killed by Owen it would seem, lifts 'distressful hands, as if to bless', like a priest, and we are told that 'Foreheads of men have bled where no wounds were', which suggests the stigmata and miracles of Catholic saints. A reference to how 'I would go up and wash them from sweet wells', and the cave-like space, might be a recollection of Lourdes. In a draft he wrote biblically, 'I would have died by my own people stoned'.[38] The poem ends – it may not be a finished poem – with lines that suggest that Owen is not just visiting Hell but has in fact died and is there to stay:

'I am the enemy you killed, my friend.
I knew you in this dark: for so you frowned
Yesterday through me as you jabbed and killed.
I parried; but my hands were loath and cold.
Let us sleep now. . . .'

In August 1915 in Bordeaux he had heard that many of the Germans he had known there were still alive, fighting in the Vosges, and perhaps the recollection of these Germans contributed to 'Strange Meeting'. Was he plagued by the thought that he could have killed a friend from Bordeaux, a German with whom he shared a café table in peacetime? The incredibly successful wartime film *The Birth of a Nation* – the big cinematic hit in London when Owen joined the Artists' Rifles in 1915 – tells a story of this kind, with close friends finding themselves fighting on opposing sides in the American Civil War. In the film, two friends meet in a skirmish: one is shot and about to be finished off by his friend with a bayonet; the friend sees it's him and, as he hesitates, he is shot; the two friends lie together on the battlefield; both are dead, as if sleeping in bed together. Then, another two friends, brothers of the other friends, come up against each other in battle.

Hell and Owen's pursuit of solitude gave him a rather similar and almost equally great poem, 'Miners', a kind of companion to 'Strange Meeting'. Owen begins alone in his turret-bedroom – with its hideous furniture but 'a comfortable bed – and fireplace'[39] – listening to his hearth in a silence that allows him to hear 'A sigh of the coal':

> I listened for a tale of leaves
>   And smothered ferns,
> Frond-forests, and the low sly lives
>   Before the fauns.
>
> My fire might show steam-phantoms simmer
>   From Time's old cauldron,
> Before the birds made nests in summer,
>   Or men had children.

When 'us' and 'we' appear at the end of the poem, they refer to a common fate rather than company in his room. But the officers' mess may have played its part in the creation of the poem: 'Miners' had been inspired by a major colliery disaster near Stoke-on-Trent, which Owen would have read about in the hotel's newspapers in the mess or have heard discussed there by other officers. 'Miners' belongs with those other great poems inspired by newspapers: Stevie Smith's 'Not Waving but Drowning', Gerard Manley Hopkins's 'The Wreck of the Deutschland', and Tennyson's 'The Charge of the Light Brigade'. That Owen should focus on this tragedy so soon after it happened suggests

that it might have been pointed out by a fellow officer. The lastlines
seem to evoke a hotel lounge or officers' mess rather than his bedroom:

> Comforted years will sit soft-chaired,
>   In rooms of amber;
> The years will stretch their hands, well-cheered
>   By our life's ember;
>
> The centuries will burn rich loads
>   With which we groaned,
> Whose warmth shall lull their dreaming lids,
>   While songs are crooned

It is a thoroughly bourgeois poem, a statement of middle-class guilt;
later, George Orwell would look at the fire and remember, with similar
guilt, where the coal in his hearth came from. Back in 1915, Owen had
written to his mother saying 'I can't help feeling the anomaly of
Parliament's cajoling the Miners to work on Bank Holiday, & them-
selves taking six weeks holiday!'[40] He had met a young scar-backed
miner in the Dunsden days. Now, in Scarborough, Owen emphasises
his distance from the miners while the poem emphasises his sympathy
and empathy. In his ivory tower, where at 10.30 p.m. on 5 January
1918 he was in front of the fire in pyjamas and his fleece, airing his
toes, which had not yet forgotten Beaumont Hamel, he travelled down
into caverns of coal.

An explosion had occurred on Saturday 12 January, at half past nine
in the morning, at Podmore Hall Colliery, Halmerend, near Stoke.
Owen's poem would have been written on 14 January, which was the
day when the newspapers covered the story in detail; for instance, *The
Times* announced, in a report dated 13 January, a 'Mine Explosion in
Staffordshire' and 'Death Roll of 160'. Owen told his mother that day,
'Wrote a poem on the Colliery Disaster: but I get mixed up with the
War at the end. It is short, but oh! sour!'[41] 'Colliery Disaster' was the
headline in that day's *Daily News*. That Owen connected the war with

a mining disaster was almost inevitable, given the press's references to survivors suffering from 'gassing', and to 'gallantry', to a message from the King, even to snow falling on the scene, as it had on the Western Front the previous year. It was a year, almost to the day, since Owen had arrived at the Western Front. And on the Front, coal miners were used for tunnelling under No Man's Land. Coal miners have been employed as siege tunnellers since at least the reign of Edward I, who used miners from the Forest of Dean. In the reign of George V, the tunnelling companies were composed of experienced miners from coalfields cross the country, such as South Wales, Durham, Lancashire and Staffordshire.[42] But by the end of the poem Owen is not simply thinking of miners in Staffordshire or the Western Front: the poem has embraced every man who served in the trenches.

Owen sent the poem to his mother, but also to *The Nation* as a topical poem that might be published as a complement to the journalists' coverage of the disaster. He had once fancied becoming a newspaper journalist as a means of earning a living as a writer. On 30 December 1917, he commented that he had been inspired to write new poems in Scarborough but his urgent need was to revise poems he had already started rather than piling up new first drafts; however, this mining disaster was to be one of the exceptions and there was no time for revision: he had sent the poem off on the evening he wrote it. On 19 January, he could write to Susan that:

> With your beautiful letter came a proof from the *Nation* of my 'Miners'. This is the first poem I have sent to the *Nation* myself, and it has evidently been accepted. It was scrawled out on the back of a note to the Editor; and no penny stamp or addressed envelope was enclosed for return! That's the way to do it.
> 'Miners' will probably appear next Saturday.[43]

He told his cousin Leslie to buy *The Nation* because 'I have at last a poem'.[44] It was somewhat brave of the weekly to take the poem because Owen had chosen to use rhymes that are not perfect and, to an eye in

1918, seemed not to work properly, from the first rhymes of hearth/
earth and coal/recall, down to lids/lads and crooned/ground in the
last lines. It was a daring new approach by Owen, who had as good as
invented a new poetic technique – one that seemed, to others, his
cousin included, to be simply bad, amateurish poetry. (Tom Owen's
attempt at poetry had rhymed 'Jerry' with 'Shrewsbury', and 'War' with
'far'.) Owen had already used this method of rhyming in 'The Show',
for instance, the poem he drafted at Scarborough in November, and in
'Exposure', begun at Scarborough in December. What he achieved was
the kind of imperfection that we might find in a child's poem. Half-
rhymes had been used before but not in such a wholehearted fashion,
although there have been some attempts to find suitable precedents –
Edmund Blunden would suggest that in his 'Evening' ode, William
Collins (he of 'How Sleep the Brave') nearly invented the half-rhyme
method. Looking at the 'Ode to Evening', we do see that poor doomed,
depressive Collins might have had an influence on far more than
just 'Asleep':

> Then let me rove some wild and heathy Scene,
> Or find some Ruin, 'midst its dreary Dells,
>   Whose Walls more awful nod
>   By thy religious Gleams.
> Or if chill blust'ring Winds or driving Rain
> Prevent my willing Feet, be mine the Hut,
>   That from the Mountain's Side,
>   Views Wilds, and swelling Floods[45]

But we could equally see the influence of the Scouse accent on Owen's
poetry in so far as his sensitivity to vowel sounds led to his use of this
'pararhyme' in his poems, where the consonants usually rhyme but the
vowels do not; so in one poem 'hair' rhymes lightly with 'hour' and
'here', and, in another, 'star' with 'stir'. Collins, or Owen's semi-
detached temperament, may have influenced his innovative use parar-
hyme, but it could well come simply from his anxieties about acquiring

a Scouse accent, or, indeed, his strong desire in Bordeaux to pronounce his French vowels properly.

The effect of Owen's half-rhymes, with those vowels that don't match, was quickly seen by some readers – 'our ear being now tuned to vowel-rhyme, the poet avails himself of our disappointment to increase the biting severity of his strokes; and so, profiting not only by what he gives but also by what he withholds, he gets an effect of total desolation'.[46] In 'Strange Meeting', the barrenness builds through 'hall/Hell', 'moan/mourn', 'spoiled/spilled' down to 'killed/cold'.

*

On the day when Owen sent 'Miners' to his mother, he announced in the same letter that he had been invited to Robert Graves's wedding in London. Owen had met Graves at Craiglockhart when the latter visited Sassoon, his friend and fellow officer in the Royal Welch. Owen walked Graves over to the golf course where Sassoon was busy with his morning round. He found Graves, who was two years younger than himself, to be 'a big, rather plain fellow, the last man on earth apparently capable of the extraordinary, delicate fancies in his books'.[47] When Sassoon showed Graves 'Disabled', Graves was mightily impressed. Graves was soon in camp at Oswestry – which in *Goodbye to All That* he calls 'Oswestry in Wales'[48] – and then moved to Kinmel Park Camp in Wales, whence he wrote to Owen in October 1917, saying, with reference to 'Disabled', that 'you have seen things; you are a poet; but you're a very careless one at present'.[49] Taking a conservative approach to metre, he lectured Owen on the need to follow the rules. Understandably, Owen had reservations about Graves, finding him rather patronising and domineering, but he was happy to have 'the silent and immortal friendship of Graves' – as long as Graves treated him as a friend rather than a 'Find!!'[50] On 22 December, Graves wrote, 'those assonances instead of rhymes are fine – Did you know that it was a trick of Welsh poetry or was it instinct?', which was again a little patronising, in suggesting that Owen was incapable of invention or real originality; and 'trick' isn't quite the best word. Graves was referring to

Owen's pararhyme, which he had taken from neither Welsh poetry nor some Celtic poetry gene. But Graves had become less schoolmasterly by now, and was genuinely admiring, writing, 'Don't make any mistake, Owen, you are a damned fine poet already & are going to be more so – I wont have the impertinence to criticize – you have found a new method and must work it yourself'.[51] Graves simply wanted Owen to cheer up and 'write more optimistically – The war's not ended yet but a poet should have a spirit above wars'.[52] As if to prove his own optimism, Graves told Owen that he was engaged to a girl called Nancy, daughter of William Nicholson the painter.

The wedding of twenty-two-year-old Graves and eighteen-year-old Nancy Nicholson took place at St James's Church on Piccadilly three days before 'Miners' appeared in *The Nation* on Saturday 26 January. The 23rd of January 1918 can be seen as one of the most important days in Graves's life, of course, but in Owen's too, not only for what happened but also for what it represented: Owen had become a man of note, and spent the day with people and places that had been until very recently entirely closed to him. The man opening the door into the secret garden was Sassoon, since it was through him that Owen met Graves and also met Robert Ross, with whom Owen spent much of the day: 'Oh! world you are making for me, Sassoon!'[53] Sassoon's little black book might not have been as valuable to Owen as *The Old Huntsman*, but it was undoubtedly part of Sassoon's charm. But Sassoon himself could not be in London for the wedding because his convalescence was over and he was back with the regiment – it seems that he disapproved of the marriage and didn't apply for leave.

St James's is one of the wealthiest districts of London, described by Stephen Fry as 'that elegant parcel of metropolitan clubland bordered by Piccadilly, Pall Mall, St James's Street and Lower Regent Street [. . .] the natural habitat of the upper class English bachelor'.[54] Owen luncheoned in St James's at the Reform Club. This building, 'preeminent among clubs for its architecture',[55] is described in Arnold Bennett's novel *The Pretty Lady*, which Owen read in the spring of 1918:

In three minutes he was in the smoking-room of his club, warming himself at a fine, old, huge, wasteful grate, in which burned such a coal fire as could not have been seen in France, Italy, Germany, Austria, Russia, nor anywhere on the continent of Europe. The war had as yet changed nothing in the impregnable club, unless it was that ordinary matches had recently been substituted for the giant matches on which the club had hitherto prided itself.[56]

The war could be studied in the splendid Morning-Room,[57] and conversations took place at dinner, where officers like Owen could converse with wealthy writers. Despite some scarcities the war left the Reform Club essentially unchanged:

Said a voice behind him:
    'You dining here to-night?'
    'I am.'
    'Shall we crack a bottle together?' (It was astonishing and deplorable how clichés survived in the best clubs!)
    'By all means.'
    The voice spoke lower:
    'That Bollinger's all gone at last.'[58]

Designed by Sir Charles Barry in 1841, nine years after the club was founded, the Reform's building is a huge High Renaissance classical Italian palazzo inspired by the Farnese Palace in Rome, and, as such, sitting in the finest hall of any London club, beneath its gallery and many pillars, was the closest Owen was to get to Italy and a rebuilt Uriconium. It was one of the male worlds of privilege, where portraits of great men stared down from the walls, although it was Liberal rather than Tory and more bookish than some other Pall Mall clubs. Henry James's journal records that it was 'the most comfortable corner of the world [. . .] I could not have remained in London without it, and I have become extremely fond of it; a deep local attachment'.[59]

Owen made several trips to the Reform Club as the guest of Robert Ross, the devoted friend of Oscar Wilde who had become a respectable and influential art expert, a key figure in the promotion of contemporary art.[60] It was Ross who had Arnold Bennett elected to the Reform, and it was through Ross that Owen met Bennett at the club in November 1917. Owen had met Ross himself when Sassoon put them in touch in November 1917. Sassoon would later recall this charismatic man:

> He emerges in the mind-portrait of memory, his face – tired and old before its time – masking the sadness of wounding experience with a mood of witty reminiscence and word-play. There he would stand, in his loose grey alpaca jacket, wearing a black silk skull-cap and smoking his perpetual cigarette in its jade-green holder, emphasizing his lively pronouncements with controlled gestures of the left hand, on the third finger of which was a fair-sized scarab ring. He more than once warned me that my own hands were somewhat over-illustrative, urging me to be less precipitate and inaudible; he added that this union of gesticulation and indistinctness was probably inherited from the paternal branch of my family.[61]

Sassoon makes him sound like one of Owen's childhood heroes: Sherlock Holmes, another 1890s bachelor. His Watson was an editor of the *Burlington Magazine*, More Adey, with whom he lived for fifteen years – not at 221B Baker Street but at 40 Half Moon Street, just off Piccadilly, a short walk from St James's Church and the Reform. (Half Moon Street was classic bachelor territory, being home to Algernon Moncrieff in Wilde's *The Importance of Being Earnest*,[62] and to Bertie Wooster and his man Jeeves.) Ross was a popular, clubbable man, but his Moriarty was Lord Alfred Douglas, Oscar Wilde's nemesis, who had become determined to destroy Ross's good reputation by outing him as homosexual. Some bachelors never feel any emotion akin to love, like Sherlock Holmes, who would not 'admit such intrusions into his own delicate and finely adjusted temperament';[63] some boyish bachelors, such as Bertie Wooster in his carefree pyjamas, are uninterested in sex; Ross and Adey were companions but their confirmed bachelordom was, outwardly at least, of the respectable kind.

Arthur Conan Doyle himself was a member of the Reform, and Holmes's brother Mycroft lives on Pall Mall, where he co-founded the Diogenes Club. Owen didn't see Conan Doyle at the Reform on 23 January, but he was excited to discover that eminent Welshman Lord Rhondda was the nearest person to him at lunch, and, after lunch, Owen had a few words with H. G. Wells, whom he had met at the club during a previous visit. Wells had cheerily waved at him from another table, and, although Owen never got to know Wells very well, when they first met at the Reform, both outsiders in that space, they got on, Wells saying 'some rare things for my edification' and telling him a lot of secrets.[64] Owen admired Wells's work, and had found *The Passionate Friends* 'astonishing in its realism' – like Owen's poetry 'it refuses to ignore the unpleasant'[65] – and Owen and Wells had similar backgrounds too, complete with puritanical Protestantism, the sportsman father, social insecurity and escapist tendencies (although Owen had been luckier in his parents). Wells was also friends with Sassoon, writing to him at the time of his protest in September 1917, asking him to be sober and sensible and manifestly sane: 'If sensitive and fine minded men allow themselves to be tormented into mere shrieks of protest then the blockheads & the blood drinkers will prevail for ever.'[66] Wells was not, however, friends with Graves, who had encountered him at the Reform in 1916, when Wells 'was "Mr Britling" in those days, and full of military optimism' and 'talked without listening'.[67] So Owen and Ross left Wells behind among the club's bores and buffers, some of them blockheads and blood-drinkers, and the two men drove off to the wedding at St James's, an elegant, refined church by Wren,[68] slightly set back from the busy pavements and general hubbub of midweek Piccadilly, and across the road from Burlington House, where Owen had had 'a joyful time' in the past when visiting the Royal Academy.[69] The groom wore his uniform, complete with sword and spurs. His father recorded in his diary that 'Robert looked fine and said his responses firmly and clearly, as did Nancy'. Nancy 'was in a beautiful blue check dress with veil and had a wonderful bouquet arranged by her good father'.[70] The conductor Leopold Stokowski played the organ – he later acquired fame with American orchestras as well as in the Disney film *Fantasia* – but whereas Graves's father felt that the choirboys 'sang beautifully',[71] Graves himself recalled that they were 'out of tune'.[72] Usually attentive to choirboys, Owen made no comment about them, but found the wedding as a whole 'nothing extraordinary'.[73]

The reception was held at Apple Tree Yard nearby. Owen arrived at the wedding as a man who knew that by the end of the week he would be a published war poet. He was introduced to the guests as a poet, and there, in St James's, he was treated as a man of some importance. In the room, alongside family and schoolfriends, a collection of worthies had assembled, including Edwin Lutyens, the architect of New Delhi, who would design the Cenotaph; Max Beerbohm, the writer and cartoonist; E. V. Lucas, the writer and editor; Edward Marsh, 'the Georgian Anthologist tho' I did not know him as such till afterwards'; artist George Belcher, dandily dressed; and publisher William Heinemann. There was enough rationed sugar and butter for a three-tier cake, although without icing, and there was champagne; all in all, it was a very different occasion from the weddings that had taken place at Dunsden.

The best man was handsome George Mallory, a Cheshireman and one-time Birkenhead boy, destined to be immortalised as the mountaineer who, before the Himalayan snow became his grave, almost became the first man to conquer Everest. (In Birkenhead Owen grew up a few streets away from Andrew Irvine, Mallory's companion on that fateful climb in 1924.) Owen saw Mallory, but whether they spoke is not recorded. Did they know they both had Birkenhead connections, and that both had seen Birkenhead as a step down when their families moved there? Did Owen talk about how his poethood was born among the Cheshire hills? Did he get the chance to tell Mallory about his mountain ancestry or his childhood desire to take up both mountaineering and the Christian education of the inhabitants? Did they get to talk about Winchester, where Mallory had been at school? At that time, Mallory was simply an officer, a schoolmaster and a small-time author, so, when writing to his mother and his cousin, Owen would not have included him in the list of luminaries encountered at the wedding. Perhaps they spoke at length. Owen had started to work on 'Exposure', and he had recently referred to 'a footsore Climber' in 'The Ballad of Many Thorns'. His poem 'Science Has Looked' describes mountains, 'the breasts of Mother Earth'; while an early poem begins 'Unto what pinnacles of desperate heights / Do good men climb to seize their good!' and ends

And their sole mission is to drag, entice
And push mankind to those same cloudy crags
Where they first breathed the madness-giving air
That made them feel as angels, that are less than men.

Mallory was a young schoolmaster at Charterhouse when Graves was a pupil there, and he had introduced Graves to Edward Marsh, who, as editor, would include both Graves and Sassoon, but not Owen, in *Georgian Poetry*. The wedding must have reminded Owen of the importance of the old boy network and the value of contacts in literary London, but, if he was hoping to network, he was only partially successful, seemingly failing to befriend Marsh and other literary luminaries even though Graves nade an effort to introduce him to useful people. The one real friend Owen made at the wedding was another literary man, but one of little influence as a writer at that time, his power being more martial: Graves introduced Owen to C. K. Scott Moncrieff, 'a very useful man to know'.[74] Scott Moncrieff had been at school with Mallory, and then a brilliant undergraduate who wrote fiction and poetry, but he was 'content to devote his delicate literary gift and wide range of scholarship to the interpretation of other men's work', and would in future years become well known as a translator, especially the translator of Marcel Proust's *À la recherche du temps perdu* (*The Times* would call him 'The Translator as Artist')[75]; however, when

he met Owen he was about to start working in the War Office in
London, having been injured in battle in 1917. He entered the
War Office in March 1918, after a spell convalescing at Eastbourne.
A successful military man from a military family, Charles Kenneth
Michael Scott Moncrieff had been awarded the Military Cross in April
1917, and later in 1918 would return to France to work behind the
lines. He became a Catholic in France in 1915.[76]

Rather than dining with this new friend, Owen dined at the Reform
again with Roderick Meiklejohn of the Liquor Control Board, but then
went to Half Moon Street with Meiklejohn, spending the evening with
Ross and Scott Moncrieff. Roderick Meiklejohn later recalled a young
officer who was first and foremost good company and only secondly
a poet:

> He had great charm but the most abiding memory I retain of him
> were [sic] his simplicity and modesty. From social intercourse to the
> stage I got with him one would never have realized the considerable
> poet he was. When I knew him I had seen very few, if any, of his
> poems & those not the most important.[77]

That reference to 'simplicity and modesty' suggests a description of
Tennyson by A. C. Benson – 'his simplicity, his modesty, were childish
virtues, matured but always childlike'[78] – while that English 'charm' is
something that recurs in descriptions of Owen, and no doubt was much
in evidence during that long day. He had that supposedly English
ability to be charming while, and as a result of, being aloof and reticent.
Again, the charm was at least partly the deployment of childlike inno-
cence. At 2 a.m. Owen finally found his way to the Imperial Hotel.
After only a few hours sleep, he took the 10 a.m. from King's Cross
back up to Scarborough feeling much refreshed.

One noticeable aspect of Owen's description of the events of
23 January is that although it was a wedding, where naturally many
women were in attendance, he seems only to be interested in describing
the men, and while this may be because he didn't want to alarm his

mother by suggesting that he had been making merry with brides-
maids, he did also describe the wedding for his cousin Leslie, the
aspiring ladies' man. Yet even in his letter to Leslie he made no refer-
ence to women, and the impression we get is that Owen didn't speak
to a woman all day. For him, the wedding was a bachelor party. It
would have been normal to have described the bride's blue dress, and
no doubt his mother would have been interested to hear about that (she
herself having been married in black), but Owen simply said that the
bride was eighteen years old, and 'pretty, but nowise handsome';[79] he
even failed to point out that after enjoying some champagne, Nancy
changed into her land-girl's uniform of breeches and smock. He made
no reference to female guests, handsome, pretty or otherwise. This
bachelor was not using the wedding to find a wife of his own. Of
course, he might have been deploying the charm with ladies all day, but
that is not the impression he chooses to give, and he did decide to
spend his evening with ageing Reform Club bachelors. His wedding
present to the Graveses was the ultimate gift from the bachelor who
spends his time with bachelors: apostle spoons, spoons depicting Christ
and the apostles, that bachelor set.

CHAPTER 13

A Public School Man

The river of death has brimmed his banks,
And England's far, and Honour a name,
But the voice of a schoolboy rallies the ranks:
'Play up! play up! and play the game!'
HENRY NEWBOLT, 'Vitaï Lampada', 1892[1]

Mad about the boy,
It's simply scrumptious to be mad about the boy,
I know that quite sincerely
Housman really
Wrote 'The Shropshire Lad' about the boy.
NOËL COWARD, 'Mad About the Boy', 1932[2]

WILFRED Owen's new friend, C. K. Scott Moncrieff, worked in London, so he and Owen were two hundred miles apart once Owen had returned to Scarborough, and yet he became close to Owen, and Owen would become an important part of his life. Born in Scotland in September 1889, Scott Moncrieff was four years older than Owen, although he had only left university in 1914. Unlike Sassoon, he seems never to have looked down on his little friend, and, in fact, rather looked up to him: after all, Owen was the genuine poet, now recognised as such by Graves and Sassoon, whereas Scott Moncrieff was a mere scholar and a dabbler in verse. There was also something of the schoolboy about Scott Moncrieff, a man with a 'curious personality'.[3] He retained a strong affection for his schooldays at Winchester College. A school contemporary wrote, 'Charles Scott-Moncrieff was one of those unusual products of a Public School, who, while thoroughly "unsatisfactory" in almost every way, and thoroughly unlikely to fit into the ordinary life, yet maintain to the very end a passionate love of their School and a memory of their school days almost tragic in its devotion'.[4] Returning to his old school during the war, Scott Moncrieff brought away 'a very happy impression of Winchester which obscures the memory of twelve rather monotonous months' soldiering';[5] and, on another occasion, writing on the notepaper of the Public Schools Club, Berkeley Street, he wrote that Winchester was 'something to remember on cold and unfriendly nights for the rest of the campaign'.[6] A poem called 'Domum', which he wrote in Flanders in June 1915 and, characteristically, sent to the school magazine, expresses deep affection for the school William of Wykeham founded in 1382, and calls the sons of Wykeham to battle.[7]

One thing Owen and Scott Moncrieff had in common was the love of a school story called *The Loom of Youth*. Critical of the public-school philo-athleticism that had contributed to the atmosphere of the war, this best-selling novel is nonetheless a love letter to the public school, a story by a teenager in love with a place and a way of life:

> To a boy of any imagination, such a place could not but waken a wonderful sense of the beautiful. And Gordon gazing from the school gateway across to the grey ivy-clad studies was taken for a few moments clean outside himself; and the next few hours only served to deepen this wonder and admiration.[8]

Its author, Alec Waugh, compared the novel to a letter written by 'a man at the end of a long and intense love affair' to 'the mistress whom he still adores, but nonetheless holds largely responsible for the rupture'.[9] Based on Sherborne ('Fernhurst' in the book), it was written by Waugh in seven and a half weeks at the start of 1916 when he was seventeen; he corrected the proofs while at Sandhurst and the book was published on 20 July 1917. Owen read it in Edinburgh soon after publication, referring to it in a letter on 7 September, and Graves and Sassoon also admired it.[10] Owen was struck by the young age of the author. On 23 October 1917, Scott Moncrieff wrote to a friend saying 'Thanks for the Loom of Youth, a curiously boring book – but it wouldn't be so clever if it weren't.'[11] Subsequently, he wrote a glowing review of the book and, as a result, a friendship developed between him and Waugh. In February 1918, he gave a lunch party for Waugh at a Pall Mall club, introducing Waugh to Robert Ross.[12] This friendship would eventually lead to Alec Waugh's attempt to have his brother Evelyn employed as Scott Moncrieff's secretary – a failed attempt that, like *The Loom of Youth* itself, would play its part in the creation of irrepressible, immoral Old Harrovian 'public school man' Captain Grimes in Evelyn's *Decline and Fall*.

Evelyn Waugh's satirical response to the public-school system might suit modern readers more (and Scott Moncrieff wrote to Evelyn Waugh praising his book), but *The Loom of Youth* was admired by many people during the war, being reprinted eight times by October 1918. Scott Moncrieff no doubt felt that it captured his own experiences at boarding school, but to Owen the book offered an alluring unknown world.[13] Book IV begins with a quotation from Owen's friend Harold Monro of the Poetry Bookshop: 'Life like an army I could hear advance, / Halting at fewer, fewer intervals.'[14] In the story, poetry (often by former public-school boys) is the alternative to playing muddy games, as it had been for Owen, who, against his father's irritated advice, chose poetry instead of 'Manly sport'.[15] The book also celebrates Oxford: Oxford is longed for, but the war leaves it out of reach. Indeed, Waugh's novel is a war novel and, like 'Disabled', written within weeks of Owen reading the novel, sees a connection between teenage athleticism and the war (although, significantly, 'Disabled' is a criticism of the war rather than the public-school system).

It is also true that homosexuality features in *The Loom of Youth*. At 'Fernhurst', the strongest, heartiest boys get the prettiest young first-year boys. It was a surprisingly open treatment of schoolboy 'immorality' for a book of that time and became, as a result, controversial; its author was struck off the list of old boys at Sherborne. But, equally, if there were many public-school men disgusted by the book, those inclined to 'immorality' could embrace the book. Thus Ross, the first lover Oscar Wilde ever had, and Scott Moncrieff, described concisely by Evelyn Waugh as 'a homosexual translator',[16] were both fans of *The Loom of Youth*. But in fact homosexuality is not the focus of the novel, and when, during a genteel afternoon tea at a palatial house in Edinburgh in September 1917, Owen found that a corpulent old lady admired the novel it would not have been homosexuality they discussed.

There are a number of admiring references to public schools in Owen's letters, as when he talks about 'Downside, (a <u>Public</u> school)', where the de la Touche boys went ('I feel flattered to compete with Downside').[17] In a letter in November 1914, Owen had quoted from 'Ode on a Distant Prospect of Eton College', Thomas Gray's poem that seems to have played a part in the creation of Owen's poem 'An Imperial Elegy'. Owen owned a 1917 edition of *The Poetical Works of Gray and Collins*, and just as Collins had influenced 'Asleep' by having attended Winchester College, so Gray's attendance at Eton was important to Owen. Gray's poem clearly had an influence on Owen's war poetry. 'Insensibility', probably drafted in late 1917, builds on Gray's poem, especially its closing message:

> Yet, ah! why should they know their fate?
> Since sorrow never comes too late,
> And happiness too swiftly flies.
> Thought would destroy their paradise.
> No more; where ignorance is bliss,
> 'Tis folly to be wise.[18]

Owen says, 'Happy the lad whose mind was never trained', but he includes himself among 'We wise, who with a thought besmirch / Blood over all our soul'. Scott Moncrieff was indebted to Gray's poem too, as can be seen in his remarkable war poem 'Au Champ d'Honneur', which ends with the hope that an Englishman might

> Quicken again with boyish ardour, as he sees,
> For a moment, Windsor Castle towering on the crest
> And Eton still enshrined amid remembered trees.[19]

Owen's poetry would seem to run against the public-school spirit, but like Alec Waugh he was genuinely in love with the public school as a place – a place to escape to in the imagination, as something that, as Scott Moncrieff put it, obscures the memory of war. In February 1918, Owen read another famous school story, *The Hill*,[20] which is about Harrow (Harrow had also been discussed in *The Loom of Youth*). Written by Horace Vachell, 'a fearsome snob with a belief in an elected band of privileged beings of whom he considered himself a member',[21] the novel offered the 'romance of friendship', with rustic walks more than games, and, all in all, beautiful escapism. It isn't a book about 'immorality', but a book about the pure, ideal friendship that a boarding school can supposedly offer, and which Owen felt he had missed out on, even though there are moments where the friendship is at least a little camp:

> 'I felt odd when you were singing – quite weepsy, you know. You like me, old Jonathan, don't you?'
> 'Awfully,' said John.
> [...]
> 'You looked at me because – well, because – bar chaff – you – liked – me?'
> 'Yes.'

When the book is mentioned in Christopher Isherwood's *Goodbye to Berlin* it is a hint at the homosexuality of its owner.

The book makes Harrow into a form of Eden. When Owen read *The Hill*, he described it to his mother as 'a tale of Harrow, and the hills

on which I never lay, nor shall lie: heights of thought, heights of friend-
ship, heights of riches, heights of jinks'. He had only had Birkenhead
Institute, alas; *The Hill* was 'lovely' but also 'melancholy reading'
because it showed what he had missed.[22] When he wrote to his mother
about Harrow at midnight on 21 February he became so 'thoughtful'
that he had to put down his pen and return to the letter the following
day ('I hope I did not <u>Harrow</u> you too much').[23] In the Artists' Rifles
in October 1915, there had been a rumour that 'the Camp is going to
move to Harrow', evoking a 'Pip-ip!' from Owen.[24] Owen might have
seen Harrow's spire from Hampstead Heath, like Gordon, the hero of
The Loom of Youth, but that was as close as he came to being a
Harrovian. He seems to have been happy enough at Birkenhead
Institute, at the time, but later in life he regretted not having gone to a
great public school. Indeed, *The Hill* is positioned against the world
Owen knew, both Shropshire ('No, my young friend, that may do well
enough in Shropshire, not here') and the demonic Mersey: 'One is
reminded sometimes,' said the Caterpillar, solemnly, 'that the poor
Demon is the son of a Liverpool merchant, bred in or about the
Docks.'[25] When one of the boys gets very drunk, it is because he comes
from poor stock, his father being a Liverpudlian.

As Owen pointed out in return, he had known one hill, Broxton
Hill, 'whose bluebells it may be, more than Greek iambics, fitted me
for my job'.[26] A comparison between hills is ultimately what *The Hill*
provides, for it is a war novel and the hill of Harrow is mirrored by a
hill in battle: from the Boer War, heroic Harry Desmond, known as
'Caesar', writes to his friend John Verney, who is still at Harrow, that
'The sight of this hill brings back our Hill' and on the eve of battle 'I
have the absurd conviction strong in me that, tomorrow, I shall get
up the hill here faster and easier than the other fellows because you and
I have so often run up our Hill together'.[27] The hill of battle proves to
be fatal:

It seemed that a certain position had to be taken – a small hill. For
the hundredth time in this campaign too few men were detailed for

the task. The reek of that awful slaughter on Spion Kop was still strong in men's nostrils. Beauregard and his soldiers halted at the foot of the hill, halted in the teeth of a storm of bullets. Then the word was given to attack. But the fire from invisible foes simply exterminated the leading files. The moment came when those behind wavered and recoiled. And then Desmond darted forward – alone, cheering on his fellows.[28]

And so *The Hill* clearly influenced Owen's own hill of battle in 'Spring Offensive', which begins, 'Halted against the shade of a last hill / They fed', and then says 'soon they topped the hill, and raced together / Over an open stretch of herb and heather'. There are many similarities between Vachell's battle and Owen's: a badly written school story fed one of the greatest war poems, its clichés being transformed into poetry, with, for instance, 'halted at the foot of the hill' becoming 'Halted against the shade of a last hill', 'a storm of bullets' becoming 'the surf of bullets'.

It was in February 1918 that Owen befriended a master from Shrewsbury School, Philip Bainbrigge, and it is likely that Bainbrigge lent *The Hill* to Owen.[29] Owen remarked that it was amusing to think of himself in the Masters' Rooms at Shrewsbury, although he was in Scarborough at the time and it seems that he never did ascend the hill to Shrewsbury School, which looked down on to the town. His friendship with Bainbrigge developed in Scarborough. Bainbrigge was a dear friend of Scott Moncrieff's, Scott Moncrieff saying of him, 'Friend – nay, friend were a name too common, rather / Mind of my intimate mind, I may claim thee lover'.[30] Philip Gillespie Bainbrigge was a Scotsman, like Scott Moncrieff, born in London in 1891, and after Eton and Trinity College, Cambridge, he had become a master at Shrewsbury School in September 1913, working there happily until March 1917. He was not obvious military material, but he eventually became a 2nd Lieutenant in the Lancashire Fusiliers. The novelist Nevil Shute would recall this remarkable man, 'a brilliant young Sixth-Form schoolmaster',[31] remembering his thick spectacles and tall, weedy appearance, which didn't make him look very martial, although his intelligence and sense of humour made him a popular officer.[32] His brilliance and humour were exactly what Owen needed in Scarborough, where he was missing congenial company. Bainbrigge provides a portrait of himself in a poem he wrote in response to Rupert Brooke's famous sonnet 'The Soldier':

> If I should die, be not concerned to know
> The manner of my ending, if I fell
> Leading a forlorn charge against the foe,
> Strangled by gas, or shattered by a shell.
> Nor seek to see me in this death-in-life
> Mid shrieks and curses, oaths and blood and sweat,
> Cold in the darkness, on the edge of strife,
> Bored and afraid, irresolute, and wet.
>
> But if you think of me, remember one
> Who loved good dinners, curious parody,
> Swimming, and lying naked in the sun,
> Latin hexameters, and heraldry,
> Athenian subtleties of δης and τοις,
> Beethoven, Botticelli, beer, and boys.[33]

Bainbrigge loved being a schoolmaster, and he had the greatest regard for Shrewsbury, finding it difficult to stay away when in uniform – Owen told his mother that Bainbrigge would be staying at the school at the start of March. He was one of those teachers who, like Owen, succeeded by being a boy himself. The boys treated him rather as a treasured friend than as a boring beak. Indeed, since the headmaster C. A. Alington had been Bainbrigge's tutor at Eton, Bainbrigge had, as near as possible, continued with his schooldays; as the headmaster said with reference to his Shrewsbury common room, 'poets and children have the greatest qualities in common'.[34]

Presumably the boys didn't know about his 'erotic' homosexual writings, although these writings too had, like his teaching, combined scholarliness and schoolboyishness, being less erotic than rudely playful, more *Carry On* than porn (and more bisexual than homosexual). The 'erudite and very funny'[35] *Achilles in Scyros*, dedicated to Scott Moncrieff, includes lines like 'How I love your soft sweet breasts and your / Front entrances to Heaven' and 'I'm certain yours is like a budding rose, / Lovelier than Ganymede's love-blossoming rod'.[36] He is also, alas, happy to joke about pederasty ('you can share your tutor's tent, my boy')[37] and celebrate school-dorm sexual fumblings ('squeeze a queer / Small snake uncoiling').[38] Bainbrigge was a very clever man who hadn't grown up:

> Here Aphrodite is not: Eros boy-like
> Plays his boy's games among the leaves so green,
> Bare-breeched[39]

There's no evidence that Owen knew about these versified 'boy's games' of Bainbrigge's, which he had written at university (and hadn't published).

*

Is Wilfred Owen's sexuality revealed by the company he chose to keep? As a schoolboy at Winchester College, Scott Moncrieff had become friendly with Robert Ross and other homosexual hangovers from the 1890s. In turn, Scott Moncrieff gathered around him younger gay men, including, by the end of the war, a teenage Noël Coward.[40] Now Owen was friends with Ross, Scott Moncrieff and Bainbrigge. Ross, who gave 'litigation' as one of his pastimes in *Who's Who*,[41] had been involved in a court case against Lord Alfred Douglas in 1914 in which there was an attempt to prove that Ross was a practising homosexual: the strong implication was that a friend of homosexuals must be a homosexual too. The judge, Mr Justice Avory, said that if Douglas was acquitted that would not condemn Ross, but he took sides in his summing-up, implying that everyone could guess what Ross was:

If a man allows himself to be associated with such a person as Oscar Wilde – I do not care what his literary genius may be – if he chooses to run that risk, can he complain if a person who is not carried away by admiration for the literary genius of Wilde says, 'A man is known by his friends.'[42]

Now Owen was close to Ross, and thus close to Wilde, and a gap of a generation was bridged: it had been in March 1893, the month of Wilfred Owen's birth, that Oscar Wilde, at the height of his fame, wrote a letter to 'Dearest of all Boys', Lord Alfred Douglas, saying 'I cannot see you, so Greek and gracious, distorted with passion' but confessing that 'You are the divine thing I want, the thing of grace and beauty',[43] and this letter would play an important part in the trials that saw Wilde disgraced and imprisoned. For Owen the Wilde scandal was a lifetime ago, but, if Wilde was long gone, here was 'poor tragic Bobby R.',[44] who had been with Wilde at the Cadogan Hotel and stood lovingly by his Oscar through the trials, imprisonment and exile. Ross had always been there to comfort him:

With luck there would be Robbie Ross round the corner. 'Oh, Robbie, I've had such a *frightful* dream!' 'What was it, Oscar dearie?' 'I dreamt I was dining in H-H-Hell! Oh, Oh, Oh!' 'There, there, Oskywosky, but Robbie's sure you were the life and soul of the party.'[45]

Yet it cannot be said that Ross and Scott Moncrieff only had gay friends and associates. H. G. Wells, enegetically and indefatigably heterosexual, was one of those friends of Ross; another was Arnold Bennett, who was also a friend of Scott Moncrieff. Admittedly, Owen and Ross only encountered Bennett and Wells at the Reform – they didn't go to Half Moon Street – but Ross was not an untouchable outcast or a man of the shadows: he lived in Mayfair, he was a devout Roman Catholic, he sat on committees, he was a guest at Downing Street, his lawyer was F. E. Smith, and he was a popular man. There

was no shame in being seen with him; on the contrary, his friendship
was something to boast about, and Owen happily name-dropped him
to Susan Owen. When Ross was persecuted by Lord Alfred Douglas in
1914, with Ross appearing in court (to be acquitted) and then Douglas
being arrested, H. G. Wells and Sir Edmund Gosse – the Establishment's
Man of Letters – gave evidence of Ross's character, and Ross also
received public support. His name is in the Gosses' visitors' book 112
times between 1892 and 1918, and it was Gosse who introduced
Sassoon to Robert Ross in 1915. Cantankerous, embittered Lord
Alfred Douglas had made an enemy of Ross, but Ross was widely
admired for 'his adroit and pleasing company, his tact and cleverness,
above all his sympathy and his witty comments on life'.[46] *The Times*
commented that 'friendship was the chief business of his life'.[47] With
Owen, as with a number of other young poets, Ross would not only
offer hospitality but also do his best to promote his poetry: 'in helping
others, Robbie became a noble and "impresario" parent fulfilling a role
for which he was eminently fitted, an adoring, forgiving and compas-
sionate friend'.[48] In February 1918, Ross had most of Owen's war
poems in his keeping, and tried to have them published by Heinemann,
while also recommending them to other friends.

Perhaps echoes of Wilde in Owen's poetry are some kind of indica-
tion of sexual preference. From visiting his cousins, even before he
moved to Dunsden, Owen had got to know Reading, where Wilde was
in gaol: Leslie Gunston said of Owen that 'I think his liking for Wilde
must have come late, as I don't remember discussing his work with
him, save perhaps the "Ballad" & of course we often passed that
building'.[49] There is no reference to Wilde in Owen's collected letters.
But Owen owned Wilde's poems and Robert Harborough Sherard's
Oscar Wilde, The Story of an Unhappy Friendship (1909), which was
dedicated to Ross, and by the time Owen was at Scarborough, Wilde
had become a detectable influence on his poetry including 'Wild with
All Regrets'. There's even a similarity between Craiglockhart's 'Anthem
for Doomed Youth' and the fourth section of 'The Ballad of Reading
Gaol', Wilde's poem about a trooper of the Royal Horse Guards:

They hanged him as a beast is hanged:
  They did not even toll
A requiem that might have brought
  Rest to his startled soul,
But hurriedly they took him out,
  And hid him in a hole.[50]

Owen was probably in London, having just met Robert Ross, when he wrote a fragment 'With those that are become' in November 1917, for which he wrote down on the page 'For each man slays the one he loves / The coward / The brave',[51] recalling Wilde's ballad:

Yet each man kills the thing he loves,
[. . .]
The coward does it with a kiss,
  The brave man with a sword![52]

Owen's poetry is open to 'gay readings'. Many interpretations of his poetry in terms of its supposed homosexuality have been reductive and unconvincing, hunting out gay innuendo in the imagery of guns and bayonets and holes, but poems such as 'The Promisers', 'Storm' and 'To Eros' can be read as homosexual poetry. The poem beginning '*Who is the god of Canongate?*' seems to be about a rent boy, 'the Flower of Covent Garden'. Is this another poem expressing Owen's concern for the downtrodden and abused, or is it a poem revealing his own sexual desires?:

Where is thy shrine, then, little god?
  Up secret stairs men mount unshod.

Say what libation such men fill?
  There lift their lusts and let them spill.

Why do you smell of the moss in Arden?
  If I told you, Sir, your look would harden.

What are you called, I ask your pardon?
I am called the Flower of Covent Garden.

What shall I pay for you, lily-lad?
Not all the gold King Solomon had.

How can I buy you, London Flower?
Buy me for ever, but not for an hour.

What shall I pay you, Violet Eyes?
With laughter first, and after with sighs.

This is probably the work of someone who had not slept with a rent boy – if he had, this enquiring or fantasising mode would have been less likely. It is someone imagining the life of a rent boy, from homosexual desire or from a desire to understand the homosexuality of his friends or from his sympathy for the oppressed (or all three).

There is enough evidence to suggest that Owen was at least attracted to the world of Wilde and sufficiently attracted to homosexuality to write about it. It can also be said that he took an aesthetic interest in male beauty. But it is not at all clear that Owen was prepared to sleep with men. Owen is usually described as 'homosexual' these days, but that shouldn't imply that he was actively so.[53] It would seem that Scott Moncrieff fell for Wilfred Owen in 1918, even addressing him as 'Mr W.O.' in reference to the 'Mr W.H.' who is often taken, not least by Wilde, to be the young man loved by Shakespeare. Exactly to what extent that interest was requited may never be known, but Robert Graves came to believe that both men were homosexuals and that Scott Moncrieff had seduced Owen. According to Graves, Owen was a 'passive homosexual' and in love with Sassoon:[54]

Interviewer: Why did you not write war poems – of your trench experience in World War I like your friend Sassoon, and like Owen?

Graves: I did. But I destroyed them. They were journalistic. Sassoon and Wilfred Owen were homosexuals; though Sassoon tried to think he wasn't. To them, seeing *men* killed was as horrible as if you or I had to see fields of corpses of women.[55]

In 1943, Graves said that 'Owen was a weakling, really; I liked him but there was that passive homosexual streak in him which is even more disgusting than the active streak in Auden.'[56] In the 1957 revision of *Goodbye to All That*, Graves described Owen as 'an idealistic homosexual with a religious background', but this description had to be deleted. However, Graves is not the most reliable witness. What Graves does in fact do is expose the difficulties involved in describing anyone as heterosexual or homosexual. It is in *Goodbye to All That* that he says,

In English preparatory and public schools romance is necessarily homosexual. The opposite sex is despised and hated, treated as something obscene. Many boys never recover from this perversion. I only recovered by a shock at the age of twenty-one. For every one born homosexual, there are at least ten permanent pseudo-homosexuals, made by the public school system. And nine out of ten are as honourably chaste and sentimental as I was.[57]

At school, Graves had developed a close friendship with a much younger boy, Peter Johnstone, who later acquired a reputation for homosexuality. Owen's homosexual experiences were probably fewer than those of the average 'heterosexual' public-school man (such as chaste Graves). One Shrewsbury boy recalled that while 'furtive sexual exploration was inevitably as common as the limited privacy allowed it to be', there were 'few "queers" in the adult sense; it was sexuality rather than homosexuality'.[58] Could Dunsden or the army have had the same effect as a public school? Graves described relations between men in uniform:

Do you know how a platoon of men will absolutely worship a good-looking gallant young officer? If he's a bit shy of them and decent to them they get a crush on him. He's a being apart . . . Of course, they don't realise exactly what's happening, neither does he; but it's a very very strong romantic link. That's why I had the best platoon and then the best company in the battalion. My men adored me and were showing off all the time before the other companies. They didn't bring me flowers. They killed Germans for me instead and drilled like angels.[59]

Sexual behaviour in Owen's time, even more than now, defied categorisation, and, equally, we cannot assume that a man's sense of himself was the same as the category that we might put him in today: it has been argued that in London 'Forms of understanding that we often assume to be timeless – the organization of male sexual practices and identities around the binary opposition between "homo-" and "heterosexual" – solidified only in the two decades after the Second World War'.[60] It is possibly more accurate to say that Owen was bisexual. But even then we have to be wary of thinking of that as a description of Owen's sexual practices. Writing about beautiful men or women was one thing; sleeping with them was another. Owen, who cherished his role as an officer and a gentleman, would have been reluctant to break the law by sleeping with men, and afraid of doing so, and he would still have considered sex with women sinful and dangerous too. Owen knew that in a time of war especially, any scandalous behaviour would have left him open to blackmail, and it was rumoured that German agents were compiling a list of homosexuals who could be seduced and blackmailed as part of the German war effort. Neither had he cast off his religious upbringing, and he was still very much devoted to his mother. Devotion to his mother could be interpreted as evidence of homosexuality but that also would be simplistic, and is more likely to be evidence that he was still somewhat childlike. Graves's sense that Owen was 'passive', a 'weakling', 'idealistic', might seem unnecessarily condemnatory, but it chimes with Maidie Gray's observation that 'individual development can hardly be said to have existed for him', and the opinion of Roland Bate, who knew Owen in the war, that all of Owen's feeling and desire were sublimated in his love for his mother.

Later in 1918, Owen met a Harrow boy, writing to his mother that when swimming he had encountered 'the best piece of Nation left in England – a Harrow boy, of superb intellect & refinement'.[61] The Harrow boy walked out of the sea and straight out of *The Hill*, a 'Caesar' or John Verney. He described the same boy to Sassoon as 'the shape, Shape I say, but lay no stress on that, of a Harrow boy'.[62] As he hints here, Owen was certainly capable of finding teenage boys attractive, but he was interested in class more than sex, the accent more than the body, and proceeds to describe the boy's accent and refinement. Owen's descriptions of boys avoid the pederasty that has been associated with Bainbrigge, Wilde and Ross – Ross himself was only sixteen, with 'the face of Puck and the heart of an angel',[63] when he met Wilde – although it isn't always clear how old Owen's boys or lads are. (Covent Garden's 'lily-lad' is young, a 'delicate bud', a barefoot 'little god', but he is not pre-pubescent and is very possibly as old as Owen, who says, 'there is too much sap in my blood' and he can 'break into fullest bloom'.) But it was clearly class – especially 'the way he spoke' – that excited Owen when he met the Harrow boy. And perhaps the boy represented an England that was worth fighting for. Owen was at heart a conservative and was delighted to encounter the rich and powerful. More than that, he wanted to be a public-school man himself; spiritually, he had become a Harrovian, rather like John Betjeman, who liked to announce that he was at Harrow 'in all but fact'.[64] Owen's aspirations were also reflected in the fact that he was collecting antiques at Scarborough, even more eagerly and successfully than in Edinburgh – if there is no ancestral home to inherit, then a gentleman must buy his own antique furniture. In February 1918, Owen went to see *Quinneys*, a play about the antiques business by the author of *The Hill*. Perhaps, ultimately, Owen was attracted to men, but he spent time with particular gay men, Ross, Sassoon, Scott Moncrieff and Bainbrigge, because they were all examples of superb intellect and refinement.

Their intellect and refinement seemed especially valuable as the war started to look as if it was turning against Britain. America had joined the war on the Allies' side, but Italy suffered terribly at the Battle of Caporetto in November 1917, the month in which the horrific Battle of Passchendaele finally came to an end, and then Russia opted for an armistice in December. So, before the American forces arrived in significant numbers, the Central Powers could concentrate their efforts on the Western Front and attempt to overwhelm the British and French forces as soon as the winter weather cleared. Towards the end of February, Owen and Bainbrigge sat in a little oyster bar in Scarborough, two epicures enjoying oysters fresh from the East Yorkshire coast, while things looked 'stupefyingly catastrophic on the Eastern Front', and Bainbrigge 'opined that the whole of civilization is extremely liable to collapse'.[65] The Treaty of Brest-Litovsk, signed on 3 March, was a victory for Germany against Russia. Bainbrigge was soon in France and it was beginning to look rather likely that Owen would be required to fight again. If oysters should be eaten only when there's an 'r' in the month, would Owen be in England for oysters in September? On 9 March, he heard that he was being sent to Ripon to do physical drill and get fit:

An awful Camp – huts – dirty blankets – in fact WAR once more. Farewell Books, Sonnets, Letters, friends, fires, oysters, antique-shops. Training again![66]

CHAPTER 14

Gallantry

This afternoon I went forth in search of adventure
WILFRED OWEN to SUSAN OWEN, 12 September 1918[1]

To die will be an awfully big adventure
J. M. BARRIE, *Peter Pan*, 1904[2]

R IPON's huge military camp spread round three sides of the town, and since 1914 it had acquired many miles of new roads and paths, a railway, and thousands of men (about 70,000 troops by 1917), many of whom found it hard to enjoy the badly run camp – J. B. Priestley recalled that 'my spirits sank as low there as they did anywhere during the whole war'.[3] The inefficiencies of the camp were highlighted on Saturday 16 March, when, despite all those soldiers, six German officers, held there as prisoners of war, managed to escape.[4] The British troops enjoyed escaping too (usually with permission), and the town was quite pleasant, Owen decided, while the Yorkshire countryside surrounding it was beautiful, so on the following day, 17 March, Owen walked to Fountains Abbey on a most pleasant pilgrimage of three or four miles along the grassy field-paths to Studley village and into the estate of Studley Royal, and then up the drive to the Victorian church and, at last, the famous ruins of the abbey. It was a Sunday, the day of the week when the Marquis of Ripon allowed free access to the abbey. Owen came back too tired to write but the adventuring on

Fountains Abbey by chance did him a world of good. Surely the area was enough to remind any soldier that England was worth fighting for? He sent his family a postcard of Fountains Abbey on 18 March, and another two days later; then, two or three days later, he sent a postcard of Fountains Hall: 'Fountains Hall is a glorious house – uninhabited too!' The Jacobean Hall, which stands next to the abbey ruins, was 'Almost worth fighting for!'[5] Armed men in stone stand at the front, including Julius Caesar and Alexander the Great, as if ready to fight to defend it.

On his way back to Ripon on 17 March, Owen noticed How Hill Tower, 'a kind of Watchtower or chapel on the top of a hill':

It arrested attention as all such towers do, and I climbed up, and finding inhabitants in it, desired tea of them. Only half the old chapel is occupied by peasants; the other is vacant. The rent would be about 2s. a week! I wish it weren't so far from here. The windows have a marvellous view (for this part of the world) & I could spend my spring evenings very pleasantly up there.[6]

It was the Chapel of Saint Michael De Monte, part of Studley Royal and once part of Fountains (although it was largely rebuilt in 1718). On it a relief carving gives the initials 'MH', for Abbot Marmaduke Huby, who built the tower at Fountains and, prominently, on both that tower and this little chapel he left his motto, 'Soli Deo Honor et Gloria'.[7] (At Ripon, Owen would famously write that his poetry is not about 'deeds, or lands, nor anything about glory, honour, might, majesty, dominion, or power, except War'.)[8] Here was his chance to return to the Church, and live in a chapel like a hermit or the unsocial Cistercians of Fountains. The tower would have been the natural place to live, after the turret at Scarborough and the topmost room at Mahim. It was, though, too far away for a man with more than just poetry to worry about. Instead, he would soon take an attic room on the edge of Ripon at Borage (now Borrage) Lane, where the celandines opened out together in the spring sunshine and there was much to be alive for. The attic was 'a jolly Retreat' where he could 'have tea and contemplate the inwardness of war, and behave in an owlish manner generally'.[9] One kind of 'inwardness' is seen in 'Mental Cases', drafted at Ripon, a poem about 'men whose minds the Dead have ravished': 'Memory fingers in their hair of murders'.

This contemplative owl was now twenty-five years old. On 18 March, his birthday, he had a quiet afternoon in Ripon Cathedral,[10] the fine building that rises high above the little market town and rests upon a crypt built by St Wilfrid, the town's saint. On 19 March, he went to Harrogate for the afternoon, but found it underwhelming, and was far more excited by the more modest villages nearby, especially Aldborough, where he encountered Roman remains: musing amid the ruins, it was as if he was back at Uriconium and Silchester, and 'If in 1913 I used to wish to have lived in the 4th Century, how much more now!'[11] In a cottage garden at Aldborough, in a tessellated pavement, there is the Greek word meaning 'Have pity'.

On 21 March the German Spring Offensive began, and, by the end of the day, 21,000 British prisoners had been taken. Owen followed the British retreat with dismay, but, as the British were pushed back, his poetry advanced. Ripon in flower that spring inspired the first half of 'Elegy in April and September', 'jabbered among the trees' in allusion to Sassoon's 'Repression of War Experience',[12] although the poem is also an Oxford-inclined poem, recalling Matthew Arnold's elegy 'The Scholar-Gipsy', the much-loved poem about the university and the country lanes thereabout. Arnold's name and the titles of Arnold's two pastoral elegies about Oxford – 'The Scholar-Gipsy' and 'Thyrsis' – appear on Owen's manuscript, and Owen says 'I will stray among these fields for him', while Arnold says 'Thou through the fields and through the woods dost stray'. 'Stray' is a very Arnoldian word.[13]

In May, he wrote 'Futility', a short and striking expression of the waste of war, although it too could be described as a kind of pastoral elegy – the sun that cannot wake the soldier's corpse 'awoke him once, / At home, whispering of fields half-sown'. It is about sensuous (even sensual) sunshine just as 'Thyrsis' is about the pursuit of light ('*The light we sought is shining still*'). 'Thyrsis' says of the dead poet that 'thine earth-forgetting eyelids keep / The morningless and unawakening sleep / Under the flowery oleanders pale', but there is none of Arnold's hard-won optimism in Owen's poem, which ends with questions that needn't be answered:

> Was it for this the clay grew tall?
> – O what made fatuous sunbeams toil
> To break earth's sleep at all?

Like 'Asleep', which Owen revised in May 1918, 'Futility' plays with both the euphemism that the dead have fallen asleep, and the sense that they are merely asleep because they are awaiting the Resurrection.

At Ripon that spring Owen also wrote 'The Send-Off', a remarkably assured and affecting poem about troops leaving by train and then returning:

> Shall they return to beating of great bells
> In wild train-loads?
> A few, a few, too few for drums and yells,
>
> May creep back, silent, to village wells,
> Up half-known roads.

The poem must have partly arisen from the call for stirring send-offs for troops: *The Times* carried an article on 27 March calling for bands for troops off to the Front, as 'An Aid to Cheerfulness' (in his draft, Owen uses both 'cheerful' and 'cheerlessly'). The article is very close to Owen's poem:

> Would it not also help to release the emotions of those who watch them go, and give a people which has been too long undemonstrative an occasion for breaking through its icy reserve? Why should we not give the lads a real send-off, instead of smuggling them out of the country, to which, perhaps, some of them will never return?[14]

Owen, too, had written of that smuggling: 'secretly, like wrongs hushed-up, they went'. *The Times* correspondent had described the same scene as Owen's:

> They were a draft, marching in full kit to the station *en route* for France. The wives and sweethearts of some marched with them. There were not a few people going about their ordinary business in the street as the soldiers passed, and one or two waved *farewell* and *God-speed* to the men. [. . .] Sometimes the women with them have fluttered small Union Jacks and tried to hide their natural feelings behind a show of gaiety.[15]

Even before the war, send-offs had always affected him. In the Bordeaux days, he visited Castelnau:

> Twenty minutes we waited at the window of the train, and the adieus were many. Rich masses of lilac encumbered the carriage, and the odour was carried by the inblowing breeze into my brain, to be an everlasting memory. Then those faces and those places fell away from me.[16]

This everlasting memory seems to have been in his brain when he wrote 'The Send-Off', where women give flowers to the men: 'Their breasts were stuck all white with wreath and spray'. And as a schoolboy he had written an essay on a railway station, which ends, 'As we turn from the last glimpse of our friends' farewell greetings, the platforms are deserted, the late scene of confusion seems almost incredible, but perhaps the sense of emptiness & solitude is increased as we think of the parted friends now speeding through the country'.[17] That essay was inspired by his railwayman father, and so perhaps, in some way, was his poem. His father was keen to see his son 'normal' again and back fighting.

Owen's journey back to the trenches had already started by the time he reached his twenty-fifth birthday. There was a sense that 'The

Send-Off' was indeed autobiographical and Owen was already on a train journey with a final destination across the Channel, saying 'I think less of leaving the Army: and more of getting fit'. He didn't think there was the least probability of demobilisation now.[18] At the Medical Board on 4 June 1918, it was officially decided that Owen had now recovered from his neurasthenia after more than a year as a disabled officer. He had improved considerably, presumably by no longer appearing to be highly strung and by now being in control of his memory; as Arthur Brock would later comment, by this stage in the war Owen had 'in the most literal sense "faced the phantoms of the mind"' but 'had *all but* laid them': 'they still appear in his poetry but he fears them no longer'.[19] Owen was fit for general service; there was no need to be examined again and he was told to report forthwith to the Manchesters at Scarborough. A railway warrant was issued.

At Scarborough, he wrote a poem that could be about either Scarborough or Ripon – both towns had a racing down above the town that was used by the army during the war:

Not this week nor this month dare I lie down
In languor under lime trees or smooth smile.
Love must not kiss my face pale that is brown.

My lips, panting, shall drink space, mile by mile;
Strong meats be all my hunger; my renown
Be the clean beauty of speed and pride of style.

Cold winds encountered on the racing Down
Shall thrill my heated bareness; but awhile
None else may meet me till I wear my crown.

'Training' expresses his sense of forward momentum towards fitness first, then France. The poem echoes Housman's 'To an Athlete Dying Young', which had also influenced 'Disabled' and was high-lighted by Owen in his copy of *A Shropshire Lad*. Housman's poem claims that it is better to die young 'early-laurelled' in one's glory than to grow old:

> Now you will not swell the rout
> Of lads that wore their honours out,
> Runners whom renown outran
> And the name died before the man.[20]

Owen's poem is also a fairly surprising echo of the athleticism of the public-school story. And although he was expecting to fight again, and might have recalled Housman's gloominess, the poem shows an optimism and ambitiousness, a hunger for the glittering prizes, that is absent from other poems of the time. Indeed, his poetic reputation was growing – this poet was going places. 'Futility' and 'Hospital Barge' were published in *The Nation* on 15 June. On 29 May, he had told his sister that 'I can now write so much better than a year ago'.[21]

'Training' is a poem about perseverance and courage too. Its cold winds even seem to recall the Antarctic adventures that had thrilled him. Owen had been working on 'Exposure', which he refers to in a letter to his mother at the end of April, and even though 'Futility' was written in May, it is a poem of snow. In bracing Scarborough in July 1918, Owen wrote, 'I'd rather be sent to the North Pole – and going out into the blizzard like a gallant gentleman than go and get spattered with the blood I am trying here to enrichen'.[22] For the second time in his letters he was referring to the famous death of Captain Oates on 17 March 1912 – the birthday of both Oates and Susan Owen, the day before Owen's birthday. The words of Oates's memorial in Antarctica had haunted Owen:

> Hereabouts died a very gallant gentleman, Captain L. E. G. Oates of the Inniskilling Dragoons. In March, 1912, returning from the Pole, he walked willingly to his death in a blizzard, to try and save his comrades, beset by hardships.[23]

Oates 'walked willingly to his death'; in 'The Next War', revised at Scarborough in July 1918, 'we walked quite friendly up to Death'.

Owen had wanted to be a hero. The First World War had given him few opportunities; it had not even given him the Italian cavalry. As W. B. Yeats would later argue, this modern war had taken the heroism out of fighting. At Ripon, Owen had drafted a preface to his poems in which he argued that 'This book is not about heroes'. But then that was only because 'English poetry is not yet fit to speak of them'. There *were* heroes, and 'Training' is the poem of a man with a thirst for heroism, despite a hatred of war. At Craiglockhart, he had written,

> I hate washy pacifists as temperamentally as I hate whiskied prussianists. Therefore I feel that I must first get some reputation of gallantry before I could successfully and usefully declare my principles.[24]

Owen was also responding to pressure from his father: his love–hate relationship with his father had now reached a point where he hated the fact that his father wanted him to fight, but was keen to win his father's approval by fighting heroically. His father had been disappointed to have an 'abnormal' shell-shocked son at home; so Owen wrote, in June 1918, that he had been 'Revolver Shooting', and 'it may be a final proof of my normality (for Father's satisfaction) that I shot better than most';[25] and, in July, he referred to 'my Father's message on hearing I was G. S.: "gratified to know you are normal again"'.[26] (The word 'normal' could be used as a synonym for heterosexual, so in *Maurice*, E. M. Forster's novel about homosexuality, written in 1913–14, Clive says to Maurice, 'I have become normal – like other men, I don't know how, any more than I know how I was born',[27] and Sigmund Freud used the term 'Normalen',[28] although that isn't what Tom Owen meant, of course.) In 'The Parable of the Old Man and the Young', written in July, Owen expresses the feeling that fathers, and especially his own, had decided to sacrifice their sons unnecessarily. The poem is more a reflection of Owen's relationship with his father than a statement of

Owen's attitude to the war. He uses the story of Abraham and Isaac, with Abraham being God-fearing Tom and Isaac as Wilfred – in the Bible, Isaac is the only son, but in the poem Owen makes it more auto-biographical by calling Isaac 'the first-born':

> Then Abram bound the youth with belts and straps,
> And builded parapets and trenches there,
> And stretchèd forth the knife to slay his son.

Owen's poem may have been autobiographical, but the same anger was found elsewhere during the war. George Orwell noted that 'by 1918 everyone under the age of forty was in a bad temper with his elders'.[29] In 1918, Osbert Sitwell wrote 'The Modern Abraham' about Abraham, the patriot, who sends ten sons to the war as a sacrifice.[30]

Owen had become friends with Sitwell that spring. The Sitwells had a home in Scarborough, but Owen met Osbert Sitwell during a visit to London; on 20 May 1918 he announced that Osbert Sitwell, a friend of Ross's, was invited by Ross round to Half Moon Street to meet him. Sitwell encountered a man 'somewhat young for his age';[31] Owen encountered a young upper-class officer, born in 1892, son of a famously difficult father – a father Sitwell would later present to the world in his stylish volumes of autobiography. Osbert Sitwell's portrait of Owen in *Noble Essences* is perhaps the best of the posthumous pen portraits of Owen by those who had known him. Sitwell's book also pays loving tribute to the kindness of Ross. Not that everyone admired Sitwell or his writing: throughout his life he had his detractors, who considered him a pretentious charlatan using his wealth and connections to create a career for himself as an avant-garde gentleman of letters. For the book of the year that combined 'the greatest pretension and the least talent', Philip Larkin and Kingsley Amis created a literary award called 'the Osbert': Larkin wrote, 'I can't remember at this date whether it ever went outside the family'.[32] T. S. Eliot would refer to them as the Shitwells.[33] The family included Osbert's sister Edith, and there was also their brother Sacheverell, who, five years younger than

Osbert and ten years younger than Edith,[34] was later to be another great
admirer of Owen's poetry, although, as Edith told Susan Owen, 'he
little dreamt that when he shook hands with your son he was shaking
hands with the greatest poet of our time'.[35] This brother was a poet,
too, and Scott Moncrieff gave Owen Sacheverell Sitwell's *The People's
Palace* (1918) that summer. The Sitwells invited Owen to contribute to
the 1918 edition of their poetry annual called *Wheels* (Owen's poetry
would eventually appear in *Wheels* in 1919): *Wheels* has been described
as 'the only true schoolboys' magazine published outside a school'.[36]

Owen and the Sitwells could share a love of Scarborough, especially
of the older end of the town, where the vulgarities of the tourist
industry were less in evidence. In a memory of childhood, Sacheverell
puts this area into its townscape: 'When we had scrambled out as far as
the rocks went, one had to turn round, of course, to come back, and
then one saw the town sweeping right round the bay with as many
windows looking on to the sea as possible; with, first of all, the long
stuccoed lines of houses, then the great bridge that joined the new town
to the old across a deep ravine, and beyond that the old town, much
smaller in scale and creeping low down to the sea so as to be near the
harbour, while right above this was the towering Castle Hill with the
ruins on it.'[37] The old town was a collection of fishermen's cottages,
historic houses, battered chapels, marine odours and ancient pubs, all
possessed by the past and inhabited by true-born locals, many of whom
looked as weather-beaten as their homes. Owen delighted in the old
streets and alleys, seeing Shakespeare in a lantern, he said, and seeing
in a balcony 'the whole of Italy'.[38] During this summer at Scarborough,
Owen wrote 'The Roads Also', a poem of four stanzas that seem to
describe the old Scarborough:

> The old houses muse of the old days
> And their fond trees lean on them and doze.
> On their steps chatter and clatter stops
> For the cries of other times hold men
>   And they hear the unknown moan.

They remember alien ardours and far futures
And the smiles not seen in happy features.
Their begetters call them from the gutters;
In the gardens unborn child-souls wail,
    And the dead scribble on walls.

That word 'scribble' seems to be a play on the word 'Scarborough', as it is in Virginia Woolf's First World War novel *Jacob's Room* (1922): 'mothers down at Scarborough scribble over the fire with their feet on the fender, when tea's cleared away'.[39]

Owen's copy of Swinburne's *Poems and Ballads* is inscribed 'Scarborough. Aug. 1918', and inside the book Owen has placed a postcard of the old end of Scarborough, a pretty painting of St Mary's Church above picturesque cottages. Owen has placed scansion marks at 'Sapphics' but his pencil highlighted lines in just one poem in the book, 'A Ballad of Burdens':

The burden of dead faces. Out of sight
    And out of love, beyond the reach of hands,
Changed in the changing of the dark and light,
    They walk and weep about the barren lands
    Where no seed is nor any garner stands[40]

In the final stanza of 'The Roads Also', he echoes Swinburne with 'love they have not lived / And passion past the reach of stairs'.

This haunting, and haunted, corner of Scarborough contrasted with the brash and bold holiday resort that continued to flourish during the wartime summers. To the annoyance of many soldiers, there were still people on holiday or in comfortable retirement, enjoying the views, the restaurants, the gardens, the beaches, promenading and even pleasure-boating. Owen wished that the Boche would have the pluck to come right in and make a clean sweep of the pleasure boats and promenaders at Scarborough's spa.[41] Owen's objection to this side of Scarborough came partly from snobbery, and certainly from a desire to escape his own origins (after all, he and his family had been Scarborough holiday-makers once). So he told his mother that he wanted to be preserved from all ships in glass bottles, plush chairs, group photographs, flowers under glass shades, shell picture frames, scene-painted boulders.[42] Whether Owen saw it or not, the ship in a glass bottle was something that captured his father, landlocked and sea-fevered, dry-docked in a suburban parlour, for whom ships were for dreams and memories. And yet Owen's rejection of pleasure boats and ships in bottles expresses the spirit of his father, the man who always seemed dissatisfied with regular suburban life and hankered after manly adventure for himself and his sons. When Owen chose to loiter in the fishing quarter, the only part of town where seagoing was seriously undertaken, he was mirroring his father's habit in Birkenhead of hanging around the docks as 'the Captain'. The Owen family had never felt comfortable in the milieu that they found themselves stuck in.

If the Victorian seaside holiday was frankly rather vulgar, perhaps those holiday-makers should have been noble creatures like the Sitwells:

> Preserve me from men in waistcoats shirt cuffs and braces of a Sunday afternoon; (and preserve them from me for I would tear their waistcoats from them, and cut their throats (open at the neck) and belt them into noble creatures.)[43]

But Owen was not simply objecting to being lower class or lower middle class, because the seaside also catered to the vulgarity of the uncivilised rich. The wealthy who might have been holidaying in Germany, Italy or France, had there been no war, had been forced by circumstances to holiday at Scarborough, a very English resort that could nonetheless offer some of the charms of the Continent, including French architecture (most noticeably the Grand Hotel on the South Bay) and French cuisine. Owen wished that the Boche would have the pluck to make a clean sweep not just of the common or garden holiday-maker but, in addition, 'all the stinking Leeds & Bradford War-profiteers now reading *John Bull* on Scarborough Sands'.[44] No doubt this remark expresses a snobbish dislike of 'trade' and the North as well as the more specific case of war-profiteering, but Osbert Sitwell had a similar dislike of the war profiteers, 'Those alchemists / Who had converted blood into gold'.[45]

One could say that poets were war profiteers, turning blood into gold by selling books about the war. Poets and publishers knew that there was, for once, money in poetry. The publication of 'Miners' in *The Nation* had been moderately lucrative – Owen felt that two guineas was good pay for half an hour's work – and when 'Futility' and 'Hospital Barge' were published Owen wrote to his mother saying he would send her the editor's cheque early in July. He was hopeful that he might be able to earn money by writing after the war. Without seeming to have any mercenary interest in publication, Owen started to put together a collection of his poems: his stated intention was to 'warn' rather than to earn money by entertaining, and if he was content to be 'a poet's poet' that rather implies that he did not expect to be a popular one. Nonetheless, his poems would not have existed without the war, and he intended to call the collection *Disabled and Other Poems*, a title that would speak to soldiers and their families. Another title considered was *English Elegies* (although in the drafts for 'Futility', Owen referred to Wales before changing it to 'home': 'In Wales, whispering of fields unsown').[46]

Owen no doubt hoped to sell many copies of his book, but he looked forward to giving copies away to a number of friends and writers. Looked at now, the list of twenty names of lucky would-be recipients could be a form of last will and testament – Owen had not written a will, and had little to leave apart from a modest amount of money and his poems. One name was 'Dr. Rayner', between Meiklejohn and Tailhade, even though he had not seen his botany tutor (who now possessed a doctorate) for a few years and they corresponded only occasionally, but her classes had grown into his war poems, such as 'A Terre':

I shall be better off with plants that share
More peaceably the meadow and the shower.

Soft rains will touch me, – as they could touch once,
And nothing but the sun shall make me ware.
Your guns may crash around me. I'll not hear;
Or, if I wince, I shall not know I wince.

At Mérignac, the heather reminded him of her, because heather was
her research specialism, so perhaps he also thought of her when in
'Spring Offensive' in the summer of 1918 he wrote of how soldiers
'raced together / Over an open stretch of herb and heather'. And he did
see her again in 1918. Her record of the meeting is revealing, despite,
and because of, its sense of things unsaid:

> He spoke with great appreciation of the time he had spent in France
> before the War & of how his feet had been set upon the right path
> towards a literary goal for himself. We kept away from the war but
> I remember the visit chiefly because of what was left unsaid & the
> impression left with me of an agonizing struggle before he had been
> able to accept the inevitable.
>
> I never saw him again & I have been conscious ever since of the
> feeling – very acutely felt at the time – that he had asked for bread
> & I had given him a stone, for our friendship had been too intermit-
> tent to allow anything like full expression of what one was really
> feeling about the world we were living in. Many of us, you know, at
> that time, were feeling rather numb, & were, if anything, glad of the
> escape to over-work and the over-fatigue that followed. I do
> remember clearly that he found a palliative in his very happy rela-
> tions with his men, & that he felt he could help many of them.[47]

'Spring Offensive' ends with the line 'Why speak not they of comrades
that went under?'; 'Strange Meeting' speaks of 'the truth untold'.
Owen's poems would fill the silence, and would speak for men unable
to express themselves, but to Sassoon too he said that summer, 'What
more is there to say that you will not better understand unsaid.'[48]
Perhaps this is the love that dare not speak its name, but it is more

likely to be a reference to Owen's feelings about returning to France. Sassoon himself had written about the 'noiseless dead' who came to him in bed in Britain and whispered to his heart about the battalion still fighting in the mud: 'When are you going out to them again? / Are they not still your brothers through our blood?'[49]

*

In the August letter in which Owen hoped to see the holidaymakers swept away by the Boche, he warned his mother that he would soon be back fighting the Boche in France because he was due to have a medical inspection with twenty-one others, ready to be declared fit for draft and to be sent on draft leave straight away:

> I may reach you even before this letter! I know not. I am glad. That is I am much gladder to be going out again than afraid. I shall be better able to cry my outcry, playing my part.[50]

C. K. Scott Moncrieff had endeavoured to get Owen a desk job, but his attempts failed. One option was that Owen could become an Instructing Staff Officer in England, possibly at Oxford.[51] According to Scott Moncrieff, the application was refused because Owen's shell-shock had been interpreted as a form of cowardice: 'the state of health in which he had come home a year earlier implied a shock to and consequent weakening of his *moral* [i.e. 'morale'], and that such "cases" were not to be put in positions, in any way privileged, at home'.[52] In fact, Scott Moncrieff suggested that the rejection was put more briefly than that, 'in words which do not look well in print'.[53] But then Owen was not convinced that he really wanted a safe job, there being within him that desire to go back to the Front for the sake of his poetry and his reputation – the war was now his subject, his poetry had been quickened by trauma, and, in addition, a reputation for gallantry would make people listen to his poetry. He also felt 'dead' to people in Scarborough, and France might be a chance to live.[54] Tom Owen wanted him to do his bit, so now he would, and gladly. He would show his father and any senior officer who thought that the shell-shocked Owen of 1917 had been a coward. But what is courage? If Owen had dared to escape from France to Spain in 1914, would that have shown courage or cowardice? Is it courage to fight or courage to refuse to fight? Is it cowardice to fight bravely when one has rejected the war in poetry and in letters to one's mother?

Sassoon had set an example by going back to the front line, rejoining his battalion at the Western Front in May after a spell serving in Palestine, and Owen would follow, even though, in July, Sassoon had returned to England wounded, accidentally shot in the head by one of his own men. In August, Owen could now see Sassoon for the first time that year; he spent a summer afternoon in the sibilant company of Osbert Sitwell and Siegfried Sassoon in Chelsea, when they sat in seclusion in Chelsea Physic Garden – 3 ¼ flowery acres, with a statue of Sir Hans Sloane, across the way from the Thames and Sitwell's home on Swan Walk. For two hundred years, the garden had been owned by the Apothecaries Company and it wasn't open to the public, so, once again, through the chain of friendships that began with Sassoon, Owen had acquired access to a secret garden. But military patients from hospitals in the vicinity were allowed into the garden sometimes, and this 'haunt of ancient peace'[55] was seen as a form of treatment for the veteran: 'Here, surely, is the very place for a few – only a few – nerve-shattered or sadly injured men to sit out in the sun and forget the din, the danger, and the pain [. . .] its formality cannot but soothe men fresh from the vast untidiness of the front; its air of quiet, beneficent growth cannot but hearten those snatched from loud orgies of destruction.'[56] Perhaps he thought of 'Disabled'. They had been to hear Violet Gordon Woodhouse, the clavichordist, and it was in this year that Sitwell published in *Wheels* 'Clavichords – To Mrs. Gordon Woodhouse':

Its pure and dulcet tone
So clear and cool
Rings out – tho' muffled by the centuries

Passed by;

Each note

A distant sigh

From some dead lovely throat.[57]

Owen also saw Scott Moncrieff, who had recently started to trans-
late *The Song of Roland*, the French poem about chivalry in the
Pyrenees, a poem that Owen had read in Bordeaux in 1915. Scott
Moncrieff had long held that ancient warfare, up to the Battle of
Flodden, was more noble and humane than modern warfare, because
courage and loyalty were pre-eminent and the slaughter was pictur-
esque. 'Ancient warriors looked upon war as a magnificent sport,' he
argued,[58] and he wrote that 'Amid the distractions of that summer in
London, where the sound of the olifant came so often and so direfully
across the Channel, Roland was a constant solace, and in the leisure
hours of that summer the first fourteen *laisses* were translated, copied,
and circulated in manuscript.'[59] As Scott Moncrieff gratefully confessed,
Owen played his part in this translation: 'I should not have begun to
translate Roland had not my friend Wilfred Owen [. . .] already made
assonant verse something more than a mere joke.'[60] So following the
example of Owen's poetry, Scott Moncrieff rhymes, for instance,
'sides', 'lie' and 'knight' or 'great' with 'break', although he doesn't
follow Owen's tendency to have the consonants rhyme and the vowels
not, as in, then, 'mystery' rhymed with 'mastery' in 'Strange Meeting'.

Owen met up with Scott Moncrieff in London after one of his visits
to Hastings, where Colin Owen, his younger brother, was now
stationed. Some of Owen's last moments in England were spent at
Hastings, famous, of course, for the battle (some seven miles away from
the town) at which Norman knights defeated the English forces of
Harold. The battle had begun with a Norman poet singing a song of
heroes before riding alone into the Saxon warriors. It is said that near
the battlefield a shower of rain can make fresh blood emerge out of the
ground as evidence of the slaughter. And now the time had come for
Owen to head into battle by crossing the Channel. He arrived in
France on 31 August. It seems he felt some trepidation, and that day
he wrote to Sassoon,

I have been incoherent ever since I tried to say goodbye on the steps of Lancaster Gate. But everything is clear now: & I'm in hasty retreat towards the Front. Battle is easier here; and therefore you will stay and endure old men & women to the End, and wage the bitterer war and more hopeless.[61]

To his mother that day, he wrote, 'Your love is my home, and I cannot feel abroad'.[62]

Owen had been given the opportunity to join the last push, for, as the summer progressed, it had become increasingly clear that the German Spring Offensive had slowed and failed, and that the tide was rapidly turning against Germany and its allies, although the German machine guns were still proving to be efficiently slaughterous. But there was still time for literature and friendship: at the YMCA rest hut in the reinforcement station at Étaples soon after arriving in France, Owen met Conal Holmes O'Connell O'Riordan, former Director of the Abbey Theatre in Dublin, who had been friends with innumerable writers, including Yeats and Edward Thomas – perhaps they spoke about Thomas's death at the Western Front in April 1917 – and was himself a writer under the name 'F. Norreys Connell'.[63] Owen confessed that he hadn't read anything by O'Riordan but that he had known his name;[64] so had he also known that O'Riordan wrote a book called *The Pity of War*, which was published in 1906? It seems likely, even if Owen was not consciously recalling the title of that book (a collection of short stories) when he wrote 'Strange Meeting' – 'The pity of war, the pity war distilled' – and drafted the preface to his poems in May 1918:

My subject is War, and the pity of War.
The Poetry is in the pity.

A popular title for books and articles since Owen's preface, 'the pity of war' was used a decade before the war by this cheery, hunchbacked army-admiring author of *How Soldiers Fight*, *The Follies of Captain Daly* and *The Young Days of Admiral Quilliam*.

O'Riordan met a boyish young officer – 'quite the youngest officer who came my way'[65] – and in the few days of their friendship he got to know a paradoxical man: 'The most remarkable thing about Wilfred was the contrast (as I saw him) between the gaiety of his extraordinarily pleasant company and the bitter melancholy of his verse.'[66] As Owen himself put it, 'You would not know me for the poet of sorrows'.[67] While inwardly full of hatred for war, he had consciously become the ideal officer, determined to help his boys and to do his bit, and capable of finding some happiness – for one thing, there was the hope that the Front would be good for his poetry. Soon he moved away from O'Riordan's convivial surroundings into the ruins of Amiens and from there he joined D Company of the 2nd Battalion of the Manchester Regiment at Corbie on 15 September. Three days later, elsewhere in the British advance, Philip Bainbrigge of the Lancashire Fusiliers 'died the death of a hero'[68] at Epehy when he 'courageously led a patrol to reconnoitre a sunken road suspected of holding the enemy'.[69] According to Scott Moncrieff, who had himself 'fought with the utmost gallantry at Cambrai',[70] Bainbrigge 'behaved with great gallantry, dear soul'.[71] Writer-priest Ronald Knox composed a poem for his old friend from Shrewsbury – at Bainbrigge's request, they were Greek elegiacs – and asked 'Who could be more worthy than you? / You, for whom the Muses lament'.[72]

After a month in France, Owen too entered into battle, and like Bainbrigge he showed courage. He was immediately awarded the Military Cross:

For conspicuous gallantry and devotion to duty in the attack on the Fonsomme Line on 1st/2nd October 1918. On the Company Commander becoming a casualty, he assumed command and showed fine leadership and resisted a heavy counter-attack. He personally captured an enemy Machine Gun in an isolated position and took a number of prisoners. Throughout he behaved most gallantly.[73]

He 'inflicted considerable losses'.[74] This might not sound like the man of the war poems. Remembering his duty and remembering his forefathers, the agile Welshmen of the mountains, he had shown the gallantry of 'gallant gentleman' Oates, and the courage of Bainbrigge, but unlike them he had survived. They were in the thick of it and for days all but surrounded by the enemy.[75] Yet he came through unscathed with his nerves intact: the recommendation for the MC noted his great coolness throughout, and his energetic devotion to duty. The blood on his uniform was not his own. On 10 October, Owen wrote to Sassoon, reporting that the battalion 'had a sheer time last week'.[76] Sassoon was in England, but even there Death had visited: Robert Ross died suddenly and unexpectedly on 5 October, and Sassoon penned a weak but heartfelt elegy to 'chivalrous' Ross,[77] saying 'death has found you kind and gay' – 'Your dextrous wit will haunt us long [. . .] O heart of hearts! . . . O friend of friends!'[78] When Owen heard the news, he told his mother that Ross's death was more affecting to him, almost, than many of the deaths that took place at his side, but when he heard that Tom Owen had been upset by an elderly friend's arm amputation in Shrewsbury, he was angered, telling his mother, 'How would Father like – No, I will spare you'.[79] Any irritation or bitterness was directed at his father rather than Germany or the government – this was somewhat unfair to his father, but Owen had shown that he was now more 'manly' than his father.

The war was coming to an end and the soldiers knew it, but they could not know when it would end, although there was increasingly a sense that the war could end any day, and, as news of successes trickled through, Owen hoped for peace before the end of 1918. He began to wonder whether he would have to fight again; he was behind the line for most of October, and wrote on the 22nd that he was unlikely to be in the fighting zone for some time yet. There was enough time for the British government to reach a peace deal with Germany before he had to fight. The government, though, were planning for the war to extend well into 1919. On 19 October, Douglas Haig predicted that the war would continue for another year because attacks were still meeting with considerable resistance and there was no sign that the German army would fold. British infantry and cavalry casualties at the Western Front from 21 August to 11 November were 264,383.[80] The killing continued, and it had in no sense quietened down while Owen was in the relative safety of rear positions. The British army advanced about thirty miles in October, but the Germans continued to fight bravely. In fact, German resistance strengthened towards the end of October. So, by the last days of the month, Owen was marching back towards the line. Like a knight going into battle, he needed the right armour, requesting new socks and '<u>any literary literature</u>'.[81]

He had been reading the opening chapters of Dickens's *Little Dorrit* carefully enough to remember them after marching 'umpteen miles'.[82] Those opening chapters mirror some aspects of his life by beginning with sunny southern France then moving to London, and by referring to ancient Egypt, Italy, Liverpool, oysters, the garret bedroom, 'the loom of his youth',[83] little children, soldiers. He had read the book before, back at Dunsden, where he imagined that Little Dorrit had the features, proportions and manner of poetry-loving Miss Wright, one of his teachers at Shrewsbury Technical School: 'I am much enjoying that Book, tho' the Bathroom Scene made me quite ill'.[84] In 1918, he had, by 20 October, only read the opening chapters, but if he then carried on reading he might have reached once again the dead man in the bath, the white marble at the bottom of the bath 'veined with a dreadful red', the physician 'dabbling his hands in water; redly veining it as the marble was veined, before it mingled into one tint';[85] still, this was unlikely to upset him now, when he had seen much worse in the flesh in France. And if he reached the bathroom scene then he also reached his beloved Venice, where, in a passage highlighted by Owen in his copy, Little Dorrit imagines her past life buried underneath the Grand Canal:

And then she would lean upon her balcony, and look over at the water, as though they all lay underneath it. When she got to that, she would musingly watch its running, as if, in the general vision, it might run dry, and show her the prison again, and herself, and the old room, and the old inmates, and the old visitors: all lasting realities that had never changed.[86]

It was to a canal that Owen was marching. He entered the line on 29 October and by the end of the month his battalion was at the western side of the Oise–Sambre Canal near Ors, ready for an attack in the first week of November. The German forces controlled the other side, and, as in some ancient war of the kind that Owen had thirsted after, the narrow water had become a boundary between two warring sides. The British were preparing to cross the canal, but, if the Germans held fast, their machine guns could turn the canal into Virgil's Tiber, 'foaming with much blood' (words echoed in 'Strange Meeting').[87] At school in Shrewsbury in 1907, Owen had written about 'The Defence of the Bridge by Horatius', and in 1918 he returned to T. B. Macaulay's long rendering of that tale of battle on the banks of the Tiber:

'Oh, Tiber! father Tiber!
   To whom the Romans pray,
A Roman's life, a Roman's arms,
   Take thou in charge this day!'
So he spake, and speaking sheathed
   The good sword by his side,
And with his harness on his back,
   Plunged headlong in the tide.

No sound of joy or sorrow
   Was heard from either bank;
But friends and foes in dumb surprise,
   With parted lips and straining eyes,
   Stood gazing where he sank;
And when above the surges

They saw his crest appear,
All Rome sent forth a rapturous cry,
And even the ranks of Tuscany
　　Could scarce forbear to cheer.[88]

In his little poem 'Schoolmistress', of early 1918, Owen wrote about Macaulay's Horatius but also his modern descendants, the men of the British army, men who are more ' 'Orace' than Horatius, more Mancunian than Roman, but now no less admirable to Owen.

For Rome itself, however, peace was nearer, and soldiers on the Western Front heard about Italy's success. For the Italian forces, including the cavalry that Owen had fancied joining, the war ended on 3 November.[89] Owen's battalion was due to mount its attack on a day when Italy could celebrate peace. He told Susan that five healthy, charming girls had died of fright one night of shelling in a village he had been to, but if Owen feared that he might end up like *Little Dorrit*'s 'carrion at the bottom of a bath', then he didn't tell his mother, she to whom he had confessed so much over the years. His last letter before the attack across the canal, a letter from a smoky cellar on the evening of 31 October, told her that it was 'a great life', and ended by saying that:

> I hope you are as warm as I am; as serene in your room as I am here; and that you think of me never in bed as resignedly as I think of you always in bed. Of this I am certain you could not be visited by a band of friends half so fine as surround me here.[90]

Owen humbly echoes here the young King's great speech before Agincourt in *Henry V* ('which I have read, and learnt, and spouted', Owen once wrote):[91]

> We few, we happy few, we band of brothers;
> For he to-day that sheds his blood with me

Shall be my brother; be he ne'er so vile
This day shall gentle his condition:
And gentlemen in England, now a-bed
Shall think themselves accursed they were not here[92]

Then, early on 4 November, Wilfred Owen and his band of friends tried to cross the canal. War veined the water with a dreadful red, before it all mingled into one tint.

CHAPTER 15

Home

SCENE: Shrewsbury

WORTHY: I'm sorry, sir, to be the messenger of ill news.

BALANCE: I apprehend it, sir; you have heard that my son Owen is past recovery.

WORTHY: My advices say he's dead, sir.

BALANCE: He's happy, and I am satisfied; the strokes of Heaven I can bear, but injuries from men, Mr Worthy, are not so easily supported.

GEORGE FARQUHAR, *The Recruiting Officer*, 1706, II.ii.90–6[1]

We went to S. Giles' yesterday. Mr. Roberts preached. 'Lo, I am with
you alway, even unto the end of the world.' *Matt.* 28. XX.
WILFRED OWEN to SUSAN OWEN – Shrewsbury, April 1907[2]

I N Shrewsbury, the Owens could read in the newspapers about the progress towards peace. On 1 November 1918 there had been 1,497,198 British officers and men in France, out of a total of 3,458,586 in the British army as a whole, and now, surely, all but an unlucky few would survive the war. Wilfred Owen had told his mother to expect him home by February 1919. The Home Front was not an entirely safe place, since the influenza pandemic – the Spanish Flu – was now killing 7,000 people a week in Britain, and killed possibly 30 million across the globe, but sons could come home and live the lives their parents wanted them to live. The papers spoke of 'Cheap Homes, not yet planned': "'For" said the paper, "when this war is done / The men's first instincts will be making homes."'[3] Wilfred Owen had had his own post-war ambitions too: a country cottage, a return visit to Bordeaux, an antiques business, flying, poetry. On 5 May 1918, Owen had laid down his future 'Projects': by 1919, his collected poems; by 1920, blank-verse plays on old Welsh themes, using Tennyson and Yeats as his models; and then work on 'Perseus' and 'Idyls in Prose'.

On 5 November, the *London Gazette* announced that Owen had been promoted from 2nd Lieutenant to Lieutenant. On that day, Siegfried Sassoon met, for the first time, Lawrence of Arabia, and Lawrence, who would also become friends with Robert Graves, can be seen as the man who achieved much of what Owen had, at times, wanted – a career in archaeology, Egypt, Oxford, escape, fame, status, solitude. And Lawrence, like Sassoon and Graves, survived the war. Soon Lawrence adopted the name Shaw – Susan Owen's maiden name, of course – as if he was another version of Owen (they were the same height, and both had boyish looks). Lawrence, for his part, envied poets, feeling that 'they had some sort of secret which he might be able to grasp and profit from'.[4] They would have become friends. Lawrence described Owen as 'remarkable'[5] and 'a very beautiful technician, with great power of saying (not to mention seeing) things':

> Sassoon has told me a lot about him. Owen was a decent fellow, very modest and not tolerant.[6]

On 9 November 1918, at the Lord Mayor's Banquet in London, the British celebrations began. The speeches were received with hearty cheers and the waving of handkerchiefs. When the Prime Minister, David Lloyd George, rose to speak, he met the cheers with joy and thanks, and spoke of victory as if it had already been achieved. He also took the opportunity to thank the mothers and fathers of soldiers for the part they had played. News of an impending armistice spread through Britain and France, and it was eventually signed at 5 a.m. on 11 November with hostilities ceasing at 11 a.m. (Britain and France being in the same time zone then). It was over. Britain was ready to celebrate when the end came. Church bells celebrated the Armistice and rang in the new era. In town squares bands played and thankful, noisy crowds gathered. In Shrewsbury, Tom and Susan Owen seem to have stayed at home, even though they had every reason to be happy – their three sons had joined the forces, but, whilst there were 723,000 British deaths in the war (from both disease and action) and a grand total of 9,450,000 had died in the conflict,[7] now all three Owens could return unharmed.[8] For four years, telegraph boys had gone down muddy lanes, up gravel drives, along suburban streets, delivering dreaded news about a son, but the Owens of Monkmoor Road had been spared, and the unexpected visitor at the door was surely no longer to be feared. But then, at noon, when the bells were still ringing, the telegram arrived at Mahim.[9] As Susan simply recalled, 'we heard the dread news <u>there</u> on Nov 11th/18'.[10] She would forever now associate her Shrewsbury home with a telegram. Owen could have sent a telegram announcing his return, but this one had come from what he called 'the W.O.', the War Office, not their W.O.[11] Lieutenant Wilfred Owen had died on 4 November.

The death of W. E. S. Owen, killed in action, was reported by the Officer in Charge of the 2nd Battalion of the Manchester Regiment on 6 November. The official report was then filled in on 11 November ('Report of Death of an Officer to be forwarded to the War Office with the least possible delay after receipt of notification of death on Army Form B. 213 or Army Form A. 36 or from other official documentary sources'). Army bureaucracy could be slow, so it was a week before the Owens heard, no doubt hearing when they did because there had been an attempt to empty an in-tray on a desk somewhere before the Armistice celebrations. The War Office would have been notified from France and then they would have sent a telegram through to Shrewsbury, presumably to the post office on Pride Hill (which sounds like a place out of *Pilgrim's Progress*), its Morse code all too familiar to the telegraph

operators. The words varied slightly from telegram to telegram but they
had been essentially the same throughout the war:

-.. . . .--. .-.. -.-- ('deeply')
.-. . --. .-. . - ('regret')
.. -. ..-. --- .-. -- ('inform')
-.- .. .-.. .-.. . -.. / .. -. / .- -.-. - .. --- -. ('killed in action')

To this they could now add '--- .-- . -.' ('Owen'), reducing the writer
to punctuation. The telegraph messenger – probably a boy, but possibly
a woman – would have taken the telegram over the Severn, past
Shrewsbury Technical School, past the Abbey, its bells still ringing,
and up to the modest suburban home where Wilfred Owen had loved
his top-floor room with a view. Shrewsbury knew about death on the
battlefield and grieving families: whether to the Battle of Shrewsbury,
or to battles against the Welsh, or to battles in the far corners of the
Empire, the town had given its sons. Ghosts returned: in August 1485,
on his way to Bosworth Field, Henry Tudor and his army stayed in
Barracks Passage and, because they received such a warm welcome, the
ghosts of soldiers killed at Bosworth are said to have returned to those
buildings – soldiers' faces appear at the windows in Barracks Passage,
peering in but unable to enter, like the ghosts in Owen's 'Exposure'.
Over the centuries, again and again, bad news had made its way to
worried wives and mothers, in a letter or by word of mouth, from near
or from far, but now in the modern age there was the telegram, with
the knock at the door, the glance at the slip of paper and a muttered
'No answer' to the uniformed messenger.

Telegrams by their nature would provide few details, but eventually
the Owens learnt about the attack and the canal, and how their son was
doing his duty bravely at the moment when he was shot. He and his
men had the task of crossing a deep ditch and then the canal itself. The
attack began at 5.45 a.m. after a night of rain and mist. Against the
German machine guns and artillery, the Royal Engineers tried to put a
bridge into place. Some men crossed the canal. Wilfred Owen did not.

When anyone dies the family must wonder whether another path could have been taken, and the many varieties of 'what if?' and 'what might have been' plague the mourner like flies. In Owen's case, if he had stayed at Dunsden he would probably have joined up at the start of the war; if he had delayed joining the forces in 1915, he would have been conscripted the following year; if he had joined the Merchant Service like his brother, he would have served in the navy. If he had gone to Oxford in 1911, he would have finished his degree in 1914 and could have stepped straight into the army: the vast majority of undergraduates joined up early in the war, and of those who matriculated at Oxford between 1910 and 1915, 29.3 per cent were killed in the war (compared with an overall death rate of 13.6 per cent for British officers).[12] Perhaps Owen would still have died; perhaps he would have died very early in the war. But what if he had escaped to Spain in 1914? Or if he had got a desk job in the summer of 1918? Or if he had got a Blighty? Or if he had made it across the canal? If he had survived the war? One who knew him suggested that 'he would have become, I hazard, a leader of some Yoga sect of Buddhism'.[13] He could have become a love poet and a poet of the Second World War. Sassoon wondered whether 'the modern intelligentsia' would have ignored Owen if he had lived.[14]

It could have been a long life. The last person to be born before Owen was Yone Minagawa, who was born on 4 January 1893 and died on 13 August 2007; and one Emiliano Mercado del Toro, the last man born before Owen, and the last war veteran born before 18 March 1893, died in 2007 too. The last known veteran of the war died in 2012. But, having once written that 'I hate old age, and there is only one way to avoid it!',[15] Wilfred Owen died at twenty-five, and, having once fancied having 'my dead name' in Westminster Abbey, 'High in the heart of London, unsurpassed / By Time for ever', Owen was buried in the humbler, more rustic surroundings of Ors Communal Cemetery, to the north-west of the village of Ors, between Le Cateau and Landrecies. The grave carries an epitaph taken from Owen's poem 'The End': 'Shall Life renew these bodies? Of a truth / All death will he annul'. The words express religious conviction whereas in Owen's poem they express religious doubt. Perhaps 'Strange Meeting' would have been more suited to his gravestone: Siegfried Sassoon, for one, saw it as Owen's own epitaph as well as his elegy for soldiers of all nations. But the epitaph at Ors was chosen by Susan Owen and the words on a grave often express the beliefs and grief of the mourners rather than the dead; the words are not insincere or misleading because they are the perfect expression of the hopes of Owen's parents, who believed that their son had gone to Heaven. In 'Asleep', Owen had wondered whether there is a Heaven of angels and 'calm pillows of God's making' – 'Who knows?' But his parents were devout Christians and had no doubts. In May 1919, Susan wrote movingly to Alec Paton, Owen's friend from Birkenhead who had lost contact with him:

> I have been in very frail health for some years and the loss of my first-born boy has been a great trial to us all – tho' we have two dear boys and Mary left – no one can ever fill his place – but then, I know I shall go to him; tho' he can never come back to me and that wonderful hope is my strength and stay – a wonderful God given strength to bear the awful sorrow. Wilfred only went to the front (for the second time) on September 1st, he won his Military Cross on Oct. 1st and on Nov 4th was taken 'Home' while leading his men, and helping to make a bridge across Ors Canal. The [sic] buried him in the grave-yard at Ors – someday I hope to be able to see it – Dear Alec make the best of the life that has been spared to you – and live to His Glory Who gave His life for you and me upon the Cross – and for those dear pals who have given their lives for us in this awful War – they will be waiting to welcome us – and some day you two will be "pals" again you were each others first boyhood friends – and that true friendship must be renewed someday, in the better and happier Home that God has prepared for all who believe, with just child-like faith, in Him – [. . .] Oh! how he hated war and all its horrors – but he felt he must go out again to share it with his boys – his nature never changed [. . .] I am sure no Mother ever had such loving letters.[16]

Alec Paton recalled the Owens' happy home, and he said that that home would be recreated in Heaven. Owen had told Susan that she was his home and that her love was his home; and now she would see him again in the home of God's love.

Catholic C. K. Scott Moncrieff was also convinced that heaven was now his friend's home.[17] When he dedicated *The Song of Roland* to Owen in 1919, he included a poem 'To W. E. S. O.': it speaks of Owen's literary immortality but also of Owen's life in Heaven, and imagines the day when 'Beyond the stars' light, in the eternal day, / Our two contented ghosts together stay'.[18] In 1921, he had written to Susan Owen, saying that her son had helped him from beyond the grave, and with her kindly 'child-like faith' she could believe him:

> What a wonderful time it will be when we all meet again. Thank you for telling me that you feel Wilfred has helped you since he was 'called home to God'. I wonder <u>how</u> much they do influence us? <u>Certainly</u> their memory does – all my memories of Wilfred are very precious and I know he is a power for <u>good</u> in the hearts and lives of his two younger brothers still, and always will be.[19]

When Scott Moncrieff died in 1930, his mother used a medium in order to communicate with her son. The infant Wilfred Owen had once wondered whether it was possible to get the evening paper in Heaven, and Scott Moncrieff was now able to answer that query, pointing out that he could read anything he wanted to read. Heaven was like a country house or boarding school, where Scott Moncrieff, reunited with many friends, was rejuvenated: 'I feel so terribly young, just as if I was beginning my life again'.[20] Wilfred Owen's description of the afterlife in 'Strange Meeting' is both more credible and more memorable, but Owen did remain young, like so many millions: 'They shall grow not old, as we that are left grow old. / Age shall not weary them, nor the years condemn.'[21]

*

Owen's other afterlife was literary. Years after his burial at Ors, he became one of sixteen poets of the First World War commemorated with a memorial in Westminster Abbey's Poets' Corner – a memorial that carries words from Owen's preface to his poems. In Ors he was buried with soldiers; in Westminster his name is remembered alongside poets. Other memorials and plaques commemorate the poet too: one at Shrewsbury Abbey carries words from 'Strange Meeting'. His immortality was ensured by his poems, so on 3 November 1919 Edith Sitwell wrote to Susan saying 'Tomorrow, his first poems in book form will be with you – the immortality of his great soul', referring to *Wheels*, which was dedicated to Owen and included a selection of his war poems.[22] Owen had, of course, been asked to contribute to 1918's *Wheels* so it was natural that *Wheels* should launch his work into a country trying to recover from the war. One of the poems in *Wheels* was 'Strange Meeting', which became for many people the greatest poem of the war. T. S. Eliot said that it was 'of permanent value and, I think, will never be forgotten', calling it 'not only one of the most moving pieces of verse inspired by the war of 1914–18, but also a technical achievement of great originality'.[23] When Owen's *Poems* were published by Chatto and Windus in 1920, with an introduction by Sassoon, 'A Portrait of the Author' and editorial work by Edith Sitwell, Edmund Blunden noted that in 'Strange Meeting' Owen was at his greatest and that the discovery of final assonances in place of rhyme might mark a new age in poetry. *The Poems of Wilfred Owen*, edited by Blunden, appeared in 1931. Owen was a man who had had no children but he had literary descendants. He left no will and had little to leave, apart from books and antiques, but there was a rich literary inheritance for those who came after, and his poems sold. Owen's descendants in poetry would include W. H. Auden, Keith Douglas, Philip Larkin, Ted Hughes, Seamus Heaney.

He is still relevant today partly because, as Larkin noted,

in the end Owen's war is not Sassoon's war but all war; not particular suffering but all suffering; not particular waste but all waste. If his verse did not cease to be valid in 1918, it is because these things continued, and the necessity for compassion with them.[24]

As a war reporter, Martin Bell used to carry Wilfred Owen's poems with him everywhere.[25] Seamus Heaney has written that 'in the wake of the Omagh bombing, I remember how grateful I was to invoke Wilfred Owen's line about "the eternal reciprocity of tears"'.[26] And quotations from poems such as 'Anthem for Doomed Youth', 'Disabled', 'Dulce et Decorum Est' and 'Exposure' are often used these days in discussions of the war on terrorism and the war in Iraq. When Harold Pinter was given the Wilfred Owen Award on 18 March 2005, he asked, 'What would Wilfred Owen make of the invasion of Iraq?'[27] Pinter was convinced that Owen's response would have been thoroughly Pinteresque, but then, in the First World War, Owen looked forward to seeing the Middle East with the army: in 1916, he wrote, 'All our draughts go to Egypt; thence to Mesopotamia. I am glad.'[28]

Wilfred Owen remains contradictory: not quite a pacifist, he even hated 'washy pacifists'; he wrote 'Dulce et Decorum Est' but he also wanted chivalry; he was the eternal boy who was a grown-up voice in an infantile war; he loved home but was eager to escape it; he was a Christian of a kind, who disliked the Church; conservative and radical, normal and abnormal; the snobbish supporter of the downtrodden; the poet of modernity who was in love with the past; the realist and romantic; he was an innovative and traditional writer who was devoted to poetry and wrote, in the preface to his poems, 'Above all I am not concerned with Poetry'; he longed for friendship and solitude; he fought gallantly, and urged his men to fight bravely, in a war he had been reluctant to join and then came to oppose bitterly. This is another part of why the man and his poems are so popular – he can appeal to everyone, and remains intriguing.

On 7 February 1954, Siegfried Sassoon had a pleasant dream about Wilfred Owen, who had returned to life: Sassoon had never had a dream of himself with Owen before, and cried 'O Wilfred, how wonderful, that you are back again alive!' Sassoon explained to him 'all that had happened about his becoming so famous'.[29] Owen is still famous. Today, he is everywhere. He's encountered in the classroom and in television programmes, in Shropshire and in songs, in Benjamin Britten's *War Requiem* and in Derek Jarman's *War Requiem*, in Westminster Abbey and in Alan Bennett's *The History Boys*, in Pat Barker's *Regeneration* and in the film of that novel. Rowan Atkinson was given an Owen moustache in *Blackadder Goes Forth* so that he looked rather like the war poet. The restaurant critic can write of 'Bayonne ham with the best celeriac remoulade: crunchy, sleek and as potent with the sting of mustard as a Wilfred Owen lament'.[30] 'Anthem for Doomed Youth' became one of the 'Poems on the Underground', so commuters could read, to the rapid rattle of the train, Owen's poem with its 'rapid rattle' of guns. He's one of the best known and most loved poets. Owen is the quintessential War Poet, one of the most famous victims of war, a representative of youth and of doomed youth. He has been a chosen book on *Desert Island Discs*, and David Cameron has chosen 'Dulce et Decorum Est' as his favourite piece of poetry: 'I still remember the first time I read Owen's poems and the incredible power and anger' – Owen's poems 'were literally an eye-opener and I still find them moving when I read them again today'.[31] They might not have been *literally* an eye-opener, but it is an appropriate idea, given that Owen's poem describes men who went 'all blind'. As the centenary of the war arrives, many people will return, or be introduced, to Wilfred Owen – to the poetry, to the young moustached face and to the story of his life.

Abbreviations

JFO I   Harold Owen, *Journey from Obscurity: I. Childhood* (London: Oxford University Press, 1963)

JFO II   Harold Owen, *Journey from Obscurity: II. Youth* (London: Oxford University Press, 1964)

JFO III   Harold Owen, *Journey from Obscurity: III. War* (London: Oxford University Press, 1965)

CPF   Wilfred Owen, *The Complete Poems and Fragments*, ed. Jon Stallworthy (London: Chatto and Windus, Hogarth Press and Oxford University Press, 1983)

CL   Wilfred Owen, *Collected Letters*, ed. Harold Owen and John Bell (London: Oxford University Press, 1967)

Unless the notes state otherwise, Owen's poems are taken from Wilfred Owen, *The Poems of Wilfred Owen*, ed. Jon Stallworthy (London: Chatto and Windus, 1990)

Notes

A Note of Introduction

1. John Kemplay, *The Two Companions: The Story of Two Scottish Artists, Eric Robertson and Cecile Walton* (Edinburgh: Ronald Crowhurst, 1991), p. 68.
2. Tuesday afternoon, 25 September 1917: 'we had a jolly dinner at the Caledonian Hotel'. *CL* 495.
3. Kemplay, *The Two Companions*, p. 68.
4. 19 September 1917. Cited by John Kemplay in a letter to the author, 3 March 2011.
5. Cecile Walton, 19 October 1917. Cited by John Kemplay in a letter to the author, 3 March 2011.
6. Edmund Blunden, 'Memoir', *The Collected Poems of Wilfred Owen*, ed. C. Day Lewis (London: Chatto and Windus, 1966), p. 170.
7. Owen claimed that he was a child until 'Beaumont Hamel' in early 1917, which was the experience that he describes in 'Exposure'.
8. Manchester, University of Manchester Library, MS DSW /1/1/4/8/9, 'Owen thesis – MSS, notes etc', notebook, pp. 64–5.
9. *JFO* III, p. 61.
10. *CL* 479.
11. *CL* 479. Monday 30 July 1917.
12. *CL* 430.
13. 19 August 1918. *CL* 569.
14. *CL* 356.
15. *CL* 274.
16. *CL* 482. Presumably referring to Coventry Patmore: 'Tennyson is like a great child'. Cited by Arthur Christopher Benson, *Tennyson* (London: Methuen, 1912; first published 1904), p. 79.
17. Author Symons, 'Ernest Dowson' (1900) in *The Poems of Ernest Dowson* (London: John Lane, The Bodley Head, 1905), p.xvii.
18. *CPF* 416.
19. *CPF* 414.
20. *CL* 590.
21. Yeats to Dorothy Wellesley, 21 December 1936. See Bernard Bergonzi, *Heroes' Twilight: A Study of the Literature of the Great War* (London: Macmillan, 1980), p. 125.
22. 'Arms and the Boy'.

1 Lands of Our Fathers

1. George Borrow, *Wild Wales: Its People, Language and Scenery* (London: T. Nelson, n.d.), p. 368. Wilfred Owen's copy is in the English Faculty Library, Oxford.
2. Herman Melville, *Redburn: His First Voyage* (New York: Russell and Russell, 1963), p. 278.
3. *CL* 581.
4. *JFO* I, p. 3.
5. Lewis Owen's wife was Margaret Puleston, said to be descended from Joan, 'the Fair Maid of Kent', wife of (among others) the Black Prince, and mother of Richard II.
6. It is near Dinas Mawddwy that George Borrow meets a fine and friendly woman and asks her her maiden name: '"Owen," said she laughing, 'which after my present name of Jones is the most common name in Wales"'. Borrow, *Wild Wales*, p. 377.
7. Also see James J. Levick, 'The Early Welsh Quakers and their Emigration to Pennsylvania', *Pennsylvania Magazine of History and Biography*, xvii, 4 (1893), pp. 385–413.
8. The 'Gwylliaid Cochion Mawddwy'.
9. Baron's Gate is three miles east of Mallwyd, the next village to Dinas Mawddwy.
10. 'T. R.', 'Gwylliaid Cochion Mawddwy; or The Red-Headed Banditti of Mawddwy', *The Cambro-Briton*, i, 5 (January 1820), p. 186.
11. Cited by E. Mary Hartley, '"Baron" Lewis Owen of Dolgellau and his Descendants', *Second Stages in Researching Welsh Ancestry*, ed. John and Sheila Rowlands (Bury: FFHS and UWA, 1999), p. 332.
12. 'owne' is perhaps a punning anagram of Owen.
13. *CPF* 472–80.
14. Manchester, University of Manchester Library, MS DSW /1/1/1/25/8, 'University College Reading', M. C. Rayner to Dennis Welland, 25 September 1947, f. 3r.
15. Different army records gave his height as 5 feet 5 ½ inches, 5 feet 5 inches and 5 feet 6 inches.
16. *CL* 470.
17. Dylan Thomas, *The Collected Letters*, new edition, ed. Paul Ferris (London: J. M. Dent, 2000), p. 967.
18. *CL* 36.
19. *JFO* I, p. 162.
20. Pym's mother, Irena Spenser Thomas, was born in Oswestry in 1886. Her father opened the ironmongery shop in Oswestry in 1865.
21. 'Strange Meeting'. 'Uriconium'.
22. See Manchester, University of Manchester Library, MS DSW /1/1/7/1, 'Typescript extracts', Susan Owen to Miss Vera Hewland, 5 July 1936, f. 3r: 'the room where Wilfred was born is still there – I saw the window some years ago – I was born there too!'
23. *CL* 329.
24. Edward Burne-Jones to F. G. Stephens 1885, cited by Penelope Fitzgerald, *Edward Burne-Jones* (Stroud: Sutton, 2003), p. 208. The baronetcy was offered on 27 January and was made public by the time *The Times* referred to 'Sir Edward Burne-Jones' on 12 February.
25. *CL* 82.
26. 'The Oswestry Flower Show', *Wrexham Advertiser, and North Wales News* (Saturday 8 September 1894), p. 5.
27. University of Manchester Library, MS DSW /1/1/7/1, 'Typescript extracts', Susan Owen to Miss Vera Hewland, 12 August 1936, f. 4r.
28. Ibid., f. 4r.

29. 'All Children'. *CPF* 428.
30. In 1895, the GWR ran 721,090 passenger trains.
31. 'The Send-Off'.
32. Lowry grew up at Caldy a few miles west of the town.
33. Malcolm Lowry, *Ultramarine: A Novel* (London: Jonathan Cape, 1963), p. 142.
34. Ibid., p. 67.
35. J. B. Priestley, *English Journey* (London: William Heinemann, 1934), p. 245.
36. Henry James, *English Hours* (Oxford: Oxford University Press, 1981), pp. 1–2. Liverpool is described in 1888. The book was published in 1905.
37. *CL* 347–8. Tranmere is the dockland area at the south end of Birkenhead, and also has a park on higher ground.
38. Cited by Niall Griffiths, *Real Liverpool* (Bridgend: Seren, 2008), p. 135.
39. Five or six miles as the crow flies. Lennon grew up at 251 Menlove Avenue, Woolton.
40. Dixon Scott, *Liverpool 1907* (Neston: Gallery Press, 1979; first published in 1907 by A. and C. Black), p. 6.
41. The Wirral, described in 'The Churchyard on the Sands' by Lord de Tabley, in Geoffrey Grigson, ed., *The Faber Book of Poems and Places* (London: Faber and Faber, 1980), p. 238.
42. Benjamin Disraeli, *Tancred: or, The New Crusade*. vol. III, book V, chapter V.
43. Rectoral Address at Glasgow University, 7 November 1923.
44. *CL* 222.
45. *CL* 412.
46. *CL* 360.
47. *CL* 411.
48. Priestley, *English Journey*, p. 245.
49. Ibid., p. 237.
50. Oxford, University of Oxford, English Faculty Library, Owen Collection, Box 3, AA 410, 'The Autobiography of a Dog'.
51. *CPF* 433.
52. W. M. Comber and D. Haworth, eds, *Cheshire Village Memories* (Malpas: The Cheshire Federation of Women's Institutes, [1952?]), p. 38.
53. At the Birkenhead Institute, he had good schoolmasters – the two headmasters during his time there were educated at Edinburgh University and London University, respectively.

2 The Struggle for Existence

1. *CL* 325.
2. Kenneth Grahame, *The Wind in the Willows* (New York: Charles Scribner's Sons, 1908), p. 102.
3. Nathaniel Hawthorne, *Our Old Home* (Boston: Houghton, Mifflin, 1900), p. 49.
4. *JFO* III, p. 61.
5. Neville Cardus, *Autobiography* (London: Collins and the Book Society, 1947), p. 60; 63; 66.
6. Oxford, University of Oxford, English Faculty Library, Owen Collection, Box 3, AA 410, 'The River Severn'.
7. Arthur Mee, ed., *Shropshire: County of the Western Hills* (London: Hodder and Stoughton, 1939), p. 190.
8. Sir Philip Sidney was a pupil at the school before the buildings in question were built.
9. *CL* 54.
10. Desmond F. T. Coke, *The Bending of a Twig* (London: Chapman and Hall, 1907), pp. 238–9.
11. *JFO* III, p. 160.

12. *CL* 53.
13. *Baedeker's Great Britain 1890: A Handbook for Travellers* (reprinted by Old House Books, Moretonhampstead), p. 262. There are varying calculations of Shrewsbury's population at the time, some giving it as about 50,000, and it depends on whether the suburbs and surrounding area are included.
14. The Shrewsbury Rail Disaster was on the front page of the *Illustrated London News* on Saturday 19 October. The disaster was also covered in detail inside. Wilfred Owen would have seen the wreckage, which was even depicted on postcards.
15. John Holloway, ed., *The Oxford Book of Local Verses* (Oxford: Oxford University Press, 1987), p. 197.
16. Cited in Wendy Moffat, *E. M. Forster: A New Life* (London: Bloombury, 2010), p. 91.
17. Manchester, University of Manchester Library, MS DSW /1/1/7, Susan Owen to Scott Moncrieff (7 February 1921), f. 5r.
18. *CL* 137.
19. *JFO* III, p. 59.
20. *CL* 31.
21. *JFO* I, p. 103.
22. *CL* 325.
23. 'To Poesy'.
24. *CL* 22.
25. University of Oxford, English Faculty Library, Owen Collection, Box 3, AA 416, 'Notes on Keats'.
26. *CL* 69. April 1911.
27. *CL* 88. From the preface to *Endymion*, dated 'Teignmouth, 10 April 1818', published May 1818. John Keats, *The Complete Poems*, ed. John Barnard (London: Penguin, 2003), p. 505.
28. *CL* 70.
29. J. A. Erskine Stuart, *The Literary Shrines of Yorkshire: The Literary Pilgrim in the Dales* (London: Longmans, Green, 1892), p. v.
30. *CL* 70.
31. Cited by C. Day Lewis, 'Introduction', *The Collected Poems of Wilfred Owen*, ed. C. Day Lewis (London: Chatto and Windus, 1966), p. 14.
32. Leonora Eyles, *The Ram Escapes* (1953), cited by Pamela Horn, *The Victorian and Edwardian Schoolchild* (Gloucester: Alan Sutton, 1989), p. 180.
33. Oxford, University of Oxford, English Faculty Library, Owen Collection, Box 29, 6, 'Reminiscences', 27 February 1970. Mr and Mrs Roy Denville Jones.
34. Ibid., 'Reminiscences', 27 February 1970. Mr A. J. Wright, fellow pupil at the Technical School.
35. Ibid., 'Reminiscences', 27 February 1970. Miss Beth Smith.
36. J. B. Priestley, *The Edwardians* (London: Heinemann, 1970), pp. 104–5.
37. George Grossmith and Weedon Grossmith, *The Diary of a Nobody* (Bristol: J. W. Arrowsmith, 1892), pp. 13, 14–15.
38. *CL* 63.
39. *CL* 125. 19 March 1912.
40. He set out on 23 September 1880, around the time when the academic year begins – his son Wilfred's departure for France in late September 1913 at the age of twenty mirrored his father's own 'gap year' at a similar age.
41. 'To the City of Bombay', 1894, Dedication to *The Seven Seas*. Cited by Andrew Lycett, *Rudyard Kipling* (London: Weidenfeld and Nicolson, 1999), p. 24.
42. Jan Morris with Simon Winchester, *Stones of Empire: The Buildings of the Raj* (Oxford: Oxford University Press, 1986), p. 133.
43. 'Smile, Smile, Smile'.
44. *CL* 46.

45. *CL* 570.
46. 'A Rhymed Epistle to E. L. G.', Canto IV. *CPF* 31.
47. *CL* 67.
48. *CL* 66.
49. 'Anthem for Doomed Youth'.
50. *JFO* II, p. 30.
51. *CL* 83.
52. 'Mental Cases'.
53. *CL* 84.
54. *CL* 74.
55. *CL* 81.

3 The Banned Word

1. Matthew Arnold, *Selected Poems and Prose*, ed. Miriam Allott (London: J. M. Dent, 1993), p. 97.
2. John Henry Newman, 'Knowledge Viewed in Relation to Professional Skill', *The Idea of a University: Defined and Illustrated* (London: Longmans, Green, 1886), p. 177.
3. Cited in Jane Robinson, *Bluestockings: The Remarkable Story of the First Women to Fight for an Education* (London: Penguin, 2010), p. 117.
4. E. R. Dodds, *Missing Persons: An Autobiography* (Oxford: Clarendon Press, 1977), p. 33.
5. *JFO* III, p. 258.
6. *CL* 191.
7. *CL* 349.
8. Oxford, University of Oxford, English Faculty Library, Owen Collection, Box 3, AA 416, 'Notes on Keats'.
9. William Spooner, cited by William Hayter, *Spooner: A Biography* (London: W. H. Allen, 1977), p. 52.
10. Cited by Evelyn Waugh, *A Little Learning: The First Volume of an Autobiography* (London: Chapman and Hall, 1964), p. 170.
11. William Spooner, cited by William Hayter, *Spooner*, p. 53.
12. *CL* 254. He was no J. R. R. Tolkien (born 1892), who not only had a remarkable aptitude for languages but also went to an excellent day-school, with the help of a fee-paying uncle, and went up to Oxford in 1911 with an Open Classical Exhibition from Exeter College, a school-leaving bursary, and financial support from his parish priest.
13. Alan Clark, *The Tories: Conservatives and the Nation State 1922–1997* (London: Orion, 1999) p. 5.
14. *JFO* III, p. 129.
15. Ibid.
16. Evelyn Waugh, 'Was Oxford Worth While?', *A Little Order*, ed. Donat Gallagher (London: Eyre Methuen, 1977), p. 17.
17. *CL* 92.
18. *CL* 75.
19. *CL* 156.
20. Kathleen E. Royds, *Elizabeth Barrett Browning and Her Poetry* (London: George G. Harrap, 1912).
21. Cited by Arthur Mee, ed., *Oxfordshire* (London: Hodder and Stoughton, 1942), p. 334. Arthur Waugh's *Alfred Lord Tennyson: A Study of his Life and Work* (London: William Heinemann, 1896) includes two pictures of Shiplake Church and one of the Rectory.
22. Jerome K. Jerome, *Three Men in a Boat: To Say Nothing of the Dog!* (London: Penguin, 1957; first published 1889), pp. 133–4.

23. 'Full Springs of Thought'.
24. Dunsden became a separate parish in 1866. Dunsden is in Oxfordshire, north of the Thames. Sonning, like Reading, is in Berkshire, south of the Thames. See James Edward Austen-Leigh, *Memoir of Jane Austen* (Oxford: Clarendon Press, 1926; reprint of a memoir from 1871), p. 24. Owen owned *Pride and Prejudice* (1906 edition).
25. Austen's maternal grandfather was Rector of Harpsden. Austen's mother, Cassandra, was born there.
26. *CL* 148.
27. *CL* 95.
28. Mary Russell Mitford, *Our Village* (London: Cassell, 1909).
29. All Saints Dunsden is just 500 metres from the Reading Borough boundary.
30. Sonning, 'the most fairy-like little nook on the whole river'. Jerome K. Jerome, *Three Men in a Boat*, p. 134.
31. *JFO* II, p. 195.
32. Eton master H. E. Luxmoore, wrote of Oxford in 1901 that 'if a very smart Science or Math man knows no Greek I don't see much harm in letting him in, but I had rather he went to Owens College or Liverpool'. Robert Cecil, *Life in Edwardian England* (London: B. T. Batsford, 1969), p. 150.
33. The library had only about 9,000 books when Owen enrolled. At the end of the 1911–12 academic year, it had 9,328 books.
34. See *The Reading University College Review*, iv (1911–12).
35. Jerome K. Jerome, *Three Men in a Boat*, pp. 134, 76.
36. See Manchester, University of Manchester Library, MS DSW /1/1/3/9/50, 'File (30 Nov. 1957–16 June 1963)', Dennis Welland to Miss E. A. Lashford, 15 December 1960, f. 1r: 'he attended classes at University College, Reading, in botany but being apparently a part-time student he does not appear in the University records, except as having entered on the 15th June, 1912 and left on the 26th'.
37. University of Manchester Library, MS DSW /1/1/1/25/8, 'University College Reading', M. C. Rayner to Dennis Welland, 25 September 1947, f. 1r.
38. See Robinson, *Bluestockings*, p. 210. Also Edith Morley's unpublished 'Looking Before and After: Reminiscences of a Working Life' (University of Reading, Special Collections, uncatalogued E. J. Morley papers, MS 5304, Box 3). Morley (1875–1964) was appointed a professor at Reading in 1908. She was Professor of English Language but taught literature.
39. 'Impressionist', *CPF* 396.
40. *CL* 129.
41. J. C. Holt, *The University of Reading: The First Fifty Years* (Reading: Reading University Press, 1977), p. 88. Cited in Jane Robinson, *Bluestockings*, p. 210.
42. Edith Morley edited Hurd's *Letters on Chivalry and Romance* (London: Henry Frowde, 1911). Her prize-winning essay on *The Works of Sir Philip Sidney* was published in 1901 (London: Hugh Rees, 1901). She joined the Fabian Society in 1908. She described herself as a feminist but not a man-hater. Although she belonged to the WSPU she was not an active suffragette.
43. Edith Morley, *The Works of Sir Philip Sidney*, the Quain Essay 1901 (London: Hugh Rees, 1901), p. 1.
44. Ibid., p. 60.
45. Ibid., p. 59.
46. Ibid., p. 3.
47. University of Manchester Library, MS DSW /1/1/1/25/9, f. 1r. Ruskin, of course, was an Oxford man, first publishing under the title 'a Graduate of Oxford'.
48. 'A Rhymed Epistle to E.L.G.', *CPF*, 31 August 1912.

49. Figures taken from Edith J. Morley, *Women Workers in Seven Professions: A Survey of their Economic Conditions and Prospects* (London: George Routledge, 1914), p. 107.
50. 'This money business was a funny thing for all of us at this period. Wilfred surprisingly was the only one whose perception told him that before life could be lived properly money somehow had to be got; that without it everyone was completely helpless and for ever subjugated.' *JFO* II, p. 55.
51. In early April 1914, he was considering entering Reading's University College as an 'Educational Student' in October, but, again, he was worrying about the financial arrangements.
52. John Keats, *The Complete Works*, vol. 4, ed. H. Buxton Forman (Glasgow: Gowars and Gray, 1901), p. 47. Keats to Benjamin Bailey, 22 November 1817.
53. George Borrow, *Lavengro: The Scholar, The Gipsy, The Priest* (London: Oxford University Press, 1904), p. 210.
54. Ibid., pp. 240, 239.
55. *CL* 316.
56. *CL* 161.
57. *CL* 187.
58. *CL* 186.
59. *CL* 127.
60. *CL* 100.
61. *CL* 92.
62. *CL* 273.
63. Cited by C. Day Lewis, 'Introduction', *The Collected Poems of Wilfred Owen*, ed. C. Day Lewis (London: Chatto and Windus, 1966), p. 14.
64. 'A Rhymed Epistle to E. L. G.', Epilogue. *CPF* 31.
65. Wilfred Owen, 'The Little Mermaid'.
66. *CL* 118–19.
67. *CPF* 437.
68. *CL* 118.
69. 'The Little Mermaid'.
70. 'I know of these romantic friendships of the English and the Germans. They are not Latin. I think they are very good if they do not go on too long. [. . .] It is a kind of love that comes to children before they know its meaning. In England it comes when you are almost men; I think I like that. It is better to have that kind of love for another boy than for a girl.' Evelyn Waugh, *Brideshead Revisited* (Harmondsworth: Penguin, 1962), p. 98.
71. *CL* 508.
72. Leslie Gunston to Dennis Welland. Manchester, University of Manchester Library, MS DSW /1/1/1/14/6, 'Gunston, E. Leslie (1951-)', f. 4r.
73. *CPF* 61.
74. University of Oxford, English Faculty Library, Owen Collection, Box 3, BB 437, 'Do Plants Think?'
75. *CL* 73.
76. University of Manchester Library, MS DSW /1/1/7, 'Typescript extracts', Susan Owen to Miss Vera Hewland, 17 February 1936, f. 1r.
77. *CL* 185.
78. 'The Roman City of Uriconium', *The Times*, 39701 (Wednesday 27 September 1911), p. 6, col. B. The date of AD 584 has since been revised.
79. 'Miss de la Touche wrote to the Headmaster of Downside on 15 December 1914: "I have taken a young tutor for them for the Christmas holidays, he is giving lessons in Bordeaux preparing for Oxford"'. *CL* 305.
80. Alfred, Lord Tennyson, 'The Lady of Shalott'.

4 L'Homme du Monde

1. Elizabeth Barrett Browning, *Aurora Leigh* (London: Chapman and Hall, 1857), p. 317.

2. Stendhal, *Memoires d'un Touriste*, vol. 2 (Lausanne: Editions Rencontre, 1961), p. 269.

3. Richard Ellmann, *James Joyce* (London: Oxford University Press, 1966), p. 224. Joyce quickly grew to hate the work, and envisaged that 'Some day, I shall clout my pupils about the head, I fear, and stalk out'.

4. Gordon Bowker, *James Joyce: A Biography* (London: Weidenfeld and Nicolson, 2011), p. 138.

5. James Joyce, *Ulysses*, ed. Jeri Johnson (Oxford: Oxford University Press, 1998), p. 675. 'family name unkown' corrected to 'family name unknown'.

6. *CL* 202.

7. *The Letters of Henri de Toulouse-Lautrec*, ed. Herbert D. Schimmel (Oxford: Oxford University Press, 1991), p. 369.

8. He 'overdid the ladies a bit'. Lautrec's friend Viaud to Maurice Joyant, 9 January 1901, in Julia Frey, *Toulouse-Lautrec: A Life* (New York: Viking, 1994), p. 487.

9. Christopher Isherwood, *Lions and Shadows: An Education in the Twenties* (London: Hogarth Press, 1938; Minerva edition, 1996), p. 188.

10. *CL* 214.

11. *CL* 252.

12. Hugo's *The Alps and the Pyrenees*, cited by A. C. Swinburne, 'Notes of Travel: Alps and Pyrenees', *Studies in Prose and Poetry* (London: Chatto and Windus, 1907), p. 214.

13. A. C. Swinburne, 'Notes of Travel', pp. 213–14. Reviewing Hugo's *The Alps and the Pyrenees*.

14. *CL* 242.

15. *CL* 205.

16. *CL* 200.

17. Near Dunsden. *CL* 159.

18. *CL* 222.

19. Henry James, *A Little Tour in France* (Oxford: Oxford University Press, 1984), p. 90. Originally 1884, describing a trip made in 1882.

20. *CL* 222.

21. *CL* 199.

22. There was a baronet called Owen, a Sir John Arthur Owen of Pembrokeshire, born in 1892.

23. *JFO* III, p. 61.

24. James, *A Little Tour in France*, p. 90.

25. *CL* 265.

26. *CL* 246.

27. *CL* 256.

28. *JFO* I, p. 7.

29. *CPF* 390.

30. 'The Ballad of Reading Gaol'. In Owen's 'With those that are become': ' "For each man slays the one he loves" ' (*CPF* 492); and 'Strange Meeting': 'I am the enemy you killed, my friend'.

31. Lines by Max Beerbohm, asking Le Gallienne to return, cited in the introduction to Richard Le Gallienne, *The Romantic '90s*, intro. H. Montgomery Hyde (London: Putnam, 1951), p. xxix.

32. 'Unto What Pinnacles'.

33. 'Science has Looked'.

34. 'Supposed Confessions'.

35. *CPF* 62.

36. Cited by C. Day Lewis, 'Introduction', *The Collected Poems of Wilfred Owen*, ed. C. Day Lewis (London: Chatto and Windus, 1966), p. 14.
37. *CL* 224.
38. *CL* 230.
39. *CL* 234.

5 Venus and Mars

1. François Mauriac, *Génitrix* (Paris: Bernard Grasset, 1923), p. 105
2. *À l'ombre des jeunes filles en fleurs* was published in French 26 days after Owen's death, but some of the book had appeared in June and July 1914 in the *Nouvelle Revue Française*. C. K. Scott Moncrieff translated *À l'ombre des jeunes filles en fleurs* (literally 'In the Shadow of Young Girls in Flower') as *Within a Budding Grove*.
3. *CL* 237.
4. *CL* 239.
5. *CL* 240.
6. *CL* 464.
7. *CL* 239–40.
8. Osbert Sitwell, *Noble Essences or Courteous Revelations: An Autobiography* (London: Macmillan, 1950), p. 104.
9. Oxford, University of Oxford, English Faculty Library, Owen Collection, Box 3, AA 410, 'Milton'.
10. *CL* 256.
11. Betty Kent, cited by Richard Holmes, *Shelley: The Pursuit* (London: Weidenfeld and Nicolson, 1974), p. 373.
12. *CL* 106.
13. Ben Jonson, 'The Epistle', *Volpone, or The Fox* (1605).
14. George Steiner, 'A Man of Many Parts', *Observer Review*, Sunday 3 June 2001, p. 15.
15. *CL* 243.
16. Ibid.
17. Ibid.
18. *CL* 245.
19. *CL* 244.
20. *CL* 247.
21. *CL* 253.
22. *CL* 257.
23. *CL* 252.
24. *CL* 511.
25. *CL* 273.
26. Philip Larkin, *Jill* (London: Faber and Faber, 1975 edition), p. 97.
27. *CL* 234.
28. *JFO* II, p. 30.
29. 'To Poesy'.
30. 'Impromptu', beginning 'Now let me feel'.
31. 'Disabled'.
32. *CL* 234.
33. Ibid.
34. John Addington Symonds, *Shelley* (London: Macmillan, 1909), p. 8. Owen's copy is in the English Faculty Library, Oxford.
35. 'Supposed Confessions of a Secondrate Sensitive Mind in Dejection'. Owen would also acquire Alfred de Vigny's book called *Chatterton* (Paris, n.d.).
36. 'Science has Looked'.

37. *JFO* II, p. 196.
38. *CL* 249.
39. Ibid.
40. *CL* 284.
41. 'A Palinode'.
42. *CL* 265.
43. Both books must also have influenced the description of the crowd at the start of *The Scarlet Pimpernel*.
44. *CL* 432.
45. See John F. V. Keiger, *France and the Origins of the First World War* (London: Macmillan, 1983), p. 145.
46. *CL* 220.
47. *CL* 265.
48. 'The King's Visit to Shrewsbury', *The Times*, Saturday 4 July 1914, issue 40567, p. 8, col. C.
49. *CL* 472. Earlier, in 1916, Owen had written, 'We have been expecting the King to visit our trenches, and have worked overtime every day this week. Our anxiety begins again tomorrow! I give an extra ten minutes to shaving every morning in consequence. It is most annoying.' *CL* 398.

6 The Valleys Shadowful

1. Charles Scott Moncrieff, *The Song of Roland: Done into English, in the Original Measure* (London: Chapman and Hall, 1919), p. 28.
2. Laurent Tailhade, *Poèmes élégiaques* (London: Mercure de France, 1913), p. 67.
3. Oxford, University of Oxford, English Faculty Library, Owen Collection, Box 3, AA 410, 'Description of a Railway Station at a busy Time of Day'.
4. 'The Sleeping Beauty'.
5. *CL* 276.
6. University of Oxford, English Faculty Library, Owen Collection, Box 3, AA 411, 'Description of a journey from Constantinople to Merv'.
7. *CL* 269. Coleridge wrote, 'A noise like of a hidden brook / In the leafy month of June, / That to the sleeping woods all night / Singeth a quiet tune'.
8. Alphonse Donné, *Change of Air and Scene* (London: Henry S. King, 1872), pp. 156–7.
9. Hilaire Belloc, 'On "Mailles"', *Hills and the Sea* (London: Methuen, 1906), p. 16.
10. 'From My Diary, July 1914'.
11. *CL* 273.
12. Scott Moncrieff, *The Song of Roland*, p. 28.
13. Ibid., p. 61.
14. The church used to hold the famous ivory horn of Roland (given to the church by Charlemagne), now lost, and it is said that some of the dead of Roncevaux were buried there.
15. Cited by Penelope Fitzgerald, *Edward Burne-Jones* (Stroud: Sutton, 2003), p. 219.
16. *CPF* 433.
17. *CL* 274.
18. *CL* 268.
19. Karl Baedeker, *Southern France, including Corsica: Handbook for Travellers*, 6th edition (Leipzig: Karl Baedeker, 1914), p. 127.
20. Hilaire Belloc, 'Preface', Johannes Jörgensen, *Lourdes*, trans. Ingeborg Lund (London: Longmans, Green, 1914), pp. xii, xiii.
21. *CL* 248.
22. Elizabeth Barrett Browning, *Aurora Leigh* (London: Chapman and Hall, 1857 edition), p. 294.

23. Ibid., p. 293.
24. This part of the building is captured by Ruskin in one of his lyrical flights of fancy in *The Stones of Venice* (1851–3). George Bull, *Venice: The Most Triumphant City* (London: The Folio Society, 1980), p. 134.
25. *CL* 76.
26. *CL* 521.
27. *CL* 481.
28. Laurent Tailhade, 'Épigramme', *Poèmes élégiaques*, p. 67: 'The town of kisses, Bagnère, to the winds of the evening / Delivers the nudity of the nymph and the female bather'.
29. Virginie Amélie Avegno Gautreau (1859–1915).
30. *CL* 279.
31. *CL* 276.
32. Ibid.
33. *CL* 280.
34. *CL* 279.
35. Manchester, University of Manchester Library, MS DSW /1/3/3/2/2, 'JC – Biographical enquiries re WO', letter from J. Loiseau to J. Cohen, 29 December 1953, f. 40r.
36. *CL* 273.
37. Ibid.
38. *CL* 271.
39. *CL* 277.
40. *CL* 490.
41. *CL* 520.
42. *CL* 280.
43. Cited by Matthew Sweet, *Inventing the Victorians* (New York: St Martin's Press, 2001), p. 168.
44. Cited, ibid., p. 169.
45. *CPF* 438.
46. *CPF* 437.
47. *CL* 277.
48. *CL* 280. Christian Sinding (1856–1941) was a Norwegian composer.
49. *CL* 277.
50. D. H. Lawrence, *The Rainbow* (London: Penguin, 2007), pp. 92–3.
51. *CL* 277.
52. *CL* 278.
53. 'M. C.', 'Passing Paris', *The Egoist* (June-July 1918), p. 85.
54. Remy de Gourmont, *The Book of Masks: An Anthology of French Symbolist and Decadent Writing based upon* The Book of Masks, trans. Andrew Mangravite (London: Atlas, 1994), p. 62.
55. See *Poèmes élégiaques* (1913): 'A Ma Chère Femme'. He was twice married.
56. *CL* 282.
57. Ibid.
58. University of Manchester Library, MS DSW /1/1/4/9, 'Annotated doctoral thesis (1950–1951)', pp. 23–4 (in French). Trans. Tim Jayne.
59. Ibid., p. 24 (in French). Trans. Tim Jayne.
60. *CL* 282.
61. Charles Darwin, *On the Origin of Species by Means of Natural Selection* (London: Henry Frowde, Oxford University Press, 1902), p. 441.
62. *CL* 282.
63. University of Oxford, English Faculty Library, Owen Collection, Box 28 (School Books), 3 (Essays), 'My Native Country', 30 September 1907.

64. Barcelona features in 'Golden Hair'.
65. *CL* 464.
66. Cited by A. N. Wilson, *Hilaire Belloc* (London: Mandarin, 1997), p. 293.
67. 10 August 1914. *CL* 274.
68. London, Imperial War Museum, Private Papers of Canon H. R. Bate MC (cat. no. 10782), MS 'The First World War Memoirs of Canon H. R. Bate MC' (1974), HRB1, p. 19. See the penultimate line of Arnold's 'The Scholar-Gipsy'.
69. *CL* 269.

7 Mist' Howin's Honied Slumber

1. Evelyn Waugh, *Brideshead Revisited* (Harmondsworth: Penguin, 1962), p. 97.
2. Cited by Zdzisław Najder, *Joseph Conrad: A Chronicle* (Cambridge: Cambridge University Press, 1983), p. 124.
3. *CL* 143.
4. *CL* 284.
5. *CL* 285.
6. *CL* 288.
7. *CL* 121.
8. Cited by Anthony Kenny, *Arthur Hugh Clough: A Poet's Life* (London: Continuum, 2005), p. 132.
9. Cited by Robert Bernard Martin, *Gerard Manley Hopkins: A Very Private Life* (London: Flamingo, 1992), pp. 331, 324, 327.
10. Osbert Sitwell, *Noble Essences or Courteous Revelations: An Autobiography* (London: Macmillan, 1950), p. 104.
11. Siegfried Sassoon, 'A Personal Appreciation of Wilfred Owen by his Friend, Siegfried Sassoon', BBC Third Programme, Sunday 22 August 1948, 10.30–11 p.m. See Manchester, University of Manchester Library, MS DSW /1/3/3/1/6, 'SS/EB 1946–1954'.
12. *JFO* II, p. 62.
13. 23 July 1915. *CL* 347.
14. Bevis Hillier, *John Betjeman: The Biography* (London: John Murray, 2007), p. 183.
15. Siegfried Sassoon, cited by Alan Judd and David Crane, *First World War Poets* (London: NPG, 1997), p. 27.
16. *CL* 257.
17. *CL* 232.
18. *CL* 233.
19. *CL* 299.
20. Ibid.
21. *CL* 59.
22. *CL* 343.
23. *CL* 291.
24. *CL* 300. This axiom was not uncommon among writers, even if Rupert Brooke and others had enlisted. D. H. Lawrence, October 1914: 'I think I am much too valuable a creature to offer myself to a German bullet gratis and for fun'. Lawrence, *Selected Letters*, ed. Richard Aldington and Aldous Huxley (Harmondsworth: Penguin, 1950), p. 76.
25. *CL* 325.
26. *CL* 205.
27. Belloc's sons were Louis (b. 1897), Hilary (b. 1902), Peter (b. 1904). The de la Touche boys left Downside in July 1916.
28. *CL* 316.
29. *CL* 237.

30. *CL* 347.
31. *CL* 348.
32. Mark Thompson, *The White War: Life and Death on the Italian Front 1915–1919* (London: Faber and Faber, 2008), p. 46.
33. Ian Kershaw, *Hitler 1889–1936: Hubris* (London: Penguin, 2001), p. 90.
34. Sir John Hawkwood (b. Essex 1320, d. Florence 1394). Commander-in-chief of the army of the Republic of Florence. He had socialised with Chaucer, Petrarch and Jean Froissart.
35. Cited by William Caferro, *John Hawkwood: An English Mercenary in Fourteenth Century Italy* (Baltimore: Johns Hopkins University Press, 2006), p. 24.
36. D. H. Lawrence, *The Prussian Officer and Other Stories*, ed. Antony Atkins (Oxford: Oxford University Press, 1995), p. 248.
37. Lawrence, cited by John Worthen, *D. H. Lawrence: The Early Years 1885–1912* (Cambridge: Cambridge University Press, 1992), p. 431.
38. Frieda, cited ibid., p. 439.
39. D. H. Lawrence, *Selected Letters*, ed. Richard Aldington and Aldous Huxley (Harmondsworth: Penguin, 1950), p. 51.
40. Edward Bulwer-Lytton, *The Last Days of Pompeii* (London: J. M. Dent, 1906), p. 35. Owen may also have seen the Italian film adaptations of the novel in 1908 and 1913, which proved to be very popular.
41. *The Aeneid* begins, famously, with 'I sing of arms and the man' (*Arma virumque cano*).
42. *CL* 339.
43. *CL* 354.
44. *CL* 343.
45. *CL* 348. 'Ragging' is rough play, pranks, riotous behaviour.
46. *CL* 477. St Ouen (*c.*600–84), bishop of Rouen 641. Feast day 24 August. Pronounced 'Oo-on' in Rouen and Normandy, but, elsewhere, as a word to rhyme with the French word *pain*.
47. *CL* 356.
48. *CL* 345.
49. *CL* 348.
50. *CL* 353.
51. *CL* 325.
52. *CL* 342.
53. *CL* 343.

8 Mother and Fatherland

1. *CL* 449.
2. *CL* 387.
3. *CL* 506.
4. *JFO* II, p. 23.
5. *JFO* III, pp. 61, 139.
6. *CL* 586, 15 October 1918.
7. *CPF* 228.
8. See Sigmund Freud, *The Interpretation of Dreams* [1900], ed. Joyce Crick (Oxford: Oxford University Press, 1999), p. 202.
9. London, Imperial War Museum, Private Papers of Canon H. R. Bate MC (cat. no. 10782), MS 'The First World War Memoirs of Canon H. R. Bate MC' (1974), HRB1, p. 19.
10. *CL* 479.
11. 19 August 1918. *CL* 569.
12. *CL* 423.

13. Cited by Max Arthur, *Forgotten Voices of the Great War* (London: Ebury Press, 2003), p. 222.
14. Siegfried Sassoon, *Collected Poems 1908–1956* (London: Faber and Faber, 1984), p. 250.
15. *CL* 150–1.
16. Richard H. Hutton, *Sir Walter Scott* (London: Macmillan, 1909), p. 6. Wilfred Owen's copy is in the English Faculty Library, Oxford, inscribed 'Wilfred E. S. Owen, July 1912'.
17. Army Form E. 501. Attestation of Wilfred Edward Salter Owen. Manchester, University of Manchester Library, MS DSW /1/3/3/2/6, 'WO – Medical Records'.
18. D. H. Lawrence, *Selected Letters*, ed. Richard Aldington and Aldous Huxley (Harmondsworth: Penguin, 1950), pp. 87, 90.
19. H. R. Bate, *Blackwood's Magazine* (1974), p. 386. Imperial War Museum, Private Papers of Canon H. R. Bate MC (cat. no. 10782), MS 'The First World War Memoirs of Canon H. R. Bate MC' (1974), HRB1.
20. *CPF* 409.
21. Lawrence, *Selected Letters*, p. 88.
22. Cited by Paul Delaney, *D. H. Lawrence's Nightmare: The Writer and His Circle in the Years of the Great War* (Hassocks: Harvester Press, 1979), p. 133.
23. *The Letters of T. S. Eliot: Volume I: 1898–1922*, eds Valerie Eliot and Hugh Haughton (London: Faber and Faber, 2009), p. 133, 18 November 1915.
24. *CL* 368.
25. *CL* 362.
26. Cited by Desmond Graham, *Keith Douglas 1920–1944: A Biography* (Oxford: Oxford University Press, 1988), p. 1.
27. Richard H. Hutton, *Sir Walter Scott* (London: Macmillan, 1909), p. 54. Acquired by Owen in July 1912.
28. 'Dulce et Decorum Est'.
29. 'A Terre'.
30. *CL* 398.
31. Manchester, University of Manchester Library, MS DSW /1/1/4/9, 'Annotated doctoral thesis (1950–1951)', Sassoon's handwritten comments in pencil facing p. 187.
32. To Eleanor Farjeon, November 1915. Cited by Eleanor Farjeon, *Edward Thomas: The Last Four Years* (London: Oxford University Press, 1958), p. 172.
33. Edward Thomas, *Selected Letters*, ed. R. George Thomas (Oxford: Oxford University Press, 1995), p. 118.
34. Edward Thomas, *Letters from Edward Thomas to Gordon Bottomley*, ed. R. George Thomas (London: Oxford University Press, 1968), p. 256.
35. Cited by Farjeon, *Edward Thomas*, p. 175.
36. Edward Thomas, *Selected Letters*, ed. R. George Thomas, p. 117.
37. Edward Thomas, *Letters from Edward Thomas to Gordon Bottomley*, ed. R. George Thomas, p. 258.
38. Cited by Farjeon, *Edward Thomas*, p. 184.
39. *CL* 301.
40. Evelyn Waugh, *Brideshead Revisited* (Harmondsworth: Penguin, 1962), pp. 390, 25.
41. *CL* 393.
42. *The Times*, issue 41170 (Thursday 18 May 1916), p. 6, col. C. On 20 October 1915, a raid had destroyed the Tiepolo fresco in the Scalzi Church.
43. *CL* 159.
44. The *Oxford English Dictionary* cites Owen as the first example of the use of 'aerobatics': 15 January 1915, 'Garross is going to engage in Aerobatics (ah-hem!) on Sunday: over Bordeaux'. *The OED* uses Owen as the first example for fourteen words, including 'motor-bicycling'.

45. *CL* 408.
46. *CL* 297.
47. University of Manchester Library, MS DSW /1/1/4/9, 'Annotated doctoral thesis (1950–1951)', p. 23 (letter in French by Tailhade), trans. Tim Jayne.
48. *CL* 553.
49. Letter to Gordon Campbell, 21 September 1914. *The Letters of D. H. Lawrence Volume II, June 1913 – October 1916*, eds George J. Zytaruk and James T. Boulton (Cambridge: Cambridge University Press, 1981), p. 218.
50. Michael Jubb, *Cocoa and Corsets* (London: HMSO, 1984), plate 29.
51. Edward Bulwer-Lytton, *The Last Days of Pompeii* (London: J. M. Dent, 1906), pp. 138, 138–9, 139.
52. Cited by Wendy Moffat, *E. M. Forster: A New Life* (London: Bloomsbury, 2010), p. 148.
53. Cited ibid., p. 147.
54. *CL* 375.
55. *CL* 560.
56. *CL* 395.
57. *CL* 395.
58. Richard H. Hutton, *Sir Walter Scott* (London: Macmillan, 1909), p. 52. Wilfred Owen's copy is in the English Faculty Library, Oxford.
59. *The Lay of the Last Minstrel* (1805), canto 2, stanza 1.
60. *CL* 396.
61. Rupert Brooke, *1914 and Other Poems* (London: Sidgwick and Jackson, 1916), p. 15. Owen's copy is in the English Faculty Library, Oxford.
62. *The Poetical Works of Gray and Collins*, ed. Austin Lane Poole (London: Humphrey Milford, Oxford University Press, 1917), p. 93. Owen owned this edition of the poems. Anatole France, a writer Owen knew of, wrote *Sur La Voie Glorieuse* during the war, translated as *The Path of Glory*. Anatole France, *The Path of Glory*, trans. Alfred Allinson (London: John Lane, The Bodley Head, 1916).
63. *CL* 295.
64. *The Poetical Works of Gray and Collins*, ed. Austin Lane Poole, p. 33.
65. C. Day Lewis, *The Buried Day* (London: Chatto and Windus, 1960), pp. 92–3.
66. F. W. Bockett, *Some Literary Landmarks for Pilgrims on Wheels* (London: J. M. Dent, 1901), pp. 52–3.
67. *CL* 71.
68. *A Shropshire Lad* XL. A. E. Housman, *A Shropshire Lad* (London: Grant Richards, 1915), p. 59. Wilfred Owen's copy of this edition of *A Shropshire Lad* is inscribed on the flyleaf 'Witley: August 1916:'.
69. Paul Fussell, *The Great War and Modern Memory* (London: Oxford University Press, 1977), p. 282.
70. Robert Nichols, ed., *Anthology of War Poetry 1914–1918* (London: Nicholson and Watson, 1943), p. 29.
71. *A Shropshire Lad* XXVIII – 'The Welsh Marches', p. 41.
72. *CL* 399.
73. *A Shropshire Lad* X, p. 17.
74. *A Shropshire Lad* IX, p. 15.
75. *A Shropshire Lad* I – '1887', p. 2.
76. *CL* 398.
77. *CL* 417.

9 The Octopus

1. *CL* 427.
2. *CL* 421.

3. *CL* 422.
4. Ibid.
5. *CL* 423.
6. *CL* 426.
7. Fusilier Victor Packer, cited by Max Arthur, *Forgotten Voices of the Great War* (London: Ebury Press, 2003), p. 83.
8. 'Dulce et Decorum Est'.
9. *CL* 427.
10. *CL* 428.
11. *CL* 427.
12. *CL* 428.
13. 'The Poet-Prophet of the Empire: Twenty Poems from Kipling', *The Times*, Wednesday 1 May 1918, issue 41778, p. 9, col. E.
14. *The Boy's Own Annual*, vol. 39 (1916–17), p. 248.
15. *CL* 428.
16. *CL* 431.
17. 'Frost-Bound Battle Front. Visit to French Quarters. Comfort by Contrast. (From Our Special Correspondent.) With the French Army, February 4', *The Times*, Thursday 8 February 1917, issue 41397, p. 7, col. A.
18. Private Leonard Haine, cited by Arthur, *Forgotten Voices of the Great War*, p. 202.
19. *CL* 430.
20. See 'Cramped in that Funnelled Hole'.
21. *CL* 429.
22. *CL* 458.
23. *CL* 435.
24. *CL* 434.
25. *CL* 440.
26. *CL* 443.
27. 'Strange Meeting'.
28. *CL* 443.
29. Derek Amato, 'Experience: A Head Injury Made Me a Musical Prodigy', *Guardian Weekend*, 13 October 2012, p. 16.
30. Augustus John, *Finishing Touches*, ed. Daniel George (London: Readers Union and Jonathan Cape, 1966), p. 30.
31. *CL* 446.
32. *CL* 452.
33. 'Anthem for Doomed Youth'.
34. *CL* 456.
35. *CL* 461.
36. William Sharp, *Life of Percy Bysshe Shelley* (London: Walter Scott, 1887), p. 134. Sharp's biography goes so far as to argue that Shelley 'was ever wont to practise as well as preach the Christian ideal'. p. 135.
37. Reverend David Railton. See Neil Oliver, *Not Forgotten* (London: Hodder and Stoughton, 2006), p. 184. Equally, Germany employed Lutheranism for patriotic purposes.
38. Cited by John Ellis, *Eye-Deep in Hell: The Western Front 1914–18* (London: Book Club Associates, 1979), p. 67.
39. 'Text of Papal Note', *The Times*, Thursday, 16 August, 1917, issue 41558, p. 7, col. G. *The Times* carried the Pope's statement on 16 August, but the statement is dated 1 August. It had carried the news of the Pope's peace proposals on Wednesday 15 August.
40. 'Text of Papal Note', *The Times*, Thursday, 16 August, 1917, issue 41558, p. 7, column G.

41. Ibid.
42. *CL* 461.
43. Ibid.
44. The Lourdes hymn begins 'Immaculate Mary / Our hearts are on fire'.
45. As was that other war poet, Ivor Gurney.
46. *CL* 447.
47. Ibid.
48. *CL* 312.
49. *CL* 424.
50. *CL* 463.
51. 'Memorare', a well-known Roman Catholic prayer dating from the Middle Ages.
52. *CPF* 228.
53. *CPF* 229.
54. *CPF* 228.
55. *CL* 457. Another Owain (or Owen) was the son of Arthur's sister Modron or Morgan le Fay and he too resisted the advance of the Angles.
56. *CL* 470. Situated next to the Royal Victoria Hospital, it cared for 9,616 patients from October 1914 to March 1919.
57. Manchester, University of Manchester Library, MS DSW /1/3/3/2/6, 'WO – Medical Records'.

10 Brock's Folk

1. George Borrow, *Lavengro: The Scholar, The Gipsy, The Priest* (London: Oxford University Press, 1904), p. 181.
2. Vincent Van Gogh, *Letters from Provence*, ed. Martin Bailey (London: Parkgate, 1998), p. 105.
3. *CL* 471.
4. *CL* 50.
5. *CL* 249.
6. 'Disabled', 'Autumnal', 'To Eros'.
7. *CL* 341.
8. Cited by Chiang Yee, *The Silent Traveller in Edinburgh* (Edinburgh: Mercat, 2003), p. 238.
9. R. L. Stevenson, *St. Ives* (London: J. M. Dent, 1914), p. 54.
10. Cited by Michael Hurd, *The Ordeal of Ivor Gurney* (Oxford: Oxford University Press, 1984), p. 111. Gurney was at Edinburgh War Hospital, Bangour. He left Scotland in November.
11. William J. Locke, *The Morals of Marcus Ordeyne* (London: Bodley Head, 1905), pp. 113, 120.
12. Ibid., p. 296.
13. *CL* 453.
14. London, Imperial War Museum, Private Papers of Lieutenant J. H. Butlin (cat. no. 7915), MS 67/52/1 (20035), 5 May 1917, 11 May 1917.
15. Ibid., 26 June 1917. Activities at Craiglockhart included the Model Yacht Club, photography, the Field Club, French, bowls, tennis, golf, concerts, the workshop, fishing, badminton, croquet, cricket, billiards, poultry and gardening.
16. London, Imperial War Museum, Private Papers of Siegfried Sassoon (cat. no. 9059), 'P. 444 Siegfried Sassoon Volume 2', MS 'SS 7 Papers Relating to Dr W. H. R. Rivers and Family', f. 301. ('Ms notes in an unidentified hand on the staff of Craiglockhart War Hospital, namely G. C. Major Bryce, Dr Rivers and some of his patients, also comments on Captain Brock, Major Ruggles, Lieutenant Macintyre. 7pp. n.d. 297–303'.)

17. Ibid.
18. See Thomas E. F. Webb, '"Dottyville": Craiglockhart War Hospital and Shell-Shock Treatment in the First World War', *Journal of the Royal Society of Medicine*, Vol. 99, No 7 (July 2006), pp. 342–6.
19. Arthur J. Brock, *Health and Conduct* (London: Williams and Norgate, 1923), p. 170. He recommended 'a return to a more primitive life – not to the letter but to the spirit in which unsophisticated country people regard and deal with their circumstances'. Arthur J. Brock, *Dreams, Folklore, and our Present Spiritual Distress* (London: April 1924), p. 499.
20. Arthur John Brock, 'The Re-Education of the Adult: The Neurasthenic in War and Peace', *Sociological Review*, Vol. 10, pp. 25–43 (1918), at p. 30. Cited by Webb, '"Dottyville"', p. 344.
21. Brock, *Dreams, Folklore, and our Present Spiritual Distress*, p. 499.
22. W. H. R. Rivers, 'The Repression of War Experience', *Lancet* (2 February 1918). Cited by A. M. Crossman, '*The Hydra*, Captain A. J. Brock and the Treatment of Shell-Shock in Edinburgh', *Journal of the Royal College of Physicians of Edinburgh*, xxxiii (2003), p. 120.
23. Brock, *Health and Conduct*, p. 262.
24. Ibid., p. 170.
25. Cited by Jon Stallworthy, *Wilfred Owen* (London: Oxford University Press and Chatto and Windus, 1974), p. 198.
26. Borrow, *Lavengro*, p. 59.
27. *CL* 472, 480–1.
28. 1902. Cited by David Cantor, 'Between Galen, Geddes, and the Gael: Arthur Brock, Modernity, and Medical Humanism in Early-Twentieth-Century Scotland', *Journal of the History of Medicine and Allied Sciences*, Vol. 60, No. 1 (January 2005), p. 6.
29. See A. M. Crossman, '*The Hydra*, Captain A. J. Brock and the Treatment of Shell-Shock in Edinburgh', p. 121.
30. Imperial War Museum, Private Papers of Lieutenant J. H. Butlin (cat. no. 7915), MS 67/52/1 (20035), 3 June 1917.
31. Ibid., 26 June 1917.
32. Brock, *Dreams, Folklore, and our Present Spiritual Distress*, p. 500.
33. 'Who is the god of Canongate?', 'Six O'Clock in Princes Street', 'I am the Ghost of Shadwell Stair'.
34. Hans Andersen, *Faery Tales*, trans. Mrs. E. Lucas, illus. Maxwell Armfield (London: J. M. Dent, 1910), p. 2.
35. In the manuscript of 'Disabled', Owen had written, 'Ah! he was looked at when he used to stand / In parks'. *CPF* 351.
36. *CL* 478.
37. Acturus, 'Antaeus, or Back to the Land', *The Hydra*, New Series, iii (January 1918), p. 3.
38. Quoted in John Kemplay, *The Paintings of John Duncan, A Scottish Symbolist* (Petaluma: Pomegranate, 1994), p. 105.
39. *CL* 495.
40. Edinburgh, National Library of Scotland, MS Acc 6866, notebook 8 (John Duncan 1917 to 1920), p. 13, 15 March 1917.
41. Ibid., p. 15, 20 March.
42. St Andrews, University of St Andrews Library, MS 45956, letter from John Duncan, RSA, to D'Arcy Wentworth Thompson, 11 May 1937, f. 1r.
43. Malcolm Foster, *Joyce Cary: A Biography* (London: Michael Joseph, 1969), p. 42. Original spells 'Rossetti' as 'Rosetti'.
44. 'Editorial', *The Hydra*, 10 (1 September 1917), p. 7.
45. Wilfred von Oven was press aide to Goebbels; Arthur Moeller van den Bruck died in 1925 but influenced Nazism and wrote *Das Dritte Reich* (1923).

46. In the 1973 film *The Wicker Man*, directed by Robin Hardy and written by Anthony Shaffer, the Scottish pagan Lord Summerisle was played by Christopher Lee.
47. *CL* 482.
48. *CL* 483, 454.
49. Oxford, University of Oxford, English Faculty Library, Owen Collection, Box 3, BB 437, 'Do Plants Think?'.
50. Acturus, 'Antaeus, or Back to the Land', p. 4.
51. Cited by Humphrey Carpenter, *W. H. Auden: A Biography* (London: George Allen and Unwin, 1981), p. 56.
52. *CL* 471–2.
53. *CL* 479.
54. James B. Salmond, ed., *Veterum Laudes: Being a Tribute to the Achievements of the Members of St Salvator's College during Five Hundred Years* (Edinburgh: Oliver and Boyd, 1950), p. 187.
55. *CL* 481.
56. Gilbert Jessop and J. B. Salmond, eds, *The Book of School Sports* (London: Thomas Nelson, [1920?]), p. 9.
57. Siegfried Sassoon, *Siegfried's Journey 1916–1920* (London: Faber and Faber, 1945), p. 58.
58. *CL* 485.
59. *CL* 488.
60. Siegfried Sassoon, *Collected Poems 1908–1956* (London: Faber and Faber, 1984), p. 83.
61. 15 June 1917. Cited by Max Egremont, *Siegfried Sassoon: A Biography* (London: Picador, 2006), pp. 143–4.
62. The MC medal itself was found in an attic on the Isle of Mull in 2007. The family assumed it had been thrown away with the ribbon in 1917.
63. Manchester, University of Manchester Library, MS DSW /1/1/4/9, 'Annotated doctoral thesis (1950–1951)', Sassoon's handwritten comments in pencil facing p. 238.
64. *CL* 461.
65. Cited by John Grigg, *Lloyd George: From Peace to War 1912–1916* (London: Methuen, 1985), p. 416.
66. *CL* 428.

11 Modern People

1. Edwin Muir, *Collected Poems* (London: Faber and Faber, 1963), p. 157. Published in *The Voyage* (1946).
2. Second Crusade, 1146, see Watkin Williams, *Saint Bernard of Clairvaux* (Manchester: Manchester University Press, 1935), p. 268.
3. Siegfried Sassoon, *Siegfried's Journey 1916–1920* (London: Faber and Faber, 1945), pp. 59, 58.
4. *CL* 494.
5. Sassoon, *Siegfried's Journey 1916–1920*, p. 60.
6. Cited in *D. H. Lawrence: Novelist, Poet, Prophet*, ed. Stephen Spender (London: Weidenfeld and Nicolson, 1973), p. 137. 'Calamus' is a reference to Walt Whitman. 'I should like to know why nearly every man that approaches greatness tends to homosexuality, whether he admits it or not: so that he loves the *body* of a man better than the body of a woman – as I believe the Greeks did, sculptors and all, by far.' p. 136.
7. Manchester, University of Manchester Library, MS DSW /1/1/4/9, 'Annotated doctoral thesis (1950–1951)', Sassoon's handwritten comments in pencil facing p. 62.
8. Ibid.
9. *CL* 499.
10. See Peter Parker, *The Old Lie: The Great War and the Public-School Ethos* (London: Constable, 1987), p. 193.

11. *JFO* II, p. 30.
12. *CPF* 351.
13. Cited by A. M. Crossman, 'The Hydra, Captain A. J. Brock and the Treatment of Shell-Shock in Edinburgh', *Journal of the Royal College of Physicians of Edinburgh*, 33 (2003), p. 120.
14. 'Editorial', *The Hydra*, 10 (1 September 1917), p. 7.
15. Siegfried Sassoon, *Diaries 1915–1918*, ed. Rupert Hart-Davis (London: Faber and Faber, 1983), p. 176. See Joseph Pearce, *Old Thunder: A Life of Hilaire Belloc* (London: HarperCollins, 2003), p. 176.
16. 3 September 1917. *CL* 489–90.
17. *CL* 491.
18. See G. K. Chesterton's *Autobiography*, and Dudley Barker, *G. K. Chesterton: A Biography* (London: Constable, 1973). Also see John O'Connor, *Father Brown on Chesterton* (London: Burns Oates and Washbourne, 1937), p. 31: 'The master of the house came home from business, a man in ten thousand for charm and integrity, as we often proved in small things and in great. Francis Steinthal, Bradford born, of Frankfurt ancestry and the Israel of God.'
19. Cited by Michael Ffinch, *G. K. Chesterton* (London: Weidenfeld and Nicolson, 1986), p. 114. Steinthal children played parts in the masque, which was written for Francis Steinthal's 50th birthday. Francis Eric, his son, was born in 1886; he later changed his surname to Petrie and served with the Royal Fusiliers. He married Maria Zimmern, born 1887. Martin Steinthal (later Petrie) was born on 3 March 1916.
20. Cecil Gray, *Musical Chairs or Between Two Stools* (London: Hogarth Press, 1985), p. 100.
21. Ibid., p. 126.
22. London, Imperial War Museum, Private Papers of Siegfried Sassoon (cat. no. 9059), 'p. 444 Siegfried Sassoon Volume 2', MS 'Siegfried Sassoon's Protest Album', p. 8. Cecile Walton Robertson of Edinburgh and Dorothy Seward of Cambridge, writing from The Old House, Newabbey, Dumfries, 18 August 1917.
23. *CL* 501.
24. John Kemplay, *The Two Companions: The Story of Two Scottish Artists, Eric Robertson and Cecile Walton* (Edinburgh: Ronald Crowhurst, 1991), p. 68.
25. Ibid., p. 69.
26. Cited by William Hardie, *Scottish Painting 1837–1939* (London: Studio Vista, 1976), p. 100.
27. John Duncan was, on the other hand, a moralist who broke off connection with Eric Robertson in 1915 because of Robertson's immorality.
28. John Kemplay, *The Two Companions: The Story of Two Scottish Artists, Eric Robertson and Cecile Walton* (Edinburgh: Ronald Crowhurst, 1991), p. 68.
29. Ibid., p. 72.
30. Cecile Walton, 19 October 1917. Cited by John Kemplay in a letter to the author, 3 March 2011.
31. 19 September 1917. Cited by John Kemplay in a letter to the author, 3 March 2011.
32. A letter to Sassoon on 5 November 1917 recalling 21 October. *CL* 506.
33. *CL* 594.
34. *CL* 495.
35. Muriel Spark, *The Prime of Miss Jean Brodie*, intro. Candia McWilliam (London: Penguin, 2000), p. 32.
36. Edmund Blunden, 'Memoir', *The Collected Poems of Wilfred Owen*, ed. C. Day Lewis (London: Chatto and Windus, 1966), p. 171.
37. Ibid., p. 170.
38. Acturus, 'Antaeus, or Back to the Land', *The Hydra*, New Series, 3 (January 1918), p. 4.

39. R. L. Stevenson, *St. Ives* (London: J. M. Dent, 1914), p. 37.
40. *Lady Windermere's Fan* (1892), Act III.
41. Lord Moran, *The Anatomy of Courage: The Classic WWI Account of the Psychological Effects of War* (London: Robinson, 2007), p. 184.
42. 'An Inmate', 'Stared At', *The Hydra*, New Series, 8 (June 1918), p. 12.
43. *CPF* 256.
44. Cited in *The Poems of Wilfred Owen*, ed. Edmund Blunden (London: Chatto and Windus, 1952), pp. 134–5.
45. See *The Times*, Monday 19 June 1916, issue 41197, p. 10, col. E. 'You can learn to use it in half-an-hour.' No darkroom was needed.
46. *CL* 497.
47. *CL* 498.

12 The Ghost and Graves

1. Richard Brinsley Sheridan, *The Rivals, The Duenna, A Trip to Scarborough, The School for Scandal, The Critic*, ed. Michael Cordner (Oxford: Oxford University Press, 1998), p. 170.
2. See Stephen Weissman, *Chaplin: A Life* (London: J.R. Books, 2009), p. 220. The song was copyrighted in 1915, but performed in 1914 and possibly earlier.
3. Manchester, University of Manchester Library, MS DSW /1/3/3/2/6, 'WO – Medical Records'.
4. Cited in *D. H. Lawrence: Novelist, Poet, Prophet*, ed. Stephen Spender (London: Weidenfeld and Nicolson, 1973), p. 72. His friendship with Morrell ended in 1916.
5. See Dominic Hibberd, *Wilfred Owen: A New Biography* (London: Phoenix, 2003), p. 340. 'Song of Songs' appeared in *The Hydra*, 10 (1 September 1917), p. 13.
6. *CL* 505.
7. *CL* 506.
8. Cited by Dorothy Eagle and Hilary Carnell, *The Oxford Literary Guide to the British Isles* (Oxford: Oxford University Press, 1980), p. 339.
9. 'A Tear Song' has been described as a poem about Ripon. Hibberd, *Wilfred Owen: A New Biography*, p. 395. Jon Stallworthy says it was probably drafted at Scarborough between November and January. Wilfred Owen, *The Poems of Wilfred Owen*, ed. Jon Stallworthy (London: Chatto and Windus, 1990).
10. *CL* 508.
11. Cited by Richard Ingrams, ed., *England: An Anthology* (London: Fontana, 1991), pp. 227–8.
12. Robert Graves, *Goodbye to All That* (Harmondsworth: Penguin, 1960), p. 211.
13. 'They want to call No Man's Land "England" because we keep supremacy there. [. . .] To call it "England"!' *CL* 429. 19 January 1917.
14. *The Poetical Works of Gray and Collins*, ed. Austin Lane Poole (London: Humphrey Milford, Oxford University Press, 1917), p. 258. Owen's copy is in the English Faculty Library, Oxford.
15. In 'Asleep' there is also an echo of Walter de la Mare's 'The Dwelling-Place' of 1912, which, like 'Asleep', ends with 'Alas!', rhymed with 'pass'.
16. *CL* 509.
17. *CL* 514.
18. Late July: 'I have just been playing a little cricket with the lads.' *CL* 566.
19. Henri Barbusse, *Under Fire: The Story of a Squad (Le Feu)*, trans. Fitzwater Wray (New York: E. P. Dutton, 1917), p. 142. Owen owned the book in the original French, *Le Feu* (1916), but referred to reading, at Scarborough, 'H. Barbusse, *Under Fire*'. *CL* 520. Sassoon lent *Under Fire* to Owen.
20. Osbert Sitwell, *Tales My Father Taught Me: An Evocation of Extravagant Episodes* (London: Readers Union, Hutchinson, 1963), p. 36.

21. Anne Brontë, *Agnes Grey* (Edinburgh: John Grant, 1905; first published 1847), p. 286.
22. London, Imperial War Museum, Private Papers of Canon H. R. Bate MC (cat. no. 10782), MS 'The First World War Memoirs of Canon H. R. Bate MC' (1974), HRB1, p. 2, 4a.
23. *CL* 509. 23 November 1917.
24. *CL* 509, 510.
25. *CL* 520. 30 December 1917.
26. *CL* 521.
27. Barbusse, *Under Fire*, p. 4.
28. Oxford, University of Oxford, English Faculty Library, Owen Collection, Box 29, 6, 'Reminiscences', 27 February 1970. Mr and Mrs Roy Denville Jones.
29. Imperial War Museum, Private Papers of Canon H. R. Bate MC (cat. no. 10782), MS 'The First World War Memoirs of Canon H. R. Bate MC' (1974), HRB1, pp. 4a, 24.
30. University of Oxford, English Faculty Library, Owen Collection, Box 29, 6, 'Reminiscences', 27 February 1970. Mr A. J. Wright, fellow pupil at the Technical School.
31. Imperial War Museum, Private Papers of Canon H. R. Bate MC (cat. no. 10782), MS 'The First World War Memoirs of Canon H. R. Bate MC' (1974), HRB1, p. 24.
32. *CL* 512.
33. Philip Larkin, 'Vers de Société' (1971), *High Windows* (London: Faber and Faber, 1974).
34. Agatha Christie, *And Then There Were None* (1939).
35. In Bordeaux in 1915, Owen used *The Song of Hiawatha* in his teaching. *CL* 320.
36. *CL* 556.
37. University of Oxford, English Faculty Library, Owen Collection, Box 3, AA 410, 'The River Severn'.
38. *CPF* 309.
39. *CL* 515–16.
40. *CL* 348.
41. Citied in *The Poems of Wilfred Owen*, ed. Edmund Blunden (London: Chatto and Windus, 1952), p. 125.
42. 115,000 miners volunteered in the first month of the war – 230,000 by June 1915.
43. *CL* 527.
44. *CL* 529.
45. *The Poetical Works of Gray and Collins*, ed. Poole, p. 274.
46. 'Wilfrid [*sic*] Owen's Poems', *Times Literary Supplement*, Thursday 6 January 1921, p. 6.
47. *CL* 499.
48. Robert Graves, *Goodbye to All That* (Harmondsworth: Penguin, 1960), p. 220.
49. *CL* 595.
50. *CL* 499.
51. *CL* 595–6.
52. *CL* 596.
53. *CL* 511.
54. Stephen Fry, *Moab is My Washpot* (London: Hutchinson, 1997), p. 10.
55. Arnold Bennett, *The Pretty Lady* (Gloucester: Alan Sutton, 1987; first published 1918), p. 53.
56. Ibid., pp. 207–8.
57. Ibid., p. 54.
58. Ibid., p. 212.
59. Cited by H. Montgomery Hyde, *Henry James at Home* (London: Methuen, 1969), p. 18.
60. In 1910, he was a founding committee member of the Contemporary Art Society, along with Lady Ottoline Morrell, Clive Bell and Roger Fry.
61. Siegfried Sassoon, *Poet's Pilgrimage*, ed. D. Felicitas Corrigan (London: Victor Gollancz, 1973), p. 90.

62. Dedicated to Ross, the first act of Wilde's play takes place in 'Algernon Moncrieff's flat in Half-Moon Street, W.'
63. 'A Scandal in Bohemia' (1891), *The Adventures of Sherlock Holmes* (1892).
64. *CL* 507.
65. *CL* 462.
66. H. G. Wells, *The Correspondence of H. G. Wells: Volume 2 1904–1918*, ed. David C. Smith (London: Pickering and Chatto, 1998), p. 521.
67. Robert Graves, *Goodbye to All That* (Harmondsworth: Penguin, 1960), p. 205.
68. Ibid., p. 49.
69. *CL* 337.
70. Cited by Richard Perceval Graves, *Robert Graves: The Assault Heroic 1895–1926* (New York: Viking, 1986), p. 191.
71. Cited ibid.
72. Graves, *Goodbye to All That*, p. 223.
73. *CL* 528.
74. New York, New York Public Library, Berg Collection, Robert Graves to Siegfried Sassoon, 6 February 1918, f. 1r. See www.oucs.ox.ac.uk/ww1lit/collections/document/3118.
75. 'Mr. C. K. Scott Moncrieff: The Translator as Artist', *The Times*, Monday 3 March 1930, issue 45451, p. 19, col. A.
76. Ronald Knox, *A Spiritual Aeneid* (London: Burns Oates, 1958; first published 1918), p. 184: 'Scott-Moncrieff, who (like Hicks) asked for my final advice, had already been received in France.'
77. University of Manchester Library, MS DSW /1/1/1/26/14, 'Various personal recollections of W.O.', f. 1r.
78. Arthur Christopher Benson, *Tennyson* (London: Methuen, 1912; first published 1904), p. 78.
79. *CL* 528.

13 A Public School Man

1. Henry Newbolt, *Collected Poems 1897–1907* (London: Thomas Nelson, n. d.), p. 132.
2. Noël Coward, *The Cream of Noël Coward*, ed. Michael Cox (London: The Folio Society, 1996), p. 123.
3. 'Mr. C. K. Scott-Moncrieff: The Translator as Artist', *The Times*, Monday, 3 March 1930, issue 45451, p. 19, col. A.
4. Obituary, *The Wykehamist*, 725 (18 March 1930), p. 247.
5. Winchester, Winchester College, MS E3/5/89/2.
6. Winchester, Winchester College, MS E3/5/89/3.
7. Winchester, Winchester College, MS E3/5/89/1. Published with alterations in *The Wykehamist*, 543 (30 June 1915), p. 428.
8. Alec Waugh, *The Loom of Youth* (London: Mayflower, 1928; first published 1917), p. 9.
9. Alec Waugh, cited by Jonathan Gathorne-Hardy, *The Public School Phenomenon, 597–1977* (Harmondsworth: Penguin, 1979), p. 335.
10. Graves, 19/1/18: 'I was immensely struck by Alec Waugh's book and so was Sassoon who sent me my copy.' Edinburgh, National Library of Scotland, MS Acc 7243, f. 2v.
11. Edinburgh, National Library of Scotland, MS Acc 12763. From hospital, SW1.
12. Alec Waugh, *The Early Years of Alec Waugh* (London: Cassell, 1962), p. 123.
13. Nonetheless, *The Loom of Youth* does refer to a number of writers and books that Owen knew and loved: *A Shropshire Lad, Jekyll and Hyde, Arms and the Man, Lavengro*, Swinburne, Keats, Shelley, Byron.
14. Waugh, *The Loom of Youth*, p. 215.
15. *JFO* III, p. 61.
16. Evelyn Waugh, *The Diaries of Evelyn Waugh*, ed. Michael Davie (London: Weidenfeld and Nicolson, 1976), p. 205, 6 April 1925.

17. *CL* 302.
18. *The Poetical Works of Gray and Collins*, ed. Austin Lane Poole (London: Humphrey Milford, Oxford University Press, 1917), p. 35.
19. Published in *The New Witness*, 23 December 1915. Martin Stephen, ed., *Never Such Innocence: A New Anthology of Great War Verse* (London: J. M. Dent, 1991), p. 183.
20. Reprinted 21 times between 1905 and 1913.
21. Adrian Wright, *Foreign Country: The Life of L. P. Hartley* (London: Andre Deutsch, 1996), p. 141.
22. *CL* 535.
23. *CL* 535.
24. *CL* 361.
25. Horace Annesley Vachell, *The Hill: A Romance of Friendship* (London: John Murray, 1905), p. 249, 58.
26. *CL* 535.
27. Vachell, *The Hill*, p. 319.
28. Ibid., p. 311.
29. See Peter Parker, *The Old Lie: The Great War and the Public-School Ethos* (London: Constable, 1987), p. 194.
30. Poem by Scott Moncrieff in Charles Scott Moncrieff, trans., *The Song of Roland: Done into English, in the Original Measure*. Intro. G. K. Chesterton (London: Chapman and Hall, 1919), p. vi. ll. 5–6.
31. Nevil Shute, *Slide Rule: The Autobiography of an Engineer* (London: William Heinemann and Readers Union, 1956), p. 27.
32. See 'Fallen Officers', *The Times*, Thursday, 3 October 1918, issue 41911, p. 3, col. C.
33. Cited in Shute, *Slide Rule*, p. 28. Martin Taylor has slightly different Greek in the penultimate line in Martin Taylor, ed., *Lads: Love Poetry of the Trenches* (London: Constable, 1989), p. 69. Michael Charlesworth offers 'Athenian subtleties of this and that' for the penultimate line in his *Heads and Tales* (Wells: Greenbank Press, 2000), p. 21. In *Stand in the Trench, Achilles*, Elizabeth Vandiver corrects the Greek particles to δη's and τoι's. *Stand in the Trench, Achilles: Classical Receptions in British Poetry of the Great War* (Oxford: Oxford University Press, 2013), p. 330.
34. C. A. Alington, preface, in Evelyn Southwell and Malcolm White, *Two Men: A Memoir* (Oxford: Oxford University Press, 1919), p. vi. Also see Evelyn Southwell and Malcolm White, *Two Men: A Memoir* (Oxford: Oxford University Press, 1919).
35. Cited by P. J. Heslin, *The Transvestite Achilles: Gender and Genre in Statius' Achilleid* (Cambridge: Cambridge University Press, 2005), p. 53.
36. Timothy d'Arch Smith, *Love in Earnest: Some Notes on the Lives and Writings of English 'Uranian' Poets from 1889 to 1930* (London: Routledge and Kegan Paul, 1970), p. 149.
37. Cited by Heslin, p. 54.
38. d'Arch Smith, p. 149.
39. Ibid., p. 148.
40. Sassoon recorded in his diary on 3 October 1918 that Scott Moncrieff arrived at Half Moon Street with Noël Coward.
41. John Campbell, *F. E. Smith, First Earl of Birkenhead* (London: Jonathan Cape, 1983), p. 306.
42. Cited ibid., p. 308.
43. Oscar Wilde, *The Letters of Oscar Wilde*, ed. Rupert Hart-Davis (New York: Harcourt, Brace and World, 1962), pp. 336–7.
44. Henry James, cited by Ann Thwaite, *Edmund Gosse: A Literary Landscape 1849–1928* (Oxford: Oxford University Press, 1985), p. 358.
45. Augustus John, *Finishing Touches*, ed. Daniel George (London: Readers Union and Jonathan Cape, 1966), p. 145.
46. Osbert Sitwell, *Great Morning: Being the Third Volume of Left Hand, Right Hand* (Basingstoke: Macmillan and the Book Society, 1948), p. 254.

47. 'Death of Mr. Robert Ross', *The Times*, 41914, Monday, 7 October 1918, p. 5, col. D.
48. Maureen Borland, *Wilde's Devoted Friend: A Life of Robert Ross 1869–1918* (Oxford: Lennard, 1990), p. 257. See also Osbert Sitwell: 'To several of us he acted as impresario, reaping no benefit for himself thereby.' Osbert Sitwell, *Noble Essences or Courteous Revelations: An Autobiography* (London: Macmillan, 1950), p. 99.
49. Manchester, University of Manchester Library, MS DSW /1/1/3/9/59, Leslie Gunston to Dennis Welland, 18 October 1960, f. 1r.
50. 'The Ballad of Reading Gaol' (1898), IV. First published anonymously. Published under Wilde's name 1899. Owen owned *Poems by Oscar Wilde* (London: Methuen, 1916).
51. *CPF* 492.
52. 'The Ballad of Reading Gaol' (1898), I.
53. 'Teachers do not say so in British schools – where the poetry of the Great War is just about the only literature in verse that students will put up with – but the three most famous war poets were either bisexual (Rupert Brooke) or homosexual (Wilfred Owen and Siegfried Sassoon). And it shows. This is, perhaps, the most popular gay literature in English culture, although many readers would be furious if they heard you saying so.' Gregory Woods, *A History of Gay Literature: The Male Tradition* (New Haven: Yale University Press, 1998), p. 121.
54. Manchester, University of Manchester Library, MS DSW /1/1/1/12/3–5 [description of a letter from Graves in 1948 that is closed to readers].
55. Interview by Peter Buckman and William Fifield for *The Paris Review*, 47 (1969). Frank L. Kersnowski, ed., *Conversations with Robert Graves* (Jackson: University Press of Mississippi, 1983), p. 96.
56. Cited by Martin Seymour-Smith, *Robert Graves: His Life and Work* (London: Abacus, 1983), p. 63.
57. Cited by Jeffrey Richards, *Happiest Days: The Public Schools in English Fiction* (Manchester: Manchester University Press, 1988), p. 194.
58. Brian Inglis, *John Bull's Schooldays* (1961), p. 93. Cited by Richards, *Happiest Days*, p. 191.
59. Robert Graves, *But It Still Goes On*, cited by Parker, *The Old Lie*, p. 245.
60. Matt Houlbrook, *Queer London: Perils and Pleasures in the Sexual Metropolis, 1918–1958* (Chicago: University of Chicago Press, 2005), p. 7.
61. 31 August 1918. *CL* 570.
62. *CL* 571.
63. Cited by Thomas Wright, *Oscar's Books* (London: Chatto and Windus, 2008), p. 167.
64. Cited by A. N. Wilson, *Betjeman* (London: Arrow, 2007), p. 36. 'I always add "in all but fact", as I like the turn of phrase'.
65. *CL* 535.
66. *CL* 538.

14 Gallantry

1. *CL* 574.
2. See J. M. Barrie, *Peter and Wendy; Margaret Ogilvy* (New York: Charles Scribner's Sons, 1912), p. 118.
3. J. B. Priestley, *English Journey* (London: William Heinemann, 1937), p. 287. 'I have most unhappy memories of Ripon – and I am not the only one, by several thousands'.
4. 'Escape of Six German Officers', *The Times*, 41740, 18 March 1918, p. 5, col. B.
5. *CL* 541.
6. Ibid.
7. 1 Timothy 1: 17.
8. 'Preface', written at Ripon, probably in May 1918.

9. *CL* 543. 'Borage' was an appropriate name – knights used to consume borage for courage before battle.
10. *CL* 540.
11. *CL* 548.
12. 'Repression of War Experience' was written in June 1917 and published in *Counter-Attack* in 1918.
13. 'The Scholar-Gipsy': 'rumours hung about the country-side, / That the lost Scholar long was seen to stray', and the blackbird has 'known thee past him stray'.
14. 'Bands for Troops Off to the Front', *The Times*, 41748, Wednesday 27 March 1918, p. 3, col. B.
15. Ibid.
16. *CL* 245.
17. Oxford, University of Oxford, English Faculty Library, Owen Collection, Box 3, AA 410, 'Description of a Railway Station at a busy Time of Day'. The mark was 17/20 – 'You would have done better to keep to the 3rd person'.
18. *CL* 542.
19. Arthur J. Brock, *Health and Conduct* (London: Williams and Norgate, 1923), p. 172.
20. *A Shropshire Lad* XIX (London: Grant Richards, 1915), p. 29.
21. *CL* 554.
22. *CL* 564.
23. Cited by Edward Evans, *South with Scott* (London: Collins, 1921), p. 254.
24. *CL* 498.
25. *CL* 559.
26. *CL* 562.
27. E. M. Forster, *Maurice* (London: Hodder and Stoughton, in association with Edward Arnold, 1971), p. 71.
28. 'Sigmund Freud came up with the noun *Normalen* ("normals"), to mean "heterosexuals", and Abraham Brill introduced this noun "normal" into English in translating works such as *The Interpretation of Dreams* (1913) and *The Psychopathology of Everyday Life* (1914).' Dot Wordsworth, 'Mind Your Language', *The Spectator*, cccxx, 9616 and 9617 (15/22 December 2012), p. 40.
29. Cited by Miranda Carter, *Anthony Blunt: His Lives* (London: Macmillan, 2001), p. 93.
30. See Jay Winter, *Sites of Memory, Sites of Mourning: The Great War in European Cultural History* (Cambridge: Cambridge University Press, 1998), p. 220.
31. *CL* 597.
32. Philip Larkin to Patrick Taylor-Martin, 14 June 1984, *Selected Letters of Philip Larkin 1940–1985*, ed. Anthony Thwaite (London: Faber and Faber, 1992), p. 711.
33. T. S. Eliot to Ezra Pound, 31 October 1917: 'OSWALD and EDITH Shitwell, Graves (query, George?) Nichols, and OTHERS'. T. S. Eliot, *The Letters of T. S. Eliot: Volume I: 1898–1922*, ed. Valerie Eliot and Hugh Haughton (London: Faber and Faber, 2009), pp. 230–1.
34. Osbert 1892–1969, Edith 1887–1964, Sacheverell 1897–1988. Osbert said that Edith never met Owen.
35. Edith Sitwell, *Selected Letters*, eds John Lehmann and Derek Parker (London: Macmillan, 1970), p. 19, 9 September 1919.
36. Beverley Nichols, *Twenty-Five* (London: Penguin, 1935; first published 1926), p. 46.
37. Sacheverell Sitwell, *Sacheverell Sitwell's England*, ed. Michael Raeburn (London: Orbis, 1986), p. 14.
38. *CL* 533.
39. Virginia Woolf, *Jacob's Room* (London: Hogarth Press, 1945), p. 89.
40. Algernon Charles Swinburne, *Poems and Ballads* (First Series) (London: William Heinemann, 1917), p. 127.
41. *CL* 568.

42. *CL* 558.
43. *CL* 557.
44. *CL* 568.
45. 'The Next War', *Never Such Innocence: A New Anthology of Great War Verse*, ed. Martin Stephen (London: J. M. Dent, 1991), p. 323.
46. *CPF* 319.
47. Manchester, University of Manchester Library, MS DSW /1/1/1/25/8, 'University College Reading', M. C. Rayner to Dennis Welland, 25 September 1947, ff. 2r-v. Matthew, 7: 9: 'Or what man is there of you, whom if his son ask bread, will he give him a stone?'
48. *CL* 571.
49. Siegfried Sassoon, *Collected Poems 1908–1956* (London: Faber and Faber, 1984), p. 78.
50. *CL* 568.
51. See footnote at *CL* 553 and Oxford, University of Oxford, English Faculty Library, Owen Collection, Box 3, DD 461. C. K. Scott Moncrieff to Wilfred Owen, 26 April 1918: 'Nichols turned up one day – and Graves's brother yesterday who wants to go and be a cadet at Oxford. We might send you to teach him.'
52. C. K. Scott Moncrieff, *The Nation* (26 March 1921). See typescript transcripts in Manchester, University of Manchester Library, MS DSW /1/1/4/8/3, 'Owen thesis – MSS, notes etc'.
53. C. K. Scott Moncrieff, *The New Witness*, 10 December 1920. See typescript transcripts in University of Manchester Library, MS DSW /1/1/4/8/3, 'Owen thesis – MSS, notes etc'.
54. *CL* 569.
55. 'Physic Garden Opened to Wounded', *The Times*, 41182, Thursday 1 June 1916, p. 11, col. F.
56. Ibid.
57. *Wheels, 1918: A Third Cycle*, ed. Edith Sitwell (Oxford: B. H. Blackwell, 1918), p. 11.
58. 'Debating Society', *The Wykehamist*, 443 (April 1907), p. 398.
59. Charles Scott Moncrieff, trans., *The Song of Roland: Done into English, in the Original Measure*, intro. G. K. Chesterton (London: Chapman and Hall, 1919), p. xiii.
60. Letter (dated 20 December 1919) from C. K. Scott Moncrieff to the editor, *The New Witness*, 2 January 1920, p. 117. See University of Manchester Library, MS DSW /1/1/4/8/7, 'Owen thesis – MSS, notes etc'.
61. *CL* 571.
62. *CL* 570.
63. O'Riordan lectured on 'Three Dead Poet Friends: Ernest Dowson, Edward Thomas and Wilfred Owen'. He knew Thomas through the Square Club, a literary dining club.
64. *CL* 572: 'a man of letters whose name I know, but whose works are not much known, Mr. O'Riordan'. *CL* 573: 'I have been seeing O'Riordan daily, "O'Riordan", as G. K. Chesterton writes, "whom all of us know and love as Norries Connell." – "All of us" means the whole clan of English writers.'
65. University of Manchester Library, MS DSW /1/1/4/8/9, 'Owen thesis – MSS, notes etc', notebook, p. 65.
66. Manchester, University of Manchester Library, MS DSW /1/1/1/26, 'Various personal recollections of W.O.', 15 May 1947, f. 2r.
67. *CL* 573.
68. Obituary, *The Salopian*, 12 October 1918, p. 10.
69. 'Fallen Officers', *The Times*, 41911, Thursday 3 October 1918, p. 3, col. C.
70. Obituary, *The Wykehamist*, 725, 18 March 1930, p. 248.
71. *C. K. Scott Moncrieff: Memories and Letters*, ed. J. M. Scott Moncrieff and L. W. Lunn (London: Chapman and Hall, 1931), p. 141, 9 October 1918.
72. *The Salopian*, 12 October 1918, p. 10.

73. *CL* 580. This citation in the collected letters differs slightly from the entry in the regimental roll of honour: 'For conspicuous gallantry and devotion to duty in the attack. On the company commander becoming a casualty he assumed command and showed fine leadership, and resisted a heavy counter-attack. He personally manipulated a captured enemy machine gun from an isolated position, and inflicted considerable losses on the enemy. Throughout he behaved most gallantly.' *The Regimental Roll of Honour and War Record of the Artists' Rifles* (London: Howlett, 1922), p. 111.

74. Ibid.

75. *CL* 581.

76. Ibid.

77. 4 August 1961. Siegfried Sassoon, *Poet's Pilgrimage*, ed. D. Felicitas Corrigan (London: Victor Gollancz, 1973), p. 91.

78. 'Elegy: 5 October 1918 / To Robert Ross'. Ibid, pp. 90–1.

79. *CL* 583.

80. Tim Travers, in David Chandler and Ian Beckett, eds, *The Oxford Illustrated History of the British Army* (Oxford: Oxford University Press, 1994), p. 239.

81. *CL* 589.

82. *CL* 587.

83. Charles Dickens, *Little Dorrit* (London: J. M. Dent, n.d.; first published 1857), p. 44.

84. *CL* 116.

85. Dickens, *Little Dorrit*, pp. 670–1.

86. Ibid., p. 445.

87. The descent into Hell is also reminiscent of Virgil's *Aeneid*, and when in 'Strange Meeting' Owen says that 'when much blood had clogged their chariot-wheels, / I would go up and wash them from sweet wells', there is an echo of the famous words from *The Aeneid* ('much blood' being a straight translation of Virgil's 'multo' and 'sanguine'). 'I see wars, horrible wars, and the Tiber foaming with much blood': 'Bella, horrida bella, / Et Thybrim multo spumantem sanguine cerno' (Virgil, *The Aeneid*, Book 6, l. 86).

88. Thomas Babington Macaulay, *Miscellanous Essays and The Lays of Ancient Rome* (London: J. M. Dent, 1910), p. 432.

89. Armistice signed with Austria 3 November. It came into effect on 4 November, but the fighting stopped on the 3rd.

90. *CL* 591.

91. *CL* 82.

92. *Henry V*, IV.iii. 57–62. The speech on St Crispin's Day, 25 October – Owen was writing on 31 October.

15 Home

1. George Farquhar, *The Recruiting Officer and Other Plays*, ed. William Myers (Oxford: Oxford University Press, 1995), p. 180.

2. *CL* 33.

3. 'Smile, Smile, Smile'.

4. Robert Graves, *Goodbye to All That* (Harmondsworth: Penguin, 1960), p. 244.

5. T. E. Lawrence, *The Letters of T. E. Lawrence*, ed. David Garnett (London: Jonathan Cape, 1938), p. 752.

6. Ibid., p. 756.

7. Niall Ferguson, *The Pity of War* (London: Penguin, 1999), p. 295. Officially 702,410. There were 2,556,014 British casualties (excluding the Empire), including the wounded, and prisoners.

8. 5,704,416 men served in the British army during the war – 4,970,902 joined after the outbreak of war, and, of those, 2,446,719 were volunteers. Peter Simkins, in *The*

Oxford Illustrated History of the British Army, ed. David Chandler and Ian Beckett (Oxford: Oxford University Press, 1994), p. 241. 'The overall total of those who served represented slightly over 22 per cent of the male population of the United Kingdom.'

9. 'They had received the dreaded telegram at 12 noon on 11 November, Armistice Day. The church bells were still ringing, the bands playing and the jubilant crowds surging together.' *JFO* III, p. 201.

10. Manchester, University of Manchester Library, MS DSW /1/1/7, f. 2r. Susan Owen to Vera Hewland, 10 May 1936.

11. For 'W.O.' see *CL* 560.

12. D. R. Thorpe, *Supermac: The Life of Harold Macmillan* (London: Chatto and Windus, 2010), p. 48; Gerard J. DeGroot, *Blighty: British Society in the Era of the Great War* (London: Longman, 1996), p. 273. A total of 2,708 Oxford men were killed in action.

13. London, Imperial War Museum, Private Papers of Canon H. R. Bate MC (cat. no. 10782), 'The First World War Memoirs of Canon H. R. Bate MC (1974)', HRB1, f. 2.

14. 'I sometimes wonder how much interest the modern intelligentsia would show in him if he was still alive. Probably as little as they show for me! Anyhow, the fact that I knew him seems to be my main claim to distinction nowadays.' Manchester, University of Manchester Library, MS DSW /1/1/1/21/3, 'Sassoon, Siegfried', 15 May 1950, f. 1r.

15. *CL* 448.

16. Manchester, University of Manchester Library, MS DSW /1/3/3/2/6, 'WO – Rare Editions', Susan Owen to Alec Paton, 27 May 1919, ff. 12–13.

17. 'I find there is but one course of action which satisfies and that is to fling oneself Body and Soul into the Love of God'. Winchester, Winchester College, MS E3/5/89/4.

18. 'To W. E. S. O.' by Charles Scott Moncrieff, in Charles Scott Moncrieff, trans., *The Song of Roland: Done into English, in the Original Measure*, intro. G. K. Chesterton (London: Chapman and Hall, 1919), p. vii.

19. Manchester, University of Manchester Library, MS DSW /1/1/7/1, 'Typescript extracts', Susan Owen to C. K. Scott Moncrieff, 14 February 1921, f. 6r.

20. *C. K. Scott Moncrieff: Memories and Letters*, eds J. M. Scott Moncrieff and L. W. Lunn (London: Chapman and Hall, 1931), p. 240.

21. Laurence Binyon, 'For the Fallen'.

22. Richard Greene, *Edith Sitwell: Avant-Garde Poet, English Genius* (London: Virago, 2011), p. 129.

23. See *A Tribute to Wilfred Owen*, compiled by T. J. Walsh, 1965. Manchester, University of Manchester Library, MS DSW /1/1/6/2, 'Magazine'.

24. Philip Larkin, *Required Writing: Miscellaneous Pieces 1955–1982* (London: Faber and Faber, 1983), p. 163.

25. Martin Bell, interviewed on *Men's Hour*, BBC Radio 5, Sunday 22 May 2011, 9–10 p.m.

26. Seamus Heaney, *Stepping Stones* (London: Faber and Faber, 2009), p. 353.

27. Harold Pinter, *Death etc.* (New York: Grove, 2005), p. 1.

28. *CL* 395. In 1918, Owen also dreamt of visiting Baghdad after the war as a dealer in antiques.

29. Siegfried Sassoon, *Poet's Pilgrimage*, ed. D. Felicitas Corrigan (London: Victor Gollancz, 1973), p. 87.

30. Cited in 'Pseuds Corner', *Private Eye*, 1330 (22 December–10 January 2013), p. 29.

31. Cited by Liz Thomas, 'Anti-war poem by Wilfred Owen is a favourite with David Cameron. (Wonder what Tony Blair's would have been . . .)', *Daily Mail* (*Mail Online*, www.dailymail.co.uk), 28 September 2010.

Further Reading

Max Arthur, Forgotten Voices of the Great War (London: Ebury Press, 2003)

Maureen Borland, Wilde's Devoted Friend: A Life of Robert Ross 1869–1918 (Oxford: Lennard, 1990)

Santanu Das, Touch and Intimacy in First World War Literature (Cambridge: Cambridge University Press, 2005)

Max Egremont, Siegfried Sassoon: A Biography (London: Picador, 2006)

Paul Fussell, The Great War and Modern Memory (London: Oxford University Press, 1977)

Robert Graves, Goodbye to All That (Harmondsworth: Penguin, 1960)

Dominic Hibberd, Wilfred Owen: A New Biography (London: Phoenix, 2003)

John Kemplay, The Two Companions: The Story of Two Scottish Artists, Eric Robertson and Cecile Walton (Edinburgh: Ronald Crowhurst, 1991)

Tim Kendall, Modern English War Poetry (Oxford: Oxford University Press, 2006)

Tim Kendall, ed., The Oxford Handbook of British and Irish War Poetry (Oxford: Oxford University Press, 2007)

C. K. Scott Moncrieff, C. K. Scott Moncrieff: Memories and Letters, eds J. M. Scott Moncrieff and L. W. Lunn (London: Chapman and Hall, 1931)

Neil Oliver, Not Forgotten (London: Hodder and Stoughton, 2006)

Wilfred Owen, The Collected Poems of Wilfred Owen, ed. C. Day Lewis (London: Chatto and Windus, 1966)

Peter Parker, The Old Lie: The Great War and the Public-School Ethos (London: Constable, 1987)

Siegfried Sassoon, Collected Poems 1908–1956 (London: Faber and Faber, 1984)

Siegfried Sassoon, Diaries 1915–1918, ed. Rupert Hart-Davis (London: Faber and Faber, 1983)

Siegfried Sassoon, Poet's Pilgrimage, ed. D. Felicitas Corrigan (London: Victor Gollancz, 1973)

Siegfried Sassoon, Siegfried's Journey 1916–1920 (London: Faber and Faber, 1945)

Osbert Sitwell, Noble Essences or Courteous Revelations: An Autobiography (London: Macmillan, 1950)

Jon Stallworthy, Survivors' Songs: From Maldon to the Somme (Cambridge: Cambridge University Press, 2008)

Jon Stallworthy, Wilfred Owen: A Biography (London: Oxford University Press and Chatto and Windus, 1974)

Jon Stallworthy and Jane Potter, eds, Three Poets of the First World War: Ivor Gurney, Isaac Rosenberg and Wilfred Owen (London: Penguin, 2011)

Martin Stephen, ed., Never Such Innocence: A New Anthology of Great War Verse
    (London: J. M. Dent, 1991)
D. S. R. Welland, Wilfred Owen: A Critical Study (London: Chatto and Windus, 1960)
Merryn Williams, Wilfred Owen (Bridgend: Seren, 1993)
Jay Winter, Sites of Memory, Sites of Mourning: The Great War in European Cultural
    History (Cambridge: Cambridge University Press, 1998)

Illustration Acknowledgments

1 The Bodleian Library, University of Oxford, Owen Collection (English Faculty Library), Box 36, f. 2A(d); 2 The Bodleian Library, University of Oxford, Owen Collection (English Faculty Library), Box 36, f. 1A(b); 3 The Bodleian Library, University of Oxford, Owen Collection (English Faculty Library), Box 36, f. 1A(d); 5 The Bodleian Library, University of Oxford, Owen Collection (English Faculty Library), Box 36, f. 2B(c); 9 The Bodleian Library, University of Oxford, Owen Collection (English Faculty Library), Box 36, f. 1C(b); 12 The Bodleian Library, University of Oxford, Owen Collection (English Faculty Library), Box 36, f. 2D(a); 14 DSW /1/1/4/5/4. Reproduced by courtesy of the University Librarian and Director, The John Rylands Library, The University of Manchester; 15 DSW /1/1/4/5/3. Reproduced by courtesy of the University Librarian and Director, The John Rylands Library, The University of Manchester; 16 © National Portrait Gallery, London; 17 The Bodleian Library, University of Oxford, Owen Collection (English Faculty Library), Box 36, f. 1E(b). Courtesy of The First World War Poetry Digital Archive, University of Oxford; 18 from the Haig papers held by the National Library of Scotland (project: *Images of War, 1916–1918*). © National Library of Scotland. Licensor www.scran.ac.uk; 19 The National Library of Scotland's collection (project: *Images of War, 1916–1918*). © National Library of Scotland. Licensor www.scran.ac.uk; 20 Ministry of Information First World War Official Collection. © IWM (Q 6475); 23 © Napier University. Licensor www.scran.ac.uk; 24 © National Portrait Gallery, London; 25 © Estate of John Duncan. All rights reserved, DACS 2013. Glasgow Museums; 26. Scottish National Portrait Gallery. © Walton Family; 27 Scottish National Gallery of Modern Art (on loan from a private collection); 28 The Bodleian Library, University of Oxford, Owen Collection (English Faculty Library), Box 36, f. 2E(c). Courtesy of The First World War Poetry Digital Archive, University of Oxford; 30 © National Portrait Gallery, London; 32 Scottish National Portrait Gallery. © Estate of Edward Stanley Mercer; 33 Courtesy of Shrewsbury School; 36 The Bodleian Library, University of Oxford, Owen Collection (English Faculty Library), Box 36, f. 1F(L). Courtesy of The First World War Poetry Digital Archive, University of Oxford; 37 DSW /1/1/4/5/7. Reproduced by courtesy of the University Librarian and Director, The John Rylands Library, The University of Manchester; Authors own collection, 4, 6, 7, 8, 10, 11, 13, 21, 22, 29, 31, 34, 35.

Acknowledgments

My first and greatest debt is to Wilfred Owen himself. I was of course unable to ask for Wilfred Owen's permission to write this book, but I am most grateful to the Owen estate for permission to quote from both published and unpublished material. I am particularly grateful to Jon Stallworthy, the senior executor, who has been most supportive and kind, while never trying to influence what I wrote – at no point did he ask to read the book before publication, and neither the Owen family nor the executors are responsible for what I have written. It is simply true that the book could not have been written without their support. And I would like to offer special thanks to Elizabeth Owen for her friendliness, encouragement and help.

Needless to say, this book also comes after nearly a century of work on Wilfred Owen by many scholars and writers, and I would like to thank them all. My book has been written in a spirit of respect for what has been written before. Jon Stallworthy's editions of the poetry have been beside me throughout, and I refer to them repeatedly in this book. A new edition of the poetry, edited by Jon, came a little too late for this book but I hope that my *Wilfred Owen* will lead readers to Jon's edition of Owen's complete poems and fragments. Jon Stallworthy was also Owen's first proper biographer in 1974, and Dominic Hibberd's detailed biography appeared in 2002. Fortunately, a biography is not like a gravestone: there's room for more than one. (Owen owned three lives of Keats.) While this book has not been written to supersede earlier biographies, it is certainly different from them: I never intended to record everything that could be said about Owen, and have attempted to give a fresh portrait of the man – to, in Owen's words, throw 'more light on the Life & Character' – by being selective and more thematic, and by placing him in new contexts.

I would like to pay tribute to Dennis Welland, one of the first Owen scholars, whose vast archive at Manchester University has been a wonderful resource, providing a good deal of new material that was unavailable until the last few years. And Harold Owen contributed so much to our knowledge of his brother Wilfred by writing his family memoir, and by editing the Owen letters with John Bell. I frequently refer to the 1967 OUP edition of the letters (in the notes, I use *CL* plus the page number), although with an awareness of subsequent changes to some of the dates of the letters.

Liverpool Hope University, Queen Mary (University of London) and the University of St Andrews have given financial support to my research, for which I am very grateful, and I would like to thank my colleagues and students at the various universities of my academic career. Liverpool Hope University has been especially supportive in the last couple of years, and the university's beautiful library supplied many of the books that I needed. My research work on the literature of the First World War began when I was a student at The Queen's College, Oxford, and it was at Oxford, in the Owen Room, that I first lectured on the war, during the time when I was a lecturer at Merton College. In my college room at Merton, there was a plaque commemorating a member of the college who died in Belgium in 1914; and this book was partly written at a desk that was presented to my great-grandfather by the British Legion – a coal-miner at twelve years old, a mental health nurse, a member of the artillery and the RAMC, he was disabled in 1917 (he seems perhaps to have been the embodiment of Owen's poetry), becoming a member of the Legion's National Executive for over twenty years and active in the care of ex-servicemen for forty years.

It has been an honour to work with Yale University Press, and I offer thanks to everyone there who has been involved with this book, especially Heather McCallum, Rachael Lonsdale, Beth Humphries and Tami Halliday. Heather and Rachael have been brilliant editors, with the patience of Job and the wisdom of Solomon, and I am immensely grateful to them: this book could not have been written without them. The errors though are my own.

I would also like to thank the following: Matthew Bradley; Guffi Chohdri and Oxford University Press; Dorothy Clayton, Alice Hendry and the University of Manchester Library; Shona Corner, Patrick Elliott, Natalie Paris and National Galleries Scotland; Santanu Das; Vanessa Davis and the Wilfred Owen Association; the estate of John Duncan; Kathryn Ferguson at Alan Brodie Representation Ltd; Alexander Field; Suzanne Foster and Winchester College; Glasgow Museums; Penny Hatfield at Eton College; Jennifer Hough; Nicola Ireland and the Royal Scottish Academy; Tim Jayne; John Kemplay; Dominika Kurek-Chomycz; Stuart Lee and Kate Lindsay of the First World War Poetry Digital Archive; the Barbara Levy agency; Liverpool University; Sara Lodge; Mike Morrogh and Shrewsbury School; Charlotte Murray and the University of Reading Special Collections; my parents; the National Library of Scotland; the National Portrait Gallery; Kenneth Newport; Simon Offord, Anthony Richards, Sabrina Rowlatt and the Imperial War Museum; Tom Owens; Michael Riordan and The Queen's College, Oxford; Nick Roe; St Andrews University Library Special Collections; the Scottish National Gallery of Modern Art; the Scottish National Portrait Gallery; Scran; Senate House Library; Richard Shenton and the Media Archive for Central England; Samantha Sherbourne and the Bodleian Library, Oxford; Colin Simpson of the Williamson Gallery, Birkenhead; Swansea University; and (last but by no means least) Sue Usher and the English Faculty Library, Oxford. The Owen collection at the English Faculty Library, especially the library of his books, has been an invaluable resource.

The poem 'Survivors' is copyright Siegfried Sassoon by kind permission of the Estate of George Sassoon. Quotations from Wilfred Owen's *Collected Letters* and quotations from Harold Owen's *Journey from Obscurity* are by permission of Oxford University Press. I would like to thank the David Higham literary, film and television agency for permission to quote from Osbert Sitwell's 'Clavichords – To Mrs. Gordon Woodhouse', published in *Wheels, 1918: A Third Cycle*, ed. Edith Sitwell (Oxford: B. H. Blackwell, 1918). I am also pleased to be able to use lines by Noël Coward: *Mad About the Boy* copyright © NC Aventales AG 1932 by permission of Alan Brodie Representation Ltd, www.alanbrodie.com. Owen's poems and fragments are from *The Complete Poems and Fragments*, ed. Jon Stallworthy (London: Chatto and Windus, Hogarth Press and Oxford University Press, 1983) and *The Poems of Wilfred Owen*, ed. Jon Stallworthy (London: Chatto and Windus, 1990) © the Executors of Harold Owen's Estate 1963 and 1983. The poems and fragments that remain in copyright are used by permission of Random House and the Wilfred Owen Estate, and with thanks to Jon Stallworthy. I quote four lines from the last stanza of Edwin Muir's 'For Ann Scott-Moncrieff (1914-1943)', taken from Edwin Muir, *Collected Poems* (London: Faber and Faber, 1963), p. 157. 'For Ann Scott-Moncrieff (1914-1943)' is reprinted by permission of Faber and Faber Limited.

If permission has not been obtained from any owners of copyright material, or if any debt has gone unacknowledged, I apologize sincerely and I will happily incorporate any missing acknowledgements into any future editions.

November 2013
Liverpool

Index